KV-191-803

A. Robert Lee

Designs of Blackness:

Mappings in the Literature and Culture of Afro-America

Pluto  Press
LONDON • STERLING, VIRGINIA

First published 1998 by Pluto Press
345 Archway Road, London N6 5AA
and 22883 Quicksilver Drive,
Sterling, VA 20166–2012, USA

Copyright © A. Robert Lee 1998

The right of A. Robert Lee to be identified as the
author of this work has been asserted by him in accordance
with the Copyright, Designs and Patents Act 1988

British Library Cataloguing in Publication Data
A catalogue record for this book is available from
the British Library

ISBN 0 7453 0643 8 hbk

Library of Congress Cataloging in Publication Data
Lee, A. Robert, 1941–
    Designs of Blackness: mappings in the literature and culture of
Afro-America/A. Robert Lee.
        p.   cm.
    ISBN 0–7453–0643–8 (hardbound)
    1. American prose literature—Afro-American authors—History and
criticism. 2. Slaves—United States—Biography—History and
criticism. 3. Autobiography—Afro-American authors. 4. Afro-
Americans in literature. 5. Afro-Americans—Civilization. 6. Race
in literature. I. Title.
PS366.A35L44   1998
818'.08—dc21   98–19975
                                                                    CIP

UNIVERSITY COLLEGE WORCESTER LIBRARY
A 67925
810.09 LEE

Designed and produced for Pluto Press by
Chase Production Services, Chadlington, OX7 3LN
Typeset from disk by Stanford DTP Services, Northampton
Printed in the EC by T.J. International, Padstow

Para Pepa, murciana, huertana

Contents

Acknowledgements

Over the years I have had the immense benefit of friendships, conversations and much correspondence with a number of the writers in this study – more than a helpful step for a white critic presuming to address black writing. Several have been the subject of BBC and other interviews with me. I thank them all, but especially the late Chester Himes, Harold Cruse, Clarence Major, John A. Williams, John Wideman, Lorenzo Thomas, Ted Joans, Ishmael Reed and Leon Forrest, whose death occurred as this book was being completed but whose friendship will always stay with me.

The late Eric Mottram of King's College, London, and a pioneer voice of American Studies in Britain, was early to alert me to the genius of Ralph Ellison as to so much else in American culture.

Advice and relevant exchanges about American multiculturalism and beyond have been as frequent as they have been forthcoming from a wide circle of friends. In this I owe warmest debts to David Murray and Brian Lee of the University of Nottingham; Clive Bush and Shamoon Zamir of King's College, London; Ralph Willett, formerly of the University of Hull; Jacqueline Kaye and Richard Gray of the University of Essex; Christopher Bigsby of the University of East Anglia; Faith Pullin of the University of Edinburgh; Epifanio San Juan of Ohio State University, Bowling Green; the late Daniel W. Bernd of Governors State University, Illinois; Harrison Hayford of Northwestern University; Barbara Fields of Columbia University; John G. Cawelti of the University of Kentucky; Rex Burns of the University of Colorado at Denver; Evelyn Hu-DeHart, Annette Dula and Ron Billingsley of CSERA, the University of Colorado at Boulder; Werner Sollors of Harvard University; Amritjit Singh of Rhode Island College; H. Nigel Thomas of L'Université de Laval; Javier Coy of the University of Valencia; Ole Moen of the University of Oslo; John G. Blair of the University of Geneva; Mario Maffi of the University of Milan; Gunter Lenz of the University of Frankfurt; Giovanna Franci, Franco La Polla and Franco Minganti of the University of Bologna; W.M. Verhoeven of the University of Groningen; C.C. Barfoot and Theo D'haen of the University of Leiden; Hans Bak of the University of Nijmegen and the Roosevelt Study Center, Middelburg; Truman Metzel and Jeff Rice, bibliophiles extraordinaires, of *Great Expectations* bookstore, Evanston, Illinois; John Yau, my Berkeley co-sojourner in 1995; Carmen Tafolla of Texas; and Mark Kinkead-Weekes, Lyn Innes, Abdulrazak Gurnah, Henry Claridge, Christine Bolt, David Turley, Graham Clarke, George Conyne and Darryll Grantley, of the University of Kent at Canterbury, my academic home for nearly three decades. I also warmly acknowledge the welcome and support given to me by my colleagues at Nihon University, Tokyo – especially Stephen Harding, Kunihiko Tamuro, Ichitara Toma, Kimitaka Hara, Takeshi Onodera and Takeshi Sekiya.

Fellow contributors (especially the late Laurence B. Holland) to my essay-collection *Black Fiction: Studies in the Afro-American Novel* (1980), and Donald J. Ratcliffe, of the University of Durham, editorial mainstay for my *Black American Fiction since Richard Wright* (BAAS Pamphlet, No. 11, 1983), helped in ways to which I still feel indebted.

Gerald Vizenor of the University of California requires separate mention for inviting me into Berkeley's Ethnic Studies Department and for every ongoing kindness and tricksterism. At Berkeley, too, I owe much to conversations with Ling-chi Wang, Joe Lockard, Dorothy Wang (who also gave stalwart help in tracking down a number of references), Donald McQuaid and, again, with Ishmael Reed.

My debt to students in Europe, America and Japan deserves its own paragraph; I offer it unreservedly.

As to the printed word, I am grateful for permission to rework past writing from Vision Press, VU Press, Rodopi, Salem Press, St. Martin's Press, Bowling Green Popular Press, *Black American Literature Forum* (as was) and the *Journal of American Studies*. For its part, Pluto Press has become a kind of Archway Road web-site in its own right, especially from the distance of Tokyo, courtesy of Anne Beech, Roger van Zwanenberg, Robert Webb and Lisa Jolliffe, along with Gemma Marren.

Above all, I owe a debt of life, and Spain, to Josefa Vivancos Hernández.

Introduction

But who does not know of literature banned because it is interrogative; discredited because it is critical; erased because alternate?

Toni Morrison, *The Nobel Lecture in Literature* (1993)[1]

Toni Morrison's queries well become a new study of African American writing. They carry all her typical acuity and toughness, the kind of edge behind a lifetime's storytelling which, in addition to a Pulitzer Prize and other awards, rightly won her the Nobel Prize in 1993. They also call attention to how she has reinterpreted the narratives of Afro-America, a world, more accurately worlds, initially turned upside down by slavery, by the Middle Passage, by every subsequent American colour line meanness, and yet also anything but mere victimry.

For Morrison has equally invoked survival, resilience, wit, belief, the tough, ironic wisdom to have come out of set-back and oppression, all of it as underwritten by a historic black creativity of self and word and music. That the award, however much a crowning of both Morrison herself and African American writing in general, aroused cavils was oddly appropriate. It gave a reminder that racism can as readily snake its way into literary circles as elsewhere, and that, for some, black authorship (especially by a black woman) still must play petitioner in matters of canon.

Despite the Nobel Committee's own conviction otherwise, the sniping implied that Morrison's prize was more a gesture to Civil Rights America, Third Worldism, anti-coloniality, or women of colour, than an earned tribute to a writer of quite singular inventive power. Morrison's formulations in her Nobel lecture as to the 'banning', 'discrediting' or even 'erasure' of 'alternate' literature included herself in answering this kind of attempted put-down.

Who better, then, from this quite personal bearing, to have gone on to reflect upon how African American written voice – an illegality under slave edict for its transgression of ownership of the word as much as the body – has so often fared in America? Has not, in this sense, all America's black writing been an answering-back, a seizing of its own rights to word, poem, novel, play, text, literature?

Morrison, moreover, brings to bear the credential not only of an accomplished fiction writer but of a case-hardened editor, first with L.W. Singer Publishing Company (1964–67), then with Random House (1967–84), along with her academic appointments at Barnard, Yale, SUNY and Princeton. Toni Cade Bambara, James Alan McPherson, Angela Davis, not to mention Leon Forrest, have been but a few to have come under her editorial purview. Almost by definition as an African American woman writer, she herself comes out of an 'alternate' culture even if, in a Stockholm far removed in time and place from her own original Lorain, Ohio, her achievement eventually would be celebrated at the international centre of things.

For all of her encompassing vision, her fiction bespeaks a massively particular sense of America's many black and inter-racial histories. So, at least, would be the witness of a literary career which announced itself with the portrait of fissured black womanhood in the person of Pecola Breedlove in *The Bluest Eye* (1970), which told the fraught, embattled story of two black girlhood mirror selves joined yet broken in *Sula* (1974), which gave a new tracing of African diaspora through the black-mythic life of Macon Dead III ('Milkman') in *Song of Solomon* (1977), which delivered a stunning memorial story of the 'haint' of slavery as infanticide in *Beloved* (1987), and which conceived a compelling Great Migration story-ballad of love gained and lost in the Harlem of the 1920s in *Jazz* (1992).[2]

In both inclusive and specific reach of story as in style she offers a vantage point, a presiding spirit, with which to begin the present account. Morrison also adds her lustre to the long, winding company of African American writers who before, and alongside, have also voiced the historic continuum which has been Afro-America. Giving literary form to so dramatic a story has indeed meant the facing, the telling, of defeat as well as conquest, of the very will to black voice or signature undermined, even erased, by a mainstream often fearful of just what it might say.

No doubt, in part, this remembrance of enjoined silence has played its role in the exuberant variety of black written idiom, a point emphasized, and reflexively embodied, in both the Prologue and Epilogue to *Invisible Man* (1952), Ralph Ellison's landmark novel.[3] Its voices have been many, vernacular and high, down-home 'black' and mainstream, Dixie-rural and citied, and, axially, every community style of the spoken made over into the scriptural.

As the sub-title emphasizes, *Designs of Blackness: Mappings in the Literature and Culture of Afro-America* seeks to develop a series of culture-studies maps, soundings, configurations. Local analyses of text play into an ongoing and contextual cross-reference, 'the word' as inscription in its own invitational right yet inevitably shaped by, and given to, a larger

African American continuity of word, and that, in its turn, linked into America's overall and ever more mosaical multicultural word.

In this respect I have not hesitated to dwell as closely upon a given passage, image or form of words (the 'Written by Himself/Herself' of slave narrative is indicative) as upon a sense of Afro-America's dialogical depths and widths. That has meant a necessary interplay with each varying concourse of American history from slavery to the 1960s of Black Power, the disenfranchisements of Reconstruction to the long overdue re-enfranchisements of the Civil Rights Act of 1964 and the Voter Registration Act of 1965, the Depression and then World War II as black experience, through to the Reagan–Bush 1980s of 'benign neglect'. It also recognizes how, whether in the issue of Martin Luther King's birthday as national holiday, or the 1992 white-racist police beating of Rodney King in L.A.'s South Central, or the Clinton concern for a new American compact and dialogue on race, history remains in the making.

Within these time-frames, and given a prime focus in literary work, I also invoke Afro-America through the turns of its talk, the dazzling plenty of its musicianship and the popular-culture dimensions of its sport, street life, film, humour, cuisine and dress styles. Nor have I sought to step round, or through, the implications of a still evolving body of theory and ideology about African American, indeed all black, writing. Whether considering the Black Aesthetic of the 1960s, or of its aftermath in the 1980s and beyond – in which names like Houston Baker and Henry Louis Gates Jr. have set the standard through their work on 'signifying' and black literary typology, along with, say, Barbara Christian and Hazel V. Carby, on issues of gender and feminism in African American writing – each is not only given its due but, to one degree or another, uninhibitedly put to critical work.[4]

The emergence of new black textual and reference scholarship has added to a fuller sense of the African American record, symptomatically *The Schomburg Library of Nineteenth-Century Black Women Writers* (1988–), *The Oxford Companion to African American Literature* (1997) and *The Norton Anthology of African American Literature* (1997).[5] All of these represent new consolidation, scale and context, a latest reproof to add to that begun in the 1960s against one-time neglect as undeserved as it was complacent or patronizing.

☆　☆　☆

Though I have hardly been shy about coverage, *Designs of Blackness* moves away from linearity or a merely sequential view of literary-cultural history.

Rather, each chapter seeks to negotiate any one era of authorial achievement, and any one African American writer or group, through a contextualizing mix of voice and cultural expression, and, at the same time, as perceived through the revisionist interpretations of later eras. The opening account, of the black literary Birth of the Nation, is meant to be indicative: 1776, and the paradox of slaveholding at American Independence, as written and bequeathed by a founding black authorship with the Augustan New England poet, Phillis Wheatley, as centre.

This inaugurating round of African American literary voice is first reinvoked through the 'black nationalist' 1960s and the kinds of ideological critique to have followed in its wake. It then comes more sharply into focus as a literary ancestry (especially for the 'New Negro' or Harlem Renaissance 1920s) running from the 1770s to the 1820s. Finally, it is taken up for its own imaginative enfigurings through four primary texts, Wheatley's *Poems* (1773), Jupiter Hammon's hymnological 'An Evening Thought' (1760), Olaudah Equiano/Gustavus Vassa's slave-autobiographical *Narrative* (1789), and David Walker's fierce, rallying abolitionist pamphlet *Walker's Appeal* (1829).[6]

The subsequent chapters work in kind. Chapter 2, an analysis of African American 'first-person singular' (in Emerson's historic phrase), takes its orientation from Frederick Douglass's slave-written *Narrative* (1845) before widening into a shared circle of Booker T. Washington, 1920s 'New Negro' autobiography, Richard Wright, James Baldwin as essayist-autobiographer, Chester Himes, Malcolm X and Maya Angelou. The emphasis, throughout, falls upon scriptural self-owning, enletterment as a dialectic of recognition, recovery, the very making and remaking of identity.[7]

Chapter 3 pursues Harlem as a city of words. Whether hub, magnet, triumph or pit, a 1920s Jazz Age clubland, a 1940s 'race riot' gathering point, a postwar home for Langston Hughes or Ralph Ellison, and James Baldwin before them, or a contemporary mixed-fare of Sugar Hill and tenement, churchly respectability and drugs, this has been Afro-America's premier metropolis. Its literary, as well as musical and visual, conspectus has shown an energy in kind with the varieties of its citizenry, cultures high and popular. Alain Locke's imagined 'race capital' of the 1920s links to LeRoi Jones/Imamu Amiri Baraka's Black Arts Theater of the 1960s, Claude McKay's *Home to Harlem* (1928) to Rosa Guy's *A Measure of Time* (1983) with the Harlemry of Langston Hughes, Chester Himes, James Baldwin and Darryl Pinckney positioned along the way.[8]

'Womanisms', Chapter 4, takes Alice Walker's historic formulation in *In Search of Our Mothers' Gardens* (1983) as a working gloss for the genealogy of a dozen woman-authored novels from Harriet E. Wilson's *Our Nig* (1859) to Toni Morrison's *Beloved* (1987), with Zora Neale Hurston's *Their Eyes Were Watching God* (1937) as a key touchstone. [9] An Afro-America of women 'authoring', 'authored', and they, in turn, 'authoring', serves as a frame. The literary womanism in view – its politics, gender concerns, lineages, sorority, is taken for a shared, yet resolutely individual gallery of signatures.

In its account of Richard Wright, Chapter 5 argues for a reading beyond the received figure of 'Negro protest' or 'black realism'. Rather, he is taken as a writer whose fiction turns upon rarer, other, landscapes, with an 'inside' storytelling to match, of the psyche, of *cauchemar* and yet also wonder, and whereby Wright can look to literary kin as much in Kafka or Poe as, say, Dreiser. On this account, with a story like 'The Man Who Lived Underground' and his novel *Native Son* (1940) as centrepieces, he invites a rethinking as naturalist-realist. Wright, runs the suggestion, can as well be thought his own kind of putative modernist.[10]

'War and Peace', Chapter 6, takes off from Wright into the 1940s as a decade both of, and itself the complex subject of, black writing, and throughout possessed of its own discrete play of paradox. In working through a span of literary texts from John O. Killens's *And Then We Heard the Thunder* (1963) to Gwendolyn Brooks's *A Street in Bronzeville* (1945), the issue becomes one of how each refracts the contradictory equation of a black soldiery at war abroad in the name of a cause, a peace, denied them and their families at home.[11]

Chapter 7 considers how to account for, in the aftermath of World War II, a Beat movement which, however counter-cultural and full of allusions to blues and 'black' existentialism, has passed into history overwhelmingly through a white (and white male) writer-cadre of Ginsberg, Kerouac, Ferlinghetti and the rest. In tackling the poetry of black Beatdom by LeRoi Jones/Imamu Amiri Baraka, Ted Joans and Bob Kaufman, the hope is to offer an amends, a literary making-good.

No other era since Emancipation has more carried the 'racial' smack, the *frisson*, of an America required to deliver its equalitarian promises than the 1960s. Jones/Baraka's *Dutchman* (1964), a play of the black, mythic, ever-circling underground, amounted to one kind of staging. Black Power, Civil Rights, the politics, militant or gradualist, respectively of Malcolm X and Martin Luther King, amounted to another. Chapter 8 explores this overlapping force of drama (not least as enfigured in the performative, powerfully iconic and continuing presence of Muhammad Ali) – a 'blackness' of both theatre and life, with playwrights from James Baldwin to Ed Bullins, Lorraine Hansberry to Douglas Turner Ward, straddling the two.[12]

Black literary writ in the novel, especially given the long shadow of Richard Wright, almost by ideological and critical rote has been taken to be neo-realist. A voice like that of Leon Forrest, the subject of Chapter 9, suggests otherwise. His trilogy of 'Forest County', and the Witherspoon-Bloodworth Chicago dynasty, *There Is a Tree More Ancient Than Eden* (1973), *The Bloodworth Orphans* (1977) and *Two Wings to Veil My Face* (1984), takes its place as a modernist feat both in its own right and as contributing to a larger black literary modernist and postmodern turn. Those sharing imaginative, fabulatory, billing with Forrest run from Ishmael Reed as the metafictional wit who bowed in with spoof science fiction and Westerns like *The Free-Lance Pallbearers* (1967) and *Yellow Back Radio Broke-Down* (1969) to John Wideman, Carlene Hatcher Polite and the story-writer James Alan McPherson and, by shared consent, the Ralph Ellison of *Invisible Man* as tutelatory narrative spirit.[13]

The final chapter takes on the vexed helix of race itself, and along with it colour, Afro-America's fictions of passing as a pathway into the altogether more enravelled, canny domains of American identity. 'Who's Passing for Who? was Langston Hughes's title for a 1945 story. It acts as a gloss, a point of entry, to the way the pluralities of self have throughout been both reduced, and traduced, by the usual racial taxonomies.

Given a context of recent multicultural controversy, from the opening of the American (and Western) literary canon through to the affrays and ethnic and sexual culture-politics of political correctness, and in texts from the first-ever African American novel, William Wells Brown's *Clotel* (1853), through to Charles Johnson's picaresque *Oxherding Tale* (1982), I suggest that race, as colour, has long been shown infinitely to deceive. They involve, on Afro-America's own abundant evidence of novel writing, and beyond, a near Melvilleian *trompe l'oeil* – the specific outward show, itself often in doubt, taken for the always more plural inner human whole.[14]

☆   ☆   ☆

People ask me why I'm always writing about the past. I don't know. I think it's probably because there's more of it. It seems infinite and inexhaustible to me, and it can bear a lot of re-imagining. Especially black American life, because it has been usurped by some people and it *needs* to be re-imagined.[15]

This, to return to Toni Morrison and an interview given in 1992, pulls together many of the threads explored in *Designs of Blackness*. Re-imagining Afro-America's past, as indeed its present and future, has of necessity been a call to word for all its writers. The study to hand, I hope, conveys my own warm, indebted pleasure in, and due recognition of, just how compelling has been the upshot.

1

Reclamations: The Early Afro-America of Phillis Wheatley, Jupiter Hammon, Olaudah Equiano and David Walker

Like the dead-seeming, cold rocks, I have memories within that came out of the material that went to make me. Time and place have had their say.

Zora Neale Hurston, *Dust Tracks on a Road* (1942)[1]

... what is commonly assumed to be past history is actually as much a part of the living present as William Faulkner insisted. Furtive, implacable and tricky, it inspirits both the observer and the scene observed, artifacts, manners and atmosphere and it speaks when no one wills to listen.

Ralph Ellison, 'Introduction', *Invisible Man*, 30th Anniversary Edition (1952, 1982)[2]

'We Shall Overcome'. 'Freedom Now'. 'I Have A Dream'. In a profile of America's earliest black writers, the great clarion phrases of the 1960s could at first look anachronistic, a vantage point all too recent. Yet if the Kennedy–Johnson years (with good reason they have also been called the Martin Luther King–Malcolm X years) signified the immediacy of Civil Rights and Black Power, the effect, at the same time, was to open Afro-America, indeed all America, to retrospect, the excavation and interrogation of almost every past configuring of the nation in black and white – not to mention of its colouration through Native, *latino* and Asian heritage.

In literary terms this has led to a timely and often celebratory process of reclamation. For the nineteenth century it spans black folklore, spirituals, verse and the early African American novel as evolved from William Wells Brown and Harriet E. Wilson to Charles Chesnutt and Frances E. W. Harper. The present century bows in with the 1920s Harlem or 'New Negro' Renaissance to be followed, in the Depression years, with the epochal figure of Richard Wright.

Black 'womanist' voice, to invoke Alice Walker's term, has its prime signatories in Zora Neale Hurston and Walker herself. Afro-America's poetry finds its best-known canon in a line from Phillis Wheatley to Paul Dunbar, Countee Cullen to Langston Hughes and, latterly, Gwendolyn Brooks to Rita Dove. Theatre can look back to Lorraine Hansberry, to Jones/Baraka in the 1960s, and thereafter to an Ed Bullins or August Wilson. And for the literary generation writing in the wake of Ralph Ellison and James Baldwin the banner names include LeRoi Jones/Imamu Amiri Baraka, poets from Audre Lorde to Michael Harper, key story writers like James Alan McPherson and Toni Cade Bambara, and a variety of novelists from Toni Morrison to Ishmael Reed.

Yet for the writers who constitute Afro-America's very earliest tier of the 1770s through to the 1820s, and in particular Phillis Wheatley, Jupiter Hammon, Olaudah Equiano/Gustavus Vassa and David Walker, matters have not been so availing. To explore why, and with what implications, a number of connected steps back and forth in time need to enter the reckoning. For as the 1960s brought about the historic Second Renaissance of black politics and the arts, the decade also reopened avenues into prior legacy – though only rarely with a view to the New Republic of 1776 as perceived and written by Afro-America.

Usually, and understandably, it has been with the great slave texts, the *Narrative* of Frederick Douglass in 1845 above all, that reclamation stops. The Age of Wheatley rarely becomes more than prelude, a literary antechamber. Yet to revisit the black writings of that age is to be faced with both an individual complexity of imagining and a case study in how modern Afro-America has come to construe its own literary-cultural formation.

The 1960s call for an ideologically committed black arts would prove as exhilarating and as vexatious as the age's politics. Yet it undeniably took on the key issues. Who had best written, and who was now best writing, Afro-America? What made for an African American usable past? Which prior touchstones, if any, were to be retained in the judgement of black art and literature? Can a linkage truly be discerned between Phillis Wheatley as the author in 1773 of the first ever black book to be published in America and, say, Ralph Ellison as the landmark novelist of *Invisible Man* in 1952?

☆   ☆   ☆

In all these regards LeRoi Jones/Imamu Amiri Baraka – poet, dramatist, storywriter, essayist, community activist, black nationalist and, thereafter, Marxist – especially serves. Never one to pull punches he called for a renewing 'black fire' in the title-phrase of the anthology he co-edited with Larry Neal in 1968.[3] An earlier taking of aim was to be found in his 'The Myth of a "Negro Literature"'(1962):

> The mediocrity of what has been called 'Negro Literature' is one of the most loosely held secrets of American culture. From Phyllis [sic] Wheatley to Charles Chesnutt, to the present generation of American Negro writers, the only responsible accretion of tradition readily attributable to the black producer of a formal literature in this country, with a few notable exceptions, has been of an almost agonizing mediocrity.[4]

The sense of let-down, even anger, at the apparent non- emergence of a truly *black* black literature was patent. Whatever the claims to be advanced for Phillis Wheatley as Enlightenment America's inaugural black poet, or for Charles Chesnutt as the Reconstruction author of the Uncle Julius McAdoo stories of *The Conjure Woman* (1899) and a classic novel of 'passing' like *The House Behind the Cedars* (1900), so much of 'Negro Literature' had apparently failed to deliver. The accusation of 'agonizing mediocrity' spoke volumes.[5]

Three decades on, a development not lost on Jones/Baraka himself, that view tends to look peremptory, more a given time's cultural reflex than a judgement for the ages. Nor could Jones/Baraka or anyone else quite have anticipated the massive recovery of past African American writing or the impact of black literary theory and scholarship with its reordering of the critical rules of engagement for black texts. Yet in the flurry of scholarly editions, histories and their trade spinoffs, the least reinstituted writings still remain precisely those embracing Wheatley, Hammon, Equiano and Walker.

The issue, then, becomes one of how best to free Wheatley and her literary contemporaries from routine charges of vapidity, imitation, flaws both ideological and expressive. Can they, as others of Afro-America's first literary age, be summoned on grounds other than merest duty, an also-ran piety? Meeting the issue lies not only in a better sense of their respective imaginative claims but also in establishing their link to quite subsequent traditions of black writing, a continuity of word and context within, and at the same time also reaching outside, Afro-America. In all of these interconnected respects each of the four offers at once a particular, and a wholly representative, case.

In Phillis Wheatley one looks to the oblique liberationist idiom of her *Poems on Various Subjects, Religious and Moral by Phillis Wheatley, Negro Servant to Mr. John Wheatley, of Boston, in New England* (1773). In the case of Jupiter Hammon's 'An Evening Thought: Salvation by Christ, with Penetential [*sic*] Cries' (1760), the challenge lies in inferring the black verse maker from within the verse, the personal accent from within the general devotionalism. *The Interesting Narrative of the Life of Olaudah Equiano, or Gustavus Vassa, the African. Written by Himself* (1789) works similarly, the 'own memoirs' of an ex-slave eclectically Ibo, American and British, whose plainstyle as often as not flatters to deceive. As for David Walker's *Walker's Appeal, in Four Articles, together with a Preamble, to the Coloured Citizens of the World, but in particular, and very expressly, to Those of The United States of America* (1829), it can be seen to put *The Declaration of Independence* as America's self-inaugurating charter of 1776 under quite the most accusatory of intertextual black auspices.[6]

☆   ☆   ☆

Paradoxically, the very cavils raised by Jones/Baraka (and the 1960s Black Arts context out of which they arose) would play their own circuitous part in the re-evaluation of Wheatley, Hammon, Equiano/Vassa and Walker. The resolve, in 'The Myth of a "Negro Literature"', 'to get at [Negro experience] ... in its most ruthless identity',[7] could not have been doubted in his own writing. The 'blackness' of his 1964 play *Dutchman*, or of his nationalist anthem-poem, 'BLACK DADA NIHILISMUS', or of his story-cycle *The System of Dante's Hell* (1965), each bespeaks precisely the dispensation he finds lacking in Wheatley and her generation. 'Black Art', from his *Black Magic: Collected Poetry, 1961–1967* (1969), gives summarizing terms of reference:

> We want a black poem. And a
> Black World.
> Let the world be a Black Poem
> And Let All Black People Speak This Poem
> Silently
> or LOUD[8]

Throughout most of the 1960s Jones/Baraka wrote as one of the prime movers of the Black Aesthetic, a cultural nationalism he shared with a number of leading black literary writers and critics. Addison Gayle Jr., whose essay-anthologies and criticism also held centreground, left little doubt of his ideological affinities when he offered the following opinion: 'The Black Aesthetic ... is a corrective – a means of helping black people out of the polluted mainstream of Americanism'.[9]

Others were quick to re-enforce the argument. Hoyt Fuller, founder of Chicago's OBAC (Organization of Black American Culture), proclaimed in 'Towards a Black Aesthetic' (1968) that 'the revolutionary black writer has decided that white racism will no longer exercise its insidious control over his work'.[10] Ron Maulana Karenga, the radical West Coast force behind the Afrocentric *US*, in his greatly influential 'Black Cultural Nationalism' (1968), laid down as criteria 'commitment to the revolutionary struggle' and a belief in 'permanent revolution'.[11] For Larry Neal, equally, in 'The Black Arts Movement' (1968), politics and art were not to be thought separate domains – 'Black Art is the aesthetic and spiritual sister of Black Power'.[12] Poets like Don Lee/Haki R. Madhubuti in his early 'community' verse collections *Black Pride* (1968), *Think Black* (1968) and *Don't Cry, Scream* (1969), or Etheridge Knight in his affecting and black-existential *Poems from Prison* (1968), together with scholar-critics like George Kent in *Blackness and the Adventure of Western Culture* (1972) and Stephen Henderson in *Understanding the New Black Poetry* (1973), added their shared weight to the ethos of commitment and militancy.[13]

It was in this spirit that the controversy over William Styron's *The Confessions of Nat Turner* (1968) arose. In *William Styron's Nat Turner: Ten Black Writers Respond* (1968), Styron as white Southern novelist could be taken to task by the editor, John Henrik Clarke, for 'distortion' and 'reducing Nat Turner to impotence', thereby denying the leader of Virginia's slave rebellion in 1831 'a literary interpreter worthy of his sacrifice'. No matter that Styron – born and raised in Tidewater country, a Southern liberal for all his own slaveholding forbears, and a long-time friend of James Baldwin – called his novel 'less an "historical novel" than a meditation on history', and would later cite archival support for his portrait, or argue for rights of imagination in his use of first-person voice; he had appropriated, and then dehistoricized (and so unheroized) a black leader.[14]

Fuller again reflected a shared sense of the changing literary politics when, on assuming the editorship of the long-time black features monthly, *Negro Digest*, he retitled it *Black World*. Magazines like Black Arts's *Black Dialogue* (1964–70) – founded on the West Coast and out of which grew Joe Goncalves's *Journal of Black Poetry* (1966–73) which published international African and Caribbean as well as African American writing – and the Oakland-based *Soulbook* (1964–76), gave a standard for the rewriting of Afro-America. Others included *Umbra* (1963–73), which published Ishmael Reed, Clarence Major and Julian Bond, *Nommo* (1969–72), published under the aegis of OBAC, *The Black Scholar* (1969–), initially issued six times a year before becoming a quarterly and a major source of black creative work, and *Black Creation* (1970–75), edited by Fred Beauford, which, however 'committed' in a general sense, also pointed to a growing unease at Black Aesthetic prescriptivism.[15]

Over time, discontents and splits had begun to show; there was a look of High Command to the ideology, a hands off to proprietary white criticism, but also an insistence that black literary work be judged only by the one required 'community' standard. Black was to mean Afrocentricity, consciously racialized writing in the name of the one revolutionary purpose, with all black writers, artists and their critics held to appropriate account. The upshot could not help but become attritional, adherence to a laid-down ideology of resistance and overturn with a corresponding indictment of supposed literary slackers, heretics or mavericks.

On this standard, among others, Langston Hughes, Robert Hayden, and on occasion Ralph Ellison and James Baldwin, found themselves judged short of the mark; theirs was a 'protest' either non-existent or too displaced to satisfy the movement's desiderata (Jones/Baraka notoriously complained of Ellison's 'fidgeting away in some college'). Ishmael Reed, whose satiric virtuosity and early postmodern textual play had been announced in his novel *The Free-Lance Pallbearers* (1967), also came in for chastisement. But when accused of turning away in his work from a politically usable, adversary, black-centred aesthetic, and thereby an 'anomaly' (Gayle) and 'bourgeois dupe' (Baraka), with typical brio he gave back as good as he got. His answering barbs spoke of 'goon squad aesthetics', 'black sheriffs', and 'neo-realist gangs'.[16] Given this kind of affray, it was perhaps inevitable that early black writing would get almost completely left out of the reckoning, an ideological and literary poor relation.

The Black Aesthetic undoubtedly played its part in ushering in the 'Second Black Renaissance'.[17] Yet with the gathering unease at such an unyielding party line it helped give rise to other critical ideologies and practices. These would circle back to a closer inspection of Afro-America's literary beginnings. Clarence Major, the novelist of *All-Night Visitors* (1969) and the poet of *Cotton Club* (1972), and one of the literary generation which inherited the Black Aesthetic, found himself writing in his essay-collection *The Dark & Feeling: Reflections on Black American Writers and Their Works* (1974):

> The racial identity of a group of writers is not grounds for a critical formula to which all may be subjected for analysis. Furthermore artistic values, red, blue, white, green, black or gold, do not have to give way to socio-political concerns ... In the Introduction to *The New Black Poetry* I speak of a 'radical black aesthetic.' ... I do not mean 'black aesthetic' as an extension of Black Nationalism.[18]

Nor was it only creative writers who took against in-house rules and regulations. A generation of black scholarship moved into new avenues of approach. Houston Baker, who readily acknowledges his debts to the Black Aesthetic generation (and who initially had taken against Reed), would propose in studies like *The Journey Back: Issues in Black Literature and Criticism* (1980) black vernacularity with its dynamics of talk, memory, folk and the blues, as quite another schema for analysis of black writing.[19] In *From Behind the Veil: A Study of Afro-American Narrative* (1979) Robert B. Stepto would argue for black typology, the core figural patterning of unfreedom into freedom, silence into word, dark into light, as derived from slave narrative.[20] Black feminism, or womanism in Alice Walker's historic term, would win its own hearings in critical accounts like Barbara Christian's *Black Women Novelists: The Development of a Tradition, 1892–1976* (1984) and Hazel V. Carby's *Reconstructing Womanhood: The Emergence of the Afro-American Woman Novelist* (1987) – both given over to the novel of a discrete other kind of black literary continuity, one of gender, mothering and daughtering, womanism/feminism, heterosexual and same-sex love, family, and private and public femininity.[21]

Henry Louis Gates Jr., the emerging doyen of black critical scholarship, would anatomize 'signifying' in its every turn and riff as at once syncretically both African and African American. In *Figures in Black: Words, Signs and the 'Racial' Self* (1987) he offers a working summary, his own balance sheet of gains and losses. While giving full recognition to the Black Aesthetic as 'energetic and compelling', 'an infectious movement of letters', he anything but denies limitations, above all the notion of the black (or any) text made subject to the one exclusive interpretative strategy or ownership.[22]

Under these evolving protocols African American literature, including its first shapings from Wheatley to Douglass, has attracted an ever greater pluralization of theory and analysis.[23] Even critics given to the rarer altitudes of deconstruction find grounds for interest. What, it is proposed, could be more artfully artless than slave narrative, coded, synecdochic, given to its own inlaid allusion and doubling? Nor has all been high solemnity. It was perhaps only a matter of time before even slaveholding would be opened to postmodern irreverence – Ishmael Reed, again, in his novel, *Flight to Canada* (1976) – 'the peculiar institution' subjected to comic but always seriously purposive daring, and replete with an 'African' (or as Reed terms it HooDoo or Vodoun) rendering of the symbology, time and space of slave history.[24]

Writers and critics alike began to see, moreover, that the taste for experiment, each different style of fable or image, in fact belonged to a long and shared black literary continuum. The Harlem Renaissance in the 1920s, for which Alain Locke's *The New Negro: An Interpretation* (1925) acted as manifesto-anthology, was symptomatic. If its writers almost vaunted their varieties of genre and voice, they were mindful of the remembered and ancestral 'texts' of slavery – stories of survival, coping, witness or belief within a context of auction-block and subsequent abuse. This spoken black-community word, its folklore, double play and humour, and whatever due allowance for the influence of a white literary-experimental 1920s, became written text, one African American generation's self-scripturalization.

The relevant footfalls can be met with in Langston Hughes's 'The Negro Speaks of Rivers' (1921), with its deft alluvial metaphor of black diaspora and blues; in Countee Cullen's 'Heritage', first published in his collection *Color* (1925), whose luxuriant, Keatsian imagery turns on a query about the references back to Africa as a mother continent of 'copper sun' and 'nakedness'; in Jean Toomer's *Cane* (1923), with its symbolist mosaics and portraiture of different women within a landscape of 'race' as southern heat and fever; in Claude McKay's *Home To Harlem* (1928) in which Harlem becomes at once historic and iconic metropole; in Nella Larsen's *Quicksand* (1928) and *Passing* (1929) and Jessie R. Fauset's *Plum Bun* (1929), in which both the race and gender implications of 'passing' are overlappingly held up for scrutiny; in the often dazzlingly memorial grain within the polemical essays of W.E.B. DuBois – or in an anti-lynch novel like Walter White's *The Fire in the Flint* (1924), the work of an NAACP (National Association for the Advancement of Colored People) stalwart with its invocation of an ancestral and yet ongoing threat against America's black population (between 1889 and World War I alone a proven 2,522 lynchings took place); and in the books, pamphlets and essays of Alain Locke himself whose every forward vista calls up a vast, historic black past.[25]

So shared a sediment of memory, of passed-down image, bind the two eras of Wheatley and Locke into an ongoing, yet always newly made-over, black lexicon. Arthur A. Schomburg, Puerto Rico-raised founder of the Negro Society for Historical Research in 1911, book collector and archivist, for whom the 135th Street branch of the New York Library with its huge and indispensable black archives is named, had every reason to say in his 'The Negro Digs Up His Past' (1925) that 'already, the Negro sees himself against a reclaimed background'.[26]

Richard Wright, successor voice to the Harlem Renaissance, offers his own kind of working retrospect. If *Native Son* (1940) signified Depression-era naturalism, did it not also imply an ancestral black psyche shaped by slave pursuit and haunting? Is the autobiography of *Black Boy* (1945) and the posthumous *American Hunger* (1977) not only the history of a Dixie childhood and migration to Chicago but also of Wright as a writer compelled to discover and then add his own voice to whole past congregations of black word?[27]

A same continuity of 'the word' finds its echo in James Baldwin's fiction and essays. Whether in his novel, *Go Tell It on the Mountain* (1953), or in his debut essay-collection, *Notes of a Native Son* (1955), he explores 'white' and 'black' less in terms of colour than as historic American power relationship. The very language of race, for Baldwin, becomes a refractive history, burdened in codes of superiority and inferiority from slavery times to modern Harlem.[28]

Ralph Ellison's *Invisible Man* (1952), along with the major essay work of *Shadow and Act* (1964) and *Going to the Territory* (1986), however scriptural, at the same time both invoke and use an oral iconography of Stagolee, Brer Rabbit, goopher, haints and signifying, along with every kind of borrowing from Afro-America's music. In every respect, Ellison insists on how black culture and especially its verbal arts have been woven into, insubstantiated within, all aspects of mainstream America.[29]

The process does not abate in recent fiction. In Paule Marshall's *The Chosen Time, the Timeless People* (1969) the echoes are those of the Middle Passage and the Caribbean landfall. Toni Morrison evokes an Ethiopia borne to America through spoken myth and child song in *Song of Solomon* (1977). Great-Momma Sweetie Reed looks back to slavery time from the Chicago of a later century in Leon Forrest's *Two Wings to Veil My Face* (1984). Black migration from the Carolinas to Pittsburgh, and its family markers of place and memory, likewise press into the stories told in John Wideman's 'Homewood' trilogy of *Hiding Place* (1981), *Damballah* (1981) and *Sent For You Yesterday* (1983).[30]

Ntozake Shange choreographs *Sassafrass, Cypress & Indigo* (1982), her novel of three South Carolina sisters, as a latterday 'spell' of music, letters and diary; Charles Johnson, reflecting a training in philosophy, subjects slave narrative to a phenomenological slant in *Oxherding Tale* (1982), and gives a science fiction or *Doppelganger* update to conjure and spirit talk in *The Sorcerer's Apprentice* (1986). Even Clay Ellis's *Platitudes* (1988), a montage of computer letterwriting, photography and menus set in New York, although it issues from a writer who dubs himself a 'New Cultural Mulatto' and so borrows freely from black and white literary tradition, turns upon an older blues-like love in its two young black writers.[31]

Not to associate this black 'tradition of the new' with its antecedents would be to fall short on the massive cross-reference, the iconographic links and interstices, of the African American literary tradition.

A consequence of all these developments has been the opportunity to see in Afro-America's first authors not only an inauguration but also a conjuncture, an affiliation, into later black literary tradition. Wheatley, African yet New Englander, slave girl yet black woman, can thus be situated inside a continuum of black womanist writing, whether the Harriet E. Wilson of her recently recovered novel of New England mulattoism and domestic service, *Our Nig; or, Sketches from the Life of a Free Black* (1859), the Zora Neale Hurston of the sumptuously vernacular blues novel, *Their Eyes Were Watching God* (1937), the Gwendolyn Brooks of a mock-epic yet always elliptical portrait of unfulfilled black womanhood like *Annie Allen* (1949), or the Rita Dove of the finely intimate and worked verse chronicle of black Ohio family, *Thomas and Beulah* (1986).[32]

Jupiter Hammon as evangelizer bequeaths a fervour, however much of its own time and place, to be heard again in accusing verse like Paul Dunbar's 'We Wear the Mask' (1895), or a keenly first-hand essay like Richard Wright's 'The Ethics of Living Jim Crow' (1937, 1940), or the existential self-making within Malcolm X's *Autobiography* (1965), or the determined historical clarifications of George Jackson's penitentiary writing in *Soledad Brother* (1970).[33]

Equiano/Vassa can credibly be placed inside a litany of quite other black 'first person singular', from Briton Hammon and his 14-page *A Narrative of the uncommon suffering and surprizing deliverance of Briton Hammon ...* (1760) as the first-known American slave writer through to James Baldwin's 'This World Is White No Longer' in *Notes of a Native Son* (1955) or Maya Angelou's break from Dixie racial and sexual silence in *I Know Why the Caged Bird Sings* (1970).[34]

The rhetorical militancy of David Walker likewise casts a long shadow. It finds one kind of echo in back-to-Africa stalwarts like Martin Delany and Marcus Garvey. It ancestralizes the addresses and sermonry of contemporary minister-politicians from Martin Luther King to Jesse Jackson, Malcolm X to Louis Farrakhan. Each, like Walker, would give a bold and persistent nay-saying to white ascendancy and divide and rule.

Taken together, Wheatley, Hammon, Equiano/Vassa and Walker can no longer remain peripheral secret sharers in the making of black literary history. They deserve better, not only founders but unmistakeable and enduring powers of voice in their own right.

☆   ☆   ☆

It is fitting, too, that a fuller sense of the immediate black literary context of their own time for Wheatley and her peers begins to win recognition. This includes, notably, Benjamin Banneker's *A Plan of Peace-Office for the United States* (1793), first published in the pages of his voluminous Enlightenment-era almanacs; the pamphlet *A Narrative of the Proceedings of the Black People during the Late Awful Calamity in Philadelphia ...* (1794) with its account of black resilience in time of Yellow Fever by the ex-slave co-authors, Bishop Richard Allen and Absalom Jones; Jupiter Hammon's own Christian-philosophical view of slavery as God's will in *An Address to the Negroes of the State of New York* (1806); and George Moses Horton's rousing verse appeal *The Hope of Liberty* (1829).[35]

Yet whatever the extension of the early African American canon, Wheatley and her literary generation still too rarely win through other than on narrow antiquarian grounds. The need persists to seize more fully upon the shared import of their work.

With Phillis Wheatley (1753–84) obliquity might well be thought all, given her practice of enfiguring imaginative freedom within a formulaic eighteenth-century poetics as the implied silhouette of literal freedom from slave ownership. The life has become familiar: the likely Gambia-Fulani, Islamic and/or animist and sun worshipping child, first sold at auction in Boston in 1761 to John and Susanna Wheatley and named Phillis for the slave ship which transported her; the slave turned maidservant educated by the Wheatleys into both letters and Congregationalism whose manumission occurs in 1773 (the same year she accompanied the Wheatley son, Nathaniel, on a six week visit to England); and the wife of John Peters whom she married in 1778, whose three children die before she does, and who, at 31, ends her own days in poverty and isolation.

Wheatley's poetry, however, offers an altogether less familiar challenge. Her Augustan verse forms, the elegy, panegyric, epic or Christian homily together with her great themes of Nature, Belief, Death, The Muse are customarily noted. But even as she emulates these forms, she also, implicitly, contests them: the imaginative will to freedom within a closed literary form is the very analogy of her historic will to freedom from within (in her phrase) the 'Afric' slave barrier.

Thus, as much as she inherits the designation of Boston's slave bellettrist brought out of pagan darkness (John Wheatley's 'LETTER sent by the Author's Master to the Publisher' speaks of her 'astonishing' ability to read 'the most difficult Parts of the Sacred Writings') she time and again insinuates a perceptible counter life. 'Attested' as her poetry was by Governor Thomas Hutchinson and his fellow Massachusetts worthies ('To the Publick'), is not the better clue to be found in the portrait which acts as a frontispiece with its encircling legend of 'PHILLIS WHEATLEY, NEGRO SERVANT to MR. JOHN WHEATLEY, of BOSTON'? There, eyes resolutely focused, quill in hand, book, ink and parchment before her, she appears to be quite certain about her own freedom of 'the word', her own self-subscription.

'On Imagination' offers a starting point. In one sense this is conventional neoclassic rhapsody ('imagination' as 'imperial queen', 'the sceptre o'er the realms of thought'). But Wheatley's hints go further. This is an 'imagination' with its subordinate 'fancy' (a nice anticipation of Coleridge's distinction in *Biographia Literaria*), which serves as a means of release from the 'soft captivity' of 'the mind'. 'Imagination' sponsors 'swiftness', the freeing of 'the mental optics'. Above all, it gives access to the 'measure' of the skies and 'the realms above', enabling those so possessed to 'grasp the mighty whole, Or with new worlds amaze th' unbounded soul'.

The pivotal phrase here is 'unbounded'. Its echo of shackles lost, flight taken, freedom won, tacitly implies the one slavery within the other. If, in the poem's last line, Nature's glories make for an 'unequal lay' between writer and subject, is there not the further hint of another order, that of owner and owned in which freedom to imagine goes unmatched with freedom to become one's own historic self-author?

This same parallel of freedom in imagination, freedom in life, underwrites 'To S.M. a young *African* Painter, on seeing his works'. As encomium, the terms again come over conventionally enough in the deployment of a visual imagery of 'breathing figures', 'balmy wings'. But the more consequential note lies in the implied fuller self-creation: the juncture of 'the painter's and the poet's fire' and of their two creatively 'free' spirits, yet also the two of them as pledged to a life realm as free as even 'fair creation'. Is not this the true 'seraphic theme' of the poem, its 'purer language'? Whatever their efforts with canvas or verse, and whatever New England Christianization, the transcending attainment for them (and, paradoxically, for their one-time captors) lies in a call to being beyond slavery's own 'solemn gloom of night'.

This liberative self-imagining in Wheatley, more urgent than the genteel Augustanism so often attributed to her, runs right through her poetry. It even takes form in her striking juvenilia, 'On Being Brought From Africa to America', with its due smack at binaries of black and white, pagan and Christian, and its terse, mock ingratiatory closing injunction:

> Remember, *Christians*, *Negros*, black as *Cain*,
> May be refin'd, and join th'angelic train. (p. 18)

It shows itself again in her careful adaptations from the Classics and the Bible. 'To Maecenas', for instance, with its strong solar invocation ('tow'ring *Helicon*'), passing allusion to the *African* 'Terence', and Parnassian hopes of emulating the Roman statesman and, in turn, the New England 'worthy' admired by Wheatley as re-embodying his spirit, carries the same note of aspirant liberation, the one self delivered out of the example of the other. 'Goliath of Gath', her own paraphrase of 1 Samuel XVII, recasts the account of David and Goliath as an overthrow of tyranny in terms whose register of 'martial powers', '*Jehovah's* name' and 'th' Almighty's hand', creates liberationist resonances later to be thought almost routine. These analogize Israel with Afro-America, the Jewish with the African diaspora.

Wheatley's 'nationalist' poetry in no way works to lesser shared purpose. 'To His Excellency General Washington', whose upshot of life imitating art took the form of her own meeting with the commander in chief, offers a Western panegyric (and African praise poem?) whose anti-'Britannia' sentiment culminates in the lines:

Ah! cruel blindness to Columbia's state!
Lament thy thirst of boundless power too late. (p. 146)

The one lexis again implies the other: 'boundless' as part of a cluster to include 'bondage', 'bound', 'binding'. Each calls up, accusingly, her own race's *American* enslavement.

In like manner, her 'On the Death of the Rev. Mr. GEORGE WHITEFIELD. 1770' moves beyond classic lamentation, not least in the reflexive implication that *his* 'music' ('We hear no more the music of thy tongue') has passed to her. A deliberately cross-racial salvationism is sounded in how she thinks of God's call as being made at one and the same time both to white America ('"Take him my dear *Americans*, he said ... "') and to black America ('"Take him, ye *Africans*, he longs for you ... "'). How has an all-inclusive Christianity – to which as convert and true believer she is committed – come to be so racially marked, two bifurcated Christianities, a white and black God? That Wheatley's poetry possesses its general historicist dimension can hardly be in doubt given verse like 'On The Capture of General Lee', with its liberty praising heroicization of the American revolutionary cause, or 'America', with its allusion to the 'Iron chain' of colonial ownership, or 'To the King's Most Excellent Majesty on His repealing of the Stamp Act' with its 'When kings do smile it sets their subjects free'. But here, too, is not her language for this history ('liberty', 'chain', 'subjects') seamed with its own not so implicit racialization, the black signification carried inside the white play of allusion?

An explicit 'Afric' dimension to this historicity can be found in two key Wheatley references. In February 1774 she writes to Samsom Occom, crossblood African-Mohegan Presbyterian minister, hymn writer and fellow New Englander: 'God grant Deliverance in his own way and Time', insisting upon a 'Vindication of ... Natural Rights' and of 'the Land of Africa' as due its 'Cry for Liberty'. The rich irony of a Christian and recently manumitted Wheatley writing to a converted Native American Occom on the issue of a Western, God sanctioned 'Deliverance' hardly needs emphasis.

In 'On The Death of General Wooster', a poem posthumously recovered, liberationism is even more explicit, albeit yoked to her own form of providential Chistianity:

But how, presumptuous shall we hope to find
Divine acceptance with th' Almighty mind –
While yet (O deed Ungenerous!) they disgrace
And hold in bondage Afric's blameless race? (p. 149)

In these lines, as in fact throughout her verse, Phillis Wheatley not only refracts but actually intervenes in the Atlantic slave history which 'made' her, an imagined freedom itself defiantly imagined. In his modern verse monologue, 'A Letter from Phillis Wheatley', Robert Hayden has every cause to imagine her on the English visit relishing 'signatures affirming me/True Poetess, albeit once a slave'.

☆   ☆   ☆

Evangelical hymnody will likely never be at the forefront of most literary preference, and no more so in the case of Jupiter Hammon (1720?–1800?) than with far better known practitioners like the English-born Charles Wesley or William Cowper. His enslavement, Long Island upbringing, Wesleyan conversion, probable unletteredness, and (in contrast with the anti-slavery stances of Richard Allen or David Walker) 'political' moderation, make for a context. Here was one of Early America's true believers walking humbly within his appointed station.

His 'An Evening Thought: Salvation by Christ, with Penetential [*sic*] Cries: Composed by Jupiter Hammon, a Negro belonging to Mr. Lloyd, of Queen's Village, on Long Island, the 25th of December, 1760', however, suggests a more combative, restless energy. This first ever black publication in America (a full-length book would await Wheatley) conveys an apparently quite unracialized religious sensibility – devotional, full of mission, pitched *ad hominem*. But is *nothing* to be heard of black religious experience, a would-be godly salvation of body and spirit as also relief from literal enslavement and in the form of a readily imaginable call and response elicited from pulpit or lectern?[36]

It is this latter which invites attention, each repetition and stress pattern, each calling up of a personal Jesus, and each sureness of heavenly freedom after earthly servitude. Piety, self-evidently, knows no single racial origin and the poem bears not a single explicit black reference. Yet it adds immeasurably to its reading when not only the subtext of slavery is brought to bear but also Toni Morrison's notion in *Playing in the Dark: Whiteness and the Literary Imagination* (1992) of 'representing one's race to ... a race of readers that understands itself to be "universal" or race-free'.[37]

In this the very first stanza points the way:

> Salvation comes by Christ alone,
>   The only Son of God;
> Redemption now to every one,
>   That love his holy Word. (p. 23)

The word, specifically God's 'holy Word', can be part of a spiritual exhortation as race-free as any. But it takes on added force when Hammon's versifying is also remembered as having been composed under African American auspices with all the habits, the communal sound and sign, of black signifying to hand.

These resonances make for a continuum throughout. 'Dear Jesus, we would fly to Thee' reads the succeeding stanza, flight from an imperfect worldly slavery to a perfect heavenly slavery. 'Dear Jesus, give thy Spirit now, Thy Grace to every Nation', in the fourth stanza, adds its own double note: selves, nations, possessed of 'the spirit', presumably more so for a captive people who are for good reason prone to slave quarter conversions and visions of Freedom's Trail as embodied in the death and resurrection of the martyred slave Christ.

These collocations of 'redemption', 'salvation', 'awakening', 'hunger' and, above all, 'freedom', which follow, do further contributing service, a process of called for spiritual transformation given added ironic urgency when read mindful of being offered in the voice of 'a Negro belonging to Mr. Lloyd'. How 'universal', that is shared and cross-racial, a transformation might be so entertained? How inclusive is the 'we' so urged to 'depart from Sin', 'accept the Word', 'magnify thy Name'?

Which meaning, finally, can be attached to the closing stanza, with its desideratum of 'Repentance here' as the prelude to Jesus's 'tender love'?

> Come, Blessed Jesus, Heavenly Dove,
> Accept Repentance here;
> Salvation give, with tender Love;
> Let us with Angels share. (p. 25)

Is this a 'repentance' simply universal or coevally (and transgressively) one to embrace black slave author and white free reader? In 'An Evening Thought', as in Hammon's other poems and addresses, these arising implications underline how poetic convention becomes unconventional, a generality of voice yet at the same time one invitingly particular, and invitingly African American.

Speaking of his 'extremely chequered' and 'various life and adventures' at the end of his *Interesting Narrative*, Olaudah Equiano (1745–1801), slave-named not after a Roman emperor but the Scandinavian monarch Gustavus Vassa, offers a disclaimer worth some pondering. With an appropriately Franklinesque show of modesty, a Christian convert's eye to the vainglory of self-history, he writes:

> I am far from the vanity of thinking there is any merit in this narrative; I hope censure will be suspended, when it is considered that it was written by one who was as unwilling as unable to adorn the plainness of truth by the colouring of imagination. (p. 178)

But whatever his own professed intention, and quite as much as Bunyan's *Pilgrim's Progress* or Defoe's *Robinson Crusoe*, which he cites as antecedents, can Equiano's 'plainness of truth' be taken simply at face value? Is his fear of 'the colouring of imagination' anything like the snare and delusion he implies, unacceptable malfeasance or falsification?

For whatever the would-be 'humble' factuality of his account, it offers at virtually every turn evidence of an often luminous imagination. The effect is to enhance the sheer historical eventfulness of the account, whether Equiano's moves in and out of African slave capture, progress from Ibo-Benin royal sibling to human chattel to manumitted freeman merchant, or transition from stasis as property to movement as mariner and North Pole explorer. It holds, too, for the unabating sea traveller who voyages from coastal Nigeria to the 'plantation' Antilles, from America to England and back, and from England to the Mediterranean of the Anglo-French Napoleonic Wars.

This imagination is evident in the gloss of the name Olaudah as 'one favoured, and having a loud voice and well-spoken', in the calculated likening of his 'Igbo' origins to 'that pastoral state which is described in Genesis' or, as the slave ship takes him to America, in the contrast of the flying fish with the 'multitude of black people, of every description, chained together'. In the latter instance, the fish as free energy (not to say sustenance denied Equiano and his fellow captives) contrasts perfectly with the stasis of the hold, a black prisoner caste immobilized and starved. Equiano's play of image and pattern takes on a 'colouring of imagination' not to be 'censured'.

This will to fabulation, however much Equiano himself may have deemed it a lapse, in fact gives the *Narrative* its best effect. The opening scenes invoke an African remembrance of sights and sounds: kinship systems, foodways, dress, politics, shamanism (holy men as 'magicians'), the role of language and ceremony, and black Islamic as against white Christian slavery. Envisaging the likely fate of his sister he calls up 'the pestilential stench of a Guinea ship', with its hint of brute sexual as well as racial enslavement. In so writing up each capture and flight, first in Africa and, thereafter, in slave America and the West Indies, Equiano's accent betrays the instinctive fabulist or poet as much as exhorter.

The geography of his life, accordingly, takes on iconographic as well as literal force (Equiano, as often observed, became one of the most travelled personalities of his time). In Virginia, he finds himself named Jacob, having been called Michael aboard the slave ship – Gustavus Vassa soon follows. In Virginia, too, he sees a slave serving woman bound in an 'iron muzzle ... which locked her mouth so fast that she could scarcely speak'. These two experiences enfable, as well as historicize, slavery. The first witnesses to slave naming as one kind of ownership over another, the second as a means to speech literally prevented. Given his own rights of text, he can repudiate both, just as he can concede his one-time fear of whites as cannibals or his alarm at their clocks and apparent control of space and time.

For he cannot but see himself as having entered precisely a kind of alien space-time. This amounts to a 'west' of 'extraordinary escape(s)' and 'signal deliverance' whose eventfulness includes the Canada of the Seven Years War, Georgia as the worst of slaveholding Dixie, 'Musquito' Central America, the Mediterranean of Gibraltar, Tenerife, Cadiz and Smyrna, and the 'uninhabited extremity of the world' as he terms the North Pole. Thus, as much as he avows 'the interposition of Providence', the 'divine hand', in his different rites of passage, his *Life* also reads for him, and is written by him, as actual and yet a species of Gulliverism, literal voyage yet the semblance of dream voyage.

Each detail suggests, knowingly or not, a career full of itinerary chance, mishap, unpredictability, contingency. His life, or at least his life's telling, unfolds as much discontinuously as continuously – from warships at anchor in the Nore to a sea battle off Gibraltar, from the story of John Mondle's *delirium tremens* to Monserrat's haunted, tremulous Brimstone Hill, from Philadelphia Quakerism to the purchase of his own freedom, and from his association with Dr. Charles Irving and their desalination experiments to his final Bible conversion and work in abolitionism. Overall, these zigzags and reversals, shifts and discontinuities, make the perfect contradiction, that of the unforeseen as norm.

Notwithstanding assertions of Calvinist predestination, or invokings of rulebooks like Foxe's *Martyrology* and the *Guide to the Indians*, nothing, not even the Bible, will wholly account for the strangeness, the alterity, of a life at different times so dramatically both free and encaptured. The vaunted modesty of his authorship, his role as God's instrument, belies the life he tells. Quite self-appetitively, whatever his disclaimers and upbraidings, he has been led to 'author' himself.

Though 'from early years a predestinarian' (p. 140), Olaudah/Vassa relishes history as random, contrary, in fact wholly unpredestinarian. His plainstyle, another would-be modesty in keeping with his turn to Christianity, likewise equivocates, exhilarated (and exhilarating) where the intention may have been to sound merely instrumental. For whatever else, it both reveals, and conceals, the one-time slave whose unowned memorialist its creator has become in the process of writing the *Life of Olaudah Equiano or Gustavus Vassa, the African*.

In the most immediate sense the *Appeal* of David Walker (1785–1830), who, though born in Wilmington, North Carolina, made a Brattle Street clothing-store in abolitionist Boston his workplace and centre of operations, takes quite the contrary path. The terms in play throughout his 76-page octavo pamphlet (understandably banned in the South) at first seem the very spirit of explicitness, polemic given uninhibitedly to the show of its begetter's anger. Rita Dove's poem, 'David Walker', calls up the response it elicited at the time as 'Outrage, Incredulity. Uproar in state legislatures.'

Throughout the Preamble, Four Articles and Conclusion, the indictment is unbounded. 'We (coloured people of these United States)', Walker's opening page declaims, 'are the most degraded, wretched, and abject set of beings that ever lived since the world began ... '. The call for divine forgiveness of enemy rings no less uncompromisingly – '*O, my God, have mercy on Christian Americans!!*'. Whether on account of thinking his work done, or of the well-taken premonition of an early death by foul play, Walker would make all of his known bow in this one pamphlet, a no-holds, truly chiliastic, voice of black reckoning.

As he builds his 'Appeal' – Article 1 on 'our wretchedness', Article 2 on enforced 'ignorance ... and abject submission to the lash', Article 3 on America's double standard of Christianity, and Article 4, on slave colonization 'in a far country' – the urgency runs at one with writing known to have been done at speed. The italicizations and exclamation points, the appeals to Biblical typology (especially the afflictions of 'the children of Israel'), the historical inserts ('Bartholomew Las Casas', for all his anti-*encomienda*, anti-Indian slavery, as a founding proponent of 'our wretchedness' as *black* slaves), and each reproachful irony of the kind he directs at the Whig Kentuckian, Henry Clay ('Is not Mr. Clay a white man, and too delicate to work in the hot sun!!'), keep the pressure wholly unyielding. This is discourse unremittingly at heat and velocity, the raised voice transferred to the page.

Not quite all, however, is apocalypse. A vital other mediating frame intervenes, that of America's own *Declaration of Independence*. He closes on the lines:

> I also ask the attention of the world of mankind to the declaration of these very people of the United States. (p. 74)

The aim is unmistakable: the lie of slaveholding America's claim to a unique 'universal' equality and shared access to 'life, liberty and the pursuit of happiness'. Despite the secular cast of the *Declaration*, Walker's *Appeal* both notes and sees the irony in its conviction of Godly exceptionalism.

This careful shadowing of his *Appeal* with the *Declaration*, the 'reason' of American constitutionality contradicted by the 'unreason' of American slavery, deepens and interiorizes the text, an achievement altogether shrewder than first appearances might indicate.

Walker's tactics, thereby, situate his *Appeal* within the larger gallery of work created by Wheatley, Hammon, Olaudah/Vassa and their contemporaries. Reclamation in name and detail, and with fuller estimation of the imagining in play, has indeed been owed to all of them. For by their writings this first literary generation bequeaths an Afro-America, an America, not only in the word of a given time and place but in so much of its own future word.

The Stance of Self-Representation: Founders, Moderns and Contemporaries in African American Autobiography

Very soon after I went to live with Mr. and Mrs. Auld, she very kindly commenced to teach me the A,B,C. After I had learned this, she assisted me in learning to spell words of three or four letters. Just at this point of my progress, Mr. Auld found out what was going on, and at once forbade Mrs. Auld to instruct me further, telling her, among other things, that it was unlawful, as well as unsafe, to teach a slave to read. To use his own words, further, he said, 'If you give a nigger an inch, he will take an ell. A nigger should know nothing but to obey his master – to do as he is told to do. Learning would *spoil* the best nigger in the world. 'Now,' said he, 'if you would teach that nigger (speaking of myself) how to read, there would be no keeping him. It would forever unfit him to be a slave ...' These words sank deep into my heart, stirring up sentiments within that lay slumbering, and called into existence an entirely new train of thought. It was a new and special revelation, explaining dark and mysterious things, with which my youthful understanding had struggled, but struggled in vain. I now understood what had been to me a most perplexing mystery – to wit, the white man's power to enslave the black man. It was a grand achievement, and I prized it highly. From that moment, I understood the pathway from slavery to freedom.

Narrative of the Life of Frederick Douglass,
an American Slave, Written by Himself (1845)[1]

When, under the imprint of the American Anti-Slavery Society of Boston, Frederick Douglass published his landmark *Narrative*, he clearly hoped it would serve a number of related ends. First, it would be an act of memorialization – of birth to his slave mother Harriet Bailey and the unknown white slave master who was his father, of a Maryland plantation upbringing, and of workskills, hirings-out, and eventual clandestine escape by land and sea to New England.

At the same time, it would be his rallying-cry against the whole unconscionable edifice of slavery, a call to moral if not physical arms in the name of abolition. His resolve lay in showing America's white, and ostensibly Christian, citizenry the profound travesty of having a slave population in whose ranks he, himself, had so recently been entrapped. The slim volume with which he made his entrance, a mere 50 cents a copy on appearance, thereby bore the larger purpose: the closing down, for ever, of America's 'peculiar institution'.

Little wonder the *Narrative* holds its place in the nation's slave history, a bestseller by the standards of the day which quickly ran to more than a half-dozen editions, which was translated into Dutch and French, and which yielded two later and considerably longer versions as *My Bondage and My Freedom* (1855) and *Life and Times of Frederick Douglass* (1881, expanded 1892).[2]

Yet along with the life it chronicles, and the high crusading purpose, another more oblique dimension also requires acknowledgement. The words *Written by Himself* here assume primary significance. A form of credential, that is, not written by abolitionist helper and defiant of required slave illiteracy, it also gives a pointer to the *Narrative* as scripted drama in its own imaginative right. For the *Narrative* not only reports Douglass's taking textual possession of his history from white proprietorship, whether John Pendleton Kennedy's *Swallow Barn* (1832), with its magnolia plantation South, or New England abolitionist writing with its high point in Beecher Stowe's *Uncle Tom's Cabin* (1852), it also gives its own unique imaginative embodiment of that process.

Douglass's evidentiary manner at once reveals and conceals. On the one hand the *Narrative* reads as a transcript from life, with an additional frisson. It had been written by an author still open to re-enslavement under the 1793 and other Fugitive Slave legislation, unrepealed until 1864, and Douglass sought to escape these provisions on publication of the *Narrative* when he took up anti-slavery lecture invitations in England. The immediacy becomes even sharper when Douglass refuses to name those who have helped him, or to give details of the flight across the Chesapeake Bay, or to reveal his own whereabouts in Boston. In its own time, and not a little headily, most readers recognized a species of outlaw writing by an outlaw slave author.

Yet the matter does not end there. Douglass knew how his very manner of writing up the escape amounts to its own constitutive act of freedom.

All the components which have made the *Narrative* a canonical text come into play: the confessional first-person format, the iconography of a journey from dark to light and, always, the memorial use not only of black history but of black speech and cadence. The effect of each is not only to report, but to actualize, a self, the 'text' of Douglass's own self now made over into a literal or scriptural 'text'.

If it is little surprise that Douglass's *Narrative* lays down track for nearly all subsequent African American autobiography, this does not for a moment detract from its uniqueness. Douglass clearly calls upon a special ingenuity (and personality) in the plotting and implementation of his escape. His rendering of scenes like the whipping of Aunt Hester, the Covey fight, or the Sabbath school he runs at Mr. Freeland's plantation, all bespeak an instinctive narrative stylist. Nor can it be overlooked that Douglass finds himself enslaved within the less typical tobacco-crop Maryland setting rather than a down-river cotton and chattel slave state like Georgia or Mississippi.

But the uniqueness also lies in the very manner of Douglass's telling. For in remembering the acquisition of his ABCs and his three- and four-letter words, he does infinitely more than invoke the 'kind' tutelage of his slave master's wife. He actually enacts the 'new and special revelation', the 'deep and mysterious things', of literacy. He performs, as it were, his access to 'the word' as if almost to vaunt his scriptural conquest over previously denied powers of defining self and reality.

This process of gaining, and then in his *Narrative* giving vent to, an illegally-won enletterment, finds a long echo in black memory. Although herself born a 'Free Negro' in Maryland, and spending her young adulthood in Ohio, Frances E.W. Harper is typical. Her novel *Iola Leroy or Shadows Uplifted* (1892) offers a byway to its main plot in the story of Tom Anderson, a slave, who is threatened with 'five hundred lashes' if his master catches him pursuing 'the key to forbidden knowledge ... in the A B C's'. Anderson goes on to fashion a cloth for his head in which he hides cut-outs of the alphabet and practises his first writing on a river beach. Enletterment again denotes transgression, risk, but above all escape from non-ownership of word as much as body.[3]

Is there not, in this respect, a truly defiant irony in the title-phrase display of Douglass's own status under law as *An American Slave*? What more accusing paradox or synopsis could there be than a 'slave' freely writing his own supposed status as property? Whether or not he writes from abolitionist Boston, and however eloquently or affectingly he does so, he would have all know that within an America of constitutionally sanctified property-rights he has been not only slavery's bodily possession or stolen goods, but also its supposed verbal thing, its object in words.

As a slave he has been forced to exist within the definitional orbit of 'nigger', 'property', 'coon', 'boy' or 'hand', together no doubt with others which propriety did not allow him to print, terms always outside his own

choosing and calculated only to de-individuate and possess. Even as an
ex-slave, if, precariously, he can so regard himself at the time of writing,
he remains within a category, however welcome, still not wholly of his
own making. His *Written by Himself* challenges both: servitude into
freedom, wordlessness into word. In the latter respect his 'own' signature
implies escape from any or all nomenclature not of his own determining.

This double textuality operates throughout. When Douglass declares
'my father was a white man' he raises the issue not only of his own
parentage (evidence now gathers of Native American forbears), but of the
whole arbitrariness of 'race'. Who ordained these rules of miscegenation
and racial genetics? When is white black, black white, and where, implies
Douglass, does that leave him?

In the Edward Covey fight, 'the turning point in my career as a slave',
Douglass achieves far more than some local set-to with his overseer. The
pugilism possesses the prose itself, each feint, grip, release or hit taken into
and made the very rhythm of the telling. In this, too, Douglass anticipates
a later history of black–white pugilism through names like Jack Johnson,
Joe Louis and Muhammad Ali in which white oppression, whiteness as
the historic code of ownership, albeit for the moment, is fought into
dispossession and defeat.

In the encounter with the two dockside Irish labourers, the text once
more takes the drama into its own being. Will they, won't they, reveal
him as runaway? In fact, as the account shifts and turns, as it gives
mimetic body to Douglass's fears they ... wish him well, and with just the
hint that under other auspices a white–black worker alliance might have
been possible.

'I subscribe myself ... FREDERICK DOUGLASS'. So he takes his bow at
the close. In fact, Douglass is playing counterfeiter, *auteur*, a name whose
very composition, and compositeness, he has every reason to emphasize.
'Frederick Augustus Washington Bailey', 'Frederick Johnson', plain
'Frederick', 'Frederick Douglass' and 'FREDERICK DOUGLASS': in each
of his previous namings he implies slavery's power as much to unauthor
as to author. In his own eventual formulation, however, he insists upon
his own newly acquired and countervailing power to shadow and reverse
the process. Is not the capitalization as FREDERICK DOUGLASS a kind of
printerly answering-back, a name now self-owned and defiantly pitched
in majuscule? That 'Douglass' as surname, he explains, came about in
consequence of a borrowing from Scott's 'The Lady of the Lake' by his
abolitionist host in Boston, adds a perfect irony, realism overlaid by
romance.

Slaves, under the so-called Black or Slave Laws, were forbidden to read
and write, an upshot of the 1739 Stono Rebellion in South Carolina.
They might finagle their own 'passes', bear witness to the iniquities of
slavery, compose (or fake) their own names, and then use each of these
to advance slave revolution. These are some of the means used in the plot

hatched by Gabriel Prosser in Richmond in 1800 and which are taken up in Arna Bontemps's meticulous, unsparing but always lyric novel *Black Thunder: Gabriel's Revolt: Virginia 1800* (1936).

In Prosser's wake the list includes Toussaint de L'Ouverture in Haiti in 1802, Charles Deslandres in Louisiana in 1811, Nat Turner in Southampton County, Virginia in 1831, Denmark Vesey in Charleston, South Carolina in 1832, Cinqué aboard the Spanish slave ship *Amistad* in 1839, and Madison Washington whose mutiny on another slave ship, the *Creole*, in 1841, on its journey from Hampton, Virginia to New Orleans with 134 slaves for sale, supplied Douglass with his own admired protagonist and fiction-of-fact narrative in *The Heroic Slave* (1853).

Slave nomenclature itself gives a further twist to ownership, the slave as human palimpsest upon whom the slaveholder inscribes himself. Even leading slave insurrectionists like Prosser, Turner and Vesey all bear their masters' names. Douglass knew well enough slaveholding's related bad-faith naming, the mock family kinship of an 'Uncle' Tom and 'Aunt' Dinah or the undermining glorification of a 'Cleopatra', 'Pompey' or 'Caesar' (the latter explicitly echoed in a later age's science fiction slave film series like *Planet of the Apes* (1969) and its sequels).

The display of Douglass's own name and accompanying text offers a counter, a writing-back. On account of Mrs. Auld's teaching of the alphabet, so alarming to her husband, there will indeed be 'no keeping' Douglass as a slave. Under his new-made signature the *Narrative* at once reports a life and Douglass's own 'speaking' of that life, and as much for his readers as himself. It serves him as a genesis, a freeing into word to act upon, and take possession of, his freeing into history.[4]

His is a recognition of the abiding connection between literacy and liberation. The appropriation of 'the word' back from those who hitherto have done the defining exactly complements the appropriation of his physical body from South to North in 1838 – 'the pathway from slavery to freedom'. For as he aptly cites Mr. Auld in words which would not have been amiss had they found voice in Mark Twain's Pap Finn: 'If you teach that slave to read ... It would for ever unfit him to be a slave.'

The *Narrative*, in other words, represents a transgressive text ('unlawful', 'unsafe') not simply because it violates slave laws or even slaveholding bans on black literacy. Rather, it lives out that very transgression as word, image, rhythm, story – an inaugural slave narrative equally as liberating in its qualities of telling as tale. The implications for all subsequent black self-chronicle are unmistakable.

Certainly these implications are not lost on the writer-narrator of Ralph Ellison's *Invisible Man* as he contemplates his own call to word:

Sometimes I sat watching the watery play of light upon Douglass' portrait, thinking how magical it was that he had talked his way from slavery to a government ministry, and so swiftly. Perhaps, I thought, something of the kind is happening to me. Douglass came north to escape and find work in the shipyards; a big fellow in a sailor's suit who, like me, had taken another name. What had his true name been? Whatever it was, it was as *Douglass* that he became himself, defined himself. And not as a boatwright as he'd expected, but as an orator. Perhaps the sense of magic lay in the unexpected transformations. 'You start Saul, and end up Paul,' my grandfather had often said. 'When you're a youngun, you Saul, but let life whup your head a bit and you starts to trying to be Paul – though you still Sauls around on the side.'[5]

Nor is the impact of Douglass, and his acquisition of the written word, lost on a contemporary like Darryl Pinckney in his *High Cotton* (1992). The narrator invokes his grandfather seated at a New York Upper East Side library reading about Douglass:

He said that what fascinated him most about the 'back years' was the story of how young Frederick Douglass, driven by the sound of his master reading from the Book of Job, stole a primer and copied the letters on pieces of pine plank ... Douglass made impudent progress in secret, he said, and, lo, one day literacy, like the fleet waters of the earth, swept him to freedom.[6]

☆   ☆   ☆

The step from Frederick Douglass to Angela Davis, 1840s Maryland slave to 1960s West Coast member of the American Communist Party and the author of *Angela Davis: An Autobiography* (1974), crosses gender as well as time and space.[7] Even so, the linkages are intimate and many, and in one respect more than most. In *If They Come in the Morning*, a political anthology of writings published in 1971, Davis reprints her address to the California court when, amid the drama of Black Power, she was charged with 'murder, kidnapping and conspiracy'. 'Only in the stance of self-representation', she responded, 'will I be able to properly and thoroughly confront my accusers'.[8]

Davis's 'stance of self-representation' and Douglass's 'written by himself' mirror one another almost to perfection, each steeped in transgression, legalism, an insistence upon respective kinds of self-authoring. Davis's formulation, however, perhaps more exactly supplies a working template for the line of autobiographical narrative from slave writing to New Negro autobiography, and, thereafter, from the modernity of Richard Wright, Zora Neale Hurston, Chester Himes and James Baldwin to the contemporaneity of Malcolm X and Maya Angelou, with still newer names like Lorene Cary and Ray Shell there to advance the tradition. However various the chronology, a concourse of shared concerns shows through, no less persistent for being posed differently the one way at the one time.

These bear upon how best to textualize the individual self within the 'exemplary' autobiography – how agreeable, after all, or husbandly, or short-tempered, or witty, in fact was Douglass? How, too, to find the unique register in the face of a pre-emptive lexicon of 'race', of colour binaries and superstitions? Where is the balance best struck between the one black life and that of the larger community with its shaping and memorial play of codes, whether Southern or city, church or street, barbershop or kitchen, menfolk or women?[9]

To take up these considerations in black autobiography's founding phase, three related tiers come into play. At the outset there is all the rest of American slave narrative (full-length or fragment, collected or not, in all an estimated five thousand texts or more). They tell a collective story: encapturement, Atlantic transportation, field or house servitude, brutalism as not only labour but sexual property, religiosity, living always on one's wits by double-talk and 'puttin' on massa', together with the sustaining dips into Brer Rabbit, Jack the Bear, 'flying' Africans, High John and each associated figure of black folklore and tricksterism. Despite the Supreme Court's Dred Scott decision of 1857 which confirmed black Americans to be 'not included under the word "citizens" in the Constitution' there persists the dream of liberation. Could any one writer tell 'all' without, in fact or imagination, soliciting the aid of the spirits, God, conjure or hoodoo?[10]

Olaudah Equiano/Gustavus Vassa speaks, animistically, iconically, in his *Narrative* (1789), of reading and writing as a will 'to talk to the books ... in hopes [they] would answer me'. William Wells Brown, in his *Narrative of William W. Brown, a Fugitive Slave. Written by Himself* (1847), alleges a 'loss for language to express my feeling' – a deficiency not true of Afro-America's first literary all-rounder, especially given the eloquence of his Kentucky to Canada *Life and Escape*, which he published as a preface to his founding novel *Clotel, or, the President's Daughter* (1853). J.W.C. Pennington in his *The Fugitive Blacksmith* (1849) avails himself of another overlap of written and spoken word in recalling the effort to capture the brute equations of slavery 'with pen or tongue'.[11]

In more or less every slave narrative this same regard for words as alchemy, an answering means to unknot in speech or script the sheer abiding abnormality of a life forbidden all choice, shows its hold. The *Life* (1849) of Father Josiah Henson, another Maryland escapee to Canada, Methodist Minister, and life-long Underground Railway worker, so bequeaths an escape story soon to become the source for Stowe's *Uncle Tom's Cabin* (1852). Henry 'Box' Bibb's *Narrative* (1849) offers the unsparing memory of Kentucky slave abuse, including the bizarre would-be escape in a box by the eventual founder of Canada's abolitionist journal

The Voice of the Fugitive. Solomon Northrup's *Twelve Years a Slave* (1853), albeit a dictated text, speaks of the near phantasmagoria in being highjacked and sold several times over in Louisiana. William (and Ellen) Craft's *Running a Thousand Miles for Freedom* (1860) turns upon a legendary cross-representation, a chronicle of escape from Georgia violating racial, sexual and class lines with Ellen in the transvestite guise of invalid white owner ('my *master* as I now call my wife') and William, the first-person voice of the text, as black nurse-cum-slave.[12]

Two black abolitionist women bequeath yet other styles of autobiographical narrative, one passed down and held in black memory, the other remembered through her own *Narrative* and legendary addresses. Harriet Tubman, slave escapee turned Underground Railway veteran, Union spy, military strategist, a woman whose 'word' was involved in rescuing more than 400 other slaves, has a name which recurs as much in the oral as the written lore of anti-slavery. Sojourner Truth belongs with her in spirit, an ex-slave (she was also known as Isabella), a physically imposing presence, a boundless black feminist. Her 'Ar'n't I a Woman?', the fierce equalitarian speech she made to the overwhelmingly white 'Women's Rights Convention' in Akron, Ohio, in 1851, together with each of the seven versions of her *Narrative*, gave live meaning to her self-freeing as African American woman in both fact and language. When she delivered her celebrated biblical riposte to a policeman who asked for her 'identity' after an anti-slavery address, 'I am that I am' (God's words to Moses on Mount Sinai), self-representation could not have been more succinct or magical.[13]

Alongside, and equally a history to match any fiction, stands Linda Brent/Harriet Jacobs's *Incidents in the Life of a Slave Girl* (1861).[14] Her seven year hiding out, or 'loophole', in all its resonances of confined, airless cargo-hold slavery and the Middle Passage, serves as both the mark of slave wordlessness (she cannot speak to, or write to, but only glimpse, her children) and of gendered wordlessness (she cannot protest to any immediate effect the ongoing sexual threat of her owner, Dr. Flint). Silence again becomes worded, a name of her own choosing operates, and literally enclosing darkness is made typographically visible. The 'dark and troubled' sense of things may still intrude into the Reconstruction South. But as newly fledged author 'Harriet Jacobs' makes clear, she perfectly recognizes the further liberation of her own text's making over of her enslavement. In one sense an obituary to her past, in common with other major slave narratives, *Incidents* co-exists as a certificate of birth for her future.

A second tier involves three turn of the century classics.[15] Booker T. Washington's *Up from Slavery* (1901) moves on from slave narrative *per se* into what he himself explicitly terms 'autobiography'. Given his uncertainty of exact date or place of birth ('I was born a slave on a plantation in Franklin County, Virginia'), virtual family anonymity ('Of my ancestry I know almost nothing'), and eventual arbitrary self-naming as 'Booker Taliaferro Washington' ('I think there are not many men in our country who have had the privilege of naming themselves in the way I have'), the self he shows to emerge is that of the destined race leader, the presiding spirit of Tuskegee Institute and postbellum Great Conciliator.

The irony of this has become well known. Washington is judged too ready in his deference to the colour line, a compromiser and time-server, an Uncle Tom at worst. An added irony, however, arises. The evidence gathers that, in fact, he was always worldlier, more tough willed and psychologically complex and divided. How far, then, does it matter that the Washington of *Up from Slavery* belongs less to history than myth, a version duly massaged with self-favouring extracts and correspondence? If the aim is one of inspiration, uplift, a 'public' story, how far can the 'my life' on offer be allowed to indulge various kinds of latitude in local detail or confirmation? How can truth be disensnared from fiction in a self-custodial leader who fashions himself as *both* tale and teller?

Undoubtedly more to later taste is W.E.B. DuBois's *The Souls of Black Folk* (1903). DuBois speaks and writes from outside the legacy of slavery. Massachusetts born, a black Yankee of Huguenot name, educated at Fisk, Harvard and Berlin, mover in the Niagara movement, editor of *The Crisis*, and a founder of the NAACP, his becomes another kind of black autobiographical voice, that of the professional social scientist. Being *Dr.* DuBois, the first black holder of an earned Ivy League Harvard Ph.D., cannot but help impart itself into the text. Although he professes himself to be 'moved' by slave songs and blues, he writes from a kind of cultural–anthropological distance, be it in the analysis of the failures of Reconstruction, the acclaimed 'twoness' of Afro-America, or the musicology of Southern black voice. A better clue to the man within the public figure lies in the less-read trilogy of *Darkwater: Voices from within the Veil* (1920), *Dusk of Dawn: An Essay Towards an Autobiography of a Race Concept* (1940) and *The Autobiography: A Soliloquy on Viewing My Life from the Last Decade of its First Century* (1968).[16] Each reflects DuBois given to more first-person inflection, speaking far more of and for himself rather than delivering case study or lecture.

James Weldon Johnson's *The Autobiography of an Ex-Coloured Man* (1912, 1927), with its shift of genre into fictional autobiography, sets a mixed-race narrator who 'passes' to negotiate a world itself matchingly full of racial code, harlequinry, double-standard.[17] If, eventually, the narrator opts for a permanent white over black identity, it adds to the novel's deft play of first-person voice. How ironic *is* the text and in which direction?

Johnson's text anticipates a considerable body of subsequent eponymous black novel writing in which Ralph Ellison's *Invisible Man* (1952) takes premier rank. As engaging as any, thereafter, would be John A. Williams's

The Man Who Cried I Am (1967), a fast-moving European-based thriller with its Richard Wright figure who has paid with his life for having discovered a genocidal white fascist conspiracy, the King Alfred plan of the Alliance Blanc, and which is remembered by a dying fellow black exile-author, Max Reddick. George Cain's *Blueschild Baby* (1970), told through the alter ego of 'Georgie', works as a modern Harlem and Brooklyn narrative of its black addict-hero's enslavement to heroin (or 'horse') and in which the needle becomes a virtual saviour-devil instrument. Ernest Gaines's *The Autobiography of Miss Jane Pittman* (1971) amounts to a small masterpiece of black memoir in the form of taped interviews with a former plantation survivor and extending from Civil War to Civil Rights; a 'slave narrative' updated from first-person page to contemporary High Tech.[18]

☆   ☆   ☆

'New Negro' autobiography, the black 1920s in first person voice, amounts to a near plenitude, though few possess a more inviting ease than Langston Hughes's *The Big Sea: An Autobiography* (1940) and *I Wonder As I Wander: An Autobiographical Journey* (1956). Hughes pitched himself as *flâneur*, a kind of international black stroller player. His account of 'the years of Manhattan's black Renaissance' is both full and compelling – all the fellow literati, the magazines like W.E.B. DuBois's *The Crisis* (launched in 1910 and in which, in 1921, Hughes published 'The Negro Speaks of Rivers'), the Urban League's *Opportunity* (1923–49), the Brotherhood of Sleeping Car Porters's *The Messenger* (1917–28) and the short-lived but lively *Fire!!* (1926) under Wallace Thurman's editorship, and the 'social whist parties', showtime and jazz. It was amid all this that he wrote his enduring 'The Negro Artist and the Racial Mountain' for *The Nation* (1926), with its pride in black accomplishment from 'the blare of Negro jazz bands and the bellowing voice of Bessie Smith' to the work of Jean Toomer and Rudolf Fisher and Aaron Douglass; it spoke, too, of a future prospect in which to express 'our individual dark-skinned selves without shame'. Even so, the laureateship behind his poems, plays, stories and columns as conducted from his one permanent home at 20 East 127 Street in Harlem, which he bought in 1948 and from which he managed continuing forays to Haiti, West Africa, France and Russia, brought its reservations. 'Fake simplicity' James Baldwin once notably called it.

To admirers, on the other hand, the two volumes of autobiography bear all his best colloquiality. The story brims in event, from his birth in Joplin, Missouri, through the passed-around boyhood in Kansas, Illinois and Ohio, the stints with his ill-spirited father in Mexico, the seamanship, the education at Lincoln University and Columbia, the long friendships (notably with his Harlem Renaissance contemporaries, the Cuban poet Nicolás Guillén and, in all its on and off collaboration, Zora Neale Hurston), and on to the doses of McCarthyite investigation on account of his leftish, anti-colonial and Russian sympathies (which, even so, many thought he deliberately underplayed). Both in substance and manner it rightly played its part in a reputation that went well beyond not only Harlem but America.[19]

James Weldon Johnson's *Along this Way* (1933) bears witness to another key 1920s presence, even if, occasionally, a certain formality enters – as if the author wanted only his public self best known. That still yields plenty: the mixed stock into which Johnson was born (his father a freeborn man of colour from Virginia, his mother French-Haitian from the Bahamas), the first black to have been called to the Florida bar since Reconstruction, the musical collaborations with his brother John Rosamond, the American consulships in Venezuela and Nicaragua, a guarded version of the situation which led to *The Autobiography of an Ex-Coloured Man*, the memorable verse addresses in *God's Trombones. Seven Negro Sermons in Verse* (1927) and a lifetime's other poetry, lyrics and translations which also includes his landmark *The Book of Negro American Poetry* (1922, 1931), the two decades he served as Field Secretary for the NAACP, and the eventual Visiting Professorships at Fisk and New York University.[20]

Contrastingly, Claude McKay's *A Long Way from Home* (1937), in offering 'the distilled poetry of my experience' from Jamaica to Afro-America with Harlem as a centrepoint, does so as a story full of self-division and in a narrative style to match. It registers an itinerant, often angry and volatile writer's life. First, however, is the light it throws on his writing, whether the steady output of fiction like *Home to Harlem* (1928) as given over to 'ragtime and blues', *Banjo* (1929) with its sailor ports-of-call and odysseys, *Banana Bottom* (1933) whose speech and peasant life came out of his own Jamaica, and *Gingertown* (1932), whose stories include 'Brownstone Blue' as a perfect vignette of 1920s cabaret Harlem, or of poetry like *Harlem Shadows* (1922) which, however lyric, at the same time catches the tougher idiom of street and tenement. As to McKay's vision of himself and his times, the story he tells is one of radicalism, class war and the colour line, with smacks at some of the Talented Tenth elitist implications of Locke's movement (he once took aim at *The New Negro* as a 'chocolate soufflé of art and politics'), frequent political and literary warring, and his own disillusioned break with Marxism and conversion to Catholicism.[21]

Although written in a far later age, George Schuyler's *Black and Conservative* (1966) gives another autobiographical version of the Harlem Renaissance. As befits the iconoclast of 'The Negro-Art Hokum', an essay he contributed to *The Nation* (1926) – Hughes's 'The Negro Artist and the Racial Mountain' was a riposte – or the irascible satirist of the novel *Black No More* (1931), with its fantasy send-up of assimilationism (Schuyler himself was contradictory on the issue), his autobiography takes few prisoners. It hits at the feuds, the grandstanding, the sexual spats and styles, the harking back to Africa, and even the whole question of a separate Black

Arts movement. *Black and Conservative* makes a virtue of dissent, the 'one man's opinion' of a tough, lifetime journalist who at different times was socialist, capitalist, and then freewheeling critic of both.[22]

Divergent as they are in pattern and voice, the autobiographies of Hughes, Johnson, McKay and Schuyler each enletter the black 1920s as an awakening, a black (and indeed cross-racial) time of awakened literary spirit. The Wall Street Crash, and the Depression in its wake, changed matters utterly. Optimism waned. Other politics intervened, those of unemployment, food-lines, shared privation. To focus selectively on blackness, or black art, was to risk missing the larger picture. It was a turn-about, too, which would find its own suitably uncompromising autobiographical register, first out of the black sharecropper South and then out of Chicago's South Side, that of Richard Wright.

☆   ☆   ☆

Towards the close of *Black Boy* (1945) Wright sounds a note which again recalls Douglass and his fellow writers of slave narrative: 'Not only had the southern whites not known me, but, more important still, as I had lived in the South I had not had the chance to learn who I was.'[23] 'To learn who I was', patently, does not implicate Wright in an actual slave escape. But it does argue a similar shedding of imposed terms of reference along the lines in play throughout Douglass's *Narrative*. Both *Black Boy*, and the posthumous *American Hunger* (1977),[24] bespeak a will to articulacy, an uninhibitable resolve to name for himself the world's contradictory plenty – racial or otherwise.

As much as the family moves through Mississippi, Arkansas and Tennessee, and then Wright's own eventual migration North to Chicago, give off a quite extraordinary eventfulness, the emphasis coevally falls upon coming authorship. In speaking time and again of his 'hunger', Wright speaks to an artist's hunger, the compulsion to 'learn who I was' as by a process of self-inscription. Effectively the black boy of earlier Southern provenance is written into being by the black adult of later Chicago South Side experience.

Nor is event only of the one kind in *Black Boy*. The volume opens with a scene of arson, the boy's not so visceral will to burn down the family house. It is this 'Richard', too, who strangles the kitten to spite the father who will eventually abscond and mockingly display his new woman, and whom Wright will recall as a spectral, uncomprehending black fieldhand. He remembers himself as child alcoholic, intimidated witness of his mother's stroke, victim of his Aunt Addie in all her pentecostal fury and of an equally vengeful Adventist grandmother, and duped deliverer of (of all things) Klan newspapers. Each becomes, as it were, an experiential vocabulary to be stored, the word as not only gain, truthsaying, but also loss, traduction.

This other self of his childhood and adolescence continues into the 'Richard' who sleepwalks, strikes back at his adult persecutors with an open knife, and who lies, cheats and hustles too much ahead of his time. His early work experiences, in turn, both at the optical company (a sight imagery to anticipate Ellison's *Invisible Man*) and at the Memphis hotel, bring him ever more implacably up against the colour line. In none of this eventfulness, however, does 'Richard' operate from his own centre, but rather in roles which signify margin, his own alterity or displacement.

The counter current, throughout, however, is Wright's attention to the boy's, to his own, nascent creativity, the literary self in waiting. A catalogue of compensatory sense impressions (among them 'the yearning for identification loosed in me by the sight of a solitary ant carrying a burden upon a mysterious journey') follows his beating for the fire. The text recalls the storybook magic 'Richard' associates as a child with the riverboat *Kate Adams*. There is a harking back to the vernacular talk of black boyhood, from conjure to black slang to games of competitive insult like 'the dozens'. The insistence on reading his own class address rather than that supplied by the Tom-like High School principal carries its own prophetic charge.

The 'redemption' derived from H.L. Mencken follows, the allures, mirrors, identifications of reading. The subterfuge of using the forged card to gain entry to a segregated local library especially applies – black reading and writing as a kind of scriptural outlawry. But it is subterfuge which works. The literary prospect so long denied him becomes his for the taking. The South graduates from actual geography to a site in imagination, to remembrance, a South which his fiction from *Uncle Tom's Children* (1938) to *The Long Dream* (1958) will confirm he 'can never really leave'.

This double current holds for *American Hunger*. For all the reality of its windswept shoreline and stockyards, and even its black South Side, Chicago strikes him as citied unreality, miasma. His jobs, whether with the Hoffmans, the Post Office, the John Reed Club, or at the fringes of the Communist Party, confirm a 'No Man's Land into which the Negro mind in America has been shunted.' He refers, insistently, to 'my excessive reading', to 'stabs of writing ... full of tension, frantic poverty and death'. He ponders the 'language' of his own difference, whether from the white shop girls with whom he works, the white medical researchers at the laboratory, his Communist Party brethren or, strikingly, his fellow blacks.

In this he avails himself of one of the volume's most haunting tableaux, that of the laboratory dogs whose vocal chords have been cut and 'who would lift their heads to the ceiling and gape in a soundless wail'. This devocalization, fact and image, grips and pursues him. *American Hunger*, word for word, acts as perfect rejoinder, a making vocal in himself of that which previously has itself been cut from voice. Both parts (it was conceived as the one sequence) of the autobiography yield, finally, Wright's own

Portrait of the Artist, 'Richard' as the begetter of Richard Wright as surely as 'Stephen Daedalus' can be said to have begotten James Joyce.

I was born in a Negro town. I do not mean by that the black back-side of an average town. Eatonville, Florida, is, and was at the time of my birth, a pure Negro town – charter, mayor, council, town marshal and all. It was not the first Negro community in America, but it was the first to be incorporated, the first attempt at organized self-government on the part of Negroes in America.[25]

On this downhome, typically beckoning note Zora Neale Hurston opens *Dust Tracks on a Road* (1942). But although it has rightly come to be regarded as the most availing of all pre-1960s autobiography by a black woman, it has also been snared in controversy. Did she anaesthetise much of the crueller racism she suffered, or as one of her main biographers, Robert Hemenway, alleges, 'camouflage' matters of 'racial segregation'? If, indeed, Hurston massages facts, omits, holds back on certain white malpractice and patronage knowing her readership would be largely white, even (as recent editions have confirmed) initially left out certain more 'political' passages, is that simply to close the account?[26]

Hardly, it has to be said. For *Dust Tracks on a Road* exhibits interests and subtleties in plenty, not least its own voice as an inspired doubling-up of the folk idiom of Eatonville (with assistance from her field trips in Haiti and the Caribbean) and of the lightly worn anthropological learning acquired at Barnard College and Columbia under the tutelage of Franz Boaz.

The immediate ease of her writing ('I have been in Sorrow's kitchen and licked out all the pots') shows through at every turn. That is not to say she tells a life more sweet than sour but rather a blend of both while at the same time paying her dues to the texturing intimacies of the black world that bred her. However easeful of her white readership she may be, that may have much to do with a genuine cross-racial generosity, the readiness to give access not only to black but to non-black readers.

She sustains this stance with every adroitness. She could, and did, infuriate a number of black contemporaries (and later nationalists) with her coolness to 'race solidarity' ('And how can Race solidarity be possible in a nation made up of so many elements in the United States? ... why should Negroes be united? Nobody else in America is'). She could inveigh against negritude ('This Negro business') and black as well as white 'race clichés' ('There is no *The Negro* here'). But how could the warmth she feels for her black origins be doubted? When, typically, she recalls with a mix of pleasure and pain her father's attitude towards her in childhood, she does so in terms to match. Her gloss runs: 'A little of my sugar used to sweeten his coffee right now. That is a Negro way of saying his patience was short with me.'

This stylish vernacularity holds throughout. Of her creative visions in childhood she says expressively: 'A cosmic loneliness was my shadow.' She recalls her Eatonville poeticizing in a suitable paradox: 'My phantasies were still fighting against the facts.' Her furious grappling match with her stepmother she encapsulates in kitchentalk, an apt alimentary metaphor: 'This was the very corn I wanted to grind.' Her 'for ever shifting', as she calls it, summons up a sense of home as stored speech or talk: 'I was a Southerner and the map of Dixie was on my tongue.'

Even her academic research into black folklore yields its homelier turn when she describes herself as 'delving into Hoodoo, a sympathetic magic'. For the closeness of her alliance with Ethel Waters, blues queen, she uses a suitably oral and same-sex metaphor, that of a French kiss: 'I am her friend and her tongue is in my mouth.' In remembering the first publication of her stories and books like *Jonah's Gourd Vine* (1934) and *Mules & Men* (1935), she observes with, again, just the right touch of sexual intimacy: 'You know that feeling when you found your first pubic hair'.[27]

These, and a tissue of sayings in shared style, particularise her recollections in *Dust Tracks on a Road*: Cudjo Lewis, for instance, as the last former slave born in Africa and alive in her time ('I lonely for my folks' she has him say, down-home and idiomatically, of his original West African family); or the Eatonville of her near-mythic kin ('Papa said he didn't have to do but two things – die and stay black'); or her own love affairs ('I did not just fall in love. I made a parachute jump'). Similarly, her willingness to tackle sexual materials produces a laconicism the equal of Dorothy Parker ('I may be thinking of turnip greens with dumplings, or more royalty checks, and here is a man who visualizes me on a divan sending the world up in smoke').

Robert Hemenway calls attention to the 'paradox of the public and private Zora Neale Hurston',[28] which is not to doubt his own clear sense of her achievement. An otherwise fervidly admiring Alice Walker can likewise discern 'oddly false-sounding' elements in *Dust Tracks*.[29] Even so, Hurston's triumph continues to lie precisely in her own affirmations and sayings, the sheer inventive spiritedness of her self-telling.

The pre-eminent motifs of Chester Himes's two volumes of autobiography, *The Quality of Hurt* (1972) and *My Life of Absurdity* (1976), are projected in his own title phrases: hurt and absurdity.[30] Himes's stance, throughout, is to tell, stably, a life of marked instability, that of a personality on his own autobiographical reckoning 'argumentative, bad-tempered, and unsympathetic'. His first volume speaks freely of 'the eccentricities of my creativity' and 'blind fits of rage', its successor of 'my sensitivity towards race' and 'the [endeavour] to find a life into which I could fit'. It would be a mistake, however, to think Himes wrote out of mere nerves, temper, whim. He shows himself at once far too self-aware and, as his Coffin Ed-Grave Digger thrillers give street-level yet surreal witness, too aware of the ways of the world, for that.

The Quality of Hurt covers the years from his birth in 1909 in Jefferson City, Missouri, to his young, handsome mulatto manhood in Ohio, through to his European exile in the early 1950s. The stopping-off places en route read like pages from his own fiction: the cruel decay of his parents' marriage which he uses in The Third Generation (1954); the freak blinding in a gun-powder accident of his brother Joseph which haunted Himes throughout his life (Joseph Himes went on to a distinguished career in sociology at the University of North Carolina); his own back injury in a lift shaft for which he was cheated of due compensation; and the Cleveland delinquency where he hung about with a hoodlum named Bunch Boy, his part in a jewel theft in 1929, and his seven year jail sentence which he would put to account in Cast the First Stone (1952). On release in 1936 he wrote poems for the Cleveland Daily News, worked on an FPA history of Cleveland, continued with crime and prison stories, spent time on Louis Bromfield's community farm at Pleasant Valley, Ohio, and saw the publication of his war industry based first novel, If He Hollers Let Him Go (1945). Himes's life, it could be said, was already long scripted; it merely awaited its literary making over.[31]

The Quality of Hurt takes Himes to his meetings in Paris with Richard Wright and James Baldwin, to Spain (he describes a tetchy encounter with Robert Graves in Mallorca), and to London where he found the petty racism especially depressing (not least on account of being with a white woman). During his time with Alva Trent, the source of 'Elizabeth Hancock' in a novel long available only in French, Une Affaire de viol (1963),[32] another kind of fugitive self-chronicle came into play: he helped write her (still unpublished) autobiography, The Golden Chalice.

Two observations in particular pick up on the slave legacy and self-scripting. In the course of describing the circumstances of his intimately autobiographical novel, The Primitive (1955),[33] he gives an unexpected and bittersweet twist to Crèvecoeur:

> The American black is a new race of man; the only new race of man to come into being in modern time. And for those hackneyed, outdated, slavery time racists to keep thinking of him as a primitive is an insult to the intelligence. In fact, intelligence isn't required to know the black is a new man – complex, intriguing, and not particularly likeable. I find it very difficult to like American black myself; but there's nothing primitive about us, as there is about the most sophisticated African. (pp. 285–6)

This kind of contrariety, hurt and absurdity entwined, does not sit easily in any camp.

The other observation concerns Himes's stance as a writer:

No matter what I did, or where I was, or how I lived, I had considered myself a writer ever since I'd published my first story in *Esquire* when I was still in prison in 1934. Foremost a writer. Above all a writer. It was my salvation, and is. The world can deny me as an ex-convict, as a nigger, as a disagreeable and unpleasant person. But as long as I write, whether it is published or not, I'm a writer, and no one can take that away. 'A fighter fights, a writer writes,' so I must have done my writing. (p. 117)

Writing as pugilism, its own compelled call to arms, looks both back (to Douglass's *Narrative* and the Covey fight) and forward (to Eldridge Cleaver's *Soul on Ice* (1968), for example, which speaks of his penitentiary wrestle with words as a means to 'save myself').[34] Ishmael Reed's essay collection, *Writin' Is Fightin': Thirty-Seven Years of Boxing on Paper* (1988), continues the tradition, the first half of its title a borrowed rap throwaway from Muhammad Ali.[35]

This embattled contrariety of blackness and word continues in *My Life of Absurdity*: the moves back and forth across Europe and America; the edgy literary friendships in Paris and elsewhere with Richard Wright, a white 1920s veteran like Carl Van Vechten, the Caribbean born George Lamming, Europeans like Jean Giono and Marcel Duhamel, African Americans from Malcolm X to John A. Williams, Melvin Van Peebles and Nikki Giovanni; his belated rise to fame with the *Série Noire* thrillers; the continuing travels and amours and eventual second marriage to Lesley Packard, the white Englishwoman and journalist with whom in his last years he made his home in Javea on Spain's Valencian coast. The upshot is black autobiography holding within itself a kind of unfinished colloquium or jousting ground, the weighing of racial paradox and contradiction.

☆   ☆   ☆

'The root function of language is to control the universe by describing it'.[36] So, in 'Stranger in the Village' (1953), written while recuperating from a nervous breakdown in the birthplace of his Swiss lover, the unnamed Lucien Happersberger, and published first in *Harper's*, then, in 1955, in *Notes of a Native Son*, James Baldwin turns his temporary sojourn to a more inclusive purpose. As the unprecedented sole black presence ('no black man had ever set foot in this tiny Swiss village before I came'), not to say a foreigner by speech, his own exile becomes the very *figura* of the larger African, and African American, diaspora behind him.

He sees refracted in himself a people initially dispossessed of their languages, then banned from writing the European tongues (English in the immediate case) of their enslavers, and further silenced by 'segregation' and 'terrorization' and the persistences of sexual myth. Where, more graphically, than in a snowclad, Alpine outpost ('this white wilderness'), should Baldwin write back into being his own black signifying, a descendant of those same first Africans illegally shipped to the Americas and now the '*Neger!*' as the village children call him (loadedly? innocently?) in *Schweizerdeutsch*.

Yet, he proposes that neither he nor those from whom he arose in Harlem or the black Dixie of an Atlantic away can be thought true 'strangers in the village'. Rather, he, like them, belongs, however ambiguously, in 'the interracial drama acted out on the American continent'. Nor, for Baldwin, can 'the Negro in America' be understood in terms that deny contradiction, even riddle, being neither wholly African nor European ('The most illiterate among them is related, in a way that I am not, to Dante, Shakespeare, Michelangelo ... '), but rather, again in an echo of Crèvecoeur, another kind of American 'new man'. 'No road whatever', he insists, 'will lead Americans back to the simplicity of this European village where white men still have the luxury of looking at me as a stranger'. Inscribing that complexity ('I am not, really, a stranger any longer for any American alive') becomes a governing cause for him, a call to moral as much as writerly imagination.

Given, as he sees it, the refusal to speak or write 'truthfully' across the colour line, Baldwin's 'self-representation' becomes also the representation of the historic blackness which made him; most notably the residues of an African past erased by colonialist requirements under slavery. If he can wonder 'what on earth the first slave found to say to the first black child he bore', 'Stranger in the Village' offers a key saying of his own answer. It also points the way to the overall witness, a favoured Baldwin term, which constitutes *Notes of a Native Son* together with *Nobody Knows My Name: More Notes of a Native Son* (1961) and *The Fire Next Time* (1963).[37]

The analogy between the implantation of black selfhood into white history and vice versa ('This world is white no longer, and it never will be white again' he concludes), and black script into the white page must have struck him as forcefully as it did the Ellison of *Invisible Man*. The insistence, at least, on making 'language' a means of 'controlling the universe' ('making it my own' he calls it in 'Why I Stopped Hating Shakespeare') lies behind each essay in *Notes of a Native Son* as they range from Harlem to Paris, Mississippi to Sweden, Atlanta to Turkey, or from praise to censure of progenitors who include Harriet Beecher Stowe, Richard Wright, Henry James and William Faulkner.

In 'Autobiographical Notes' he speaks of 'appropriating these white centuries', of ending his 'racial bastardy' (his own illegitimacy no doubt an animus behind the image), and of 'unlocking' his 'being a Negro' in order 'to write about anything else'. In 'Everyone's Protest Novel', then 'Many Thousands Gone', he famously argues the limits of, respectively, *Uncle Tom's Cabin* and *Native Son*; his criterion, itself revealingly, 'the power of revelation'.

In arguing that it has been 'only in his music ... that the Negro in America has been able to tell his story', Baldwin personalizes his own matching literary sense of mission. 'Notes of a Native Son' recalls his Harlem deacon stepfather reluctantly conceding to the then boy preacher, 'You'd rather write than preach, wouldn't you?'. And in 'A Question of Identity', with, as so often, Henry James most in mind, he calls up the imaginative returns of expatriation for an American writer: 'From the vantage point of Europe he discovers his own country.'

Nobody Knows My Name extends the process, its very title a working brief for the inscription of 'self and the world' as he calls it in the Introduction. From 'The Discovery of What it Means to be an American', in which he gives his rueful admiration of the European as against American status of the writer's 'vocation' ('A European writer considers himself to be part of an old and honorable profession ... the tradition does not exist in America') through to his closing thoughts on authorship in the Baldwin–Mailer skirmish ('His [the writer's] work, after all, is all that will be left when the newspapers are yellowed'), the same impetus holds, black self-authoring as repossession and memorialization.

The time, thus, can be early 1960s Afro-America as in 'East River, Downtown' ('the American Negro can no longer, nor will he ever again, be controlled by white America's image of him'). The place can be colour line Mississippi as in 'Faulkner and Desegregation' ('It is apparently very difficult to be at once a Southerner and an American'). On a different tack it can turn, as in 'The Male Prison', to Gide and homosexuality with all the implications for his own sexual preference ('it was clear to me that he had not come to terms with his nature'). Yet each essay carries a shared impress: the word as both an urging of revelation and, in Baldwin's making over, itself a revelation.

Something of an autobiographical summary lies in 'Down at the Cross: Letter from a Region of My Mind', from *The Fire Next Time*, where he again considers the private and public racial fissures of language both in the world and as the world:

For the horrors of the American Negro's life there has been almost no language. The privacy of his experience, which is only beginning to be recognized in language, and hence is denied or ignored in official and popular speech – hence the Negro idiom – lends credibility to any system that pretends to clarify it. And, in fact, the truth about the black man, as a historical entity and as a human being, *has* been hidden from him, deliberately and cruelly; the power of the white world is threatened whenever a black man refuses to accept the white world's definitions. (p. 83)

Doubts, often enough, have arisen about Baldwin's later discursive powers (as they have about the fiction after *Go Tell It on the Mountain* (1953)), from *A Rap on Race* (1971), his colloquy on black and white as American iconographies with Margaret Mead, through to *The Evidence of Things Not Seen* (1985), his 'state of the union' rumination on the Atlanta black child murders – for which Wayne Bertram Williams was indicted in 1981 – and on Atlanta itself as one-time slave world, black South and eventual Civil Rights arena.[38] But the unique and vindicating contribution of *Notes of a Native Son*, *Nobody Knows My Name* and *The Fire Next Time* remains. As essays cum autobiography they themselves both rebuke 'the white world's definitions' and yield a repository of necessary counter definitions; they do so, too, with the bonus of a rare, exhilarating fluency.

As they contemplated 'Jimmy' with cigarette in hand, the breathy deliverer of 'the word', moralist yet sexual adventurer with his warm, gap-toothed smile (in childhood he was tagged 'Frog Eyes' on account of his protrusive stare) and capacity to dip into raciest Harlem idiom, there were always those who thought him overexposed and thereby tamed by the very media which once lionized him. Yet when the news of his death from cancer at 63 went out from the farmhouse in the Riviera's St-Paul-de-Vence where he had made his home since the 1970s, it gave a dramatic reminder of just how singular and bold of spirit he had been all along. Harlem to the South of France might have been thought an unlikely journey for one of his origins. But as confirmed in his omnibus *The Price of the Ticket: Collected Non-Fiction 1948–1985* (1985) it produced a landmark African American, a landmark body of first-person African American writing.[39]

☆   ☆   ☆

No black autobiography makes the 'stance of self-representation' more contemporary than *The Autobiography of Malcolm X* (1965).[40] Full of dire if accurate prophecy ('If I'm alive when this book comes out, it will be a miracle'), made in political *media res*, its voicing is shot through with challenge, combat, an ideological blackness ('"The white man is a devil" is a perfect echo of the black convict's experience'). To his amanuensis, Alex Haley – still to write *Roots* and the long-time journalist and contributor to *Atlantic*, *Harper's*, *Saturday Evening Post* (for whom he did a series on Elijah Muhammad) and who first interviewed Malcolm for *Playboy* – he stresses the language of race as a species of anti-language:

I'm telling it like it *is*! You *never* have to worry about me biting my tongue if something I know as truth is on my mind. Raw, naked truth exchanged between the black man and the white man is what a whole lot more of is needed in this country – to clear the air of the racial mirages, clichés, and lies that this country's very atmosphere has been filled with for four hundred years. (p. 276)

His own passage into self-elucidation against these 'mirages' and 'clichés', he locates, like Douglass and others before him, in yet one more paradigm of names. 'Malcolm Little' represents the self who leaves for Detroit from Omaha, Nebraska. There he becomes 'Red', zoot suited, conked, a restless hustler of drugs and street crime. In Boston, with his step-sister Ella, he becomes 'Homeboy'. In Harlem he graduates even more into the full-time pimp, numbers man, drug pusher and thief ('I had seen a lot, but never such a dense concentration of stumblebums, pushers, hookers, public crap shooters, even little kids running around at midnight begging for pennies') and on account of his 'marinny' hair acquires the monicker of 'Detroit Red'. The 'robberies and stick-ups' ('I can't remember all the hustles I had during the next two years in Harlem') land him, at not yet twenty-one, with a ten year sentence, seven of which he serves under the name of 'Satan' as conferred upon him by his cellmates for his blasphemy.

His transforming encounter with the Nation of Islam gives him the name by which he will be known in history. Correspondence with Elijah Muhammad, a ready belief that Christianity has 'taught the "negro" that black was a curse', a convert's remorse at 'the very enormity of my previous life's guilt', and an education won from the prison library leads on to release and his Black Muslim incarnation first as 'Brother Malcolm', then 'Malcolm X', and eventually, 'Minister Malcolm X'.

His rupture with Elijah Muhammad has become the stuff of legend. Having preached black separatism, black nationalism, and the whole devil counter-genesis of Yacuub and satanic whiteness, he discovers in his *hajj* to Mecca a more 'orthodox Islam' of tolerance, inclusivity. Prince Faisal tells him 'The Black Muslims have the wrong Islam.' Reborn into a new Islamic identity he becomes El-Hajj Malik El-Shabazz, though also, and finally, after his journeys through Beirut, Cairo, Ghana, Liberia, Senegal, Morocco and Algeria, the 'Omowole' of Nigeria's Yoruba, 'the son who has come home'.

'I hope the book is proceeding rapidly, for events concerning my life happen so quickly' Haley witnesses Malcolm as saying, as if he somehow always knew the assassin's bullet awaited him at the Audubon Ballroom in 1965. But the comment also throws light on the textual disposition of the *Autobiography* itself, a 'life' always dictated on the move, compositionally unfixing and fixing its contours (if not its very meaning) even as it was being filtered through Alex Haley on to the page. This is black self-representation as both an act of map-making and map, an improvization both in life and in its literary register to match the volatility, and yet the resoluteness, of the self which became Malcolm X.

☆   ☆   ☆

With the 1960s, Civil Rights to Black Power, a near flood of black autobiography emerges, as often as not a mix of manifesto and self-telling. In the first instance emerges Malcolm's own legacy, a whole body of politically militant, convict or ghetto autobiography. None could have been more unaccommodating than Eldridge Cleaver in the Black Panther and West Coast prison essays of *Soul on Ice* (1968), *Post-Prison Writings and Speeches* (1969) and *Conversation with Eldridge Cleaver, Algiers* (1970).[41] But if this was the Cleaver who, on hearing of Malcolm's assassination, thundered from his Folsom, California cell, 'We shall have our manhood. We shall have it or the earth will be levelled by our attempts to gain it', it was also the Cleaver who comes to see writing, the word as self-representation, as a means to 'save myself', to slough off the self 'who came to prison'.

Cleaver had no want of autobiographical company. Bobby Seale in *Seize the Time* (1970) and *A Lonely Rage* (1978) and Huey Newton in *To Die for the People* (1972) would tell the Black Panther story as one of legal margins and periphery; H. Rap Brown would offer a self-vaunting latterday 'slave narrative' in *Die Nigger Die!* (1969); Hoyt Fuller anticipated the black 'roots' phenomenon in *Journey to Africa* (1971); and Angela Davis, one of the few women to feature, in *An Autobiography* (1974), would construe her life under Marxist-historicist terms as shaped by Herbert Marcuse and her membership of the Communist Party. None, however, quite matches George Jackson's autodidact's triumph of Gramsci-influenced prison letter writing, *Soledad Brother* (1970), autobiography as 'black revolutionary' self-authoring.[42]

Post-1960s black autobiography equally looks to a plenitude of authorly lives. Nikki Giovanni's *Gemini: An Extended Autobiographical Statement on My First Twenty-Five Years of Being a Black Poet* (1971) offers one kind of bidding.[43] Its imagistic account of womanism *avant la lettre* invokes an upbringing in Cincinnati, Ohio, education at Fisk, and a black gynocracy centred in Knoxville, Tennessee, but extending its family branches into a far wider South. At quite another reach *Beneath the Underdog: His World as Composed by Mingus* (1971) takes the form of a talked life, episodic and full of the kind of controlled dissonance to be heard in Mingus's jazz.[44] Less performative, though no less determined a writing-in, Vincent O. Carter's *The Bern Book: A Record of a Voyage of the Mind* (1973), echoing Baldwin's 'Stranger in the Village', tells the rite of passage of a Kansas City expatriate who becomes 'the only black man' in the Swiss capital.[45]

Other writerly self-representations pursue the nature of black shifts, even fissures, in allegiance. Julius Lester's *All Is Well* (1976), a life which reaches adulthood in the ferment of Black Power, even so finds its balance in the Catholic quietism of Thomas Merton (Lester subsequently has moved on to Judaism).[46] June Jordan's *Civil Wars* (1981), a serial of linked autobiographical essays, delineates her life as Bedford-Stuyvesant child, Harlemite, wife to a white husband, single mother, bisexual, activist, planner (with Buckminster Fuller) of a new architecture for Harlem, and writer. Her Foreword provides an echoing rumination on the autobiographical 'word':

> Early on, the scriptural concept that 'in the beginning was the Word and the Word was with God and the word was God' – the idea that the word could represent and then deliver into reality what the word symbolized – this possibility of language, of writing, seemed to me magical, and irresistible.[47]

John Edgar Wideman's *Brothers & Keepers* (1984) tells a two-track sibling narrative: Wideman himself, the University of Pennsylvania basketball star and Oxford Rhodes Scholar, as against Robbie Wideman, his street raised, vernacular brother currently serving life for murder in Pennsylvania's Western Penitentiary. Wideman's *Fatheralong: A Meditation on Fathers and Sons, Race and Society* (1995), with its story told as father–son journeyings from Pittsburgh to Amherst, Massachusetts, and to South Carolina, supplies a coda, an essay-history on the historic issues of the black father as role model, nurturer or, for whatever historic complex of reasons, absentee.[48]

Audre Lorde's 'biomythography', *Zami: A New Spelling of My Name* (1982), broke further new ground: a black lesbian autobiography constructed as a collage, perhaps a novel, in kind with her own cross-boundary sexual and literary identity.[49] *The Autobiography of LeRoi Jones/Amiri Baraka* (1984) pursues a Newark and then Harlem 'growing up' within an American 'maze of light and darkness', each phase from Beat to Black Nationalist to Marxist a stage of unfolding in the will to an overall or totalizing meaning of self and world.[50]

A later body of fictionalized autobiography, equally as various, has also shown its paces. Lorene Cary's *Black Ice* (1991) explores a kind of black privilege, a young black woman's entrance into a formerly all-white, all-male, New Hampshire private school and the self-awakenings it engenders.[51] Darryl Pinckney's *High Cotton* (1992), besides its Douglass and other intertextual reference, offers the wry, stylishly ironic chronicle of the 'Also Chosen' (a take on DuBois's 'Talented Tenth'), a rite of passage neither out of Dixie nor the ghetto but Middle America as experienced through suburban Indianapolis, NAACP supporting parents, Columbia University, secretaryship to Djuna Barnes, and the Southern but fiercely articulate and Harvard-educated Grandfather Eustace. In keeping with its cross-ethnic story it hovers teasingly on the line between autobiography and first-person novel.[52] Ray Shell's *Iced* (1993) offers contrastingly darker fare, the harrowing, stream of consciousness autobiographical fiction of a black crack-cocaine addict's life told in italicized line measure and in which dependency is imaged as, alternatingly, euphoria and Dostoevskian lower depth.[53]

☆   ☆   ☆

'In Stamps the segregation was so complete that most Black children didn't really, absolutely, know what whites looked like'.[54] Such is just one of several opening strikes in Maya Angelou's *I Know Why the Caged Bird Sings* (1969), the first of five volumes of self-portraiture told from her beginnings in Stamps, Arkansas, carried forward into her life in California and elsewhere in the States, and eventually to Europe, the Caribbean and, most of all, Egypt and postcolonial Africa.

Her inaugural memories are of dreaming she is a white child, a contradictory fantasy all her subsequent history will flesh out and highlight. At eight, a child as woman, she is raped by her mother's black fancyman, Mr. Freeman ('A breaking and entering when even the senses are torn apart ... I thought I had died'). The trauma itself, and the belief that her voodooed word has led her uncles to kill Freeman, causes her to will her own speechlessness for years; voluntary or not yet another self-enclosing black silence. The writer within is eased in part by her grandmother's love and that of her brother Bailey, and yet also by the will to self-invention which lies behind the Douglass-like proliferation of names, whether Margaret, Marguerite, Marguerite Johnson, Ritie, My, or, eventually, Maya.

She moves out to her mother in California, 'foggy days of unknowing for Bailey and me' yet also a time of 'newly awakening sexual appetite'. The birth of a son, Guy, as she recognizes, also marks the end of her own childhood. If the 'tripartite crossfire of masculine prejudice, white illogical hate and Black lack of power' has done its best, or worst, to create silence, *Caged Bird* enacts Angelou's own unsilencing, a representation of self and community as black volubility, energy, history, speech, text.

Gather Together in My Name (1974) opens with her un-euphoria amid the euphoria of America's World War II victory ('I was seventeen, very old, embarassingly young, with a son of two months').[55] Job-hunting up and down the West Coast, at one point seeking entry to the Army, she embarks upon a series of near gothic adventures, among them Madam of a heterosexual brothel serviced by two lesbian women. None of her men, or different employments (cook and waitress serving Creole food, singer and actor at the edges of show business), gives her stability. 'My life had no center' she acknowledges. Sexuality becomes the only commodity left; she takes to tricking for mainly hispanic clients, the property of an exotic pimp named L.D. Her gloss again carries its own rueful epilogue: 'Survival was all around me but it didn't take hold.'

The succeeding volumes witness to the increasing repossession of her life. *Singin' and Swingin' and Gettin' Merry like Christmas* (1976) depicts her love affair with a Greek American, her subsequent career as shake dancer in San Francisco, her theatre success in *Porgy and Bess*, and her picaresque tour of Europe. If still 'an assembly of strivings' motherhood supplies a still centre, a fulcrum. *The Heart of a Woman* (1981) equally calls up this zigzag of motion and repose. On the one hand there is her life amid the Harlem literary set, stage appearances at the Apollo, participation in King's SCLC (Southern Christian Leadership Conference), a role in Genet's *The Blacks*, and marriage and life in London and Cairo with the South African freedom politician Vusumzi Make. On the other, and despite his near fatal car crash, there is Guy's enrolment at the University of Ghana, a mother contemplative in her pride and for the moment at rest.[56]

All God's Children Need Traveling Shoes (1986) brings her African odyssey up to date, an affectionate memoir of Ghanaian culture and landscape, of the literary circle headed by the expatriate black novelist Julian Mayfield, and of Malcolm X's visit.[57] Above all it offers her a profound sense of continuity with the African, the African American, women in whose lineage she places herself ('despite the murders, rapes and suicides we had survived'). She equally acknowledges that, in line with all other African American autobiography, hers, too, signifies a transcending black survival of life and word: self-representation lived for real and then, as it were, imagined for real.

Harlem on My Mind:
Fictions of a Black Metropolis

Here in Manhattan is not merely the largest Negro community in the world, but the first concentration in history of so many diverse elements of Negro life. It has attracted the African, the West Indian, the Negro American; it has brought together the Negro of the city and the man from the town and village; the peasant, the student, the business man, the professional man, artist, poet, musician, adventurer and worker, preacher and criminal, exploiter and social outcast. Each group has come with its own separate motives and for its own special ends, but their greatest experience has been the finding of one another. Proscription and prejudice have thrown these dissimilar elements into a common area of contact and interaction. Within this area, race sympathy and unity have determined a further fusing of sentiment and experience ... In Harlem, Negro life is seizing upon its first chances for group expression and self determination. It is – or promises to be – a race capital.

Alain Locke, 'Introduction',
The New Negro: An Interpretation (1925)[1]

There are, I suppose, contained within the central mythology of Harlem, almost as many versions of its glamour, and its despair, as there are places with people to make them up. (In one meaning of the name, Harlem is simply a place where white cab drivers will not go.) And Harlem means not only Negroes, but, of course, whatever other associations one might connect with them. So in one breath Harlem will be the pleasure-happy center of the universe, full of large, hippy mamas in electric colors and their fast, slick-head papas, all of them twisting and grinning in the streets in a kind of existential joyousness that never permits of sadness or responsibility. But in another breath this same place will be the gathering place for every crippling human vice, and the black men there simply victims of their own peculiar kind of sloth and childishness. But perhaps these are not such different versions after all; chances are both these stereotypes come from the same kinds of mind.

But Harlem, as it is, as it exists for its people, as an actual place where actual humans live – that is a very different thing. Though, to be sure, Harlem is a place – a city really – where almost anything any person could think of to say goes on, probably does go on, or has gone on, but like any other city, it must escape any blank generalization simply because it is alive, and changing each second with each breath any of its citizens take.

LeRoi Jones, 'City of Harlem' (1962),
Home: Social Essays (1966)[2]

Historically, Harlem begins with the very settlement of America itself, the village enclave founded just north of New Amsterdam in 1658 by the tough-willed, often maverick, Dutch ex-Governor of Curaçao, Peter Stuyvesant, and given the name of Nieuw Haarlem. But, overwhelmingly, black Harlem has been a child of the present century, the indisputable First City of Afro-America whose six or so crowded square miles lie between the East and Harlem Rivers to the one side and Morningside and St. Nicholas Avenues to the other with 125th Street as the great arterial thoroughfare. It is this Harlem, iconic yet always sharply local in its human nuance, which has so installed itself in the world's imagination, its very mention a prompt to interest if not fascination.

In the immediate, visual sense, Harlem from the 1920s onward has never been less than tangibly 'there', an internationally acknowledged city of black life and memory. It supplies a mirror, too, for American racial and urban politics at large, whether viewed through its vintage, Jazz Age years, or through the wrack of the Depression, or through the swirling 'race-riot' era of the 1940s (Harlem, like Detroit, blew up in 1943), or through the 1960s dramas of Black Power and the calls to militancy by leadership like that of Malcolm X, or, for all the individual human resilience and style, its subsequent ghettoization and poverty.

But simple chronology, narrative history, could not possibly give the whole account. For more than Chicago's South Side, or Los Angeles's Watts and South Central, or black Atlanta, Harlem has carried the banner of black urban America, the American 'race capital' as Locke called it. And in this respect, it has eluded definition, as unique yet at the same time as utterly symptomatic as any city in America; commentary from Alain Locke to LeRoi Jones/Baraka reaffirms both.

Harlem rightly has been judged hardworking, respectable, indubitably religious, a community keen to state and maintain its own respectability. It has also been a Harlem edged with crime and violence, whether from racketeering, narcotics, gangs and hustle in general, or the everyday abrasion of a people often made to feel pressured and boxed in to the point of implosion. Nor would it ever be denied that Harlem has been a world of showtime, whether the supposed 'doorstep Bohemia' of visiting white nightclubbers in the 1920s, or the music, entertainment and fashion capital both created and then sought out by generations of black Americans.

A further paradox for a Northern city within a city lies in how Harlem has always been a Southern place in its talk, churches and music. So, at least, would be the testimony of any black elder with roots in delta Mississippi, sharecropper Georgia, cotton Alabama or the tobacco Carolinas, and with memories variously of intimate family kin and yet also of the insults and ravages of Jim Crow. The process extends to an eclectically Caribbean Harlem, one of Jamaican/Rastafarians, Trinidadians, Barbadians ('Bajans'), St. Lucians and Guyanese; or to an African Harlem whether Yoruba or Ibo from Nigeria, Kenyan, Ghanaian, Liberian, or pre-Independence South African, with its ANC (African National Congress) and other exiles in flight from Johannesburg's apartheid, and speaking languages from Xhosa to Zulu; or even to Black-Jewish Harlem in the form of its several Ethiopian Hebrew Congregations. No one signature prevails. The multifaceted fact of Harlem lies in its immense cultural widths and depths, the undiminishing play of its different peoples and histories.

So insistent a mix shaped and energized historic Harlem. Its beginnings lie in the initial move up-town from the West Side of black families in the years immediately prior to World War I and into homes once owned by Irish, Italian and Jewish residents. Another announcement of Harlem's coming of age takes place with the sight of the heroic, all-black Fifteenth Regiment back from Europe and marching in deserved triumph up Fifth Avenue in February 1919.

Who could doubt Harlem's astonishing gallery of personalities – from the Jamaica born Marcus Garvey in the 1920s with his heady, if financially disastrous, 'Back to Africa' movement, the UNIA (Universal Negro Improvement Association) with its Black Star Line ships destined for Liberia, to Adam Clayton Powell Jr. in the postwar years as Harlem's own flamboyant Congressman; or from Josephine Baker, whose vaudeville genius for song and dance in Jazz Age shows like *Shuffle Along*, and on-stage sexual daring, she transferred from 'Renaissance' Harlem to Paris in 1925, where she continued to hold sway at the *Folies Bergères* and other *boîtes de nuit* and to work in anti-racist causes and UNICEF, to Paul Robeson, in whom the spirituals found new voice and concert performance, whose roles as O'Neill's Emperor Jones and Shakespeare's Othello launched him into serious mainstream theatre, and who maintained a lifetime's radicalism which brought down on him ongoing FBI and other government persecution; or from a minstrel-actor like Bojangles Robinson through to the luminous trumpeter and 'race man' Miles Davis; or from A'Leila Walker, the 1920s haircare heiress and salon queen, through to Katherine Dunham whose School of Dance (founded in 1944 in New York) has made her a decisive force in the modern American arts? To all of these might be added each athlete celebrity from Joe Louis to Willie Mays, Muhammad Ali to Carl Lewis who, even if they did not originate in Harlem, gave its citizenry meaning and pride.

Harlem's physical ecology, likewise, has become a necessary source of identification, whether the characteristic brownstones, the tenements, the storefront and AME (African Methodist Episcopal) churches, or the few affluent neighbourhoods like Sugar Hill and the Stanford White-designed Striver's Row, early on used as a Harlem place reference in *Plum Bun*, Jessie Fauset's 1929 novel of 'passing'. [3] To these have to be added the subsequent *barrios* of Spanish or Puerto Rican (and now other *latino*) Harlem dwellers, each with their own differences of language, religion, family, dress and foodways. The shared conviction continues among nearly all Harlemites that against the odds, whether poverty, racism or the recent calamity of drugs, America's first and self-availing black city can still survive and thrive. [4]

All of this dense human current of change has inevitably bred, and then become entwined in, its own spiral of mythologies, a Harlem prodigiously to be imagined and reimagined. This also holds true, never more so than in the 1920s, for inter-racial Harlem, a frequent meeting and gathering point despite any number of built-in constraints across the colour line. [5] Whether in high or popular culture, mainstream allusion or rap, Harlem has come to signify a kind of figurative or emblematic community replete in specific, yet at the same time legendary, names, associations and rites. [6]

Harlem has also long established its identity in every kind of music, from the choirs and gospellers to the jazz and blues played in a myriad of clubs, bars, cellars or lofts. Duke Ellington's 'Take the A Train' or 'Drop Me Off in Harlem' typically serve as musical signings-in and are as much to be heard in some 'round midnight' watering hole as concert hall. Harlem musicianship yields a simply dazzling roster of names, besides a vintage Harlemite like Ellington who made Sugar Hill his home, which include Count Basie, Cab Calloway, Ethel Mills, Louis Armstrong, Charlie Parker, Dizzie Gillespie, Thelonius Monk, Ella Fitzgerald, John Coltrane, Miles Davis, Dexter Gordon, James Brown or Aretha Franklin. Harlem may not have been the only stopover in their lives, but it ranks among the most important, especially in venues like the Cotton Club, the Lafayette Theater, and the Apollo Theater.

In the visual arts a similar virtuosity holds. One early instance would be the woodcuts, prints and graphics of Aaron Douglas, some of which Alain Locke included in *The New Negro*. Harlem also becomes the organizing reference in James Van Der Zee's Talented Tenth family and social photographic portraiture, the shrewd, versatile, Bootsie cartoons of Ollie Harrington, and the latterday portfolios of camera work by John Taylor and Gordon Parks. The achievement equally extends into the allied arts of painting, notably Romare Bearsden whose canvases frequently serve as book covers for black-authored texts, or Beauford Delaney,[7] in whom

James Baldwin found an early Village mentor, friend and sexual ally; of ballet, now virtually synonymous with the Dance Theater of Harlem; and not least of sport, the swerve and slam dunk of entertainment basketball as performed by the Harlem Globetrotters, however much they, as other black players and teams, began in an era when the NBA (National Basketball Association) operated a white-only regime.

In each of these manifestations Harlem has been the locus of a historic and ever continuing body of black creative self-expression.[8] In popular terms, particularly, it is virtually written into America's music and dance, whether 1920s cabaret (with Ellington, Basie and Calloway in the line of succession), a postwar Harlem tuned in to Lena Horne, Ray Charles or The Platters, or, through the 1960s and after, the CD and video worlds of Michael Jackson, Lionel Richie, Whitney Houston or Ice Cube and a latterday current generation of rappers. Then there has been film: early WPA (Works Progress Administration) 'shorts' with PBS and other network documentaries to follow; screen adaptations of Chester Himes's Coffin Ed/Gravedigger Jones detective stories filmed on location and directed by Ossie Davis, such as *Cotton Comes to Harlem* (1970), with a follow-up, based on Himes's *The Heat's On*, and retitled *Come Back Charleston Blue* (1972); black action movies like the immensely popular Richard Roundtree 'John Shaft' series – *Shaft* (1971), *Shaft's Big Score* (1972) and *Shaft in Africa* (1973); and, latterly, a full length bio-pic like Spike Lee's *Malcolm X* (1992) with Denzel Washington in the title role.

Harlem, in consequence, has properly come to be seen as a kind of life theatre in its own right, a working arena of street culture, churches, eateries, dress, shoestands, barbershops and clubs, even of graffiti and turf markings and, as always, the vital seams of talk from preaching to rap, kitchentalk to youth slang. Much of the latter has been added to the store of Harlem community and other related African American material held in archives like those of the Schomburg Library, an increasingly appreciated black popular culture. For some, in fact, this populist Harlem should be even more emphasized. Not only is Harlem held to have been the occasion of an extraordinary mix and range of art, its dynamic amounts to a kind of social or urban art form, a black, citied *tableau vivant*. By the 1990s Harlem would even feature in advertisements for tourist walking tours.

Nor, from its beginnings to the present, has Harlem been anything other than a *written* city, a city made over into a plurality of literary forms. Its poets run from Countee Cullen and Claude McKay in the Harlem Renaissance of the 1920s through Melvin Tolson (whose consciously modernist *Harlem Gallery*, published in 1965, offers a landmark) to the voices found in black nationalist collections like the LeRoi Jones and Larry Neal anthology *Black Fire* (1968).[9] Its drama has been both early vaudeville and modern Harlem-centred pieces like the musical gospel satire adapted from his own novel of Langston Hughes's *Tambourines to*

Glory (1958) and the later church fable of word and flesh of James Baldwin's *The Amen Corner* (1968).[10]

To these might be added Chester Himes's still unused screenplay *Baby Sister* (1961), a kind of Brechtian cartoon-strip which points forward to his later thrillers.[11] The iconography includes poverty, switchblades, dilapidated houses, numbers, black matrons, street brothers, Jesse Simple bars, the Apollo Theater, shiny big cars; in all, Harlem as cannibal territory wired with hustle. Himes builds the glittery vulnerability into the piece's very idiom:

> This is Harlem, U.S.A., a city of contradictions. A city of Negroes isolated in the middle of New York City. A city of incredible poverty and huge sums of cash. A city of the meek and the violent. A city of brothels, bars and churches. Here is the part called Sugar Hill, where the prosperous live – the leaders, the professionals, the numbers barons. Here is the part they call the Valley, where the hungry eke out an existence and prey upon one another. The Valley is like a sea filled with cannibal fish. Put in your hand, and pull out a stub. This is the story of a good-looking, healthy, voluptuous, seventeen-year old black girl, called BABY SISTER LOUIS, who lives in the Valley. She lives with her family; her mother MAMA LOUIS, and her three brothers: SUSIE, twenty-two years old, BUDDY, twenty years old, and PIGMEAT, fourteen years old. Her elder sister, LIL, a blues singer, lives with her man on Sugar Hill. BABY SISTER is a juicy, tasty lamb in a jungle of hungry wolves. And in the Valley there is no good shepherd. Only the will of the inhabitants of this community, restricted, violated and violent, timid and vicious, living in their rat-ridden, hotbox, stinking flats, are either the hungry wolves themselves, or are struggling desperately to save themselves from the hungry wolves. And it is perfectly reasonable and natural that these people should be hungry, the wolves and the sheep alike. If your own food – food for the soul and food for the spirit as well as food for the stomach – has been held just out of your reach for three hundred years, or longer, you would be hungry too. And one way to keep from starving in this land of plenty when you have no food is to eat your baby sister.

Not for Himes any dewy eyed or nostalgic picture; rather, as though in the style of an adult nursery story, this is Harlem as warground, preyed upon and yet always self-preying.

Harlem journalism and essay work equally enter the reckoning, especially that of key black newspapers like the *Amsterdam News* and of which LeRoi Jones's 'City of Harlem' marks one symptomatic instance. James Baldwin, too, plays his part in the company, as vividly as anywhere in his early, compelling, 'The Harlem Ghetto' (1948), Harlem again as 'congestion', an 'insistent, claustrophobic pounding in the skull'.[12]

Then there has been the Harlem imagined and carried in fiction, and nowhere more so than in the novel. For though Harlem has had its remarkable short-story tellers, among them Langston Hughes in any of his Simple pieces, or James Baldwin in his lyric, jazz-like 'Sonny's Blues', along with John A. Williams, Alice Childress, Toni Cade Bambara or Rosa Guy among others, it has been the novel which by scale if nothing else has sought out Harlem's completeness and plurality as a city. Nor has Harlem been only the preserve of black writers. A white, along with a *nuyorriqueño*, line of authorship, from Carl Van Vechten in the 1920s to Warren Miller, Shane Stevens, Edward Lewis Wallant and Piri Thomas in the 1950s and after, invites its own recognition.

If the focus here falls mainly upon the novel, that, in part, is because its elasticity and length have been especially hospitable to the telling of Harlem's complex singularity. At the same time, it is a novel to be seen in the context of the associated range of other expressive and cultural forms, for it shares with them the sense of challenge to the narrative imagination, a Harlem on the Mind metamorphosed and transferred to the written page.

☆   ☆   ☆

Alain Locke's insistence upon Harlem as 'the largest Negro community in the world', a coming 'race capital', is a reminder that despite poverty and the colour line the 1920s were indeed its best, or at least its best celebrated, years. It was then, probably more than at any time since, that Harlem was in vogue. *The New Negro: An Interpretation* (1925), born of *Survey Graphic*'s special Harlem number in 1924, helped to underline how Harlem had come to express much of Afro-America itself – an international black city of art, spirit, memory, music and word. So, at least, was the literary witness of its ministry of all, or nearly all, the talents.[13] And so, too, from a later age, would be the witness of Ishmael Reed in his *Mumbo Jumbo* (1972) with its mock-history of the Jazz Age, using Dyonesian-Greek and Pharaonic-Egyptian myth, as caught up in the liberative fever called 'Jes Grew' – dance, food, talk, honkytonk, showtime, sex, the whole free play of the senses – as against the puritanism which led to Prohibition, Hooverism, white masonic and Main Street America.[14]

Harlem would also have its own full-length, and greatly contrasting, chroniclers. James Weldon Johnson, in his *Black Manhattan* (1930) speaks of 'the recognized Negro capital', 'the Negro metropolis'. But his emphasis (as maybe befitted a lifelong Republican) falls less upon black migration and the struggles and costs than the high-cultural story – Harlem as a literary and theatre tradition recorded as through a personal diary, a memoir.[15]

For Claude McKay, in his *Harlem: Negro Metropolis* (1940), albeit by then an ex-Marxist and Catholic convert with old scores to settle, even the retrospect of the Depression does nothing to dim Harlem's importance.

He insists upon its role as a 'magnet', a black urban self-mirror, a first, true gathering place of the varieties of black modernity. If, then, the 1920s offer a place to begin, they do so precisely because they indicate a Harlem from the outset resistant to the kind of 'blank generalization' excoriated by LeRoi Jones.[16]

Of all the Jazz Age fiction which takes on Harlem, no two novels captured its perceived style more than Carl Van Vechten's *Nigger Heaven* (1926) and Claude McKay's *Home to Harlem* (1928), the former a source of enormous controversy on publication and written by Harlem's probably best-known white patron of the arts who would also bequeath an important photographic archive of its writers and people, and the latter, whatever the author's Jamaican origins, a lyric, on the pulse and 'down home' salute.[17] Earlier novels point the way, whether Paul Laurence Dunbar's *The Sport of the Gods* (1902) with its portraits of black life and rooming on West 27th Street and a drinks and clubland gathering-place like The Banner club, or James Weldon Johnson's *The Autobiography of an Ex-Coloured Man* (1912, 1927) whose 'passing' drama also takes on 'Sixth Avenue from Twenty-third to Thirty-third streets' as a black enclave with its own ragtime 'Negro Bohemia'.[18]

Even if it does not deal exclusively with Harlem, one would also invoke Nella Larsen's *Quicksand* (1928) which explores black Manhattan through the eyes of its almost white Danish-American and deeply self-divided heroine. On her arrival from the South, and then Chicago, Helga Crane finds herself seized by 'the continually gorgeous panorama of Harlem'. In Rudolph Fisher's two novels, *The Walls of Jericho* (1928) and *The Conjure Man Dies: A Mystery Tale of Dark Harlem* (1932), the note turns more laconic – the former a witty, cryptic satire of Harlem 'society' manners, and the latter of modern-day 'conjure' replete with a wondrous, self-purporting African con man and a detective pair to anticipate Chester Himes's Grave Digger and Coffin Ed.[19]

Wallace Thurman's *The Blacker the Berry* (1929) offers the Harlem portrait of Emma Lou Morgan, a black woman in revolt against her own colour and whose life borders on a pathology of black self-hate. George Schuyler's *Black No More* (1931) takes an attractively scabrous tilt at the workings of colour hierarchy and the urge to whiteness not only in Harlem but in Afro-America at large. Countee Cullen's only novel, *One Way to Heaven* (1932), the doomed love story of Sam Lucas and Mattie Johnson and at the same time a panorama of Harlem religiosity, shows a flair for painterly image wholly befitting Harlem's then best poet.[20]

It was, however, the novels of Van Vechten and McKay which set the standard, relative bestsellers and required reading for anyone in the 1920s and early 1930s with an eye to matters uptown. It may seem odd that Harlem's first chronicler in fiction should have been white, but Van Vechten's *Nigger Heaven* can be located within a context in which other white writings had turned to black America with a quite new kind of relish, whether in O'Neill plays like *The Emperor Jones* (1920), a Sherwood Anderson novel of race like *Dark Laughter* (1925), or Faulkner's Yoknapatawpha cycle of mixed Southern dynasties begun with *Sartoris* (1929).[21] In 1934 so grand a patron as Nancy Cunard made a considerable splash with *Negro: Anthology*, her wide-ranging compendium of black writing, art and photography.[22] Van Vechten, thereby, in a sense was doing no more than extending this general upsurge of white literary interest in both black America generally and Harlem in particular.

But what writer, especially a white one, could use 'nigger' in his title without arousing profoundest offence? No matter that 'Nigger Heaven', a phrase which refers to the topmost gallery of 'mixed' theatres where blacks were assigned seats, and often to be heard as shorthand for Harlem itself or at least for its clubs, was fairly common parlance. No matter that the novel would be endorsed by James Weldon Johnson, Langston Hughes and, most importantly, Claude McKay (who thought it the work of an author 'not a bit patronising' and indeed would use the phrase in *Home to Harlem*). W.E.B. DuBois spoke for the majority when he gave it a drubbing as 'an affront to the hospitality of black folk', a 'caricature'.[23]

The truth is that, well meant or otherwise, *Nigger Heaven* offers too slight an achievement to have other than representative significance. Its plot borders on the mawkish, a formula love story and murder with touches of yet other melodrama as embellishment. It renders Harlem itself as a kind of unexplored social territory, not quite exotica but something near. Van Vechten does better, however, in situating some of the action in the *Black Venus*, a typical nightclub catering to white patrons and an instance of cabaret Harlem. He is also highly germane in the depiction of the workings of racism both at street level and in publishing. He tries, not without success, to emulate something of Harlem speech, its vernacular ease and invention. This he takes to the length of actually including a glossary of then everyday terms like 'ofay,' 'daddy' and 'snow'. It is also perhaps to his credit that he recognized his own ambiguous position in writing *black* Harlem fiction. He has one of his characters, a white magazine editor, say:

> I have visited Harlem in two capacities, as a customer in the cabarets and as a guest in my friends' homes. The whole place, contrary to the general impression, is overrun with fresh, unused material. Nobody has yet written a good gambling story; nobody has touched the outskirts of cabaret life; nobody has yet gone into the diverse tribes of the region ... Well, if you young Negro intellectuals don't get busy, a new crop of Nordics is going to spring up who will take the trouble to become better informed and will exploit this material before the Negro gets round to it.

Locke himself could not have put things better, a call to arms from a perhaps unexpected quarter. Although *Nigger Heaven* belongs in the most minor league as fiction, it does have importance as a clue to the Harlem in the minds of outsiders, an image of Harlem which undoubtedly played to, and re-enforced, what white America wanted (or even needed) to believe about its emerging premier black city.

Far closer to Harlem's feel, its heat and energy, though with its own form of exoticizing, is Claude McKay's *Home to Harlem* published two years later. Jamaican by birth and upbringing McKay may have been, but as his poetry collection, *Harlem Shadows* (1922), and his history, *Harlem: Negro Metropolis* (1940), confirmed, he could call upon a long intimacy with Harlem as black community life. He had no hesitation in acknowledging his debt to the example of Carl Van Vechten. *Home to Harlem* seemed instantly a taking-up of Van Vechten's and Locke's shared call, a black-insider witness to the sight and sound, the ease and jazz, of 1920s Harlem. At last, said admirers, Harlem had found its laureate, even if certain self-appointed black guardians of respectability deplored the scenes of sex and drink. This admiration, however, trod lightly round the issue of whether the ostensible protagonist, Jake, gets eclipsed by his Haitian friend Ray, or whether the plot reads too segmentally, or whether McKay had allowed his lyricism to risk turning lush or indulgent.

The Harlem which most caught the attention is established early in the novel as Jake, a longshoreman, deserts his regiment in Europe and works his passage back to Harlem via Marseilles. He ponders, blues-like: 'Jest take me 'long to Harlem is all I pray.' The note is taken up in self-musings like the following, a vision of Harlem as a world warmed by affection and memory:

Oh, to be in Harlem again after two years away. The deep-dyed colour, the thickness, the closeness of it. The noises of Harlem. The sugared laughter. The honey talk on its streets. And all night long, ragtime and 'blues' playing somewhere ... singing somewhere, dancing somewhere! Oh, the contagious fever of Harlem. Burning everywhere in dark-eyed Harlem ... .Burning now in Jake's sweet blood.

Within this 'familiar Harlem', McKay acknowledges that Harlem can also be violent, abrasive, even murderous. Jake moves through Harlem's 'thickness' and 'honey' as to the manner born, relishing its licence and especially its women. But during stopovers from working on a Pullman with Ray he also gets embroiled in its dangers, eventually after a fight leaving for Chicago with his new-found 'brown-sugar', the appropriately named Felice. Who would deny that this is a male Harlem, the women either endlessly compliant and decorative or hardedged madams? Even so, it is Jake himself as one of Harlem's own who embodies the novel's true spirit. A passage like the following unfolds a near impressionistic Harlem, an irresistible black city of appetite and the senses:

Dusk gathered in blue patches over the Black Belt. Lenox Avenue was vivid. The saloons were bright, crowded with drinking men jammed right around the bars, treating one another and telling the incidents of the day. Longshoremen in overalls with hooks, Pullman porters holding their bags, waiters, elevator boys. Liquor-rich porters, banana-ripe laughter. ...

The pavement was a dim warm bustle. Women hurrying home from day's work to get dinner ready for husbands who worked at night. On their arms brown bags and black containing a bit of meat, a head of lettuce, butter. Young men who were staggering through life, passing along with brown-paper packages, containing a small steak, a pork chop, to do their own frying.

From out of saloons came the savory smell of corned beef and cabbage, spare-ribs, hamburger steaks. Out of little cook-joints wedged in side streets, tripe, pigs' feet, hogs' ears and snouts. Out of apartments, steak smothered with onions, liver and bacon, fried chicken.

If this is blue collar and after work Harlem, warm-heartedly given to the evening meal, so a more genteel 'New Negro' version can be found in Jessie Fauset's *Plum Bun* (1928). Its middle-class 'race story' of the Philadelphia born Angela Murray which ends in her move from New York to Paris delivers the more standard 1920s version, Harlem as almost anthropological surprise:

> On an exquisite afternoon she went to Harlem ... she was amazed and impressed at this bustling, frolicking, busy, laughing great city within a greater one. She had never seen coloured life so thick, so varied, so complete ... Unquestionably there was something very fascinating, even terrible, about this stream of life ... Harlem was a great city. [24]

In this novel, and in each of the era's companion texts, Afro-America could be said to have given its own textual imagining to Harlem.

1929 and its economic aftermath burst the bubble. Just as the Depression gripped America at large, so in Harlem and other black communities the poverty which had always threatened grew especially brutal. Harlem, in particular, edged increasingly towards slum, a ghetto. As quickly as it had come into vogue so Harlem went out of vogue. The image became one of citied unaffluence, a black urban people under duress and a far cry from the trumpeted gaiety of the preceding decade. And fiction, like all the arts, reflected the process.

Social realism became the rallying cry, usually associated with Richard Wright in the guise of 'Negro Protest'. Yet Wright's black city world was to be not Harlem but South Side Chicago, at least as depicted in his landmark novel *Native Son* and in the driven, divided figure of Bigger Thomas. Of the literary school attributed to Wright, principally Chester Himes, Willard Motley and Ann Petry, it would be the last who bequeaths a Depression and Harlem period novel of great importance.

Published in 1946, and set against a World War II background, Petry's *The Street* carries the mark of the Depression at every turn, a tough, deterministic story as far away as imaginable from the brave optimism of Alain Locke and his contemporaries of a generation earlier.[25] It also depicts Harlem through the viewpoint of a woman, Lutie Johnson, forced to shift for herself and her son Bub within a web of circumstance which leads her to an almost inevitable and fatal act of violence. Harlem, as it were, narrows down precisely to a street, and within it the commodifying reduction of its people and their lives.

This threat-laden Harlem gains especial edge in Petry's focusing of things through Lutie. Caught out by a bad marriage, struggling to stay respectable given her looks and relative youth, surrounded by offers to hustle, she finds herself at first drawn to a smalltime musician, Boots Smith, who promises to help her into a singing career. But he, too, reveals himself as yet another sexual threat, a would-be rapist. In him, and in all the pressure of the street, Harlem closes in on her, incarceratory, dangerous, anything but communal. One hears just the right echo of urban blues in this sample of how she is made to react:

> She glanced up at the gloomy flats where the heads had been. There were row after row of narrow windows – floor after floor packed tight with people. She looked at the street itself. It was bordered by dustbins. Half-starved cats prowled through the bins – rustling paper, gnawing on bones. Again she thought that it wasn't just this one block, this particular street. It was like this all over Harlem wherever the rents were low.

Although the novel uses precisely 'this particular street' to locate all the 'rustle' and 'gnaw' of an impoverished Harlem, Petry offers more than a mere diagram. She develops a full, various fictional cast: Mrs. Hedges, the tough, fire scarred madam, who operates to her own well-intended standard of morality; the furtive and near pathological tenement supervisor Jones of whom Mrs. Hedges remarks, 'You done lived in basements so long, you ain't hardly human no more'; Jones's intimidated mistress Min who resorts to a Harlem roots doctor in the hope of making Jones desire her; Bub's white teacher Miss Rinner, always frightened by Harlem and to whom teaching there amounts to a stigma; Boots Smith, scarred with a knife wound from one of his past women, dangled by the club owner Mr. Junto (a name which obliquely refers back to the white slavocracy elites), made to serve as his general runner and pimp, and never able to rise above low-grade musical jobs; and, outside Harlem, the affluent white Connecticut family who first employ Lutie as a maid and are so embroiled in their own money and domestic violence that they fail to see in her anything but another unremarkable black serving woman.

Around this street, too, Petry implies a further lattice of other similar streets and tenements each with its boxed-in humanity to match. She also successfully evokes the ambiguous glitter of Harlem club life, especially the Casino where Lutie works and the Junto Bar and Grill where she hopes to establish a singing career. But it is, inexorably, to the street, 116th Street, that Lutie returns, Harlem as a determining ghetto and menace.

Within its world Bub eventually is sent to Reform School for theft, and Lutie, like Claude McKay's Jake before her, heads out to Chicago after the killing of Boots. Harlem's implacable urban geometry and the behaviour and state of mind it engenders is captured graphically in Lutie's reaction to a young girl she sees in hospital:

> She felt she knew the steps by which that girl landed on the stretcher in the hospital. She could trace them easily. It could be that Bub might follow the same path.
>
> The girl probably went to high school for a few months and then got tired to it. She had no place to study at night because the house was full of lodgers and she had not incentive anyway, because she didn't have a real home. She found out that boys liked her and she started bringing them to the apartment. The mother wasn't there to know what was going on.
>
> They didn't have real homes, no base, no family life. So at sixteen or seventeen the girl was fooling around with two or three different boys. One of them found out about the others. Like all the rest of them, he had only a curious supersensitive kind of pride that kept him going, so he had to have revenge and knives are cheap.
>
> It happened again and again all through Harlem ...

Petry's vision of Harlem here as throughout in *The Street* reads clear-eyed and unsentimentally, a community both injured and self-injuring.

1930s Harlem under economic siege also lies behind the vision of Louise Meriwether's retrospective juvenile novel *Daddy Was a Number Runner* (1970).[26] Written as the first person story of 12 year old Frances Coffin, it tells a Harlem coming of age, a self-awakening forced ahead of its time on a burgeoning black adolescent girl. Replete with period Depression references to Father Divine, Dutch Schultz, Roosevelt and the Fireside broadcasts, it locates in Francie a Harlem which finds itself obliged to sell itself short on its own evident best promise. Francie bears witness to her father's hustle as a numbers man, to her peers who have taken to prostitution and pimping, to a catalogue of petty crime, welfare and street culture, and yet, throughout, also to the warmth and extraordinary human colour of her family and neighbourhood. Meriwether's achievement rests upon her ability to take up this Harlem paradox. In the very ingenuousness of Francie's idiom she measures the contradiction of Harlem's vital richness forced to exist – in the Depression as rarely at any other time in American history – within a devitalizing poverty.

The Harlem fiction by which Langston Hughes has come to be best-known cannot in any strict sense be thought of as a body of novel writing. Yet the Jesse B. Semple or Simple stories begun in 1943 in the Chicago *Defender* give precisely that impression. Eventually to run to five collections, in turn *Simple Speaks His Mind* (1950), *Simple Takes a Wife* (1953), *Simple Stakes a Claim* (1957), *The Best of Simple* (1961) and *Simple's Uncle Sam* (1965), these immensely subtle, ingenuous seeming pieces of black folk narrative turn upon the figure of Simple as the voice of street corner and domestic Harlem, its own immediate postwar *griot*.[27]

Spoken as if to an often incredulous Hughes himself, they touch on American race issues as read in the paper, heard on the radio, carried by word of mouth, and mulled over in the work place and bar. A man of many apparent foibles, Simple especially features as the put upon Harlem family man, by his ex-wife Isabel, his current glamour girl Zarita, his country cousin Minnie, and his kinsman F.D. (for Franklin Delano). A one-time Virginian who in time-honoured fashion has stepped North to Harlem, his puzzlement and general sense of being always caught on the wrong foot act as Hughes's wry, ingenious mode of taking bearings on an America shot through with racial double standards. Not that he ever allows Simple to become too sermonish, rather the genial, often self-contradicting man of the Harlem average.

Harlem itself features characteristically for Simple in outbursts like the following from 'A Toast to Harlem':

No, I would not go back down South, not even to Baltimore. I am in Harlem to stay! You say the houses ain't mine. Well, the sidewalk is – and don't nobody push me off. The cops don't even say, 'Move on,' hardly no more ... Here I ain't scared to vote – that's another thing I like about Harlem. I also like it because we've got subways and it does not take all day to get downtown, neither are you Jim Crowed on the way. Why, Negroes is running some of these subway trains. This morning I rode the A Train down to 34th Street. There were a Negro driving it, making ninety miles a hour. The cat *were really driving* that train! Every time he flew by one of them local stations looks like he was saying, 'Look at me! This train is mine!' That cat were gone, ole man. Which is another reason I like Harlem! Sometimes I run into Duke

Ellington on 125th Street and I say, 'What you know there, Duke?'
Duke says, 'Solid, ole man.' He does not know me from Adam, but he
speaks. One day I saw Lena Horne coming out of the Hotel Theresa
and I said, 'Hubba! Hubba!' Lena smiled. Folks is friendly in Harlem.
I feel like I got the world in a jug and the stopper in my hand! So drink
a toast to Harlem!

Simple's mix of standard American and down-home black idiom, his
assumed community oneness with Duke Ellington and Lena Horne, his
relish at the thought of a black brother 'flying home' at the controls of
the A train, and his folk reference to 'the world in a jug' add up to a
community voice, a voice at once itself and yet that of a larger Harlem.

Hughes, however, always knew better than to make Simple some
uncritical laureate of Harlem. Simple speaks as perfectly familiar with its
poverty and dangerous crowdedness ('A Million – and One'), its sheer daily
threat ('Enter Cousin Minnie'), its ambiguous religiosity ('Simple Prays
a Prayer'), its case-hardened experience of white America ('There Ought
to be a Law'), its own recent riots, violence and police harassment ('Name
in Print'), and even its extremes of weather ('Letting Off Steam'). But
throughout he comes over as yet another type of Harlem insider, un-Jim
Crowed as he says, and at ease with the customs and talk of his people.
Hughes's own posture of the liberal fall guy, seemingly taken unawares
by Simple's prejudices and values, makes for a perfect counter and point
of access. He can be amused, put out, frequently astounded by his Harlem
crony, but he also finds himself, as indeed do we, obliged to learn from
Simple. Their colloquies, thereby, become a kind of Harlem speaking, a
community in dialogue with itself, yet never too inward or hermetic.
Harlem, immediate postwar Harlem at least, can rarely have been more
congenially voiced or overheard.

☆　☆　☆

'"How do you get to Harlem?" "That's easy," he said, "You just keep
heading north."'[28] That, precisely, is what the un-named narrator of Ralph
Ellison's *Invisible Man* (1952) does, a journey which takes him from Dixie
to black Manhattan's Promised Land, from darkness to light, and from
unseeing to vision.[29]

Two of his essays give bearings on the point. In 'Harlem Is Nowhere'
(1948) he writes:

the most surreal fantasies are acted out upon the streets of Harlem; a
man ducks in and out of traffic shouting and throwing imaginary
grenades that actually exploded during World War I; a boy participates
in the rape-robbery of his mother; a man beating his wife in a park
observes Marquess of Queensberry rules ... Life becomes a masquerade,

exotic costumes are worn every day ... For this is a world in which the major energy of the imagination goes not into creating works of art, but to overcome the frustrations of social discrimination.[30]

In 'Harlem's America' (1966), however, Ellison indicates how these Harlem rites of surrealism and transformation at the same time point to, and complement, the writer's art:

Harlem is a place where our folklore is preserved and transformed. It is the place where the body of our Negro myth and legend thrives. It is a place where our styles, musical styles, the many styles of Negro life, find continuity and metamorphosis.[31]

As he speaks out of his border cellar, illegally irradiated by light siphoned from the Monopolated Light & Power Company, the narrator of *Invisible Man* calls up not only his own journey but that of nearly all Afro-America, the history of slavery into freedom, South into North, the erasure into the finding of identity. Harlem becomes a focal expression of Ellison's deft play of folklore, jazz and blues, a whole register of light and darkness, tease and counter-tease, within the workings of racial vision. As his narrator very quickly recognizes:

This really was Harlem, and now all the stories which I had heard of the city-within-a-city leaped alive in my mind ... For me this was not a city of realities, but of dreams; perhaps because I had always thought of my life as being confined to the South. And now as I struggled through the lines of people a new world of possibility suggested itself to me faintly, like a small voice that was barely audible in the roar of city sounds. I moved wide-eyed trying to take in the bombardment of impressions. (p. 142)

Harlem as dream, a black American dream which vacillates between euphoria and nightmare, touches base with history clearly enough: in the Garveyite figure of Ras, in the reference to the 1940s riots, in the ambiguous contribution of the American Communist Party ('The Brotherhood') to black politics, and in the fraught sexual agenda between white women and black men. But the Harlem which Ellison most insists upon is that eventually carried in the mind of the narrator, one simultaneously on the defensive and the attack, full of tricks and pitfalls and doubletakes. As the narrator says, here is a 'Heart of Darkness' Harlem, made surreal by American history and in which strange, hallucinatory identities like those of Ras, Tod Clifton, Brother Jack, the looter Dupre and, above all, those visited on or adopted by the narrator himself, exist as if by some strangely ordained transhistorical writ.

Like Harlem itself, the narrator exists in and across time, a voice of 'now' yet which comprises all the increments of black time to have gone into that 'now'. For whether as the bearer of false promissory notes (his college scroll, the letters from Bledsoe), or as an *apparatchik* in the Brotherhood, or as the confidence man B.P. Rinehart, or as the voice of the Prologue and Epilogue, the narrator speaks at once to, of and from behind Harlem, one bound up in all the prodigal contradictions of American history. Emerging, as he says, from a hole in which he and his black ancestors found themselves brutally deposited 'some time in the nineteenth-century', he assumes the almost custodial voice of Harlem, witness perforce to its historic evolution and mysteries. For him, and the readership he seeks to win over, Harlem exists as America's black *cité fourmillante*, an urban fact located in actual time and place, yet also a place lodged deep and challengingly within the American racial psyche.

So multifarious a Harlem could hardly have found a more attuned chronicler than Ellison, or at least than his narrator persona. The latter, meeting up with the Boston philanthropist Mr. Norton to whom, as a student in his Tuskegee-like college, he has shown the Trueblood family and taken to the Golden Day, tells him he has 'made' him. That is, by becoming a writer, a mythologer, a man of 'underground' creativity, he has come to serve as the surrogate of all Americans, black, white and in-between, who in effect dream American reality, and Harlem as one of its essential loadstones. So that whether Heaven or Hell, history or myth, Harlem in Ellison's assured fashioning becomes an archive of localized life yet the metaphor of an Afro-America at the edges of fantasy.

A companion Harlem is to be found in James Baldwin's *Go Tell It on the Mountain* (1953), a Harlem of Pentecostal rites, coming of age, and the ever immediate past of black Southern dynasty.[32] John Grimes, still young during the Depression, provides the human link to three black generations, a Harlem remembrance of things past. In part, this frame calls up the Great Migration, the Northward shift of black families out of Klan-fed hate and Dixie injustice. More emblematically, it calls up the Old Testament: John's preacher-stepfather, Gabriel, as a flawed Abraham, with Sarah, Hagar and Ishmael re-enacted in the lives of the unloved first wife Deborah, the alluring homegirl Esther, and the wayward prodigal son Roy. The Harlem interwar years with Gabriel's second wife Elizabeth, and John as her own illegitimate son by the murdered Richard, then take up and echo this earlier tier, the Northern story as an implied retelling of the Southern.

Rarely since, whether in his too amorphous *Another Country* (1962), or his Harlem-Puerto Rico novella *If Beale Street Could Talk* (1974), or his broad-canvassed *Just Above My Head* (1979), which contains a number of key Harlem scenes, has Baldwin's fiction – again 'Sonny's Blues' offers the exception – quite caught the fervour and cadence of embattled ghetto life. In part, this is due to the tightness of design in *Go Tell It on the Mountain*, its counterpoint of 1930s time-present and memory and of boy and adult.[33]

It is also due to Baldwin's sureness about the particular Harlem he is dramatizing, the Harlem of his best essay work marked by the authority of personal experience. This is a Harlem which, for John, has itself become his stepfather's Temple of the Fire Baptized, apocalyptic, ablaze in visions of the Fall and the Redemption, and which leaves his own already uncertain sexuality caught midways. The Grimes family, and the Temple's church people, like Praying Mother Washington and the lithesome, androgynous Elisha, personify Harlem as of this world yet with the promise of the next, and amid whose competing human frailties John must negotiate flesh and spirit.

Baldwin, even so, keeps his novel firmly tied into history. 'The Prayers of the Saints', the three memory pieces of Gabriel as flawed patriarch, of Florence, his embittered, literally cancered sister, and of Elizabeth as guardian mother, are eventful in their own right. But they also play off Depression-era Harlem against an earlier Dixie while showing the threads of hope and despair which bind both into the same story. The Harlem of the novel, thereby, takes on a personal yet historic signification, as John's own immediate place of becoming and at the same time that of the larger community whose journeyings across time and family have been the making of him.

☆   ☆   ☆

To move from Ellison and Baldwin to Chester Himes, one-time jewel thief, Ohio State student, California war-worker, jailbird, European literary exile, autobiographer and novelist, is to engage in another postwar register of Harlem, one quite sumptuously audacious in its *bizarrerie*.[34] Throughout Himes's prior fiction – the considerable output of prison and street stories begun in the 1930s and the five principal novels he wrote between 1945 and 1955 and which culminate in *The Primitive* (1955) – the hints were always there (especially in *Pinktoes* (1961) as a comic sexual spoof of Harlem inter-racial revels) of the paired detective storytelling to follow.

Begun in 1957, Himes's eight Coffin Ed Jones/Grave Digger Johnson novels (only *Run Man Run* in 1966, the story of a psychotic and racist cop, does not use the pair) were first translated from English into French as *romans policiers* in Gallimard's celebrated *Série Noire*. These 'Harlem domestic tales', as he once termed them, were the upshot of Himes's expatriation to Paris and his friendship with the French writer Marcel

Duhamel, and when subsequently issued in America in their original English they took a while to overcome initial disfavour if not hostility.

But given the shifts of racial consciousness in the America of Civil Rights and Black Power, Malcolm and Stokely, the process then reversed itself. Himes, suddenly, was judged to have caught the pathology of the times. Not only had he written plots, with a language to match, of genuine inventiveness, he had written Harlem as no one before him, a surreal and violent urban box, a counter-order of drugs and crime, a black city of the absurd. Increasingly likened by admirers to Dickens's 'other' London, Himes's Harlem was seen to serve as a locale in which literally almost anything could happen.

Each of the books offers a milling population of preachers and politicians, sober matriarchs and mock religious prophets, pimps and their chippies, drug pushers and wheel thieves, transvestites, con men and shysters of every kind and sex. Grave Digger and Coffin Ed feature as adepts, unravellers, of a territory prone to the wildest species of plot or caper whose violence frequently includes knifings, acid throwing, throat cutting and torture. At once Harlem's familiars and yet hard put to fathom its every human knot and spiral, theirs is a spiralling, often about-face world, a black (and sometimes white) hall of mirrors.

Almost invariably each novel derives from an act of macabre violence, an event outrageous to at least one of the senses. In an early magazine profile Philip Oakes offered the following sampling of Himes's imaginative wares:

A hit-and-run victim, jammed against a wall, and frozen stiff on a sub-zero night, is stripped of her finery and revealed as a transvestite. Dr. Mubutu, inventor of an elixir distilled from the mating organs of baboons, rabbits, eagles and shellfish, is butchered while arguing the true cost of rejuvenation. A white homosexual, whose jugular has been severed, expires on the sidewalk remarkably only because he's not wearing trousers.[35]

To these choice items, which describe in turn *All Shot Up* (1960) and *Blind Man with a Pistol* (1969), can be added the corpse of a headless tyre thief riding the Harlem streets on a motorcycle and crashing into a pawnbroker's shop bearing the motto 'We Will Give Credit To The Dead' (also *All Shot Up*); a white King Cola salesman, the flagellant of teenage black girls, impossibly killed by the zip gun belonging to the doped-out leader of a Harlem Muslim gang (*The Real Cool Killers*, 1959); the death by 'religious ecstasy' of Alberta Brown, a follower of one Sweet Prophet Brown, which puts in train the murderous search for a Numbers fortune hidden in an armchair (*The Big Gold Dream*, 1960); and a bale of cotton dumped in a Harlem street around which Himes weaves an astonishing spiral of drugs, politics and sexual adventure (*Cotton Comes to Harlem*, 1966).

In engaging with these, and kindred mysteries, Coffin Ed and Grave Digger unveil a Harlem as labyrinthine, equivocal and direly comic as any so far made over into literary fiction.

☆   ☆   ☆

Himes's *Blind Man with a Pistol*, perhaps appropriately the last novel published in his own lifetime, ends on a note of apocalypse, a berserk blind man spraying bullets in every direction on the New York subway. His is the virtually inevitable and absurd gesture within a Harlem tense to breaking-point. *Plan B* (1993) adds the posthumous finale, Coffin Ed killed by Grave Digger from within a Harlem enravelled in graft, paranoia, a power-politics both black and white, and as though by destiny turned cruelly against both itself and its own.[36]

Himes supplies a key to other fiction which has given its attention to postwar Harlem, not least four intersecting narratives, three white written and the other a *latino* 'fiction of fact' autobiography. Warren Miller's *The Cool World* (1959), told in the first person voice of Richard 'Duke' Custis, a gang leader adult before his time, dramatizes a Harlem of territorial divides and inevitable group violence. It compares illuminatingly with Shane Stevens's *Go Down Dead* (1967), also centred around a gang and black adolescent Harlem, a 1960s revolt novel told as a week-long episode in the life of Adam Clayton 'King' Henry.

More consequentially, Edward Lewis Wallant's *The Pawnbroker* (1961) envisages in the image of Sol Nazerman's pawnshop a Harlem itself the repository of sold-out lives and property. Sol survives, reluctantly, as the witness both to his own Jewish and European catastrophe and to that unfolding in the Harlem about him. For him, whether the past of Belsen or the present of the ghetto, both make for hell. In Piri Thomas's *Down These Mean Streets* (1967), *barrio* Harlem is told as a Puerto Rican life, a cycle of gang violence, prison, drugs and the struggle for manhood pressured by an 'anglo' colour line and language.[37]

In all of these Harlem offers the contradiction of stasis and vitality, at once urban enclosure yet at the same time a site of immense wellsprings of life. Nor has recent black-written Harlem fiction itself been any less aware of the paradox. For it lies deep within the continuing variety of design, genre, styles, novels as markedly distinct from each other as they were throughout the New Negro years of McKay and Toomer, Fisher and Thurman, Larsen and Fauset.

☆   ☆   ☆

Charles Wright's *The Messenger* (1963), centred on the wayward life of its writer-protagonist within a Manhattan of midnight-cowboy sexual hustle and drugs, might be a diary novel – as episodic, as full of cuts and fades,

as the city in which it is set.[38] The confessional style provides just the right
thread and edge to its world of queens and johns, 'street' neighbourhood,
bars, a remembered black boyhood in Missouri, and Charlie's life as a
message-deliverer across the five boroughs. Above all it tells a writer's life,
the will to subdue the city to the word. Within all of this Wright manages
a perfect cameo of Harlem as at once many cities in one:

> Tonight I caught the A train, went up to Harlem. Kenya, the Iron
> Curtain ... As I walk down 125th Street, I see young men, sharp as
> diamonds in suits they can't afford, leaning against flashy cars that don't
> belong to them, or stepping smartly as if on their way to a very high-
> class hell. 125th Street is Forty-Second Street, Broadway, Times Square,
> Fifth Avenue all combined into a jungle of buildings. It is a prayer
> meeting with a hand-clapping, tambourine 'Yes Lawd.' It's Blumstein's
> Department store, the Harlemite's Macey's. It's the Apollo, with the only
> live stage show in Manhattan. It's the smart bars catering to Big Time
> wheeling and dealing Negroes and downtown whites, who want a
> swinging Harlem night. (p. 141)

William Melvin Kelley's *dem* (1967), a title which means 'them' or white
folks, takes on Harlem through a complex mesh of dark, inventive satire.[39]
Kelley sets up white suburbia and black Harlem as two zany, opposite
worlds, each run to its own confounding play of rituals and language.
Mitchell Pierce, a white advertising executive fixated by TV soap-opera
and fast losing the ability to differentiate between media and reality, finds
himself faced with his wife's having given birth to twins, one black, one
white. Setting out to discover his black co-father, an Ellisonian trickster
named Cooley, he finds himself drawn deeper and deeper into a Harlem
wholly beyond his imagining. Kelley, in other words, offers yet another
species of 'black' black comedy, Harlem as still *terra incognita* to most of
white America, a great enclave of life unseen, unencountered.

Robert Deane Pharr's *S.R.O.* (1971) drives realism to yet another kind
of furthest reach.[40] Harlem becomes a ghetto vortex, a self-circling
tenancy of drugs, need, relief. Presided over by the supplier Sinman, it is
a Harlem which 'fixes' itself at every turn, its ravages held only momentarily
in abeyance by the needle. Claude Brown's *The Children of Ham* (1976),
a follow-up to *Manchild in the Promised Land* (1965), his bestselling
autobiography, depicts Harlem through the den life of a group of young
black drop-outs, a story of literal survival under the rules of Harlem
ghetto culture.[41]

Whether Harlem comes over as violent-absurdist as in Himes, a *terra
incognita* as in Kelley, predatory in body and spirit as in Pharr, or sociological
as in Brown, there can be no doubting the continuing variety of its novels.
This continues in Toni Morrison's adroitly memorial novel *Jazz* (1992),

set in 1926, and told against a backdrop of the Great Migration. [42] The lyric, doomed love of middle-aged Joe Trace, salesman of Cleopatra Beauty products, for 18 year old Dorcas who refuses to name him even as she lies dying when he shoots her after discovering her affair with a younger man, and his wife Violet's violent reaction and eventual calm, makes their Harlem world into a ballad, the stuff of black urban legend. Morrison's feats of multiple narration, the remembrances of coming North, setting up home, becoming Harlemites, gives a wonderful, bracing resonance to the novel.

A conspectus of these different, if frequently overlapping, fictions of place is also engagingly developed in Rosa Guy's *A Measure of Time* (1983), the life and times of 'sassy' Dorine Davis, who comes up from the Jim Crow South of her youth in the 1920s to be a survivor in the Harlem of the 1960s. [43] At successive phases in the novel she is one of the Jazz Age's black glitterati, a 'booster' pulling off spectacular store heists, a Depression era hustler, and a prison inmate who emerges to a world where Malcolm X and Martin Luther King offer the touchstones, and throughout she serves as a carrier of Harlem at its ambiguous best and worst.

Certainly Harlem's ambiguities are not lost on Darryl Pinckney in *High Cotton*. His narrator, Columbia University student and 'Also Chosen' black middle-class witness, allows himself to ponder:

> The Negro Capital of the World, the old-timers' Seventh Avenue, which boasted 'fifty-two Easters a year,' I knew had moved, long before, to the rare-books desk of the Schomburg library. The Hotel Theresa was dead, the Apollo was in a coma, and the lush exchanges between neighbors in the pretty town houses of Stanford White had to wait in a nourishing obscurity, like a piece of music whose neglect makes its revival all the more rapturous. The voyeuristic possibilities of the remains, the bad corners, were more animating to me than the dissertation-giving ardor for the ruins of melanophilia. [44]

For Rosa Guy, then, as for Darryl Pinckney, and all the succession of Harlem novelists, the rich, human *rumor* of Harlem, as García Lorca names it in his *Poeta en Nueva York* (1940), continues to press for literary expression. [45] The only *fact* about Harlem in this respect may indeed be its dense, necessary irreducibility, an undiminishing refusal to be accommodated by the single account. This, one supposes, helps to identify why there have been so many varieties of 'Harlem on My Mind' – be they expressed in the novel or in any of the abundant literary, visual, popular-culture and other forms inspired by the enduring black First City of America.

Womanisms: Harriet E. Wilson to Toni Morrison, Zora Neale Hurston to Alice Walker

Fiction is of great value to any people as a preserver of manners and customs – religious, political and social. It is a record of growth and development from generation to generation. *No one will do this for us; we must ourselves develop the men and women who will faithfully portray the inmost thoughts and feelings of the Negro with all the fire and romance which lie dormant in our history.*

Pauline Hopkins, 'Preface', Contending Forces (1900)[1]

Someone is always at my elbow reminding me that I am the granddaughter of slaves. It fails to register depression within me. Slavery is sixty years in the past. The operation was successful and the patient is doing well, thank you. The terrible struggle that made me an American out of a potential slave said 'On the line!' The Reconstruction said 'Get set!'; and the generation before said 'Go!' I am off to a flying start and I must not halt in the stretch to look behind and weep. Slavery is the price I paid for civilization, and the choice was not with me. It is a bully adventure and worth all that I have paid through my ancestors for it. No one on earth ever had a greater chance for glory. The world to be won and nothing to be lost. It is thrilling to think – to know that for any act of mine, I shall get twice as much praise or twice as much blame. It is quite exciting to hold the center of the national stage, with the spectators not knowing whether to laugh or to weep.

Zora Neale Hurston, 'How It Feels to Be Colored Me'(1928)[2]

Womanist 1. From *womanish*. (Opp. of 'girlish,' i.e., frivolous, irresponsible, not serious.) A black feminist or feminist of color. From the black folk expression of mothers to female children, 'You acting womanish,' i.e., like a woman. Usually referring to outrageous, audacious, courageous or *willful* behavior. Wanting to know more and in greater depth than is considered 'good' for one. Interested in grown-up doings. Acting grown up. Being grown up. Interchangeable with another black folk expression: 'You trying to be grown.' Responsible. In charge. *Serious.*

Alice Walker, *In Search of Our Mothers' Gardens* (1983)[3]

The publication of *The Schomburg Library of Nineteenth-Century Black Women Writers*, first issued in 1988 and running to thirty volumes and nearly fifty texts in all, gives timely emphasis to how the variety of woman-authored black literary voice showed itself from the outset. Proof positive lies in included volumes such as Phillis Wheatley's *Poems on Various Subjects, Religious and Moral* (1773), the evidentiary, slave–centred *Narrative of Sojourner Truth* (1850), each spirited Civil War and abolitionist entry in the *Journals* of Charlotte Forten Grimké (1838–1914), or an 1890s Woman's Era egalitarian-feminist classic like *A Voice from the South* (1892) by Anna Julia Cooper.[4]

The Schomburg series has also reissued fiction by a founding tier of novelists. This, notably, includes Frances E.W. Harper (1825–1911), author of *Iola Leroy or Shadows Uplifted* (1892), who was early to use the phrase 'Woman's Era' in an address to the World's Congress of Representative Women in Chicago in 1893, and the prolific Boston-raised Pauline Hopkins (1859–1930). Hopkins would become the author not only of *Contending Forces* (1900), but of the highly inventive serial novels she wrote for *Colored Magazine* (1900–09) like *Hagar's Daughter* with its webs of racial conspiracy and impersonation in Washington D.C., *Winona*, a portrait of antislavery black heroism, and *Of One Blood*, the near science fiction adventure fantasy of a woman-ruled underground African Lost Empire.[5]

Along with *Our Nig* (1859) by the newly rehabilitated Harriet E. Wilson (1827?–?), and the novels of girlhood and family of Amelia E. Johnson's *Clarence and Corinne; or, God's Way* (1890) and Emma Dunham Kelley's *Megda* (1891), this fiction deservedly has come to win for their authors the soubriquet of 'literary foremothers'.[6] All of these names, moreover, in their welcome new availability, confirm the intertextual genealogy of African American literary women begun as early as the brief, historic 'Bars Fight' (1746), by Lucy Terry, slave girl to the Wells family of Deerfield, Massachusetts, a poem of the 'Indian Wars' and the first ever known writing by a black American.

Theirs has been the missing prologue to the efflorescence which has followed. It would be difficult, not to say inaccurate, to think otherwise in the wake of 1920s 'New Negro' voices like Jessie Fauset and Nella Larsen, the genius for vernacular fable of Zora Neale Hurston, or the postwar storytelling of Ann Petry, Dorothy West, Gwendolyn Brooks and Margaret Walker. The expressly formulated literary 'womanism' which follows, with its impetus in 1960s Black Power and Black Feminism, finds its own proven idiom not only in Alice Walker, but in Toni Morrison, along with a host of their contemporaries from Paule Marshall to Gayl Jones and, in turn, a burgeoning younger generation of literary successors.

Womanism itself, as ideology, was and remains Alice Walker's own way of historicizing the gendered toughness and passed-down wisdom which, from slavery onwards, has underwritten the survival of African American women against the double odds of racism and sexism, be the latter white or black. The term implies a womanhood at once individual yet mutual, the refusal of patriarchal exclusion first from literacy, then from literature itself (one 1960s usage was *Afra*-American) and, accompanyingly, a vast experiential savvy with its own self-vaunting sass and wit.

All of these elements play into Walker's warm, daughterly affiliation with Zora Neale Hurston whose bold spirit has long served her as inspiration and model. This holds for Walker's essay work as much as her fiction. *In Search of Our Mothers' Gardens* (1983), a manifesto and working set of definitions of womanism, reprints her 'Looking for Zora' (1975), a handsome act of tribute in which Walker, famously, lays claim to being Hurston's niece. *Warrior Marks* (1993) bears yet further traces of Hurston as an anthropological excursion through African female circumcision into the more inclusive forms of power over black female lives. *The Same River Twice* (1996) exhibits its own Hurstonian feistiness in Walker's riposte to past criticism of her work, especially the accusation of being 'unloyally' negative about black men.[7]

None of this sidesteps black women's shared experience with black men, or with other women of colour, of how American history has worked in matters of family, migration, class, stereotype or discrimination. But nor is it to eclipse a history possessed, often headily, of its own life idioms and nuance. Within backcountry Dixie, or the tenement North, or a rising black suburbia, and whether churchwoman, professional, domestic worker, wife-mother or single-mother, Civil Rights veteran or public official, black femininity in America as a unique complexity has been, and remains, undeniable.

There have inevitably been overlaps with the lives of American white women. Given issues of equal rights, work equality and opportunity, homemaking, health or law, could it have been otherwise? Nor is inter-racial friendship or love to be in any way discounted. Al Young's *Who Is Angelina?* (1975), to use a male-authored text, with its black–white companionship of Angelina with Margo Tanaka, or Alice Walker's own *Meridian* (1976), with its Civil Rights-era triangle of black Meridian Hill, white Lynn Rabinovitch and black Truman Held, offer two versions. Walker's personal intimacy with Gloria Steinem, and their important editorial collaborations in *Ms* magazine, add a further confirmation from life.[8]

There are other kinds of overlap, however, whether remembered as the residual power relations from slavery carried down through years of domestic service, or through segregated Woman's Era feminism, or through pre-Civil Rights 'separate but equal' practices. American black women have, and have had, every cause to look to their own styles of mothering, daughterdom and sisterhood in a slave shadowed America.

Alice Childress's novella, *Rainbow Jordan* (1981), for instance, affectionately explores the black-womanly nurture of a girl abandoned by her own mother yet given enablement by surrogate community mothers. Rosa Guy's lively trilogy of black girlhood, *The Friends* (1973), *Ruby* (1976) and *Edith Jackson* (1978), takes on the complex intergenerational transition from Caribbean motherhood to African American young womanhood. Kristin Hunter's *The Soul Brothers and Sister Lou* (1968), *Boss Cat* (1971) and *Guests in the Promised Land* (1973) offer reminders of black woman-written fiction not only about, but in detail and with obvious affectionate relish for, children.[9]

Jamaica Kinkaid's *The Autobiography of My Mother* (1996), pitched at the interface of family history and fiction, sensitively excavates an Antiguan American mother and daughter love from 'the islands' to the New York mainland. Toni Morrison's *Sula* (1974), on the other hand, the story of a black *alter ego* friendship of 'two throats and one eye' between Sula Peace and Nel Wright, dramatizes the odd, paired contrast of young womanly disorder and order, a bond of sharing yet disjuncture.[10]

If black women have evolved their own recognizable styles of relationships, whether with men or, as siblings, friends or lovers, with other women, that has had its reflection in their literary fiction. Carlene Hatcher Polite's *The Flagellants* (1967), a novel configured as the 'reeling' colloquy of Ideal and Jimson, a black couple in 1960s Greenwich Village put to examine their own relationship against a backdrop of Civil Rights, Black Power and a changing perception of women's rights, tells one version. Alice Walker's *The Color Purple* (1982), with its redemptive same-sex love of Celie and Shug Avery, tells another. Similarly, there are traditions both actual and symbolic of midwifery and womanly herbal and 'root' medicine. A virtuoso memory novel like Gloria Naylor's *Mama Day* (1988) echoes *The Tempest* while at the same time delving into these woman-centred rites of conjure and healing as imaginatively set on Willow Springs, an unowned and half-magical barrier island, between South Carolina and Georgia.[11]

Likewise, the politics of black femininity, whether out of choice or necessity, has for the most part pitched itself at a distance from its white counterpart. That has held from Sojourner Truth's address to the 1851 Akron convention on Women's Rights with its call for equality of black with white women, through the founding of the National Council of Negro Women (NCNW) in 1894, through each AME, Baptist and other African American women's church group, and on into 1960s and 1970s womanism and black lesbian activism.

The latter finds its rallying points and beacons in fiction like Audre Lorde's autobiography-novel *Zami: A New Spelling of My Name* (1982) and Ann Allen Shockley's same-sex writing like *Loving Her* (1974), with its portrait of two styles of 'marriage' – Renay's for Terry as one woman for another in the aftermath of her earlier heterosexual liaison with Jerome Lee, which has produced a daughter, Denise, and *Say Jesus and Come to Me* (1982), with its portrait of a gay black woman evangelist.[12]

A more traditional politicized novel, however, would be Kristin Hunter's *The Lakestown Rebellion* (1978). Not only does it redeploy the satiric skills which went into *The Landlord* (1966), Hunter's Himesian comedy of zany, racial misunderstanding with its figures of the well intending white landlord Elgar Enders, sexually obsessive Madam Margarita and black con man Eldridge DuBois, but it puts a strong black woman at its very centre. Bella Lakes leads a black community's effort to sabotage a highway scheme which will destroy the town. Hunter's novel thereby retraces all the past ways black Americans have tricked, duped and out-talked both their past and present white overseers.[13]

This historic nuance calls into play a special custodianship of 'the word', a spectrum of black woman-to-woman spoken intimacy, styles of address ('hey, girl', notably, both in speech or letter writing), slang, namings, story, kitchentalk, stored wisdom, and each show and turn of humour. 'Woman's word' finds any number of its own stylings in the novel, whether the vibrant folk vernacular of Zora Neale Hurston's *Their Eyes Were Watching God* (1937); the competing life idioms of Barbadian mother and African American daughter in the Brooklyn-based Boyce family saga told in Paule Marshall's *Brown Girl, Brownstones* (1959); the Africanist 'spirit talk' within the story of Velma Henry's would-be suicide and eventual recovery through a politics of sisterhood and community against a polluting chemical corporation in Toni Cade Bambara's *The Salt Eaters* (1980); or the mobile phone and lunchclub fast talk of Terry McMillan's middlebrow 'buddy' bestseller of four black women each with their own kind of man trouble in *Waiting to Exhale* (1992).[14]

It is a complexity which both shapes and has itself been shaped by a dense black-feminine popular culture of family, religious work, foodways, quilting, choir and other music (spirituals, blues, soul through to pop), and dress styles from dashikis and turbans to the wearing of kente cloth.[15] One expression lies in hair styling as visible self-presentation in the form of Afros, braids, cornrows and, sometimes controversially, wigs and straightened hair. Around Afro-hair, in fact, there has grown a voluminous body of folk and literary imagery. Zora Neale Hurston's figure of the long-tressed and lavishly sexual Janie in *Their Eyes Were Watching God* (1937) offers one instance. Ntozake Shange's celebration of 'your hair' as 'the tell-tale sign of living' in her verse-collection *nappy edges* (1972) offers another. Many African American women will speak of talk circles in which one woman family member or friend will 'scratch', almost caress, the hair of another, a sign of mutual affection and sorority.[16]

How, then, has this legacy found its imagining in a select dozen or so of the novels written by African American women? Is not each story distinctive yet, however fugitively, bound into a shared provenance of other black women's lives and memory? Has not another kind of interplay been involved, especially given the working cues of Pauline Hopkins, Zora Neale Hurston and Alice Walker, one of authoring, women-authored and, in turn and for its own part, the life 'authored' by each imagined woman?

The refinding, and reissue, of *Our Nig; or, Sketches from the Life of a Free Black, in a Two-Story White House, North. Showing that Slavery's Shadows Fall Everywhere* (1859), to give Harriet E. Wilson's title in its challenging entirety, has aroused a revisionist flurry. By its title alone it calls up a revealing play of signification: 'Our Nig' as mock family affection yet ownership; 'Free Black' as wholly bitter parody given Frado's life; and 'two-story white house' as the symbol of a clapboarded Massachusetts, for all its rectitude, capable of cruelty not out of place in any down-South slave plantation.

The text also pushes back by over thirty years the date of the first ever known novel by an African American woman, long taken to be Frances Harper's *Iola Leroy* (1892), itself then superseded by the recently refound Emma Dunham Kelley's *Megda* (1891). It tackles not so much Dixie slavery but, whatever its status as the citadel of abolition, New England's own racial double standards. It invokes racially binaried Christianity, the supposed spectre of inter-racial marriage, child abandonment, black domestic indenture and the generally unwritten capacity of women for physical violence towards other women. Little wonder the rediscovery caused a stir, a posthumous literary debut as eventful as almost any in American literature.

If *Our Nig* has its admixtures of sentimentality, even lachrymosity, that is not to underplay the complexity of Frado as heroine. First, there is the question of voice. Frado appears to disclose her life in the first person ('*by "Our Nig"*'), but folded into the third person ('Enough has been unrolled to enlist your sympathy and aid'), and the whole glossed by Harriet Wilson as author and appellant ('I am forced to some experiment which shall aid me in maintaining myself and child without extinguishing this feeble life' she says in the Preface).

Is *Our Nig*, accordingly, novel or autobiography, even a Northern 'slave narrative'? Whose 'own' story is it: Frado's in first and third person voice; Wilson's; or a kind of simultaneous co-authorship made the more ambiguous by the volume's designation as 'sketches'?

Frado, 'beautiful mulatto', 'wild frolicking thing', an outlaw child on account of a white mother, Mag Smith, and her briefly-known but fond black father, Jim (who subjects 'race' to Twainian pastiche in his opposition of 'black heart in a white skin' and 'white heart in a black skin'), serves throughout as Wilson's enfigurement of a single and yet representative black woman's story. She becomes variously foundling mulatto child, New Hampshire bondservant driven to physical depletion in the white Bellmont family and at the hands of the ogrely Mrs. Bellmont, might-be lover of the dying, religious James Bellmont, twice over abandoned wife and mother and, eventually, subsistence bonnet-maker.

As importantly, however, she is obliged to become her own creative *alter ego*, the will to invention expressed in girltime and school high spirits, games, reading and love of her dog Fido. This authorly self typically reveals itself in her observation to the kindly Aunt Abby on the death of the cruel Bellmont daughter, Mary. In a line worthy of a Flannery O'Connor story like 'Revelation', Frado speculates: 'Wouldn't mistress be mad to see her a nigger!'. The touch is exquisite, an imagined reversal of skin, womanhood, anticipated religious destiny and, above all, word.

Wilson's feat, allowing for stock uses of plot devices like orphaning and fever, along with the limits of her plainstyle, is to put in view a heroine caught to her cost within an American confusion of realms. Class becomes entramelled in race as white Yankeeism exploits black domestic servitude. White religion, for all its prompt to abolitionism, also sanctions race contempt as Mrs. Bellmont bears out in her 'religion was not meant for niggers'. Black religion speaks to escape from this world to the next. As Frado's child servitude gives way to her own arriving black womanhood, the life she has lived in fear raises its own fear and accusation in Mrs. Bellmont and her daughter. Mr. Bellmont similarly doubles as head of household yet absentee, his white Christian fatherliness for black Frado always shadow not substance.

Frado, herself, suffers an aloneness which, paradoxically, becomes the very grounds of her own rise to voice. The upshot is that *Our Nig* writes, and in its newfound recovery rewrites, unique portraiture: Wilson's double (even triple) self-authoring. It gives a more faceted literary start than ever might have been anticipated to the novel's ensuing gallery of, and by, African American women.

☆   ☆   ☆

For all the recent warmth of greeting given *Our Nig* it has also been taken to confirm mulattodom as one of the staples of early black women's writing. That arouses old controversies. Tragic or not the mulatto (sometimes given as mulatta) first of all gets rebuked as a sop by black genteel authorship to a largely white readership. The deeper sexual-racial implications of birth, concubinage, flesh, sexual transgression, the 'othering' of the biracial female body, are so thought to have remained largely unwritten.

Did not most 'black' black women face more immediate concerns than those of a narrow and often far from unprivileged caste? Three novels, written in the wake of *Our Nig* between the Woman's Era and the closing years of the 'New Negro' 1920s, supply grounds for a reconsideration.

'A woman as white as she is a slave?' So Dr. Gresham, white New England abolitionist, doctor, and would-be husband of Iola, speaks of Frances E.W. Harper's beauteous heroine in *Iola Leroy*. His query goes to the core of Iola's history as a life lived within racial contradiction: the Creole-quadroon daughter who loses her white privilege and is sold as a black slave; the nurse to Civil War black 'Lincoln soldiers' who gives up sexual for religious intensity and the uplift of 'the race' in her marriage to the similarly light-black Dr. Latimer; and the seeming 'tragic mulatto' who reverses type and enjoys a last, harmonious coming-together of her grandmother, mother, brother and uncle (the valiant soldier ex-slave Robert Jackson) as 'the once severed-branches of our family'.

Harper sets herself a number of tasks around Iola. Slavery gets its indictments, along with white postbellum revanchism, denial of suffrage to women, and drink (Harper was a worker for temperance). She also was clearly seeking a route forward for the Talented Tenth elite, hence also Harry Leroy's eventual work with his wife Lucille as a black teacher of black children in the South. None of this, however, has freed Harper of charges of piety, a dismaying earnestness, and assimilationist compromise.

But if idealized, the portrait of Iola does not entirely give in to formula. Iola is shown to be caught at a turning point of freedom and bondage as much in gender as race. She refuses, throughout, to disguise her mixed-race origins and 'live under a shadow of concealment'. If she embodies black gentility, that is not at the expense of her connection back into vernacular and dialect worlds of field and house ex-slave women like Aunt Linda. Harper can be more than a touch preacherly. But in Iola Leroy she poses a genuine issue: what role, or as much to the point, what autonomy, is most relevant to African American women of education in an America after slavery?

Sappho Clark, around whose life Pauline Hopkins weaves an even more complicated white-black dynastic story in *Contending Forces*, might well be kin to Iola Leroy. In an immediate sense she also personifies ideality, another beautiful Creole made victim of inter-racial rape and who serves to link an antebellum North Carolina past into a postbellum reformist Boston. In marrying Will Smith, DuBois-like black philosopher and activist, and through a tangled circuit of disguise and false trails, she finally helps bring together the two family lines of the white Montforts and the black Smiths. Like *Iola Leroy* Hopkins's novel has taken its knocks as contrivance, supposedly 'race' melodrama.

Contending Forces, however, can also be seen to have achieved more. The implications of American slavery as both sexual and cross-racial proving ground are tackled with some boldness (not least the persuasively mean view of the original Mrs. Montfort as 'half white nigger' by the family's plantation neighbour). If black urban and middle-class life as schooling, home, church, 'rights' debate and meetings, together with female etiquette and courtship, gets its full rendering in Hopkins's account of the New England Smith family, so, too, does sexual assault, rape, the prostitution of black women by white men in Sappho's 'dire hell' of New Orleans and Dixie. All these genuinely entwine as 'contending forces'.

Sappho herself may well veer close to angel-like victim, the exemplary mulatto. But she also suggests a more richly embodied ambiguity. For in working through each turn of *Contending Forces*, and although Harper ends her novel in a set piece marriage, Sappho is confronted with a double challenge. She seeks a life both beyond her brute sexual disempowerment and then, having chosen against appearance to be black, beyond the limits of her own racial marking.

Nella Larsen's *Quicksand* (1928), in the figure of Helga Crane – born, like her progenitor, to a black father and Danish mother – massively interiorizes and problematizes this female experience of mulattodom.[17] The novel has not had an easy passage; its critics regularly condemn it as the not-so-camouflaged racial self-hate of Larsen herself with some sexual phobia thrown into the mix. This is to give way to superficiality, something close to a cartoon of the book. For Larsen's narrative in fact utterly takes charge of Helga's psychological zigzags, each euphoria, depression and fluctuation.

Helga from the outset seeks to appropriate 'colour' for her own ends. The lavish, baroque stylishness of dress and decor so obviously at odds with the black-puritan etiquette of Naxos – the Deep-South school where she is located at the start of the novel – gives the clue. The step North into a borderline bohemia, both in 'teeming black Harlem' and white Manhattan, adds weight. Larsen then faces more profound vacillation between becoming the exotic plaything of her blanched, utterly Scandinavian-white relatives, the Daals, in Copenhagen, and her eventual destiny as wife and acquiescent breedmare to the Rev. Pleasant Green in his fundamentalist and deepest Dixie-black outpost.

Helga's story is far from merely plaintive. Rather, Larsen manages a portrait of credible hysteria, both in Helga's contrasting would-be love affairs with the black James Vayle at Naxos and the white portrait painter Axel Olsen in Denmark, and as a woman caught at the still larger end-zones of both black and white worlds. Pursued to her own destructive cost by the inability to be psychologically or emotionally at ease, a state anticipated in her childhood parentlessness and rejection by her Nilssen relatives, Helga collapses into a last and desperate 'religious' episode.

Quicksand speaks persuasively of Helga's 'bruised spirit', her 'suffocation', a harlequinry always equally sexual as racial and the source of a destiny she believes renders her if in appearance beauty then also beast. Larsen, through her, develops headier portraiture than she has been granted: Helga Crane as a woman turned inward against herself by a colour system which literally has been the making of her yet which she can neither embrace nor escape.

☆　☆　☆

With Zora Neale Hurston's *Their Eyes Were Watching God* (1937) a wholly changed dispensation enters the reckoning – oral made over into written story, a black folk idiom of Gullah and other Africanisms through to Bible phrase, a free sexuality, and a setting within Florida-Georgia landscapes the equal of Jean Toomer's *Cane* (1923).[18] Even more to the point, no black novel better anticipates, nor better confirms, Alice Walker's womanist ethos, as much through its feats of voice as story: a text, a chronicle, to meet precisely the life it tells.

'Ah wants to utilize mahself all over', Janie, whose history this is, tells Pheoby, her friend in the all-black township Hurston created in the image of her own Eatonville, Florida. The history of Janie's taking of autonomy assumes a parallel, a rich human ply, of self and saying. In the one circuit she becomes the seasoned veteran of her liaisons with, in turn, the dour, older sharecropper Logan Killicks, Joe Starks, the patriarchal Mayor of 'Eatonville', and finally, the loving, liberative gambler-poet Vergible Woods or Tea Cake. In the other she turns her own tongue into vernacularity itself, a sustained treat of phrase, image, wit or signifying ('She got so she could tell big stories herself from listening to others').

These interwoven rites of passage Hurston uses to often compelling effect. If her Grandmother thinks 'De nigger woman is de mule uh de world', Janie herself will counter that to perfection. She looks to 'the words of the trees and the wind' as a poetry to compensate for lovelessness with Killicks. She fights back 'with her tongue' against Starks's requirement of wifely submission ('You're getting too moufy, Janie'), telling him 'we ain't natural wid one 'nother' and speaking of their marriage bed as 'no longer a daisy-field ... to play in'.

Above all she thinks of her oneness with Tea Cake ('So you aims tuh partake wid eveything, hunh?' he asks her at the outset). Life with him means bean picking by the shores of the Seminole-named Lake Okechobee, the blues and dancing to the jukes, the worker community talk and josh, their sheer togetherness ('We ain't got nothin' tuh do but do our work 'nd come home and love' Tea Cake tells her), even her jealousy of the girl Nunkie – it bespeaks idyll, a warm, uncoerced and down-home love. She remembers Tea Cake, having caused his death after his rabies-induced dementia, as a figure of song, imagination, poetry:

Of course he wasn't dead. He could never be dead until she herself had finished feeling and thinking. The kiss of his memory made pictures of love and light against the wall. Here was peace. She pulled in her horizon like a great fish-net. Pulled it from around the waist of the world and draped it over her shoulder. So much of life in its meshes! She called in her soul to come and see. (p. 286)

In all these respects, as again Pheoby observes, 'You looks like youse yo' own daughter.' If once herself destined to be mule, then, emphatically, Janie has become mule owner, mule storyteller.

Janie serves as a gathering point. Her sayings draw from and affirm a diverse, ongoing community of blackness as word (not least in the names of the fellow workers she meets with Tea Cake – Stew beef, Sop-de-Bottom, Bootyny, Motor Boat). She can witness almost at will to vodoon or legend ('Nature and salt. Dat's whut makes up strong man lak Big John de Conquer'). She tells her own folk stories ('Sometimes she thought up good stories on the mule'). She becomes a kind of performative poetry in herself (for Joe's funeral she 'starched and ironed her face'). She speaks folkishly, anthropomorphically, of the advent of the Everglades hurricane as 'the monstropolous beast', 'HIM-WITH-THE-SQUARE-TOES', adding, with a nod towards fetish, 'Havoc was there with her mouth wide open.' She reflects Hurston's own refusal simply to perpetuate piety when she hears her new acquaintance, Mrs. Turner, for all her preferred light-over-dark colour hierarchy, say of Booker T. Washington 'All he ever done wa cut de monkey for white folks.'

The 'hungry listening' that Janie arouses in Pheoby makes every kind of sense. Hurston's heroine is feistiness, warmth, ease and, once 'back home again', the very custodian and embodier of the story – *Their Eyes Were Watching God* as at once her own story and that of the local Afro-America about her. Hers, in truth, has been the final, generous rise to her own custodianship, to her own easeful womanism, as both life and word.

☆   ☆   ☆

Dorothy West holds an important cross-generational place in black literary history. A Boston-raised veteran of the Harlem Renaissance (she was close to Wallace Thurman, Langston Hughes, Paul and Eslanda Robeson, Zora Neale Hurston and, especially, Countee Cullen), and founder of the journal *Challenge* (later *New Challenge*), she has continued to write into the 1990s. Her novel, *The Wedding*, and story collection, *The Richer, the Poorer*, though both largely completed earlier, appeared in 1995.

The Living Is Easy (1948) thus stands midway, a portrait of the redoubtable Cleo Jericho Judson yet, at the same time, a detailed geography of caste and class in the 1920s and sited where Boston's black South End reaches into white Brookline.[19] The frequent charge against West has been that her vaunted 'Old Colored Families' scenario in *The Living Is Easy* offers too rarefied, or partial, an aspect of African American life. Yet there is more to be said than that.

In Cleo she tells the dynastic story of a black Carolina childhood, a Boston wifedom to Bart Judson – the self-made fruit importer twenty years her senior – the life of a woman among a woman's clan, and the fierce, manipulative route into would-be class quality with white Boston matriarchy. West opens her story to a spectrum which embraces WASP (White Anglo Saxon Protestant), Irish and Scandinavian as well as 'coloured' New England.

'Nobody can't never catch me' says Cleo in childhood, and, for the most part, so at first it proves. But if her finaglings initially win through, they also cost her sisters their happiness and her husband ('Mister Nigger' as she calls him) his 'King of Bananas' business. West invests Cleo with ambiguity, the black woman of strength pledged to outmanoeuvre or match white privilege yet the climber who wins only to lose.

Cleo's story acts as a centre for others: the subplot of a 'white' uppercrust Boston marriage shadowed by unacknowledged colour, hidden families and abortion; the pauper death of her father and her brother-in-law's rigged trial and escape from a white Dixie conspiracy; and, given a household of children, the prospects for a next Boston generation of mixed black and white lineage. West's best feat, however, lies in having embodied in Cleo black caste as at once a war for, and yet always against, itself.

Gwendolyn Brooks's title figure in *Maud Martha* (1953) inhabits a wholly opposite social order, that of 1930s and immediate postwar black working-class Chicago, the South Side as 'Bronzeville'.[20] Though not short on length, this lyric, imagistic telling of girlhood to womanhood gives an impression of miniaturism, a cycle of story vignettes each pitched to intersect, contrast and balance. In this, Brooks's novel does justice to Maud Martha's life as quotidian yet singular, full of other people's voice yet also, almost quizzically, her own.

It is very much a poet's novel, seamed in images ('What she liked was candy buttons, and books, and painted music (deep blue, or delicate silver) and the west sky' reads the opening), a narrative of inner sensation played against an outwardly moribund life of marriage, domestic work and motherhood. Brooks conveys Maud Martha's early aspirations, appropriately, as a kind of prose lyric:

> What she wanted was to donate to the world a good Maud Martha. That was the offering, the bit of art, that could not come from any other.
> She would polish and hone that.

The novel takes virtually all its bearings and style from this. In childhood Maud Martha gives herself to fantasy over fact at the sight of an escaped gorilla, food like sweet potato pie, and the stark, abrupt, incomprehensible hospital death of her grandmother Ernestine. Girlhood becomes an excitement of boys, the Chicago *Defender*, fashion, her own as against her sister Helen's hair, her first beaux, and 'New York' as the advertising razzamatazz of a Michigan Avenue store. She reaches eighteen awaiting the world to 'caress her'. Marriage to Paul leads into a spare Depression-era kitchenette, a dreamed-of happiness veering into dismay, each venture into white Chicago (despite the pleasures of hearing Ellington on the radio and an occasional ballroom night out), and the dangerous, convincingly fraught birth of her daughter Paulette.

As in the poems in *A Street in Bronzeville* (1945), Brooks catches perfectly the human variousness and pitch of Maud Martha's fellow kitchenette tenants, not to mention a world of hair manicure, domestic service on the North Side, subsequent children, black press reports of Georgia and Mississippi lynchings, or an era closing with the return from World War II of her brother Harry.

But she also has Maud Martha's own sense of life end on anything but a note of closure. Maud Martha, Maud, Maudie, ponders and celebrates with an unself-aware poet's touch, the still active call of her own powers of imagining ('The weather was bidding her bon voyage').

☆   ☆   ☆

In *Jubilee* (1966), Margaret Walker's black counter story to *Gone with the Wind*, the mode becomes popular history romance.[21] Would-be slave epic, it has its centre in the life and survival of Vyry, offspring of Dixiecrat white owner and bonded black mother, house servant until the end of the Civil War, eventual matriarch replete in spoken Christian faith and family, and, depending on how slave 'marriage' is construed, unwitting bigamist with Randall Ware, her 'Free Negro' blacksmith husband, and Innis Brown, her loyal black homesteader.

For all its canvas of antebellum to Reconstruction America, or its slaveholding detail, *Jubilee* offers essentially formula narrative – the Gothic, ghostly decline into madness of the white Dutton plantation family in the form of 'Big Missie' and 'Miss Lillian', the Simon Legree-like poor white overseer Grimes, the magnolia myth of the Confederacy, and the trek through small town and rural Dixie of Vyry and her clan in the aftermath of the Fall of Atlanta.

Vyry herself, however, merits consideration. Walker has been eloquent about how Margaret Duggans Ware Brown, her own great-grandmother, served as a model, and in her, undoubtedly, there presides a truth to history.[22] This is evident in the clannish, black-womanly protection of Vyry's sexual vulnerability in girlhood, as well as in her domestic servitude, her life in the quarters and Big House, her paradoxical loyalty to Miss Lillian, her mothering of Jim, Minna and Harry, her old-time bible Christianity, and her appalled witness to the hanging of two alleged women murderers.

On occasion a nicely complicating vernacular snap of anger adds its weight, as when the hardworking Innis Brown criticizes Vyry for seeking to take Jim, her son by Ware, off the land and into college – 'I knows your kind of dicty Big House Miss Ann's nigger servants.' Whatever the flatness of *Jubilee*'s general telling, here, as occasionally elsewhere in the novel, life underwrites fiction. A figure from actual slave time is to be glimpsed, albeit fugitively, behind the page's imagined Georgia former slave woman who presides at the close of the novel.

Gayl Jones's *Corregidora* (1975) both tells, and itself assumes the design of, a blues. Few woman-authored black novels have been more unrelentingly sexual, the black female body under historic male ownership as slave *thing*, a reduction to a fleshly orifice. This history finds its embodiment in Ursa Corregidora, singer, of Bracktown, Kentucky, who as much carries about her as narrates an ancestry bequeathed from the original Corregidora, the Brazilian-Portuguese *mestizo* slaver whose monstrous sexual rule is at once deadly yet also a near masochistic bewitchment.[23]

Her own sexual damage – she has her womb removed after a stairway fall at the hands of her husband Mutt Johnson – casts a dire, ironic shadow over the inherited slave injunction to 'make generations' and so give continuing witness. Even the brief love affair with Tadpole, owner of Happy's, the café-club in which she sings, leads to betrayal with a younger woman. That Ursa realizes, finally, how Great Gram acted in revenge for all four generations of them (Great Gram herself, then Grandmother and Mama – each prostituted by, and the latter two fathered by, Corregidora), by orally dismembering Corregidora, serves, even as she returns to Mutt, both as sexual revenge in kind and to bring the novel to its bitter-sweet point of rest.

It is this story that Jones has Ursa (a woman in her forties writing from the 1960s) enseam within the accusing riffs and cadence of the blues she sings, a shrewdly well-aimed and darkly reflexive touch. In its dialogues of memory *Corregidora* offers a portrait of black womanhood given to hurt, and with it to anger, yet also, in Ursa's slow, reluctant healing, and however provisionally, to self-repossession.

Paule Marshall's *Praisesong for the Widow* (1983) links an Afro-America of Dixie, Harlem, Brooklyn and suburban North White Plains into an

'African' Caribbean. It might as much be thought meditation as chronicle, the life of Avey Johnson, its black matronly heroine, as a past and yet a rebirth through her encounter with the Africanist remembrance, patois and worship-ritual of tropical Carriacou island. Marshall tells essentially an odyssey in kind with Langston Hughes's 'The Negro Speaks of Rivers', whose lines of imagery Avey calls up from childhood. The 'Carriacou Excursion' becomes a route into a self recentred and, at last, Avey's own.[24]

The novel's feats are many, not least its assured, engagingly paced telling of Avey's history as a blend of memory and ongoing event. The middle-class widowhood which takes her with her friends, Thomasina Moore and Clarice, on their annual Caribbean cruise nicely captures a life, its accoutrements of dress, pearls, luggage and cabin all in place, at rest, and yet not. Her suburban gentrification becomes, first, a source of vague inward, alimentary discontent, and then, physical bodily rejection and disgorgement ('her entire insides erupted').

Avey's remembrance of life with her husband Jay, Jerome Johnson, in his dire, heroic struggle into self-sufficiency as accountant, can call up fond sexual intimacy – the two of them dancing at home to 'Flying Home' or 'Cotton Tail', their sexual talk and lovemaking – yet also, in its very upward mobility, a marriage's deadening compromise. Similarly, Avey's dedicated mothering of her daughters, Sis, Annawilda and Marion, admits pain, discontent, a body gnawed by childbirth and imposed childrearing.

In thinking back, lyrically, to her aged kinswoman, Great-aunt Cuney, of Tatem Island, South Carolina, however, she acquires a first inkling of the larger history which has made her through the black church community's 'ring shouts' and the 'Ibo Landing' where enchained slave ancestors were brought ashore. These increasingly resonate for Avey, her full name Avatara, in her role as child, wife, mother and widow, each, as Marshall renders them, stations into a far older, fuller understanding of her identity.

This realisation is achieved for Avey at the 'out-island' of Carriacou, under the guidance of the Grenada grog-shop owner Lebert Joseph and his daughter Rosalie Parvay. First she experiences a cleansing and rest, then a night-time journey into the island, and, finally, a summoned black history in the names ('euphonious' and 'lyrical') and the 'nation dances' of peoples known as Temne, Banda, Arada, Moko, Congo or Cromanti. She finds herself invited back into her own history, its languages, dances, echoes, beliefs, dreams, in all the freeing rebuttal of any anonymous past Africa.

As she takes part in the circle of the 'Beg Pardon' and 'Juba' (in the novel's phrase 'sublime memories'), she comes to see this past as having lain within, and tacitly shaped, every Harlem ragtime of her girlhood, every fibre of her own 'educated' black speech. In Avey's quest for a forgotten axis to her black womanhood, *Praisesong for the Widow* does justice to her passage back, as her passage forward, a life story in all senses told as journey, soliloquy, Paule Marshall's close-spun fable of awakening.

To the Spirit:
Without whose assistance
Neither this book
Nor I
Would have been
Written.

I thank everybody in this book for coming.
A.W., author and medium.

Both Alice Walker's dedication, and her brief epilogue of thanks (wry, a writer-hostess's politeness), do precise service in *The Color Purple* (1982). Celie's story gives every reason to be thought a summoning of spirits, unanswered petitions finally answered. Each of the letters, Celie's to God, then to her sister Nettie, and Nettie's in return from her missionary life in West Africa, serve as story vignettes, life-panels. They reveal a kind of modern African American rescue narrative, Celie's restoration from the shadow of child rape and unremitting domestic abuse, into the visible evidence of her own black, womanly unsilencing.

The letters, first hidden by Celie's husband, Albert, then recovered with the aid of the magical, generously sexual singer and artist Shug Avery (typically, in her red dress, Albert's 'Queen Honeybee') become, across the thirty year separation of the sisters, messages both from, and into, history. Celie embodies, at one and the same time, a first ancestry of African diaspora, a past of almost ungendering sexual ravage (to which she responds with 'Most times mens look pretty much alike to me'), and, eventually, a 'present' of her own homemaking, and power of word, inside the Georgia which once allowed her no more than a life at the margins.

That the novel gives drama, a vernacular human nuance, to womanism, lies behind the 1983 Pulitzer Prize and the Whoopie Goldberg/Spielberg screen triumph. For Walker's storytelling shows its verve at every turn. The easeful, mutual sexuality which binds Celie to Shug not only through their bodies, but through their shared quilting, makes a perfect restorative. The very genitalia which once signified to Celie only pain, and all too early motherhood, she is encouraged by Shug to re-see as the source of health, pleasure. Albert's hate, in succession to Celie's stepfather's, so meets an opposite and enhancing order of sexuality ('Shug says, Us each other's peoples now, and kiss me').

The startling letter-declaration from Nettie, 'I love you I am not dead', plays directly to Celie's own eventual 'I'm pore. I'm black, I may be ugly and can't cook ... but I'm here.' Backcountry Georgia, once only grief to Celie, in turn becomes a refuge – of Harpo and his pugilistic wife, Sophia, and their tavernish, blues and dance 'jook' world, of Jack and Odessa who raise Sophia's children, of the singer Mary Agnes ('Squeak'), and of a Shug back from adventuring with beaux like Grady and Germaine. It acts, too, as an Afro-America finally twinned with Nettie's African-Olinka village, a culture whole in itself, yet now under threat of European colonization, and between which Celie's children, Adam and Olivia, act as living Atlantic linkage.

When Celie speaks back to Albert, the assurance of her own clothes-design business and house soon to follow, she might well call up a voice from Zora Neale Hurston: 'You a lowdown dog is what's wrong ... It's time to leave and enter Creation. And your body just the welcome mat I need.' Only in her self-restitution and voicing, and amid women who love her, will Celie also be able to say of a penitent Albert, 'He ain't Shug, but he begin to be somebody I can talk to.'

Her last letter, with its embrace of 'God, trees, skies, peoples, everything', confirms a Celie far from unforgetting of inherited pain yet, at last, the maker of her life, the subject not object of each verb which once enclosed her. Walker has her ponder this enhancing new black womanhood – her own, that of the women about her, and through them the prospect of a returned 'family' of equals. In a perfect about-face image of time, Celie sees all of them as 'old', and yet, 'the youngest us ever felt'.

The sheer gravitas of Toni Morrison's subject in *Beloved* (1987) – Sethe's throat-cutting of her infant child 'Beloved' to save her from a life of Kentucky enslavement – might have run all kinds of narrative risk: too plaintive a call to the feelings, Gothicism. In the event, this is not the case, as tact is but one part in the massive, spectacular virtuosity of the novel.[25]

'Ohio 1873', and the haunted '124' of Bluestone Road just outside Cincinnati, serve to perfection as local time and setting for a story full and vivid, in actual-seeming, yet also visionary, given to the signs and wonders of the slavery encrypted on the novel's post-title page as 'Sixty Million and more'.

Through the dense narrative of the lives of Sethe, her mother-in-law Baby Suggs, her daughter Denver, and the implacable Beloved, at once incubus and succubus, *Beloved* unravels women caught in a slave web so murderous and ravening that it threatens any sense of quiet or balance for all post-slave styles of the present. Nor does this underplay Beloved's vampirism of the returnee figure of Paul D., slave friend of Sethe's husband Halle from the Granger plantation and Sethe's eventual lover. This is slavery told as 'ghost company', 'red baby blood', Sethe's 'serious work of beating back the past' – her own back bears whip scars resembling a chokeberry tree – as for ever precarious, at risk of being overwhelmed.

'Not a house in the country ain't packed to its rafters with some dead Negro's grief' says the 'holy' Baby Suggs at the outset. Nowhere is this truer than in '124'. First it draws to itself Beloved, martyred lost child, chimera, daughter legatee of Sethe's body (despite Sethe's belief that 'what she had done was right because it came from true love'), drainer of Paul's semen, exploiter of Denver's will to sisterhood, above all, playful, hungered, ever thirsty claimant to life. As Sethe becomes 'worn down, speckled, dying, spinning', Beloved demands a mothering (although at one point she herself appears as mother to Sethe), a sexual destiny (she so taunts Paul), even a large, swollen pregnancy, and ever her own inerasable right of presence.

In her lies a still larger haunting. How else can we construe Baby Suggs's refusal to risk loving her children in the knowledge of their pending sale? How else can we imagine Sethe's own feeling as 'mossy-toothed' white boys drain her of her breast milk in a barn – all of it witnessed by Halle and the cause of his unhingement? Is not 'rape' given a more inclusive resonance than its usual gendering in Paul D.'s memory of how he, and fellow black male prisoners, have been required each morning to fellate their white guards? Is not, above all, the handsaw killing of Beloved, Sethe's traumatic act of love to avoid a daughter's 'dirtying', an impossible remembrance, a 'haint' as calvary? Even the exorcism of Beloved, as led by Ella and the townswomen, calls up Ella's own enghosting father-and-son rape, 'the lowest yet' as she calls it.

As *Beloved* closes, so, in a quite necessary way, it leaves its many implications open. Beloved has moved on from Sethe, from Denver, from Ella, from Paul D., as though she embodies too great a burden for any single consciousness. Yet she remains, communally, in history, as 'footprints', 'water', 'winds in the eaves', 'spring ice' – in Morrison's inspired fashioning as slavery's ghostchild, its unresting *anima*.

Wilson to Morrison, Hurston to Walker: 'womanism' throughout has found its own stirring litany of voice in the novel. Still later signatures arise as in stylish Haitian American storytelling like Edwidge Danticat's *Breath, Eyes, Memory* (1995) and *Krik? Krak!* (1996) or A.J. Verdelle's *The Good Negress* (1995) with its intimate play of two black dispensations – inner city Detroit and rural Virginia.[26] They, and their literary company, give continuity, a latest energy and sweep of implication, to the phrase 'written by herself'. For in them womanist authorship and authorings can look from a shared past into the future.

Richard Wright's Inside Narratives

All my life had shaped me for realism, the naturalism of the modern novel, and I could not read enough of them.

Richard Wright, *Black Boy* (1945)[1]

I picked up a pencil and held it over a sheet of white paper, but my feelings stood in the way of my words. Well, I would wait, day and night, until I knew what I wanted to say. Humbly now, with no vaulting dream of achieving a vast unity, I wanted to try to build a bridge of words between me and the world outside, that world which was so distant and elusive that it seemed unreal.

Richard Wright, *American Hunger* (1977)[2]

If something of a high flourish with which to round out each of his two volumes of autobiography, neither of these observations should detract from Wright's more consequential purpose: the momentousness, as he saw it, of his call to a literary career. A life 'shaped for realism', and then itself resolved 'to build a bridge of words between me and the world outside', invokes both an authorial past and its still to be unfolded future, a sense of personal history and yet as he looks back also a working credo. But it is the term 'unreal' which most of all carries import, a crucial, often overlooked, index to the writer he would actually become.

Wright's first observation, easily misconstrued, points less to the kind of fiction he himself would eventually *write* than to the liberating shock of recognition he experienced on *reading* the likes of Theodore Dreiser, Stephen Crane, William Dean Howells and the busy, inaugural current of American literary realism. For in their different anatomies of America he saw not exactly the mirror of his own life – how could any of them have written with authority of a black Southern boyhood lived hard against the colour line and under permanent threat of white racist violence? –

but human existence depicted as an oppressive power web likely to damage, if not actually consume, the individual.

The second observation arises out of Wright's 1930s Depression and Chicago years, the era of his brief membership of and departure from the American Communist Party which (together with his increasing disenchantment with America and subsequent FBI and State Department harassment) led to his permanent European exile in 1947. His sense of elation on opting out of the Party's *dicta*, even though it had helped him towards what then seemed a credible ideology of racelessness and anticapitalism, almost exactly parallels the sense of self-possibility he reports in *Black Boy* on leaving the Dixie South for his own migration northwards.

To 'build a bridge of words' between himself and America, and then worlds beyond, for a veteran of Mississippi-style racial custom and, if briefly, a former CPUSA (Communist Party USA) sympathiser, must in the light of that background have seemed an 'unreal' notion. For in claiming the right to use words to his own design Wright not only gave notice of his chosen path as a writer, he also affirmed that he intended nothing less than to take on, and to beat at its own scriptural game, a white-run and proprietary world accustomed as if by right to doing most of the defining of reality.

To emphasize Wright's passage into authorship, his belief in writing as a crucial liberative and existential rite, is, moreover, to imply a great deal about his fiction itself. Although he was held to be a 'committed' writer, he never in fact wrote to any single protocol, assuredly influenced by Marxism (and later Sartreanism and Freudianism) but keeping always his own imaginative distance. The praise for *Native Son* (1940), the novel which most established his name, however welcome to him in a general sense must also have been somehow inadequate. Were not review comments pronouncing him America's first 'Negro protest writer', its 'black Dreiser', the custodial voice of 'black anger' always far too reductive?[3]

For though Wright frequently assumed a departure point of deep abiding dissent, a personally endured bitter intimacy with American racial hypocrisies, this kind of phraseology, well intended or not, ultimately proves diversionary, even unhelpful. Among other deficits, it has locked his and a whole tradition of African American writing into too diagrammatic a series of oppositions: black protest against white oppression, ethnic against mainstream. He especially saw that 'protest' could give validation, intended or not, to the very terms of the racial ascendancy and subordination it sought to challenge.

In all these respects, and like Ralph Ellison and James Baldwin after him, Wright can be found insisting that binary versions of race would not take him or his reader very far. Some anger might indeed be ventilated. Black grievances might or might not win a sympathetic hearing, especially where white liberal guilt was involved. But more elusive racial complexities, the sexual and psychological components, built-in taboos, alternations of offence and defence, the utter constructedness of 'race' (as against culture) would simply get bypassed. Fiction especially risked being rendered down into sociology, documentary or treatise rather than worlds taken from life and transformingly then given their own imagining.

For Wright's grasp of complexity, his own as much as the world's, has still rarely won sufficient notice. Throughout the Depression years and even into the 1940s he was almost by rote taken to reflect the Communist Party view that Marxism pointed a way supposedly beyond race and towards the holistic view of history he calls the 'vast unity' in *American Hunger*. Then, during the Eisenhower 1950s, and as an expatriate in Paris, he frequently found himself castigated as some kind of ungrateful black anti-American voice in league with an intellectual class still enamoured of Soviet Russia and unacceptably out of sorts with America's predilection for domestic-suburban consensus at home and the Cold War abroad. In the 1960s, even as he held sway as dean of Paris's expatriate African American colony, the generation raised on Civil Rights, Selma, Watts, or the rhetoric of Malcolm X or the Panthers, seized on him as a standard bearer of either-or black militancy. In this he was to be set off against assumedly acquiescent 'native sons' like a 'conservative' Ellison, a gay Baldwin or a non-violent Martin Luther King – sometimes meanly jibed at as Martin Luther Queen.

None of these versions, however vivid or summary, in fact gives anything like Wright's overall measure. But, to one degree or another, they have persisted. His 'bridge of words', for instance, is taken to imply some kind of generic or at least Dreiserian standard of realism-naturalism. Marxist interpretation, taking a cue from *New Masses* (and with Adorno and Gramsci increasingly brought into the reckoning) continues to see Wright as a proponent of materialist history and, thereby, Afro-America's equivalent of Mike Gold or John Reed. There has been Freudian Wright, not least under French auspices like that of his most assiduous biographer, Michel Fabre, who considers Wright, whatever his creative self-command, as genius also shadowed by split, sexual demons, regressive hates and compensations.

The 1960s delivered yet another version, that of the Black Aesthetic view of Wright, the author of *Native Son* and volumes like *12 Million Black Voices* (1941) and *The Color Curtain* (1956) as the voice of a separatist black consciousness and value bent upon resistance to prying or appropriative white eyes.[4] Wright himself, in fact, nowhere argues for an exclusionist aesthetic of this or any other kind, which is not to fail to acknowledge that this ideological blackness did not play a key part in repositioning Wright at the forefront of African American literary achievement.

Few in the Black Aesthetic camp can be said to have taken on Wright's own considerable eclecticism. Could the Southern-born 'Black Boy' utterly possessed of black cultural legacy not also be considered as existentialist author whose imaginative cues equally derive from Heidegger, Dostoevski and Kafka or, in American literature, from Poe, Hawthorne and Melville, explorers of alterity, the displaced self? Wright's ambivalences about pan-Africanism and global notions of blackness equally remain to be sifted, not to mention his estimate of his own partly welcome, partly unwelcome, position as a black exile in still-colonialist France under the patronage of Jean Paul Sartre, Simone de Beauvoir and the circle of *Les Temps Modernes*. These factors yield no single settled picture, rather a Wright of competing shifts and turns and in which to take one or another part for the whole is simply to sponsor, and then perpetuate, a distortion.

The same holds true for each of the writings. There is a paradox in the deceptive clarity of Wright's work, the ease of access tempting the incautious into too ready a final version both of the man and his word. For an author taken to lack the finish of, say, Hemingway or Fitzgerald, or, among black authors, of Ellison, Herman Melville's drily sage observation in *Moby-Dick* offers just the right cautionary note: 'I have ever found your plain things the knottiest of all.'[5]

☆   ☆   ☆

Loosening Wright and his fiction from these interconnecting biographical, ideological and literary-critical myths becomes even more difficult in the light of the role he was called upon to play for other African American writers. First, there is the question of his vaunted school, the constellation which begins in novels like Chester Himes's *If He Hollers Let Him Go* (1945), with its wartime ship industry of California as scenario for a race and sex episode, Ann Petry's *The Street* (1946) with its Harlem rules of female sexual survival and odds, Alden Bland's *Behold a Cry* (1947) which looks back to the World War I Chicago race riots, or Willard Motley's *Knock On Any Door* (1947), the supposedly 'raceless' (because Chicago-Italian) novel of citied vice, drugs, murder and execution.[6]

At a slightly later remove the line includes, notably, the fiction of John A. Williams, above all his early work like *The Angry Ones* (1960), based largely on Williams's experience of the publishing world and its besetting codes of racism, *Night Song* (1961), loosely a version of the life and musical genius of 'Bird', Charlie Parker, and *Sissie* (1963), the story of two black siblings, the sister a singer based in Europe, the brother a playwright, and their sense of black family and kin. John O. Killens was frequently thought a Wrightian fellow-spirit, whether in *Youngblood* (1954), a pre-Civil Rights, liberal-accommodationist story set in the Georgia of his origins, or in *And Then We Heard the Thunder* (1963), the 1940s wartime story of a black Georgia regiment drawn into a vicious race fight with white GIs in allied Australia.[7]

Others, likewise, enter the Wrightian lists at an angle, among them William Gardner Smith's *Last of the Conquerors* (1948), the ironically titled story of black army experience in Occupied Germany; Lloyd L. Brown's *Iron City* (1951), a consciously Marxist and proletarian antiprison drama; Julian Mayfield's *The Hit* (1957), the world of Harlem numbers told as the black community dream of a once in a lifetime gambling success; and Herbert Simmons's *Corner Boy* (1957), whose locale of St. Louis, Missouri, supplies a ghetto and drugs nether world which traps its hero into a wrongful prison conviction, and *Man Walking on Eggshells* (1962), the vernacular, street-wise story of a jazzman turned militant. [8]

However markedly different in interests and manner, all of these writers have been gathered into the fold of Wrightian realism, of, however worn the phrase, 'Negro protest'. Nor can theirs be thought the only kind of eventual Wrightianism. There may be yet another, to be seen in the writing of Ralph Ellison, then Ishmael Reed, Leon Forrest and their contemporaries, which takes black narrative into the realms of irreality, a whole modernist, even postmodern, aesthetic.

That Wright, whether during the Chicago and *New Masses* 1930s, or as the presiding resident of the Paris black literary colony, or as the eventual student of the pan-African black Third World, did exert an extraordinary influence is not doubted. 'Wrightian', if it proposed no one single programme, was taken justifiably to signify a militancy of consciousness, theme, image. But to credit him with exerting a custodial influence over writers as conspicuously individual as Chester Himes and Ann Petry, James Baldwin and Ralph Ellison, amounts to yet another misreading, a skewering of the imaginative facts.

Himes's relationship with Wright, for example, especially as set out in *The Quality of Hurt* (1972) and *My Life of Absurdity* (1976), pays a far more complicated tribute to his fellow-exile than that of some disciple.[9] He loved, yet found himself frequently warring against, Wright, drawn to the apparent ease inside French intellectual life yet as often suspicious of the black spokesman status, the egotism. As to influence, the gallows humour laconicism of his thrillers if nothing else bespeaks both a massively different creative temperament.

James Baldwin and Ralph Ellison represent a similar complexity of influence and response. The two Baldwin essays which most apply, 'Many Thousands Gone' (1951) and 'Alas, Poor Richard' (1961), in all their stylish self-disaffiliation from Wright, need to be decoded also as acts of the most especial intimacy, a freedom sought as much from Wright's hold on the white world's version of American blackness as from Wright himself.[10]

Ellison, for his part, gives equally contrary witness. In 'Richard Wright's Blues' (1945) and his subsequent 'The World and the Jug' (1964), he speaks of simply 'stepping round' Wright, perhaps understandably the remark of the creator of the multivocal, eclectically mixed-form novel *Invisible Man* (1952).[11] Yet just as *Invisible Man* transforms for its own purposes the many backward glances to Dostoevski, Melville, Poe, Joyce, Malraux and the other figures Ellison mentions as influences in *Shadow and Act* (1964)

and in several interviews, so it calls up Richard Wright as the author of
the adroitly subterranean narrative of identity and revelation 'The Man
Who Lived Underground' (1945). In 'Remembering Richard Wright'
(1971) he offered a still later bead, Wright as 'sometimes too passionate',
too message-laden at the expense of a more transcending art, but at the
same time a model of unyielding black ambition. Ellison's terms aptly cite
another kind of black fighter and long-time breaker of barriers: 'In him
we had for the first time a Negro American writer as randy, as courageous,
and as irrepressible as Jack Johnson.'[12]

The saga of Wright as assumed black literary touchstone continues most
dramatically into the 1960s in Eldridge Cleaver's *Soul on Ice* (1968).
Here, in 'Notes of a Native Son', he uses the begetter of *Native Son* – 'the
Richard Wright [who] reigns supreme for his profound political, economic,
and social reference' – to berate James Baldwin – the incarnation not only
of sexual but political effeminization, ever willingly knee-bent to the
white man in a damning two-way sense.[13] But Cleaver's admiration of
Wright as the tough heterosexual black warrior, and condemnation of
Baldwin as the castratus and hater of his own blackness, however
eyecatching, does not give the whole case. With understandable cause
Cleaver might have been seeking a mythology suited to the polemical needs
of the Black Panther challenge to America – the call to African Americans
to cease being the compliant and all too literal prisoners of a history
begun in slavery and continued in the nation's ghettos and penitentiaries.
But a mythology is what it was, and remains, and not encompassing the
full human texture of *either* Wright or Baldwin.

From another angle there has been the Wright of John A. Williams. In
his fast moving political-existentialist thriller, *The Man Who Cried I Am*
(1967), Wright exists clearly as the begetting presence behind the
protagonist, Harry Ames, whose canny, born of experience (and sacrificial)
black legacy is offered as one of necessary vigilance against destruction
by white power interests. In *The Most Native of Sons* (1970), however, a
biography for children, Wright becomes a figure of tenderness, a writer
against the odds but, throughout, a caring father and husband.[14]

Williams's depiction of Ames as the victim of FBI and CIA machinations
working in some kind of harness with various white supremacist groups
in turn points forward to the Richard Wright revealed in Addison Gayle's
Richard Wright: Ordeal of a Native Son (1980), a piece of excavation
(however dully written) to complement Michel Fabre's standard biography,
The Unfinished Quest of Richard Wright (1973).[15] By gaining access to most
of Wright's government files under the Freedom of Information and
Privacy Acts of 1966 and 1974 Gayle shows how Wright suffered both
McCarthyist redbaiting and, thereafter, continued government surveillance.
The rumour still persists in some Paris and black circles that his death of
a heart attack did not come about by natural causes. Gayle's account, in
line with his prior Black Aesthetic ethos, assumes a stance that only a black

biographer and critic with the right blackness of outlook (however sympathetic a white Parisian biographer like Michel Fabre) could understand Wright's place within an America 'racial' to its historical core.

A late entry into Wright biography came with Margaret Walker's *Richard Wright: Daemonic Genius* (1988), depicting a fellow Southerner, Depression-era Chicagoan and novelist.[16] From her early meeting with Wright at the South Side Writers Group in the mid-1930s, she both drew inspiration from him and helped in supplying material from the Robert Nixon case on which he based parts of *Native Son*. The Wright she portrays is one who carried at no small cost the psychic freight of Dixie into adulthood yet, at the same time, was able to use it as the wellspring for his best writing.

Realist, naturalist, black protest writer: these have been the standard terms in the critical lexicon about Wright as literary figure. Not the least part of their inadequacy lies in the fact that Wright, in a quite different way, does link to his successors, but, to put things minimally, as his own kind of post-realist. Ellison again enters the frame in this respect, *Invisible Man* as Wrightian in its ostensible 'underground' theme yet anything but in how it transforms history into fantasy, a mythopoeic working of the black on white of writing as itself a trope for Afro-America's emergence into visibility.

Chester Himes can be brought to bear in similar terms, the Harlem of a novel like *The Primitive* (1955) or the Coffin Ed/Grave Digger Jones *romans policiers* as literal place yet at the same time quite magical shadow-territory. Another contextualizing style of Wrightian hyper realism is to be found in Hal Bennett's violent, drug-centred *Lord of the High Places* (1971).[17] This latter dispensation, not customarily granted to Wright, especially adds to the perspective for the present account: a realism, if such it be, given to covering its own traces, more semblance than not, or in the half-title of Melville's *Billy Budd* always (or almost always) the bearer of 'inside narrative'.[18]

For in line with the myths and counter-myths which have enclosed Wright and likely always kept his true self out of view, much of Wright's fiction (and autobiography) has likewise gone if not missing then awry – whether the 'Richard' he himself invents in *Black Boy* and *American Hunger*, and deftly perpetuates in reportage like *Black Power* (1954), *The Color Curtain* and *Pagan Spain* (1957), or on the evidence of his contribution to *The God that Failed* (1949) the half-in, half-out, Chicago Marxist, or the Greenwich Village and New York personality and author of *Native Son*, or, still later, the Paris expatriate and observer of postcoloniality and the Third World.[19]

It may well be that Wright, man and oeuvre, have become irrecoverably fixed inside one or another of the customary versions. From the 1940s through to the Civil Rights era, Wright is taken to operate as the simply inveterate, and so heroic, realist. His writings bequeath black militant testament, naturalist or revolutionary fare untainted by the siren calls of modernism. But however congenial the brevity or politics of this view, it amounts to no more than the easy option, a reduction of the Wright endemically and from the outset altogether more elusive in racial and every other kind of complication. Fortunately, as a first counterstep, one can again profitably turn to Wright's account of things, his own sense of idiom and working terms of reference.

The kind of writer Wright believed himself to be is nowhere better signalled than in his celebrated Preface to *Native Son*, 'How Bigger Was Born'.[20] Here, as in essays like 'The Literature of the Negro in the United States',[21] he insists on his inclination to see in black history not only a literal past scarred by oppression and survival, defeat and gain, but a matchingly inward and emblematic drama, one remembered within the collective African American psyche and in blues and black oral tradition. The last paragraph of 'How Bigger Was Born' especially insists on this kind of inheritance:

> we have in the Negro the embodiment of a past tragic enough to appease the spiritual hunger of even a James; and we have in the oppression of the Negro a shadow athwart our national life dense and heavy enough to satisfy even the gloomy broodings of a Hawthorne. And if Poe were alive, he would not have to invent horror; horror would invent him.

In so claiming James, Hawthorne and Poe as *semblables* (again an essay like 'The Literature of the Negro in the United States' which avers that 'The Negro is America's metaphor' shows how conscious he was of *black* literary tradition), he points precisely in the direction of his own species of inside narrative. Wright as realist may have been standard writ, the received wisdom, but rarely has it said anything like enough.

In this respect, the stories collected in *Uncle Tom's Children* (1938) and *Eight Men* (1961) especially offer a bearing, each on the surface circumstantial, real, but at the same time subtly parabolic, a glimpse into both white and black psyche.[22] This dual purpose telling is encountered at the outset of 'Big Boy Leaves Home', the first of the tales in *Uncle Tom's Children*. Contemplating the events which have left his friends Lester, Buck and Bobo dead and himself a terrified northwards bound fugitive from Dixie lynch law, Big Boy observes, 'It all seemed unreal now.' On the surface the story appears to offer a straightforward episode of Southern racist violence, the account of four black boys whose swim at a summer water hole leads on to death and flight. But the story's virtual every detail activates far more ancestral resonances from deep within Southern racial history, the rites whereby black manhood is killed or at least mutilated for its stereotypic desiring of white womanhood and in which the South, as in William Faulkner's mythical kingdom of Yoknapatawpha, becomes both a bucolic domain of river and pinewood and a brute inferno of lynch and castration.

Told as a classical five act sequence, the story opens with the boys' banter, their snatches of black bawdy and 'the dozens' and general rough-housing all the marks of time as adolescence. The landscape of the woods, the 'cleared pasture' and the 'tangled vines' initially serve as actual landscape and as nature's seeming stamp of approval. But at the swimming hole, they encounter the first discord within this summer-time boyhood harmony, the sign put up by Ol' Man Harvey, 'NO TRESPASSIN', its frank illiteracy at one with the intrusion of white property ownership into natural free space. Then, with the arrival of the white woman and her soldier lover, the story calls into play the South's darker if familiar racial equation: Big Boy, 'black and naked', a screaming belle, and the avenging white manfolk with blood on his lips after the first tussle, gun in hand, and vowing death to 'you black sonofabitch'.

Paradise thereby turns to nightmare. Fecklessness gives way to a new burden of consciousness. As Big Boy flees after the death of Harvey's soldier son back to family and community (to the bluesy chorus of his mother 'This is mo trouble, mo trouble'), and then away again into hiding at the kilns to await his escape in a truck owned by the emblematic 'Magnolia Express Company', so a latest black underground comes into play. 'Six foot of snake', serpentine racism given biological shape, greets his entry into the hell-like kiln. Big Boy kills the snake with a stick even as he imagines 'whole nests of them', each 'waiting tensely in coil'. His underground hole, like Fred Daniels's sewer in 'The Man Who Lived Underground' or the narrator's manhole in Ellison's *Invisible Man*, tacitly memorializes a still larger enclave – that brought on by the colour line hate which has pursued not only Big Boy and his three friends but their ancestors in an earlier slaveholding South.

Even so Big Boy can think back to a more benign black order of home, school, train, songs and 'long hot Summer days', in all, memory as a shared terrain of twelve-bar blues, guitar and briarpatch. At the same time he plays out in imagination his fantasy revenge on the white race, would-be heroism of the kind he thinks will make headlines like 'NIGGER KILLS DOZENS OF MOB BEFO LYNCHED'. Meanwhile the posse hunts down and captures Big Boy to the refrain of 'We'll hang ever nigger t' a sour apple tree.' Big Boy, in turn, burns to the chorus of 'LES GET SOURVINEERS' and 'HURRY UP N BURN THE NIGGER FO IT RAINS!' As he dies, another black boy martyred to white hate, Big Boy chokes the cerberean dog belonging to his white pursuers, displaced redress for the butchery of his friend and yet also the necessary killing of all residual innocence.

Wright's language throughout carries its own historic iconography. Big Boy's insides are drawn 'into a tight knot'. He rightly senses that the home he is leaving is a South both his and not his. The overall rite of passage has been one of the same kind of 'horror' and 'shadow' which will pursue his near namesake Bigger Thomas. Big Boy, as it were, has been forced to learn and internalize the far older configuration within the white American South of being both black and yet blackness, both normative sexual being and yet sexual phantom.

Wright's story, accordingly, tells an escape or flight narrative to match. Black and white exist as literal, visible pigmentation, even culture, yet also terms which have come to exist internally within the psyche – ancient, phobic, polarized. Wright makes Big Boy into the very embodiment of black American experience as fugitivism, whatever Big Boy's own sense of self in the eyes of the white South a figure of darkest otherness, fascination, threat. Does not 'Big Boy Leaves Home' echo Cain's fratricide against Abel, the first, most archetypal killing replayed as white against black?

The story acts as a frame for all these elements, at once dramatic yet cautionary, specific yet emblematic. The outward show contains a mutual and inside countershow, whether the black boy–white man contrast, the day into night transition, or the depiction of nature as alternatingly heaven or hell. Given the sum of these considerations to call a story like 'Big Boy Leaves Home' simply naturalistic overlooks Wright's true claim, the virtuosity of pattern, cadence, image, memory, masquerade, typology.

Each of the other pieces in *Uncle Tom's Children*, even if not equally successful, operates in kindred manner. In 'Down by the River', true to the classic blues from which Wright borrows his title, the ostensible story of a black drowning and white ingratitude for help given during a Southern flood yields another inside parable. Its black main figure, perhaps too obviously called Brother Mann, as so often under Southern writ, is in every sense 'sold down the river' by unfair racial odds. As Mann drowns, the story describes his body as 'encased in a tight vase in a narrow black coffin that moved with him'. This flood might be the flood of history itself, Southern-style, a murderous white stream of time in which black skin has been made into the garment of death.

Similarly, in 'Long Black Song', again a blues reference, the actual terrain becomes as languidly Southern-mythic in texture as the Georgia of Jean Toomer's *Cane* (1923). A black woman gets tricked into giving her sexual favours to a white salesman. Her husband, Silas, finally chooses to burn to death rather than be hanged cravenly for the revenge he enacts against the white use of sexual privilege which has so cheated him. He follows 'the long river of blood', but more a black martyr hero of his own choosing than the devil villain of the system which both literally and figuratively has denied him (and black men before him) their manhood.

'Fire and Cloud', a story equally mythic though perhaps sentimentalized in Wright's wish to envisage a cross-racial resistance to racism, tells the story of Reverend Taylor, an Uncle Tom preacher and black community leader, who after a vicious beating comes to reject passive black Christianity in favour of implacable opposition to arbitrary white authority in his Southern small town. The beating itself, which Wright dramatizes powerfully as Klan-style crucifixion, serves both as an instance of brutality and a rite of deepest inward liberation for the Reverend Taylor and the past standard he represents. The story also reflects Wright's own move from nominal Christianity to a more Marxist view of real salvation, change through historic consciousness and solidarity.

In 'Bright and Morning Star', another of Wright's stories with a Marxist and cross-racial element (which appropriately was published as a separate piece in *New Masses* in May 1938), he sets the warm maternal presence of Aunt Sue, the black mother of two activist sons, against Southern law-and-order thuggery. An' Sue, to give her her black name, represents a Faulknerian Dilsey figure no longer available as black servant to the white Compson dynasty. Rather, she incarnates the black woman as protectress, warrior, avenger. In shooting the stoolpigeon who has brought on the torture and death of her son, Johnny Boy, she passes into legend, the exemplary myth. In her own death she becomes 'the dead that never dies'.

Wright's prose is again pitched to call up black Bible cadence and a past racial history told and retold to the point where it becomes parable. Typical is the following: 'But as she had grown older, a cold white mountain, the white folks and their laws, had swum into her vision and shattered her songs and their spells of peace.' The inside narrative of 'Bright and Morning Star' resides perfectly in the collocation of 'cold white mountain', 'songs' and 'spells of peace', a black pictographic community speech to tell of life snatched from death and which derives from the blues music of the heart.

In this respect, Wright wrote no better story than 'The Man Who Lived Underground', the centrepiece to *Eight Men*. Its journey form has won praise for how it calls up Dante's *Inferno* and Dostoevski's *Notes from Underground*, yet also for how it cannily anticipates *Invisible Man* and LeRoi Jones/Amiri Baraka's *Dutchman*. For in Fred Daniels's underground odyssey, Wright develops both a literal drama of escape, a manhunt, and the parable of a black American hidden yet able to see all, invisible yet visible. In descending via the manhole cover into his underground existence, Daniels perceives the paradox of an America of both plenty and waste, which withholds as it offers its bounty.

Each glimpse of this America he experiences as one previously denied access, a kind of black underworld trespasser or scavenger forced to live at the margins of or underneath the white mainstream of the nation's history. Little wonder that his first sight is that of a glistening sewer rat, anticipating that which Bigger Thomas kills at the beginning of *Native Son* and which prefigures his own rodent fate in the final police chase. Everything Daniels sees, and on occasion steals, Wright sets against the spirituals being sung by the black congregation, America's black history as carried in the historic touchstone of its music.

As Daniels flees down into the sewer, he appears to step free of time itself and to become a traveller through all single versions of time. The story's questions properly include: 'How long had he been down here? He did not know.' He sees the dead abandoned baby 'snagged by debris and half-submerged in water', a Blakean innocent, eyes closed, fists clenched 'as though in protest', its mouth 'gaped black in soundless cry'. Such mute human frailty links directly to Fred Daniels's own fate, his self also essentially stillborn and an object of repudiation. As he 'tramps on', one particular black figure in history yet also the personification of all past black 'tramping', he next sees an embalmer at work, his 'establishment' ice cold, white and diabolic. The embalmer's own 'throaty chuckle' underlines the point trenchantly, whiteness as Hell.

Each subsequent encounter confirms this coded, quite literally visionary, landscape. The coal-bin conjures up not only real fuel but the whole underground fire of black life itself. The movie house, and its flickering screen, offers visual movement of a kind with Daniels's own miasmic perceptions of the world seen from his black underground. Life flickers like a moving image, a cinema reel. The fruit and vegetables he steals might also be thought painterly, food transposed into surrealist nourishment as on a Dali canvas. Similarly, the jewels he takes glisten hypnotically in the dark, real plunder yet also Gatsbyesque fantasy wealth. Even the newspaper heading, 'HUNT NEGRO FOR MURDER', assumes an air of disjunction, language as some foreign cryptogram which encodes reality within its own system. The same note applies to the Aladdin's Cave Fred makes of the stolen banknotes, and his tentative first efforts to write out his name. In writing *freddaniels* and other words he becomes like the first cave dwellers, a human presence, a newly literate slave, obliged by past history to begin again the finding and inscription of his own signature.

Daniels himself resembles Melville's Bartleby, another prisoner of walls: 'What was the matter with him? Yes, he knew it ... it was these walls; these crazy walls were filling him with a wild urge out into the dark sunshine above ground.' He is finally shot because the story he resurfaces momentarily to tell cannot be credited by the police, any more than that of Ralph Ellison's narrator in *Invisible Man* or Jones/Baraka's Clay in *Dutchman*.

Wright's naturalism once more secretes inside narrative, the visceral underground sediment of black American history. 'The Man Who Lived Underground' undoubtedly offers the best of the *Eight Men* stories, yet each of the others (especially 'The Man Who Was Almost a Man' and 'Man of All Work') invites a similar decipherment. For as so often in Wright's storytelling, surfaces equivocate brilliantly, an outward show, an inside truth.

☆   ☆   ☆

This inside dynamic applies equally to the longer works. All five of Wright's novels – *Lawd Today* (1963), *Native Son* (1940), *The Outsider* (1953), *Savage Holiday* (1954) and *The Long Dream* (1958) – yield their respective inlaid skeins, at once covert yet emblematic.[23] *Lawd Today*, to take Wright's probable first novel and which, ironically, was not submitted for publication for want of a clearly discernible Marxist orientation, outwardly tells a twenty-four hour day in the life of Jake Jackson, black Chicago postal worker. Its surface bristles in the detail of a Lincoln Day Holiday, Wright's informed sense of Chicago's South Side street and bar life, community dreams of a magical Numbers fortune, black vernacularity, bar drinks, meals of grits and sweet potato, and sexual opportunism. In other words it seeks to recreate the pace, the crowdedness, the ready and always overlapping contingency, of everyday black city life.

At the same time, however, *Lawd Today* explores more inward terrain, Jake Jackson as a man close to psychological split and eruption. The increasing hatred he shows his wife, the valetudinarian Lil, and his inability to control his temper, mark a man near the edge, spooked by ill-chance, a sense of odds, entrapment, frustration. In fact Jake veers increasingly towards murderousness, the violence of the internal ghetto Chester Himes once strikingly termed 'the prison of my mind'.

The brighter side of reality is conveyed in the Lincoln Day Holiday, Roosevelt Firesides on the radio, 1930s popular songs and a busy scenario of commercial hustle. But for Jake, fissured, inwardly as much as outwardly enghettoed, reality also resides in a beleaguered psyche likely to erupt into violence at the barest provocation. *Lawd Today*'s documentary format dissembles. Jake's history becomes increasingly disjunctive, a stream of normal event set against abnormal consciousness.

☆   ☆   ☆

Whatever its status as a naturalist classic the same holds even more for *Native Son*. For all its crime and punishment drama, it tells an 'inside' story as 'dense and heavy' and full of 'shadow' as Wright hoped it might in the Preface, 'How Bigger Was Born'. At the immediate plot level *Native Son* offers the drama of Bigger Thomas's tenement upbringing, the half-witting murder of his white patron's daughter, the subsequent disposal in the furnace of Mary Dalton's body and in turn the flight, murder of his girl Bessie, and trial and defence as developed through the dialectics of Mr. Max, his Jewish and Marxist lawyer. This, however, is to leave the fuller achievement of *Native Son* seriously unmet.

Ironically, *Native Son* has been criticised for not being naturalist enough. James Baldwin, notably, spoke of the novel's attenuation, Bigger and the others as figures more charade than three-dimensional portraiture.[24]

This begs the question of the kind of novel Wright in fact writes. For is not *Native Son*, against the usual assumption, more Dostoevskian than Dreiserian, *Notes from Underground* rather than *An American Tragedy?* Wright aims to convey a condition of mind, a self, a black self, made quite irretrievably alien.

Bigger's violence, from the opening episode with the rat and his bullying of his pool hall friends through to the murder and incineration of Mary and his flight, mimetically follows the course of the cracks and splits deep within his own consciousness. *Native Son* virtually asks to be read as an exploration of human personality in the mould of Dostoevski, or indeed Céline or Kafka. For the true Chicago of the novel resides more in the splintered city or tenement pent up inside Bigger's feelings and psyche than in the Windy City of The Projects or Hyde Park. In arguing for this more symbolist reading of *Native Son*, three supporting kinds of allusion must do duty for the novel's procedures as a whole: they have to do with sight, with the image of Bigger as rat, and with exactly the kind of city depicted in *Native Son*.

Native Son, like 'The Man Who Lived Underground', anticipates *Invisible Man* in its handling of sight as paradigm. The point is born home especially in a passage like the following in which Bigger considers the implication of having killed Mary:

No, he did not have to hide behind a wall or a curtain now; he had a safe way of being safe, an easier way. What he had done last night had proved that. Jan was blind. Mary had been blind. Mr. Dalton had been blind. And Mrs. Dalton was blind; yes, blind in more ways than one ... Bigger felt that a lot of people were like Mrs. Dalton, blind.

Just as Bigger's black world sees him one way (merely wayward if his hard pressed mother is to be believed, a tough street companion according to his pool hall buddies, a lover in Bessie's eyes) so to the white world he is seen only through part of his identity, as some preferred invention like the recipient of Mr. Dalton's self-serving largesse, or the proletarian black worker imagined by Mary and her lover Jan, or Mr. Max's example of how 'scientific' history shapes the individual consciousness.

Even the final chase scenes across run-down, wasteland Chicago against which he is silhouetted by the police cross-lights show him only in part, the formulaic rapist murderer. Bigger's full human self, even at the end probably ungrasped by the victim himself, lies locked inside 'the faint, wry bitter smile' he wears to his execution.[25] Perhaps, too, it lies teasingly present in the white cat that watches him burn Mary's body (an inversion of Poe's 'The Black Cat'?), the emissary of the white world which has hitherto so defined Bigger but, just as plausibly, the rarest glimpse of his own whited identity.

The rat killed by Bigger in the opening chapter also sets up a motif which resonates throughout the novel. Its belly 'pulsed with fear', its 'black beady eyes glittering', at once a creature of offence and defence, it might be the very *anima* of Bigger himself. Will not he become a kind of Darwinian reverse? His own life, its strike or be struck alternations, its would-be love yet eventual deadly impact on both Mary and Bessie, acts as the pendulum swings of hunter and prey. Within Chicago's urban race maze Bigger doubles, or rather self-divides, his own familiar and yet his own stranger.

These inside meanings also lie behind Wright's three-part division of 'Fear', 'Flight' and 'Fate', as much notations of *Native Son*'s parabolic meanings as the apparent drama at the surface. Bigger's extended last colloquy with Mr. Max implies that he has his glimmerings of how this triangular rite has made him into encaptured human rodent (Wright's version of Kafka's beetle?). This, again, is the predator himself trapped by predatory laws of survival. Wright cannily images Bigger's life as not one but a series of enclosures – tenement, basement, hideout, prison cell, his own psyche, each, in the novel's haunting last phrase, 'steel against steel'.

In 'How Bigger Was Born', Wright speaks of Chicago as 'huge, roaring, dirty, noisy, raw, stark, brutal', that is as the city of the historic stockyards, oppressive summer humidity and the chill polar winds of a Lake Michigan winter. But he also speaks of Chicago as a city which has created 'centuries-long chasm[s] of emptiness' in figures like Bigger Thomas. *Native Son* internalizes this same black city, one of feelings half-understood, incarceration, revenge, the need to strike and maim. To discern in *Native Son* only an urban-realist drama again evades the dimensions of the novel Wright himself knowingly calls 'the whole dark inner landscape of Bigger's mind'.

Though in no sense failures, both *The Outsider* and *Savage Holiday* go adrift and for connected reasons. In the former, Wright cannot resist loading his story of Cross Damon as the black twentieth-century man of alienation, with an accompanying (and intrusive) set of explanations about angst and the eclectic tradition of outsiderness. Not only does he repeatedly invoke founding figures like Heidegger and Kierkegaard, he also glosses Damon's different murders and assumptions of identity with allusions to Dread, Will, the Absurd. To this end he imports into the novel another ranking (and suitably articulate) outsider, the hunch-backed District Attorney, Eli Houston, to whom it falls as it does to Mr. Max in *Native Son* to analyse the processes which have made Damon what he is: death-in-life.

In *Savage Holiday*, Wright's touchstone becomes Freud, human personality in the form of Erskine Fowler, an ex-insurance man eased out of his job to make way for the boss's son and the victim of an almost absurd turn of events which results in the death of a neighbour's young boy. His own glaring sexual repression culminates in murder, the stabbing of the boy's voluptuous mother whose easy sexual style causes him torment. As in *The Outsider*, Wright manages a range of strong local effects, but more often he sounds tutorly, essayistic. The relative failure of both books lies in the fact that he simply will not trust his own tale to do the work. Whether the keystone is existentialism or Freudianism, the inside narrative is made damagingly explicit. Wright's philosophical interests tilt the novels too much towards idea or thesis over design, their inside workings all too readily available.

☆   ☆   ☆

Fortunately, Wright's last novel *The Long Dream* (a sequel *Island of Hallucination* remains unpublished) shows no radical fault of this kind. In part this is due to Wright's return to the materials he drew from so convincingly in *Black Boy*, the Deep South as memory, history, first origins. For Wright organizes the story of *The Long Dream*, that of Fishbelly Tucker's childhood and passage into adult identity, without the overintrusion which flaws *The Outsider* and *Savage Holiday*.

A major part of the novel's success lies in Wright's meticulous recreation of Fishbelly's childhood, at once the wholly individual childhood of a black boy in the South whose undertaker father takes care to educate him as best he knows into the wiles needed to survive in the treacherous world of small town Dixie, and at the same time a version of black childhood itself, the dynastic re-enactment of what it means to be black, curious and permanently at risk from white authority.

From the first acquiring of his folk name through to his first sexual awakenings, Fishbelly learns about the world from Tyree, his father. But he also comes to know that his father's business exists on deals struck with the Chief of Police, Cantley, and that the town's tacit and demeaning lines of agreement have been arranged on the basis of white power and black deference. Further, Fishbelly perceives that his father, by running a Numbers racket and brothel, is also 'embalming' his people in life just as he embalms them literally in his undertaking business.

The chain of events which finally leads to Tyree's death and Fishbelly's jailing on a trumped-up sex charge involving a white woman again assumes an interplay of meanings. Fishbelly's story, in all its twists and detail, offers the chronicle of a life, but also of the ritual of black coming of age, the shared perception of what it is to be man and 'nigger'.

Fishbelly's story undoubtedly plays off Richard Wright's own. For, like the portrait Wright created in *Black Boy* and *American Hunger*, it refracts in the one life the more collective story of black community in the American South – of 'black' as a marker of intimacy, language, family, and of a counter tactic against the untiring spiral of Dixie racism. Thus the impression of the South that Fishbelly carries away with him (once again, in Wright's own footsteps, to Europe) signifies a history, a geography, of outward experience and inner consciousness which, to good imaginative purpose, Wright locates in 'the locked regions' of Fishbelly's heart.

The Long Dream returns to Wright's best equipoise of outer and inner narration. Both exist, competingly, as a memorial interplay within Fishbelly's mind: a literal South of black survival against white Dixie phobia and a South as shadow, echo, the ongoing mixed feeling at a world at once home and yet a kind of alien world.

In his Introduction to George Lamming's *In the Castle of My Skin* (1953), Wright revealingly calls attention to the human layerings which have marked out black experience in the white west. He also implies how impossible it would be to render that experience to any single measure, be it protest, a version of naturalism, or Marxism, Freudianism, or even existentialism. But one observation in particular throws light on the multiple reaches of his own best storytelling:

> the Negro of the Western world lives in *one* life, *many* lifetimes ... The Negro, though born in the Western world, is not quite of it; due to policies of racial exclusion his is the story of *two* cultures: the dying culture in which he happens to be born, and the culture into which he is trying to enter – a culture which has, for him, not quite yet come into being ... Such a story is, above all, a record of shifting, troubled feelings groping their way towards a future that frightens as much as it beckons.[26]

Such a story, one story intricately drawn from many, amounts exactly to the nature of the inside narrative on offer in Richard Wright's fiction.

War and Peace: Writing the Black 1940s

The treatment accorded the Negro during the Second World War marks, for me, a turning point in the Negro's relation to America. To put it briefly, and somewhat too simply, a certain hope died, a certain respect for white Americans faded ... You must put yourself in the skin of a man who is wearing the uniform of his country, is a candidate for death in its self-defense, and who is called 'nigger' by his comrades-in-arms and his officers; who is always almost given the hardest, ugliest, most menial work to do; who knows that the white G.I. has informed the European that he is subhuman (so much for the American male's sexual security); who does not dance at the U.S.O. the night white soldiers dance there, and does not drink in the same bars white soldiers drink in; and who watches German prisoners of war being treated with more human dignity than he has ever received at their hands ... You must consider what happens to this citizen, after all he has endured, when he returns – home: search, in his shoes, for a job, for a place to live; ride, in his skin, on segregated buses; see, with his eyes, the signs saying 'White' and 'Colored' and especially the signs that say 'White Ladies' and 'Colored *Women*'; look into the eyes of his wife; look into the eyes of his son; listen, with his ears, to political speeches North and South; imagine yourself being told to 'wait.' And all this is happening in the richest and freest country in the world, and in the middle of the twentieth century.

James Baldwin, *The Fire Next Time* (1963)[1]

The risks in mapping by decades have long grown familiar. History, and the cultural styles of expression it gives rise to, rarely falls into place by some ready-made symmetry of arithmetic or calendar. This does not imply that American periodizations like the 1890s or the 1920s, along with terms like interwar or postwar, do not have their uses as shorthand.

One decade, however, that of the America of the 1940s, more than usually challenges: a single period yet seemingly separated into two parts, a single place yet for many Americans abroad on war duty also an America carried into Europe and Asia. Within it, and even more beset with contradiction, lie the black 1940s.

At first sight nothing could look clearer than a period in which war literally alternates with peace. The attack on Pearl Harbor on 7 December 1941, and in its immediate wake Hitler's declaration of war on the United States, inaugurates America's entry into the Atlantic and Pacific Wars. The conflict ends with GIs entering Berlin, the Pacific campaign, Hiroshima and Nagasaki, and Japanese surrender to General MacArthur. On the American homefront, the presidential baton passes from Roosevelt to Truman in April 1945, the troops return, and war production and Lend Lease continue to drive the economy. The order becomes one of ever greater boom and recovery.

So spare an account, however, revealingly falls short in what it fails to say about the era's complex racial spirals and dispositions. War talk readily applied a domestic lexicon of stereotypes to the enemy – Japs and Nips, Huns and Krauts, Wops and Dagos; in mirror fashion it equally did so to Americans born of these origins. Executive Order 9066 of 1942, drawing on a long history of anti-Asianism, led to the internment in the wake of Pearl Harbor of 120,000 West Coast Japanese Americans with matching action taken in Canada and Peru (Chinese and Korean Americans took to wearing badges saying 'Not Japanese'). The fact that not a single case of Japanese treason was proven, or that the all-*nisei* 442nd Regimental Combat team would become the most decorated American unit of World War II, or that Japanese American army units would be responsible for the liberation of villages in northern France, bears its own irony.[2] For many German and Italian Americans, though there was no internment, there were 'enemy alien' labels, curfews and hounding.[3]

Other American ethnicities, *chicanos* most notably, also found themselves drawn into this circle of suspicion. In 1942–43 the Zoot Suit riots in *barrio* Los Angeles erupted, partly the upshot of the Sleepy Lagoon murders but, equally, of the would-be ascendancy of one kind of America (Anglo, Navy, largely rural-Southern, English speaking, Protestant) over another (*latino*, civilian, urban-*barrio*, Spanish speaking, Catholic). Each fought as uniformed opponents, white servicemen in regular military cut against brown skinned *chicano* youth, or *pachucos*, in their baroque cutaway coats, long watch chains, pegged trousers and broad brimmed hats. 'Symbolic' as these skirmishes have been called, they convey yet another contest of wartime American racial will.[4]

Nor did the 1940s do better by America's longest standing peoples, Native Americans. The Indian Removal Act of 1830 and after it the Dawes Allotment Act and related legislation bequeath their dire legacy of deterritorialization. The massacre of nearly 300 peaceably encamped

Minneconjou Sioux at Wounded Knee in 1890 is subsumed into the Last Indian War and the Winning of the West (for Native America, however, it becomes the My Lai of its time, a memorial to white frontier paranoia). That process takes an ironic form during the World War II era in the person of Tonto in *The Lone Ranger* as 'good Indian', begun on Detroit's station WXYZ in February 1933, then aired throughout the 1940s for no less than 3500 episodes (the comic book series also began in 1940), and eventually made into ABC's massively successful 1949–58 TV series. As the ever unswerving and silent (or at best monosyllabic) shadow to his white lawman master, Tonto re-enforced a belief that 'Indians', whatever their diversity as Plains or Pueblo, Woodland or Coastal, on or off Reservation, were ever subtly unsuited to modernity, a kind of leftover wisechild. That Tonto aids and abets in the return of land, gold and other mineral acquisitions to their 'rightful' white owners, a frequent plotline, underscores the point – 'Indians' as no longer main players but retainers. The programme did its share, too, in eclipsing Native wartime service, whether those in regular enlistment or 'special service' trackers and users of code.[5]

☆   ☆   ☆

For black Americans, however, World War II meant an explicitly segregated Army, black units, even whole black regiments, each invariably under a white officer class. The extent of racial abuse in wartime bases, and the frequent insurrections it provoked, to this day awaits its full airing. By early 1943 more than 500,000 blacks were in the Army but less than 80,000 overseas and, even then, usually in support or labour battalions on the racist-stereotypic grounds of being thought unreliable for frontline duty.

Navy enlistment overwhelmingly meant serving as mess attendants ('in the best interests of general ship efficiency' argued Admiral Nimitz) while the Air Force, after many shows of reluctance, gave the go-ahead to 'The Tuskegee Airmen' of the all-black 332 Fighter Corps which saw action over North Africa but whose officers were refused entrance into segregated base clubs, practices extended, in kind, to separate nursing and billeting.[6] The American Red Cross even established a segregated blood bank in order, as a vintage segregationist like Congressman Rankin of Mississippi said, to prevent the 'mongrelization' of 'our wounded white boys'.[7] The grounds for provocation and resentment were extensive. A 1940s column in the black-run *Pittsburgh Courier* put matters succinctly – 'Our war is not to defend democracy, but to get a democracy we have never had.'[8]

That Thurgood Marshall, the longserving NAACP lawyer who had been Chief Counsel in Brown *v.* Board of Education and who in 1967 became the Supreme Court's first black Justice, would look back to discrimination cases he first conducted during the war even as he conducted others after it, confirms how the one conflict always bore the embryo of the other. None of this is to deny wartime black–white, and especially black–Jewish, alliances as in the NAACP, or in the more progressive Unions, or governmentally as through a liberal force like Eleanor Roosevelt. But it suggests how the war resulted in a considerably different experience for its black compared to its white GIs and officers, an ongoing domestic conflict within the larger foreign conflict. Walter White's *A Rising Wind* (1945) as an account of World War II black soldiering confirms precisely the turnings of bias and double-standard. [9]

The Armistice signed, and Truman's Fair Deal installed as successor to Roosevelt's New Deal, America's citizenry, black as much as white, had reason to anticipate just reward for battles fought bravely and well, a step into the future. Yet the signs, economic and consumerist, again overwhelmingly favoured white America: full or near full employment, suburbanization, tract homes, cars, TVs, phones, washing machines, and cheap abundant food and clothing. For black America, the return from the fight for democracy, for Roosevelt's 'Four Freedoms' as they became known, meant largely a continuance of the *status quo ante*, a nation still reluctant to dismantle its own ingrained habits of segregation.

However often denied at the time, race in fact features throughout most of the immediate postwar upbeat. Market capitalism as freedom involved both bravura and fear, a Cold War (with the bomb as last resort) pledged to outrun both Stalin's Russia and the China of Mao, the Red Army and the People's Republic of China. The latter arouses yet more Yellow Peril phobia (so reminding Chinese Americans of the 1882 and other Exclusion Acts), a viral, conspiratorial ideology pledged to subvert the American Way. Korea did surrogate duty for an attack on China, a racially loaded Asian communism held back at the 38th Parallel and only dimly guessed at as the beacon of wars to come, whether Vietnam, Cambodia or Laos.

Korean Americans, often made heirs to Jewish pawnbroker or storeowner myth, were to become the latest targets in the wake of the Rodney King beating during the 1992 South Central riots in which they and their stores were attacked and looted. Despite abundant white misbehaviour a lot of the reporting selectively suggested that it was only a black versus Korean flair-up, more trouble among 'ethnics'. Martin Luther King was said to have most courted danger when, having publicly declared himself against the Vietnam War in 1967, he connected racial abuse of African Americans with racial abuse of the Vietnamese.

If America had become the standard bearer of the Free World (through the relaunch of the League of Nations as the United Nations in San Francisco in 1945 or Marshall Aid to Europe in 1947), that little included most black populations. The State Department was no more effective in its stance against apartheid in South Africa, or Europe's continuing

African empires (be it 'British' Nigeria, 'French' Chad, the 'Belgian' Congo or 'Portuguese' Angola), than Congress was for Jim Crow in Alabama and Mississippi or segregation in housing in New York and Chicago.

At home other anxieties had begun to show. If the icons of white Middle America were the Corporation, Main Street, the PTA (Parent Teacher Association), The Elks, a comforting diet of Bing Crosby or *Reader's Digest* (tellingly the first phase of *Negro Digest*, 1942–51, would be made in its image), doubts had begun to arise about conformism, the social gendering of men and women into businessman or housewife. Did the Babbitry of the grey flannel suit or the nice girl image of Shirley Temple cover all bases?

The Kinsey Reports (*Sexual Behavior in the Human Male* in 1948 and *Sexual Behavior in the Human Female* in 1953) invoked regimes far from the innocent American family image; they spoke of inhibition, premarital sex, deviance, a realm far from genteel desire. Nowhere, however, was it assumed that black sexual behaviour (other than as white fantasy) came into the reckoning.

Alongside all of these rose the gathering, and increasingly impatient, energies for a change in the racial order. The word had gone up for integration – full voter registration, an end to separate schooling, hirings, restaurants, buses, toilet facilities (with all its loaded biological implication) and, in terms of America's best-loved sport, the notorious white-only major baseball leagues. The latter took its most memorable turn in Jackie Robinson's lonely, and often fiercely resented, triumph in being signed for the Brooklyn Dodgers at Ebbet's Field in 1947, as a popular tune like 'Baseball Boogie' bears out, though he had to endure wilful in-game spikings and racist name callings. Another turn of the screw, however, lay in Robinson's HUAC (House Un-American Activities Committee) condemnation of Paul Robeson.

The spectre of racial intermarriage also loomed. It would take a Supreme Court Decision in 1967 formally to overturn state and local laws against it. Hollywood, whether from 'liberal' conviction or simply an eye to the main chance, in the same year delivered Stanley Kramer's film *Guess Who's Coming to Dinner?* Sydney Poitier played the highly eligible, middle-class doctor, a model of overwhelming suitor etiquette. The widespread fear of 'alien' takeover carried yet another kind of racial *frisson* begun in the 1940s: the blurring of ideological (meaning, for the most part, communist) with biological miscegenation, reflected, eventually, in films like Don Spiegel's science fiction classic, *Invasion of the Bodysnatchers* (1956), with its space born pods and doublings, or *The Manchurian Candidate* (1962), with its Cold War warning of communism as China-manipulated fifth column.

Women, that is white and especially college-educated women, had bridled at returning from war work to the role of mother and homemaker. Their generational discontents would lead in due course to Betty Friedan's very naming of 'the problem that has no name' in her *The Feminine Mystique* (1963).[10] However, the sexual politics of black women, high school or college graduate, fieldworker or domestic, not to mention warworker, would await both a later telling and hearing.

In 1940 60 per cent of all employed black women were domestic servants (in 1997, by contrast, 60 per cent of all employed black women are white-collar workers). It was, symptomatically, to that world that Zora Neale Hurston would be obliged to return after the commercial failure of her literary career. The 1940s and 1950s experiments with the contraceptive pill which, at serious cost to health and fertility, used women of colour in Puerto Rico and Mississippi as guinea pigs, provides another kind of benchmark.[11]

Yet the 1940s did not lack its own considerable line of literary witness by black women. Zora Neale Hurston, who now belatedly emerges as the age's doyenne, novelist, folkteller, poet, historian, vernacularist, gave voice to a range of feisty, personable women – for whom Janie in *Their Eyes Were Watching God* (1937) supplies the best-known embodiment.[12] Similarly, there can no overlooking women figures like Ann Petry's Lutie Johnson in *The Street* (1946), Dorothy West's Cleo Judson in *The Living Is Easy* (1948) or, from a novelist like Margaret Walker who came of age in the 1940s, Vyry in *Jubilee* (1966), a 'neo-slave' novel as its author called it, written as a riposte to Margaret Mitchell's *Gone with the Wind* (1936), and which anticipates another and later African American 'genealogical' bestseller, Alex Haley's *Roots* (1976).[13]

American youth overwhelmingly meant a white image, Mickey Rooney as bow-tied Junior or Judy Garland as bobbysoxer with James Dean as 'rebel without a cause' soon to follow. The process for their black compeers would take far longer (in the 1940s, for the most part, they were simply not 'seen'), an eventual visibility, however, shot through as always with every kind of contradiction as in the case of Dorothy Dandridge. Her route to becoming 'the black Marilyn' in *Carmen Jones* (1954), Hollywood's first siren of colour (the code word was 'tan'), meant crossing all kinds of previously closed screen colour-and-sexuality lines. She made her 1940s debut as the 18 year old singer of 'Chattanooga Choo Choo'.[14]

Historical events and role models have been no less ambiguous since the 1940s, from the mutilation and drowning of 14 year old Emmett Till in the Tallahatchie River in 1955; the televised jeering at the Little Rock Nine in 1957; the elegant sprinting of Wilma Rudolph first in the 1956 Melbourne Olympics, then, triumphantly, in 1960 in Rome; the four children killed in the Birmingham church bombing of 1963; teenage frontline 'bloods' on war service in 1960s Vietnam and teenage single mothers in the tenements; the male gang world of, say, John Singleton's 1991 South Central L.A. movie, *Boyz N the Hood*; and a black youth music from Motown to rock to rap as variously performed, from the 1960s on, by a young Diana Ross in buffooned Motown mode, a young Michael Jackson once all black baby cuteness in the Jackson Five, or (to the selective indignation and actual campaigning against rapper 'violence' of Tipper Gore, wife of Clinton's Vice President) a young Sister Souljah.

However much Afro-America inevitably shared the overall currents of the 1940s, it was always as deepened by the sourer workings of evasion or discrimination. In war, the American military had permitted, and often actually required, every kind of black–white divide in duties and rank, until formal desegregation of the Armed Forces was enforced in 1948 under an Executive Order from President Truman. In peace, the same double standard applied. Despite a margin of increase in black political and economic leverage (some of it payback by Truman for NAACP and other black electoral support), or the various 1940s and 1950s Civil Rights Acts including the pivotal ruling of Brown v. Board of Education in 1954, it would take the activism of the 1960s to achieve a genuinely radical breakthrough. In or out of uniform, wartime or peacetime, the 1940s for Afro-America in virtually all its dealings with the mainstream meant largely unrelieved and continuing colour segregation.

One literary response lay in so-called 'raceless' fiction. Frank Yerby opened a long pulp fiction career (he has spoken of himself as a writer of 'costume novels') with *The Foxes of Harrow* (1946), formula derring-do with heiresses, rakes and villainy in *Gone with the Wind* mould. Willard Motley's *Knock on Any Door* (1947), with its Italian-American saga of murder in the figure of Nick Romano and *ad hominem* courtroom addresses, does a reprise of Bigger Thomas and *Native Son*. Ann Petry's *Country Place* (1947), though not without a black maid figure in Neola, essentially concerns a white New Englandism turned inward and provincial. Zora Neale Hurston's *Seraph on the Suwanee* (1948), to the dismay and reproof of many black followers, substituted rural poor-white for black life, a supposedly misguided attempt at 'universalizing'. The process occasionally worked the other way, nowhere more visibly than in Paul Robeson's 300 performances in the 1943 production of *Othello* and Canada Lee's admired role (in whiteface) of Webster's Bosola in *The Duchess of Malfi* in 1945.[15]

Few black soldiers or their families, however, failed to see the overall contradiction of fighting the tyranny of nazism or Japanese imperialism on behalf of an America itself the source of continuing racial oppression. Homecoming merely underlined the point, one racism for another. Ralph Ellison, recalling his own short story of a downed black airman which led on to *Invisible Man*, offers the following summary:

> historically most of this nation's conflicts of arms have been – at least for Afro-Americans – wars-within-wars. Such was true of the Civil War, the last of the Indian Wars, of the Spanish American War, and of World Wars I and II. And in order for the Negro to fulfill his duty as a citizen it was often necessary that he fight for his self-affirmed right to fight.[16]

Albert Murray, Ellison's friend, former Major in the US Air Force, novelist, and the tough, sharp essayist of both *The Omni-Americans* (1970) and *South to a Very Old Place* (1971), the former given over to the endemic Americanness of black experience and the latter to a 'state of the nation' conceived as an itinerary from New York to Mobile, Alabama, makes the link in terms as graphic as any. He, too, invokes the experience of the Tuskegee Airmen:

> It is a ... fact that Negro pilots for the 332nd Fighter Group who were captured during World War II preferred the treatment they received from the Nazis to that which they received from their fellow countrymen in Alabama, whose solicitude of German internees was beyond reproach! Qualified citizens of no other democratic nation in the world encounter more deviousness or nearly as much outright antagonism in the routine process of local, state, and federal government.[17]

☆　　☆　　☆

How, then, within these vexed equations of war and peace, has Afro-America written the 1940s? One of the most encompassing canvases of the war itself lies in John O. Killens's *And Then We Heard the Thunder* (1963).[18] Eventful, pacily naturalist in style, the portrait it develops of Sol Saunders, newly married and intending law school student, takes him through enlistment, red clay Georgia bootcamp training, a cadre of black buddies, Monterey's Fort Ord, soldiering in the Philippines, and on to eventual involvement in a race fight in Bainbridge, Australia, where he has been hospitalized. This is the American Army as Pacific fighting force yet also 'cracker army', with Solly's own story as vantage point and centre (his love of three women, his relations with different white officers from Dixie General through to the Jewish Lieutenant Samuels, and Pacific frontline service).

'You ain't on a Hundred and Twenty-fifth Street now' a black sergeant tells Sol on entering the Army. It serves as both reproach and prophecy. For Harlem becomes a kind of sustaining mnemonic for the world of the Apollo Theater, Hotel Theresa, The Ink Spots, Josh White, Lena Horne, Paul Robeson and, always, the blues. Killens plays this bulwark of black memory against both the 'wilderness of hostility and un-democracy' (as Sol describes the US Military in a controversial letter to the newspapers) and island combat and death in the Philippines.

The imagery of the war itself may well be neither 'black' nor 'white', more in kind with the classic American line of Bierce, Crane or Hemingway (planes hover 'like ghostly buzzards', platoons and regiments are seen 'awaiting Death's convenience'). But Killens nevertheless also assiduously gives the war its own black 'text': the use of down-home argot, the dozens, the sass and updates of putting on massa, even Sol's black–Jewish exchanges on race and power with Samuels.

In Sol, Bookworm, Scottie and the rest, whatever their in-group contrariety, the fellowship is one of offence and defence against two 'enemy' armies, Japanese but also American. The matter reaches its closing focus in the Australian race shoot-out 'turning Bainbridge into Georgia'. The novel's rendering of this key event provocatively confirms World War II, Afro-America's World War II at least, as foreign war inverted into civil war (an added twist lies in events being located in the allied Antipodes). As Sol and comrades engage in the messy and murderous fight with white GIs ('Bloody Yankees fighting Yankees' observes an Australian townsperson), 'enemy' extends to fellow Americans as much as Germans or Japanese.

The novel no doubt opens itself to cavils. The running black–Jewish debate about gradualism and militancy tends to intrude. Sol's love affairs with Millie, Fannie May and the white Australian, Celia, can seem paradigmatic, in turn homegirl, NAACP activist, and (across the racial divide) nurse. Is there not also a certain wishful thinking in setting up Australia as free of racism?

But the novel earns its plaudits. World War II as a refraction of America's racial double standard, 'Mr. Charlie's Army' as against Sol's 'No peace till freedom', is given drama, pace, a frame. For what *And Then We Heard the Thunder* manages to enact, the title phrase aptly made over from Harriet Tubman as one of Emancipation's most influential presences, is a 1940s Afro-America 'at war' on quite anything but the single front.

World War II's black soldiering has its distant reflection in prime American war texts like Norman Mailer's *The Naked and the Dead* (1948) and James Jones's *From Here to Eternity* (1951).[19] But in John A. Williams's *Captain Blackman* (1972), a narrative time chronicle of black war experience from Independence era to Vietnam to a 'black' nuclear take-over of America told as the serial hallucination of the wounded Abraham Blackman, the 1940s can look to a cameo written wholly from a black vantage point and possessed of its own kind of virtuosity.[20]

In section 'Five', Williams portrays segregated barracks life just outside Chicago, embarkation from Ford Ord, action in the South Pacific and, finally, the notorious waste of a black regiment in Tombolo, Italy. Blackman's memorialization of his World War II all-black unit again emphasizes race malpractice across America's military bases. This, however, the novel tells as stream of consciousness, a transcription quite as much of feeling as event.

The stopping-off points do imaginative good service on connected fronts. The mythic 'Joadie Grinder' recurs as the expression of every black

soldier's feared replacement lover man. A rendering of *The Signifyin'
Monkey* serves as black colloquial parable of survival in war and peace.
Blackman's top grade in the army's placement test loses its importance
for him as his girl betrays him and he becomes involved in a race fight at
the base. He undergoes both 'the smell of death' at Tombolo with its
needless sacrifice of black soldiers and outrage at statistics showing the
disproportion of black troops sent overseas. Even his despairing final bid
to fight in the Battle of the Bulge as volunteer, the only means of entering
racially mixed ranks, is denied on grounds of race, the Military's final,
discriminatory turn of the screw.

At a supposed staff conference he overhears a white officer say: "'*If we
don't integrate, the Europeans'll think we don't have anything but a black
army.*'" Set within the weave of black talk and commentary which,
echoing Whitman, Williams calls *drum-taps* and *cadence*, this presiding
paradox is held up for how it jars and rankles: an American Army hardly
more amenable to the interests of its own black ranks than of those they
have been sent to fight.

William Gardner Smith's *Last of the Conquerors* (1948) moves on to late
1940s Occupied Germany, black soldiery in the very homeland of
Aryanism, yet for its protagonist, Hayes Dawkins, a Germany still more
cross-racially open than his own Philadelphia.[21] This, as he moves with
sidekicks in his truck detachment ('the only colored company in Berlin')
to an eventual base in Bremburg, he finds born out in his love affair with
the German born Ilse, the relationship a taboo to white American troops
yet, in contrast, unforbidden by Ilse's family. If it dips occasionally into
flatness, a first effort after all, the novel nonetheless casts a shrewd eye
over the racial double standard as norm.

'Odd ... that here, in the land of hate, I should find this one all-important
phase of democracy' muses Hayes. The writ extends in a number of
directions. An accepted 'mixed' *German* child, Sonny, of black father and
white mother, and the discovery of a long-standing expatriate black
community, intrigues and beckons him. A white captain, sympathetic to
black needs, suddenly launches into virulent anti-Semitism. Given the much
expressed moral high resolve of the American war cause, officers and ranks
catch VD with telling regularity. These contradictions become design, the
novel's working shape.

Ilse, for her part, negotiates a sectored Germany to be with Hayes.
Hayes, however, has another kind of sector to negotiate to be with her,
that of the American racial dispensation brought from America to
Germany. The situation is compounded when he catches out a racist and
corrupt army officer and is finagled back to America ostensibly to pursue
his education under the GI Bill. His mind, dividedly, fills with images of
Southern lynchings and Northern black job layoffs, as against Ilse and
the post-racial Germany she embodies. Where race enters, for him, as for
the rest of his black company, peace has not ceased to be war.

☆   ☆   ☆

Richard Wright's *Native Son* (1940) was quick to become one of the presiding black texts of the 1940s: its brute, tenement Chicago of the Depression countered the hoped-for metropolitan Harlem of Alain Locke's 'New Negro' generation. Here was a black city of mind as much as body, not only of Bigger Thomas but of an altogether more inclusive language, memory, history, accusation; Wright deservedly won recognition. He could look to notable literary company, whether Zora Neale Hurston as self-chronicler in *Dust Tracks on a Road* (1942), James Baldwin as the passionate, rising essayist of the 1940s pieces contributed to *The Nation*, *Commentary* or *Partisan Review*, or the Ralph Ellison of mythy, allusive stories like 'King of the Bingo Game' (1944) and 'Flying Home' (1944). They, and others, help fill out, indeed create, a more inclusive sense of era.[22]

Chester Himes's first novels, *If He Hollers Let Him Go* (1945) and *Lonely Crusade* (1947), bear home the point as well as any.[23] Told against a backdrop of the 1940s California defence industry, shipbuilding in the one, aircraft in the other, both were considered 'black realism', hard-edged, urgent, recognizably actual in locale and timescale. Within the rape and run frame-up of the first, and the West Coast Unionism of its successor, however, they anything but won recognition for how Himes had explored a terrain of the black male sexual psyche as of the everyday workplace or street.

In this respect Himes's style works to immediate good purpose, cryptic, abbreviated, full of seriousness yet as often as not abruptly dark and funny. This same regime holds for all of the ensuing full length fiction: *Cast the First Stone* (1952), his claustrophobic, 'raceless' prison novel; *The Third Generation* (1954), a fictionalization of his troubled early family life in the South and prison sentence for jewel theft in Cleveland; *The Primitive* (1955), a novel of sexual and racial will fought through to murder during a near-hallucinatory Manhattan lost weekend; *Pinktoes* (1961), his amorous and inter-racial *jeu d'esprit* first issued by the Olympia Press; *Une Affaire de viol* (1963), involving an apparent sex murder, with a legal imbroglio to follow, but also a purposely cyphered story of expatriate black literary Paris; and *Plan B* (1993), his unsentimental, darkly conspiratorial, last rites to the Coffin Ed/Grave Digger Harlem detective fiction.[24]

Nor is this to overlook Himes's short story prowess as borne out in 1940s pieces like 'Marihuana and a Pistol' (1940), a violence and drugs episode told as haze-like dream and first published in *Esquire*; 'Cotton Gonna Kill Me Yet' (1944), a snappily pitched 'jive' story of hustle and lost love; or 'Mama's Missionary Money' (1949), with its rich eddies of black argot and comic blend of theft and religious signifying. Ishmael Reed dedicated his anthology of 'conjah' writing, *19 Necromancers from Now* (1970), to Himes as 'The Great Mojo Bojo', which refers, playfully, to a kingly maker of magic, an African trickster, and this again confirmed Himes as anything but casebook realist.[25]

In the case of Bob Jones in *If He Hollers Let Him Go* his life virtually personifies race as war and peace, a conflict lived feverishly in the feelings, nerves and body. In a number of quarters, and despite the laconicism and wit, Himes was criticised for writing with too much pathologic detail. But when Frantz Fanon cited *If He Hollers* in *Peau noire, masques blancs* (1952) as a pointer to how any black male, under racism, might indeed be driven to hit back at the icons of a white world, to violate sexually if need be, he did so in full recognition that this was overwhelmingly a text full of literary design.[26] Richard Wright, likewise, was shrewd enough to emphasize the carefully turned play of oppositions in the novel when he reviewed it for *PM* in 1945:

> He sees too clearly to be fooled by the symbolic guises in which Negro behavior tries to hide, and he traces the transformations by which sex is expressed in equations of race pride, murder in the language of personal redemption and love in terms of hate.[27]

The storyline, then, supplies no more than a frame: Bob Jones, black shipyard leaderman, already frayed by wartime racist hostility and taunt, as caught out, eventually, in the spurious rape charge of a peroxide blonde migrant, Madge Perkins ('She was pure white Texas. And I was black ... '). Beaten to near coma by her white male co-workers, hauled off by the police, he accepts a judge's summary and wholly cynical offer of the Army rather than prison. But the novel's true edge, its animation, derives from Himes's altogether more inward portrait of a man coping with his own unmanning.

To this end dreams, especially, proliferate, jolting him from 'absolute impotence' to euphoria. Three open the novel: of a wiry but unloved black terrier, of a police ruse to catch out a black murder suspect as 'coon', and of a black jobseeker jeered at mercilessly by two white workers for not having tools. In other dreams he is endlessly beaten by 'the president of the shipyard corporation dressed in the uniform of an Army general'; he imagines himself stampeded by swine and mistakenly shooting with a .45 revolver his girl Alice (whose light-skinned gentility, contrarily, lies behind her playing down race and urging him to college and the middle class) to the 'sympathetic smiles ... of millions of white women'; he watches a white boy laughingly knife a black boy to death; and, with 'the crazy exultation', and in the guise of a Western Union employee, he guns down a white shipyard worker who has made him the subject of racist taunt. Each dream acts as a displacement or shadow of his conscious life, a warring 'racial' sleep as much as a 'racial' wakefulness.

In this respect there is an overlap with experiences which might themselves be dream, whether going to the Lincoln Theater with Alice and watching 'a black audience clapping its hands for a blind white acrobat', or being recommended to read a liberal, caring Mrs. Roosevelt in *Negro Digest* even as his own life implodes, or being caught in a sexual 'death embrace' with the love-hate icon of Madge. Inner and outer man meet, too, when, recurringly, he has to struggle to wake from sleep to consciousness, or finds himself 'getting ready to die before I left the house', or confronting 'all that tight, crazy feeling of race as thick in the street as gas fumes'.

Under these conditions, for Bob, even commonplace reference, be it to the Joe Louis–Max Schmeling fight, the music of Art Tatum or King Cole, L.A.'s Central Avenue, or the Zoot Suit riots, takes on a kind of otherly bearing, a world to hand yet not. Pearl Harbor is said to have led to a racially underwritten 'crazy, wild-eyed unleashed hatred'. The shipyard suggests 'a littered madhouse', its heavy duty cranes 'one-legged, one-armed spiders'. 'Bile', 'electric shock', 'fever' and other motor responses well up in Bob, not least when, so unmanned, he is eventually charged under the rape statutes with brute mannishness.

Despite first hand experience of race lived, as it were, always as inwardly as not, he hears Herbie Frieberger of the Union explain it as merest footnote to Marxist laws of history and class. A restaurant 'filled with solid white America' gives him a note which reads '*We served you this time but we do not want your patronage in the future.*' Conscription ('G.I. Blues' as Peaches, one of the shipyard's women, calls it) promises more of the same, a war in the name of freedoms denied at home. Towards the close of *If He Hollers* Himes has one of the Atlas's black workers observe: 'As long as the Army is Jim Crowed a Negro who fights in it is fighting against himself.' Bob's own arbitrary, not to say abrupt, entry into the ranks could not underline the point more, a war of psyche, self-esteem and the American codes and counter-codes of black and white, to be carried into the wars of Europe and the Pacific.

Lonely Crusade, longer, fuller, pursues a more political canvas, but not without Lee Gordon as a man also pushed to the edge. 'Fear was the price for living' the novel observes at the outset. When, after a run of unemployment, he becomes a union organizer, his elation and the apprehension to which it gives way, again reverse into a fear which in turn then feeds on itself:

> when he boarded the streetcar crowded with white Southern warworkers that war spring of 1943, being a Negro imposed a sense of handicap that Lee Gordon could not overcome. He lost his brief happiness in the sea of white faces ... he had once again crossed into the competitive white world where he would be subjected to every abuse concocted by the white mind to harass and intimidate Negroes ... And be afraid, and hate his fear, and hate himself for feeling it ... The fear in him was something a dog could smell ... he could see the hostile faces of the white workers, their hot, hating stares; he could feel their antagonisms hard as a

physical blow; hear their vile asides and abusive epithets with a reality
that cut like a knife.

This concourse of 'handicap' and 'brief happiness', 'fear' and 'hate', he
initially allows to become sexual aggression towards his wife Ruth. But
it also invades Lee's whole experience of the wartime 1940s.

At Comstock he is set to decipher the true face from the false: Louis Foster
as capitalist boss, Luther McGregor as black Communist Party stooge and
psychopath, Jackie as alluring white decoy, and Joe Ptak, Marvin Todd
and Smitty as stalwarts of the Union. At each Hollywood venue he
struggles to separate substance from shadow, especially when Rosie,
Jewish-Marxist theoretician in the mould of Wright's Mr. Max, argues a
materialist view of race. He meets, contrastingly, both a black political
confidence man like Bart and a black would-be revenge killer like McKinley.
Each cross-racial marriage beguiles yet confuses him. Which is show,
fashion, which not? Then there is Los Angeles itself, mundanely a network
of freeways and neighbourhoods with Central Avenue as its main artery,
yet also, phantasmagorically, a 'bloated, hysterical, frantic, rushing city'.

Caught out one way, then another, Lee opts, finally, for the flag of
Unionism. Yet the novel leaves little doubt of each continuing war within
the larger war against Germany and Japan. White Southern workers
resent a Union urging them to transfer their hate from blacks to the white
rich. Black workers find themselves sold out by a purportedly raceless
Communist Party leadership and by its black as much as white
apparatchiks. Comstock's owner-management unhesitatingly plays each
against the other, capitalist divide and rule against an already divided
workforce. In a review full of admiration for the panorama of viewpoint
at work, Ishmael Reed once shrewdly observed that, in *Lonely Crusade*,
'Himes is on no one's team'.[28]

The novel has been said to risk *longueurs*, especially Himes's
pronouncements on communism and capitalism, the Party and the
Union, and the on-off alliances between Jews and blacks (even though
his views on black anti-Semitism and Jewish racism have a discomforting
sharpness).[29] However, this overlooks his continuing turns of speed with
dialogue, voice, wit and ability to take more than one shot across the bow
at any one time. Most of all, it fails to recognize how *Lonely Crusade*
extends and energizes the very genre of war fiction: Lee Gordon's own
parlous interior warring as intimately, phobically, of a kind with the
larger 'racial hell' (Himes's term in *The Quality of Hurt*) within America's
own World War II industries.

A related pathway into the black 1940s is to be found in the remembering
of an immediate past and, from a 1990s perspective, in how the 1940s
themselves become remembrance. In the former respect William Attaway

as memoirist of the Great Migration in *Blood on the Forge* (1941) and Owen Dodson as the child-biography novelist of *Boy at the Window* (written in the 1940s, published in 1951) and the considerable poet of *Powerful Long Ladder* (1946) supply bearings.[30] In Walter Mosley's *Devil in a Blue Dress* (1990), the first of his Easy Rawlins crime series, with its mainly black and so other than the 1940s of Raymond Chandler's mainly white Los Angeles (be it of the monied or of the city's low life), one can look to a retrospect.[31]

Blood on the Forge understandably won immediate favour with an American Left yet further radicalized by both the 1929 Crash and the Depression. Its portrait of black Southern migrancy, the Great Migration, from sharecropper Kentucky to the Pennsylvania steel mills of the Monongahela Valley in the first decades of the twentieth century, seemed the very instance of ideological history. The three Moss brothers, the stentorian Big Mat, gold-toothed Chinatown and guitar-playing Melody, whose interlinked lives it tells, surely confirmed class over race as the necessary forward path in American politics.

In fact the novel draws as much upon other seams, a five-act pageant whose black folk stylings transform the story itself into the 'hungry blues' played by Melody at the outset. An opening scene suggests a despoiled pastoral – topsoil blown away, the miscarriages of Mat's woman Hattie, a cheat over mules by the white Kentucky 'bossman' – glossed by Mat in the words 'Jest as well I was a nigger. Got more misery than a white man could stand.' The 'sealed boxcar', 'a solid thing of darkness', which takes them North, calls up the Middle Passage, a new inland slave ship. The mills they work in, steel foundries, give off a Blakean satanic resonance, as predatory as the cancer which has invaded the black girl they first meet, or as Anna, the Mexican girl-whore who Mat takes as a lover.

Each subsequent event, the vicious dog fights, the drinking, the explosion which blinds Chinatown, Melody's self-inflicted wound to his playing-hand, the strike, and Mat's destructive final enlistment against the Union in the name of the owners, the novel glosses in its own ongoing and intimate black Southern idiom. Each of the brothers becomes actor and chorus. In this sense, and however much a period 'history' of black migration North and the heat and fire of industrial mill life, *Blood on the Forge* can equally be thought a vernacular (and highly original) narrative blues or ballad.

Boy at the Window turns upon 'growing up black', the coming of age of Coin Foreman in a 1920s mixed Brooklyn neighbourhood, with a coda set in Washington D.C. after he is taken on by his bibulous, sightless and itinerant Uncle Troy. For the most part it manages lyricism without sentimentality, a linking world of remembered siblings, religiosity, school, the lacerating death of Coin's mother, a father's hard-fought but failing efforts to keep the family above subsistence, and an immigrant melee of voices (Irish, Italian and Jewish as well as black).

Coin's epiphany lies in his unfathoming of the word 'nigger', a human *reductio* all his surrounding life contests, whether his own inner imaginings, school and street play, his growing dissent at bible-driven millennialism, the bar and show-time crowd he glimpses in D.C., and, finally, the dream he harbours of a writerly, itinerary life alongside Ferris, the worldly, Huck-like friend he meets from Kentucky. In its best moments the portraiture suggests the Joyce of *Dubliners*, a religion-laden black childhood yet toughly secular in its revelations of gain and loss. In the same sweep Coin's story implies the very silhouette of 1940s adulthood, the boy's intimate fathering of the man.

That eventual 1940s, for Afro-America always a 'war' fought on multiple fronts, has its voice in Dodson's *Powerful Long Ladder*, five verse sequences of which few read more poignantly than 'Black Mother Praying'. Intoned as though a spiritual, and duly buttressed with references to Babylon, Zion and Jesus as sacrificed son, it moves from the mother's absent soldier offspring ('Last month, Lord, I bid my last boy away to fight') to 'war' at home as much as abroad ('they's draggin us outa cars/in Texas and California, in Newark, Detroit'). The effect is one of a churchwoman's spiritual, black youth 'fightin in lands as far as the wind can go' yet also 'in the city streets and on country roads'. Whether 'sisters stitching airplane canvas' or 'a black boy lyin with his arms huggin the pavement in pain', American war and peace again prove contradictory terms: the impact localized in the mother's 'I'm gonna scream before I hope'.

Half a century on, and in the stirring debut of *Devil in a Blue Dress*, Walter Mosley situates his gumshoe, Easy (for Ezekiel) Rawlins – raised in Houston, a 28 year old war veteran recently fired from Champion Aircraft – in the summer-time Los Angeles of 1948. When Easy meets the deathly DeWitt Albright, Texan lawyer turned psychopathic fixer with the eyes of the 'undead', white-suited with white cadillac to match, it puts in train a cross-plot of searches for the blue dressed Daphne Monet and a $30,000 treasure trove.

This is vintage, well-paced mystery, a full and inventive recipe of false trails, sleaze, murder and sex. Each *film noir* surface works to deceive, above all Daphne Monet herself in her role as French accented white New Orleans belle. Double dealers, black and white, make appropriately shadow-laden, predatory entrances and exits: the ex-bruiser barman Joppy, or Easy's zoot suiter Houston sidekick Mouse, or the liquor black marketeer 'Knifehand' Frank Green, or the paedophile politico Matthew Teran, or the mean-spirited white cops Miller and Mason ('the police have white slavery on the brain when it comes to colored men and white women'). Not since Himes has black detective fiction had a keener human cast or showing.

Mosley's triumph, however, lies equally in his attentive recreation of place and time. Los Angeles means Watts, Compton, Central Avenue ('a giant black alley and I felt like a small rat, hugging the corners and looking out for cats'), 103rd Street, 89th Place, bars which have evolved out of an earlier time's speakeasies, a 'Mexican' East L.A. remembered as once also Jewish, together with an outlying Japanese American farm world. Santa Monica and Malibu carry the insignia of white, monied California, a suburbia, however, always for Easy as inlaid with racial threat and danger as affluence.

The 1940s are, throughout, deftly signalled: the Billie Holiday and jazz and hornmen references; Easy's own immediate war memories (typically, 'I had spent five years with white men, and women, from Africa to Italy, through Paris, and into the fatherland itself' and 'I volunteered for the invasion of Normandy and then I signed on with Patton at the Battle of the Bulge'); and, not least, the characteristic bars, drink, smokes, music and restaurants ('Chow's Chow was a kind of Chinese diner that was common back in L.A. in the forties and fifties'). Mosley keeps this sense of black period, and of its white and California-ethnic counterpart, firmly in view, the first of his Easy Rawlins novels made over into yet another American time of peace as war.

☆   ☆   ☆

If black poetry in the 1940s supplies a matching register (its key anthology has to be *The Negro Caravan* (1941)),[32] Robert Hayden's 'Middle Passage', initially published in *Phylon* in 1945 and, after several revisions, given final form in *A Ballad of Remembrance* (1962), holds a special place.[33] The 'voyage through death' of the Atlantic slave ships ('shuttles in the rocking loom of history'), and the 'life' of the *Amistad* rebellion as led by Cinquez at sea and then 'upon these shores', Hayden encloses in a mosaic, almost Poundian, design. To a later 1960s generation, especially at the Black Writers' Conference at Fisk in 1966, this little endeared him – allegedly, his poetry was too white-imagist or 'uncommitted'; his revival, deservedly, has come again.

Each of his poem's congregated voices of 'traders' and 'deponents', the memories ('a charnel stench, effluvium of living death'), and even the underpinning mysticism (he writes as a Baha'i), brilliantly suggests enslavement's figural and continuing shadow, an American racial armistice still to be attained.

Melvin Tolson's *Rendezvous with America* (1944), *Libretto for the Republic of Liberia* (1953) and *Harlem Gallery* (1965) pitch for an even more conscious modernism.[34] Whether T.S. Eliot, or Harlem Renaissance luminaries like Cullen and Toomer on whom he once did graduate work at Columbia, the footfalls are deliberate. A 'New Negro poetry for the New Negro' would be his formulation in 1948. Only an aesthetic as multiple in voice as 'The Waste Land', Tolson argued, could offer a right and complete counter-tongue to misrepresentation and even erasure. 'Dark Symphony', the centrepiece of *Rendezvous with America*, makes the point uncompromisingly:

The New Negro
Breaks the icons of his detractors,
Wipes out the conspiracy of silence,
Speaks to *his* America ...

Margaret Walker's *For My People* (1942) signals another kind of accent, that of matrilineage both as the sign of black women's enduring and as the issue of a challenge. A poem like 'Lineage' ponders disjuncture yet a next generation of womanly continuity and word:

My grandmothers are full of memories
Smelling of soap and onions and wet clay
With veins rolling roughly over quick hands
They have many clean words to say.
My grandmothers were strong.
Why am I not as they?[35]

It had taken war service, paradoxically, to give many white and black Americans their first 'equal' close encounters, a major spur to the emerging novel of 'race relations'. George Wylie Henderson's *Jule* (1946) can be thought typical, however slight a work when compared, say, with an earlier *Bildungsroman* of black family (and midwestern) upbringing like Langston Hughes's *Not Without Laughter* (1930).[36] But it does explore options beyond any all-one or all-another racial binary.

It opens as Southern pastoral, a black child's intimate memory of corn pone, sorghum, salted possum, roasted sweet potato, hogs skilfully butchered and smoked. But just as a series of black vignettes play into the portrait of Jule's boyhood – the visit of his cantankerous Aunt Kate, the doings of the diminutive but tough fieldworker 'Dr. Mootry', the kindnesses of the black landowners Alex and Caroline, the relationship with Jule's first and eventually last love Bertha Mae – so, too, and against Dixie writ, does his relationship with a white boyhood hunting friend, Rollo.

A similar racial-ethnic mix of regime holds for Jule's life in the North, to which he flees after a fight over Bertha Mae with the white landowner Boykin Keye. 'You're in Harlem now' the club owner, Jake Simmons, tells him. Yet as he progresses from dishwasher to headwaiter to printer with his own union card won in spite of the racial line, he again manages a middle ground. He has the black worlds of Sugar Hill and Harlem ('always their laughter rose in thick swells, like homemade thunder'), but also white friendships in Long Island. Even a blonde girl's exoticized perspective on black clubland ('This is fun! This is Harlem!') does not daunt him. His sexual progress, from Maisie to the older, married Anne, who, unbeknown to him, carries his child, to the cheating Lou Davies, adds its own pace and variety of focus. Whatever the dips of style or pace *Jule* portrays an America of racial pluses and minuses.[37]

William Demby's *Beetlecreek* (1950) turns upon an altogether darker note, one of displacement, the deepening self-distance of a boy caught out by racial closure.[38] 'Everything he had done since he arrived in Beetlecreek had the feeling of being an episode in a dream.' So the novel describes Johnny Johnson, adolescent son of a dying, consumptive mother in Pittsburgh, sent to his aunt and uncle, David and Mary Diggs, in their race-divided West Virginia township.

The boy's encounter with Bill Trapp, former carnival performer, magus of sorts, loner, amounts to a bold use of *volte face* on Demby's part: a reversal of Twain's Huck and Jim in which black boy ('Pittsburgh Kid' to the town's black boy gang) pairs with, and then betrays, a kindly older white man. That, together with David Biggs's dead marriage, suffocation and false dream of love with Edith Johnson, tarnished street girl back for her adoptive mother's funeral, closes the circle.

Entrapment, coffin, stasis – each image works to shared effect. The point is emphasized in David Biggs's reaction to a picnic proposed by Trapp to mark his breaking free of past isolation:

There was no way to explain to the old man how complicated this story was, how Negro life was a fishnet, a mosquito net, lace, wrapped round and round, each little thread a pain ... too complicated.

Johnny's coming of age takes its own place as a thread within this weave or fishnet. His mother's haemorrhaging becomes fact yet also fantasy for him, a prophetic consumption. The gang leader's act of throwing a baby pigeon against a wall startles and then haunts him, a mean, brute denial of beginning life. The Biggs's earlier stillborn child positions another death against his own will to break free and survive. His aunt's relish of the church festival he perceives as parodic, spiritual trifle over substance.

It is, however, the false rumour of child molestation against Bill Trapp, and the township's temporizing black–white agreement to let things stand, which further perpetuates the deathly *status quo*. The final burning of Trapp's house, the outcome of Johnny's required gang initiation, dramatically inverts a momentary cross-racial garden into burnt out wasteland. If *Beetlecreek* has sometimes been thought too unrelenting, this, and Demby's related imagery in the novel, confirms the verve behind his envisioning of race division as endgame.

Ann Petry's *The Narrows* (1953), almost Jamesian in size and variety of cast, and full of ancillary incident, turns on one of the oldest racial staples: the supposed rape by a black man of a white woman.[39] Yet the events which join Link (for Lincoln) Williams with Camilo Williams (for Camilla Sheffield), respectively Dartmouth College educated, Phi Beta Kappa and

Navy veteran, and genteel Treadway munitions heiress and fashion reporter, belong anywhere but to Dixie melodrama.

Theirs becomes a love turned sour, begun by accident one midnight in the Monmouth fog, continued in a New York of white Manhattan and black Harlem, and brought to bitterest recrimination as Link discovers Camilla's 'secret' married and monied identity. Where Link sees himself as 'bought and sold', latterday silver-collar boy, blackamoor or stud, Camilla, in her own hurt, and as the white Treadway dynasty closes ranks, falls back on the ritual, and unfounded, charge of rape. The one story contains others, a continuing gyre of bias and taboo as Link recognizes. 'Objective about race?', he thinks, 'Hell, no. Nobody was. Not in the USA.' Petry's achievement is to make Monmouth a source of both present and serial history as 'told' from 1951–52: slavery, Salem and the Caribbean magic of Tituba, Abolition, interwar New England, the 1940s race riots, World War II and, finally, Korea.

The novel's different lives give embodiment to this trajectory. The genteel and churchgoing Abbie Crunch ('Miss Abbie'), who adopted Link, counters Bill Hodd, owner of The Last Chance Saloon, who teaches Link to refuse black gentility. Malcolm Prowther, fastidious black butler to the white Treadways, devotes himself to a wife whose sexy, blues-like Big Mama fecklessness will always betray him. Weak Knees, Hodd's kindly short-order cook, lives in a world as haunted as real (his tag of 'Stay away Eddie' is born of the belief that he had killed a one-time friend). Frances K. Johnson, black mortician, even so gives her life and friendship to Abbie. Others live at once in both Link's world, and yet below it, like the legless, rodent-like Cat Jimmie, the 'writing man' Cesar with his obsessional sidewalk bible warnings, or the religious quack the Rev. Dr. H.H. Franklin Longworth. None, in turn, escapes the unsentimental recording eye, the lens, of the photographer Jubine.

Dumble Street, for its part, serves as centre and symbol:

> It was now ... a street so famous, or so infamous, that the people who live in Monmouth rarely ever referred to it, or the streets near it, by name; it had become an area, a section, known variously as The Narrows, Eye of The Needle, The Bottom, Little Harlem, Dark Town, Niggertown – because Negroes had replaced those earlier immigrants, the Irish, the Italians and the Poles.

Its accoutrements serve a dual purpose, especially the giant maple-tree known as 'The Hangman', named by a remembering slave escapee, and the presage of Link's eventual destiny as he is accused and then summarily shot dead by Camilla's philandering husband and his Air Corp accomplices. The river works to supporting effect, an actual run of water yet the ongoing racial time and tide of the township, an eventual burial pool for Link yet a moonlit winter photograph for Jubine. The fog which opens the novel implies a larger befoggedness, the inability to see beyond racial stereotype or myth.

At the close of the novel Peter Bullock, the combustible, yet finally craven, editor of *The Monmouth Chronicle* (he sells out to Camilla's mother Mrs. Treadway), speculates on what he terms 'truthlie, lietruth'. The hybrid phrasing points exactly to Link's life, variously the gifted black child whose white schoolmates once shouted 'lookitthecoon', the adopted child pulled conflictingly between Abbie and Bill who represent two kinds of black class manners, the would-be college historian of slavery who continues to write during service in a segregated Navy, and the black lover transposed into black rapist. For it is these contrary markings of race as 'truthlie' and 'lietruth' which underwrite, and are then written into, the story Ann Petry most seeks to tell in *The Narrows*.

When Langston Hughes entered the 1940s with *Shakespeare in Harlem* (1942), his status as admired veteran of the 'New Negro' years did not allay a number of misgivings.[40] How could he have opted for ballads given the hurt of the Depression or the continuing shadow of Jim Crow both civilian and military? Nor did his Introduction help:

A book of light verse. Afro-Americana in the blues mood. Poems syncopated and variegated in the colors of Harlem, Beale Street, West Dallas, and Chicago's South Side. Blues, ballads, and reels to be read aloud, crooned, shouted, recited and sung. Some with gestures, some not – as you like. None with a far-away voice.

For those who demanded sterner black fare Hughes had taken a downward turn into sentimentality, a charge that continued despite the antisegregation tenor of the verse pamphlet he published a year later – *Jim Crow's Last Stand* (1943).[41]

Shakespeare in Harlem, however, offers a wholly richer achievement than this suggests, a graph of intimate, everyday, but always highly various black feeling. The form can be an ironic self-musing like 'Daybreak':

> You know I believe I'll change my name,
> Change my color, change my ways,
> And be a white man the rest of my days ...

It can become a two-liner like 'Little Lyric':

> I wish the rent
> Was heaven sent.

'Southern Mammy Sings', one of a grouping of 'mammy songs', can issue its own version of war and peace as it contrasts 'The nations they is fightin'' with

> Last week they lynched a colored boy.
> They hung him to a tree.
> That colored boy ain't said a thing
> But we all should be free.

A poem like 'Ku Klux' offers the tyranny of a robed clansman over his black victim:

> 'Nigger,
> Look me in the face –
> And tell me you believe in
> The great white race'.

'Death in Harlem' gives new idiom to the Frankie and Johnny fable, full of high-energy, exuberant riffs and cameos:

> Arabella Johnson and the Texas Kid
> Went bustin into Dixie's about one a.m.
> The night was young.

'Evenin' Air Blues', contrastingly, works to a wry, self-sorry note:

> if you was to ask me
> How de blues they come to be,
> Says if you was to ask me
> How de blues they come to be –
> You wouldn't need to ask me:
> Just look at me and see!

These, and each of the collection's other love snippets, 'out-of-work poems', quarrels, partings, brags and regrets make for a galleried yet diverse whole. Each carries a sense of location and period, whether Lenox Avenue or the Harlem River, Count Basie or the WPA. But the true unifying factor lies in Hughes's command of voice, from the spry loverman ('Letter') to the wearied, all-hours worker in 'Mississippi Levee', and from a poet-onlooker's admiration for the sheer colour variety of Sugar Hill women ('Harlem's Sweeties') to the voice of the street girl ('Midnight Chippie's Lament').

Rarely, however, does he manage better than in the question-form child register of 'Merry-Go-Round' with its challenge to not only the mean-spiritedness but the farce of Jim Crow:

Where is the Jim Crow section
On this merry-go-round,
Mister, cause I want to ride?
Down South where I come from
White and colored
Can't sit side by side.
Down South on the train
There's a Jim Crow car.
On the bus we're put on the back –
But there ain't no back
To a merry-go-round!
Where's the horse
For a kid that's black?

Hughes's short stories of the 1940s invite similar recognition. Each carries a savvy, and with it a sting, in excess of all the apparent lightness of touch. The effect is one of turn-about, an ironic challenge to expectation. In 'Breakfast in Virginia' (1944), typically, an older white passenger aboard the Florida to Washington Express, his own son an overseas soldier in North Africa, offers breakfast to two black corporals. But he, like them, is caught out by the refusal to serve black servicemen as the pullman journeys through a segregated state like Virginia. Hughes tells the episode as the perfect silhouette of the larger war-time double standard.

In 'Who's Passing for Who?' (1945), set in Harlem as 'literary bohemia', Hughes targets the impersonations of identity according to the darks and lights of skin colour. The story works as a hall of mirrors, 'black' and 'white' as a kind of spoof race-semiotics. The touch, again, may be light, easeful, but it hits the target unerringly; for Hughes understood the racial contraflows of the age.[42]

However the canon of African American poetry is to be construed, from Phillis Wheatley to Rita Dove, Paul Dunbar to Michael Harper, there can be no diminishing, or sidelining, the contribution of Gwendolyn Brooks. She emerged in the 1940s with *A Street in Bronzeville* (1945), written out of, and about, 'Bronzeville', or black Chicago, whose wars, as ever, are as much being fought at home as abroad.[43] To this end she brings the stamp of her own language and measure, whether off-rime and elliptical in the manner of early T.S. Eliot and the English Metaphysical poets or imagist, recalling Countee Cullen or Jean Toomer. Equally, she shares with Langston Hughes a facility for blues and talk-poems. Whichever the vein, however, her poetry is full of slant, life caught at an unsettling angle.

Annie Allen (1949), its central verse-sequence 'The Anniad', gives a typical linguistic density to the life of a quotidian brown-skinned girl whose dreams of romance die in the tenement South Side:

> Harried sods dilate, divide,
> Suck her marrowfully inside.

Maud Martha (1953), Brooks's only novel, tells a black Chicago life from girlhood to motherhood and domestic service as linking vignettes of inner feeling and dream. *The Bean Eaters* (1960) strikes a memorial and again Eliot-like note, especially in 'In Honor of David Anderson Brooks, My Father':

> A dryness is upon the house
> My father loved and tended.

In the Mecca (1968) delineates Chicago as both white and black multiverse, whether 'The Chicago Picasso', with its 'Art hurts, Art urges voyages' or 'The Blackstone Rangers', with its:

> There they are.
> Thirty at the corner.
> Black, raw, ready.
> Sores in the city
> that do not want to heal.

In *Report from Part 1: An Autobiography* (1972), written in the light of her Black Nationalist 'awakening' and Black Arts friendships with Don Lee/Haki Madhubuti and Jones/Baraka, she speaks wryly (and as imagistically as ever) of 'a surprised queenhood in the new black sun'. And *Primer for Black* (1980), one in a round of post-1960s later work, suggests, exhortingly:

> Blackness
> is a title,
> is a preoccupation,
> is a commitment Blacks
> are to comprehend –
> and in which you are
> to perceive your glory.[44]

Each of these has a beginning in *A Street in Bronzeville*, a gallery of verse portraiture inspired by black Chicago. In 'the old-marrieds' (Brooks often favours lowercase titles) long-time intimacy finds a perfect measure in a line like 'But in the crowding darkness not a word did they say'. In 'the mother', with its opening line of 'abortions will not let you forget', she imagines a woman haunted by the accusing spirits of lost, if at the time unaffordable, progeny as 'voices in the wind'. In 'when Mrs. Martin's Booker T.' she writes a species of gossip poetry, a Bronzeville neighbour's remembrance of the mortified Mrs. Martin whose son 'ruined Rosa Brown' and whose only wish was for him to

> take that gal
> And get her decently wed.

In 'the date' the note is lighter, a half-comic vignette of resentment and sexual impatience as a housemaid with 'somethin' interestin'' on my mind' is kept working late by her employer. 'The Sundays of Satin-Legs Smith', one of the volume's baroquely fine-wrought poems, portrays a zoot-suited Romeo whose dandyism masks an irredeemable emptiness of spirit. By contrast 'Queen of the Blues', reflexively a blues in itself, gives voice to the shake-dancing 'Mame' who seeks her own kind of dignity even as she plays out cheapest burlesque.

Two poems offer an especially apt finale to the black 1940s as war and peace. 'Negro Hero', spoken in the first person of a black Army veteran, remembers war's physical, acoustic horror:

> my first swallow of the liquor of battle bleeding
> black air dying and demon noise
> made me wild.

The poem does not flatter a peace in which 'white gowned democracy' honours the speaker even as it denies him:

> it was hardly The Enemy
> my fight was against
> but them.

A run of ensuing questions takes up this double-seam, the undead racial shadow in the face of war's killing:

> am I good enough to die for them, is my blood bright enough to be spilled,
> Was my constant back-question – are they clear
> On this? Or do I intrude even now?
> Am I clean enough to kill for them, do they wish me to kill
> For them or is my place while death licks his lips and strides to them
> In the galley still?

'Gay Chaps at the Bar', *A Street in Bronzeville*'s twelve-sonnet sequence, resorts to an even more abridged irony. The seventh sonnet, 'the white troops had their orders but the Negroes looked like men', is written in what Brooks herself calls 'off-rhyme', and its parodying of the formal order of the sonnet catches at, and mimics, the time's own break-down into war. It offers a further cryptic comment on the relative trivia of race as difference in the face of war's own indifference:

> They had supposed their formula was fixed.
> They had obeyed instructions to devise
> A type of cold, a type of hooded gaze.
> But when the Negroes came they were perplexed.
> These Negroes looked like men. Besides, it taxed
> Time and the temper to remember those
> Congenital iniquities that cause
> Disfavor of the darkness. Such as boxed
> Their feelings properly, complete to tags –
> A box for dark men and a box for Other –
> Would often find the contents had been scrambled.
> Or even switched. Who really gave two figs?
> Neither the earth nor heaven ever trembled.
> And there was nothing startling in the weather.

Encoffined, interchangeable, what ultimate meaning attaches to the colour of one or another dead soldier? Brooks's sonnet offers her own synoptic, challenging version of life over death, peace over war, a poet's recognition from out of the black 1940s – out of all America's 1940s – of necessary priorities.

Black Beats: The Signifying Poetry of LeRoi Jones/Imamu Amiri Baraka, Ted Joans and Bob Kaufman

Already well known and virtually revered in ultrahip literary circles, Roi had become by then a Greenwich Village luminary. Along with New York's Ted Joans and San Francisco's Bob Kaufman, he was among a handful of mid-century African American poets whose early reputations are identified with the Beat Generation. We're talking here of course about a literary movement shaped, loosely speaking, by Whitmanesque confessionalism, the modernist iconoclasm of Ezra Pound, T.S. Eliot and William Carlos Williams, as well as by abstract expressionist painting, Eastern mysticism, drug culture, and jazz.

> Al Young, 'Amiri Baraka (LeRoi Jones)', in J.J. Phillips, Ishmael Reed, Gundars Strads and Shawn Wong (eds), *The Before Columbus Foundation Poetry Anthology* (1992)[1]

Williams was a common denominator because he wanted American Speech, a mixed foot, a variable measure. He knew American life had out-distanced the English rhythms and their formal meters. The language of this multi-national land, of mixed ancestry, where war dances and salsa combine with Country and Western, all framed by African rhythm-and-blues confessional.

> *The Autobiography of LeRoi Jones/Amiri Baraka* (1984)[2]

I cannot deny that I am Ted Joans Afro American negro colored spade spook mau mau soul-brother coon jig darkie, etc.

> Ted Joans, *Tape Recording at the Five Spot* (1960)[3]

Let us blow African jazz in Alabama jungles and wail savage lovesongs
of unchained fire.

Bob Kaufman, 'Jazz *Te Deum* for Inhaling at Mexican Bonfires',
Solitudes Crowded with Loneliness (1965)[4]

Allen Ginsberg's 'Howl' (1956), the Grand Anthem of Beat poetry, has
'the best minds of my generation ... dragging themselves through the negro
streets at dawn'. In *On the Road* (1957) Jack Kerouac invokes Harlem as
quintessential 'Jazz America' while his narrator in *The Subterraneans*
(1958) recalls 'wishing I were a Negro' when in Denver's 'colored section'.
In 'The Philosophy of the Beat Generation', a key manifesto first published
in *Esquire* in 1958, John Clellon Holmes eulogizes Charlie Parker, Bird,
as black godfather to the movement. Gregory Corso, for his part, puts him
alongside Miles Davis in 'For Miles' (*Gasoline*, 1958), recalling a set

> when you & bird
> wailed five in the morning some wondrous
> yet unimaginable score.

Norman Mailer, whose 'The White Negro' (1957) served as apologia
for Beat and hipster alike, found himself arguing that 'the Negro's equality
would tear a profound shift into the psychology, the sexuality, and the
moral imagination of every White alive'. Could it ever be doubted that in
virtually all white-written Beat poetry and fiction, or associated manifestos,
Afro-America supplied a touchstone, a necessary black vein of reference
and inspiration?[5]

Yet black Beat writers themselves might well be thought to have gone
missing in action. Only LeRoi Jones, still to metamorphose into Imamu
Amiri Baraka, was reported in dispatches. That, however, had as much
to do with his Greenwich Village sojourn – and to an extent the small
magazine publication of his Projective early verse – as with any fuller
recognition of the life begun in Newark, New Jersey, continued in the Air
Force as gunner and weatherman, and given an ambiguous education
in the ways of the black middle class at Howard University. Rather, he
seemed a literary one-off caught in the shadow of an already senior Beat
pantheon of Kerouac, Ginsberg, Burroughs, Corso, Ferlinghetti, Clellon
Holmes, Di Prima and the rest.

But Jones/Baraka, in fact, did have company: Ted Joans, self-styled
surrealist troubadour; Bob Kaufman, 'Abomunist', born into a large New
Orleans black Jewish family (a lineage acknowledged in his 'Bagel Shop
Jazz'), seaman, Zen practitioner yet San Francisco rowdie, and above all
jazz and performance poet; A.B. Spellman, the poet of *The Beautiful Days*
(1965) and the jazz historian of *Four Lives in the Bebop Business* (1966);
and Archie Shepp, verse-writing jazzman.[6] Yet despite all of these, and

whatever its varied borrowings from black culture, the Beat phenomenon rarely seemed to speak other than from, or to, white America.

Jones hardly failed to acknowledge, at the time or later, this oversight towards his black fellow-writers. Thinking back on his founder and co-editor role in the journals *Yugen* (1958–62) and *The Floating Bear* (1961–63), which published not only Beats but Black Mountaineers like Charles Olson and Robert Creeley, and New York School virtuosi like Frank O'Hara and Kenneth Koch, he recalled in his *Autobiography*:

> I was 'open' to all schools within the circle of white poets of all faiths and flags. But what had happened to the blacks? What had happened to me? How is it that only the one colored guy?[7]

The same held not only for *Yugen* but for the host of other magazines which printed his early work, whether *Kulchur*, *Penny Poems*, *Locus-Solus*, *Nomad/New York*, *Fuck You: A Magazine of the Arts*, *Naked Ear*, *Quicksilver*, *Combustion* or *Red Clay Reader*.[8] It was no doubt further symptomatic, or at least some continuance of the assumed *status quo*, that he made himself the only black contributor to his own anthology of 'popular modernism', *The Moderns* (1963).[9]

This 'white social focus', as he came to term it – which also included his marriage in 1958 to Hettie Cohen, white, Jewish, his editorial collaborator on *Yugen*, and recently the affecting, unrecriminatory memoirist of *How I Became Hettie Jones* (1990) – would bring on a major turnabout in both his life and art.[10] The process notably gained impetus from his transforming visit to Cuba out of which, and against America's usual Cold War stance, he found himself inveighing in 'Cuba Libre': 'the Cubans, and the other *new* peoples (in Asia, Africa, South America) don't need us, and we had better stay out of their way'.[11] Then, as Watts exploded in 1962, Harlem, Chicago and Bedford-Stuyvesant in 1964 (and all the cities in their wake), and as Dixie racism led to the Birmingham school-bombing in 1963 and newly emboldened Klan and White Citizens Councils activity (the latter first begun in Mississippi in 1954), so Jones/Baraka himself increasingly took to black nationalism.

His poem 'BLACK DADA NIHILISMUS' bore the mark of this new Africanism, a millennial black resolve and threat:

> may a lost god damballah, rest or save us
> against the murders we intend
> against his lost white children
> black dada nihilismus.[12]

Dutchman (1964), his celebrated one act play, would further explore the myth of white and black America locked in unending subterranean contest.[13] This transformation had been much foreshadowed in his voluminous essay work, whether *Blues People: Negro Music in White America* (1963) and *Black Music* (1967), which paid homage to Afro-America's unique jazz and blues, or *Home: Social Essays*, his wide-ranging, activist expressions of social and ideological critique.[14]

His personal life took its own symbolic turn when he moved from Greenwich Village to Harlem, breaking not only with white bohemia but with Hettie Jones (née Cohen) and their daughters. Suddenly he became a black figure of controversy. The media typecast him as a voice of black terrorism, race hatred, the politics of accusation and hate. By 1965 the proof seemed conclusive: the FBI were called in to investigate his Harlem theatre work and its funding through the HARYOU-ACT (Harlem Youth Act), arrested him and, among other things, accused him of building a gun arsenal. The Black Arts Movement was deemed to be cause for alarm, his own leadership a danger.

Ginsberg, Kerouac and their fellow Beats may well have aroused shock by their language, their sexual and other mores, for a Middle America which twice had voted Eisenhower into office (in 1952 and 1956) and had become gridlocked in consumerism and Cold War ideology. But even they did not anticipate the sheer headiness and impact of Black Power. Not without cause, Robert Lowell, in his WASP confessional poem, 'Memories of West Street Lepke', called the 1950s 'tranquillized',[15] and J.D. Salinger, in *The Catcher in the Rye* (1951), supplied Holden Caulfield's 'phony' as the *mot clef* for generational ennui.[16]

Afro-America had not lacked markers. Baldwin, Ellison, Brooks, Hayden, Hansberry and a young LeRoi Jones himself all counted. But the kind of politics and affiliation which caused Jones to Africanize (and Islamize) his name to Baraka, become a founder of the Black Arts Movement, take up the cause of Black Power first through community activism (initially in Harlem, then Newark) and, from 1974 onwards, through Third World Marxism, had yet to be fully embarked upon. Black, at this stage, conveyed more a style of consciousness, a source of being cool. There was a while to go before a piece like Ted Joans's 'TWO POEMS' could assume widespread assent when it spoke of:

> those TWO
> beautiful words BLACKPOWER.

All three poets, rather, typically took up the Beat interest in Zen and Eastern transcendental spirituality – though linking it to blues and to Africa as a prime source of reference. Similarly, if their poetry could be sexually celebratory and playful, in the style of Ginsberg, it could also broach the racial taboos of sex, a Beat articulation (long continued in Joans and Kaufman) of the purported black senses. Given a heritage derived from slavery and formed as much by jazz, spirituals and rap as by Blake, Whitman, Williams and Pound, who was culturally better placed to have adapted Beat to a black dispensation, or in that honoured African American usage, to have made it signify?[17]

A number of linked references-back help situate Baraka as Beat poet. First, in the *LeRoi Jones/ Amiri Baraka Reader* (1991), he himself (or his editor William J. Harris) supplies precise dates for his Beat phase, namely 1957–62.[18] These, in his *Reader*'s words constituted 'bohemian' years before 'ethnic consciousness' gave way to 'political consciousness'. The *Autobiography*, however, gives the circumstances and flavour of his relationship to the movement:

> I'd come into the Village *looking*, trying to 'check,' being open to all flags. Allen Ginsberg's *Howl* was the first thing to open my nose, as opposed to, say, instructions I was given, directions, guidance. I dug *Howl* myself, in fact many of the people I'd known at the time warned me off it and thought the whole Beat phenomenon a passing fad of little relevance. I'd investigated further because I was looking for something. I was precisely open to its force as the statement of a new generation. As a line of demarcation from 'the silent generation' and the man with the ... grey flannel skin, half brother to the one with the grey flannel suit. I took up with the Beats because that's what I saw taking off and flying somewhere resembling myself. The open and implied rebellion – of form and content. Aesthetic as well as social and political. But I saw most of it as Art, and the social statement as merely our lives as dropouts from the mainstream. I could see the young white boys and girls in their pronouncements of disillusion with and 'removal' from society as related to the black experience. That made us colleagues of the spirit.[19]

A 1980s interview sets these remembrances within a wider historical perspective:

> Beat came out of the whole dead Eisenhower period, the whole of the McCarthy Era, the Eisenhower blandness, the whole reactionary period of the 50s. The Beat Generation was a distinct reaction to that, a reaction not only to reactionary politics, reactionary life style of American ruling class and sections of the middle class, reaction to conservatism and McCarthyism of that period. Also reaction to the kind of academic poetry and academic literature that was being pushed as great works by the American establishment. So it was a complete reaction: socially, politically, and of course artistically to what the 50s represented. That whole opening and transformation of course had its fullest kind of expression in the 60s in the Black Liberation Movement.[20]

There also remains the Beat aesthetic as Baraka fashioned it in the late 1950s, published under the rubric 'How Do You Sound?' in 'The Statements on Poetics' section of Donald Allen's *The New American Poetry* (1960).[21] Revealingly, Black Power, black cultural nationalism at least, nowhere features in an explicit way. Rather, Baraka takes aim at New Critical academicism, with its emphasis on formal prerequisites and design, advocating open forms and fields of expression. The formulation, right down to the abbreviations and punctuation, shows the residual mark of Charles Olson, together with a Ginsbergian, and behind that a Whitmanesque, will to inclusiveness:

'HOW DO YOU SOUND??' is what we recent fellows are up to. How *we* sound; our peculiar grasp on, say: a. Melican speech, b. Poetries of the world, c. Our selves (which is attitudes, logics, theories, jumbles of our lives, & all that), d. And the final ... The Totality of Mind: Spiritual ... God?? (or you name it): Social (zeitgeist): or Heideggerian *umwelt*.

MY POETRY is anything I think I am. (Can I be light & weightless as a sail?? Heavy & clunking like 8 black boots.) I CAN BE ANYTHING I CAN. I make a poetry with what I feel is useful & can be saved out of all the garbage of our lives. What I see, am touched by (CAN HEAR) ... wives, gardens, jobs, cement yards where cats pee, all my interminable artifacts ... ALL are a poetry, & nothing moves (with any grace) pried apart from all these things. There cannot be closet poetry. Unless the closet be wide as God's eye.

And all that means that I *must* be completely free to do just what I want, in the poem.[22]

Given the self-liberative urgings, the affirmations and the learning lightly worn (or, as it were, spoken), this might be thought virtually a Beat poem in its own imaginative right, or at least a prose equivalent. Certainly it links directly to the poems which make up his *Preface to a Twenty Volume Suicide Note* (1961), the volume which taken in retrospect has most become associated with his part in the Beat movement.[23]

> You are as any other sad man here
> american

Jones has his speaker confide in 'Notes for a Speech', the collection's closing poem which ruefully, ironically, echoes Countee Cullen's 1920s-written 'Heritage':

> What is Africa to me: ...
> *One three centuries removed*
> *From the scenes his fathers loved,*
> *Spicy grove, cinnamon tree,*
> *What is Africa to me?*

Jones's black bohemian would seem to have lost touch not only with Africa but with African American life and origins. Yet even as he considers this double deracination, the measure of his lament sounds blues-like and drawn from the most intimate repertoire of his own blackness. This also applies in 'Preface to a Twenty Volume Suicide Note' as title poem, which opens proceedings on a note of generalized alienation ('Nobody sings anymore') only to have that same alienation challenged by the sight of his young, cross-racial daughter, Kellie Jones, at prayer.[24]

Other poems in *Preface* do a similar about-turn. In 'For Hettie', his affectionate, roistering mock complaint at his pregnant wife's 'left-handedness' obliquely suggests the different pushes and pulls of his love for her. In 'For Hettie in Her Fifth Month' he attempts, with a hint of William Carlos Williams's 'The Red Wheel Barrow', to catch both the otherness of pregnancy itself and of the unborn child – the latter as

> one of Kafka's hipsters,
> parked there
> with a wheelbarrow.

A related kind of otherness, that of inter-racial sexual life with all its supposed mystique and taboos, shows through in blues vignettes like 'Symphony Sid' ('A man, a woman shaking the night apart') or 'Theory of Art' ('blackness, strange, mocked').

At a different level are the poems dedicated to his co-Beats. 'One Night Stand', for Ginsberg, teases the triumphalist fervour of the New Bohemia ('We entered the city at noon! The radio on ... '), a funny-wry vision of Beat's legions dressed in motley fashion and full of pose:

> We *are* foreign seeming persons. Hats flopped so the sun
> can't scald our beards; odd shoes, bags of books & chicken.
> We have come a long way, & are uncertain which of the masks
> is cool.

'Way Out West', for Gary Snyder, explores perceptual process from:

> As simple an act
> as opening the eyes

to:

> Closing the eyes. As
> simple an act. You float ...

Whether an America of Sheridan Square or a Greece of Tiresias, in the poem's span of reference, the poet's vision doubles as always mutualizingly outer and inward. Snyder's Zen affinities undoubtedly had aroused an answering note in Jones.

The most Beat cum 'projective verse' composition in *Preface*, however, is to be found in 'Look for You Yesterday, Here You Come Today', its title taken from an old blues, as if to give added emphasis to the memories of an American childhood fast giving way to a meaner, tougher adult human order. The note is nostalgic yet a nostalgia itself chastised and mocked. The speaker, duly bearded, literary, confides:

> I have to trim my beard in solitude.
> I try to hum lines from 'The Poet in New York'

Similarly, he acknowledges that his own pose can hardly keep up with an undermining diversity of experience:

> It's so diffuse
> being alive.

'Terrible poems come in the mail'. A dark Strindbergian feeling comes over him at his wife's pregnancy. Frank O'Hara, the poem reports, prefers the importance of his own silence to 'Jack's incessant yatter'. The poet's own thoughts, in a Baudelairean put-down of self-consciousness, in turn become:

> Flowers of Evil
> cold & lifeless
> as subway rails.

Only 'dopey mythic worlds hold', a childhood pop culture arcade which includes Tom Mix

> dead in a Boston Nightclub
> before I realized what happened

and other heroes from Dickie Dare to Captain Midnight, Superman to the Lone Ranger ('THERE *MUST* BE A LONE RANGER!!!' runs his insistence). These stalwarts (they have company in the title-figure reference to a Dashiell Hammett hero in 'The Death of Nick Charles' and to Lamont Cranston as The Shadow in 'In Memory of Radio') lag behind in time and place, tokens of a lost, simpler, altogether more secure childhood order. The nostalgia is palpable:

> My silver bullets all gone
> My black mask trampled in the dust
>
> & Tonto way off in the hills
> moaning like Bessie Smith.

One just about hears a Jones ready to move on from Beat self-absorption into politicization, with Bessie Smith, blues, *black* popular heritage as a route towards more committed ends and purposes.

In this respect few poems in *Preface to a Twenty Volume Suicide Note* assume a blacker animus than 'Hymn for Lanie Poo' (the nickname for his sister, Sandra Elaine). Freely associative in range, it develops a montage of skilfully parodic, if at times rueful, slaps at white social norms and their emulation by America's black middle class. Rimbaud's *Vous êtes de faux Nègres* offers the point of departure, with sequences to follow guying, in turn, white America's taste for primitivizing superstitions about sunburnt black skin, Lanie's Gatsbyesque

> coming-out party
> with 3000 guests
> from all parts of the country

and the typical superficiality of most culture talk about race. Jones's ending takes especial aim at black bourgeois assimilationism and, as he sees it, the inevitable outcome of so obviously wrong a cultural turning:

> Smiling & glad/in
> the huge & loveless
> white-anglo sun/of
> benevolent step
> mother America.

If the form (and tone) can be said to be Beat, it rests in the poem's spontaneous voices and transitions. Certainly the playful iconoclasm can scarcely be missed in

> The god I pray to
> got black boobies
> got steatopygia ...

Similarly the poem's 'I' vaunts a touch of self-irony in

> it's impossible
> to be an artist and bread
> winner at the same time.

With a perhaps irreverent eye, or ear, to Ginsberg and Snyder, there is also a show of mock oceanic feeling:

> Each morning
> I go down
> to Gansevoort St.
> and stand on the docks.
> I stare out
> at the horizon
> until it get up
> and comes to embrace
> me. I make believe
> it is my father.
> This is known
> as genealogy.

'Hymn for Lanie Poo' yields a kind of flyting, at once regretful and angrily comic, at how black America has begun to buy into and imitate white middle-class American life. The phantasmagoria is not only plentiful but apt:

> A white hunter, very unkempt,
> with long hair,
> whizzed in on the end of a vine.
> (spoke perfect english too.)

From the start, and some time ahead of his Black Nationalist and Marxist phases, Jones's poetry clearly involved a subtle overlap of both personal and a more inclusive racial feeling. As brief an affiliation as it may have been for the then LeRoi Jones, Beat – Beat poetry – had assumed its own mediating black textures.

☆   ☆   ☆

Black Beat writing yields no more companionable a presence than Ted Joans. 'Afro-surrealist', jazz adept, trumpeter, painter by early training, and lifelong performance poet, even into his sixties he continues to maintain the role of international stroller player with alternating bases in Manhattan, Paris and Mali. His insistence has always been upon an oral poetry, a talking blues or jazz, by his own count one of 'funk' and 'afrodisia'.

The connection to the Beat Movement began with his arrival in New York City in 1951, from Indiana, and an early link-up with Jack Kerouac. Their friendship, evidently full of warmth and unhampered by racial lines, Joans recalls in 'The Wild Spirit of Kicks', written to commemorate Kerouac's death in October 1969, and marked out by allusions to blues and jazz (including Kerouac's own 'Mexico City Blues') and to the Beat icon of 'the road':

JACK IN RED AND BLACK MAC
RUSHING THROUGH DERELICT STREWN
   STREETS OF NORTH AMERICA
JACK IN WELLWORN BLUE JEANS AND
   DROOPYSWEATER OF SMILES
RUNNING ACROSS THE COUNTRY LIKE A
   RAZOR BLADE GONE MAD
JACK IN FLOPPY SHIRT AND JACKET
   LOADED WITH JOKES
OLE ANGEL MIDNIGHT SINGING MEXICO
   CITY BLUES
IN THE MIDST OF BLACK HIPSTERS AND
   MUSICIANS
FOLLOWED BY A WHITE LEGION OF COOL
   KICK SEEKERS
POETRY LIVERS AND POEM GIVERS
PALE FACED CHIEFTAIN TEARING PAST

THE FUEL OF A GENERATION
AT REST   AT LAST

JK SAYS HELLO TO JC
JOHN COLTRANE, THAT IS[25]

Joans's prolific output, almost thirty titles in all beginning from *Jazz Poems* (1959) and *All of Ted Joans and No More* (1961) and running through to *Wow: Selected Poems of Ted Joans* (1991), has perhaps met its best success in two late-1960s (and still available) collections, *Black Pow-Wow: Jazz Poems* (1969) and *Afrodisia* (1970).[26] Both exhibit Joans's quickfire wit and wordplay, a largely free-form poetry in which blues, jazz, sex, Black Power, Africa and surrealist motif (his debt to André Breton is acknowledged in 'Nadja Rendezvous') plait one into another.[27]

His own working credo especially shows through in 'Passed on Blues: Homage to a Poet', a celebration of Langston Hughes, which opens on the following mellow note:

    the sound of black music
    the sad soft low moan of jazz ROUND ABOUT MIDNIGHT
    the glad heavy fat screaming song of happy blues
    That was the world of Langston Hughes.

The poem works its way through a montage of references to Harlem nights, Jesse Simple bars, downhome food (whether 'pinto beans', 'hamhocks in the dark', 'grits' or 'spareribs'), 'the A-Train', 'the dozens', 'the rumping blues', 'migrated Dixieland', 'the jitterbug', 'rent parties',

Fats Waller's 'Ain't Misbehavin'' and 'sweaty, hard-working muscle'. These, as he says, constitute:

> THE WORLD OF THE POET LANGSTON HUGHES
> BLACK DUES!
> BLACK NEWS!

This is both a homage to Hughes's lyric genius and to Afro-America's first city, a 'sonata of Harlem'. It also bespeaks Joans's own considerable inventive talent, his ventriloquist fusion of Beat and jazz.

This fusion extends throughout most of *Black Pow-Wow* and *Afrodisia*. In the former, in 'O Great Black Masque', for instance, he invokes a negritude embracing Bouaké and Alabama, Mali and Manhattan, which suggests the cadences of the black spiritual and of Whitman. In 'For the Viet Congo', an indictment of black Third World exploitation set out in capitalized typescript, he simulates what might be a newspaper 'Report from the Front' made over into verse form. The comic, teasing side to Joans comes through in his 'No Mo' Kneegrow', written while flying over Dixie ('I'M FLYING OVER ALABAMA ... WITH BLACK POWER IN MY LAP') and which, according to his own gloss, 'can be sung to the tune of "Oh! Susannah"', a short but apposite piece of satiric word play on the price of racial deference; or in 'Uh Huh', a line-up of seemingly muttered banalities which take aim at 'THE COLORED WAITING ROOM'; or in 'Santa Claws' which opens with 'IF THAT WHITE MOTHER HUBBARD COMES DOWN MY BLACK CHIMNEY ...' and goes on to lampoon Santa as some white patriarchal 'CON MAN'.

Nor can there be any mistaking the angrier Joans in his well-known 'The Nice Colored Man', which offers a column of therapeutic, detoxifying variations on the word 'nigger', beginning from 'Nice Nigger Educated Nigger Never Nigger Southern Nigger' and working through to:

> Eeny Meeny Minee Mo
> Catch Whitey by His Throat
> If He Says – Nigger CUT IT!

This gathers yet greater force from the fact that Joans's own father was killed by whites in a 1943 Detroit race riot; the schoolyard race ditty is sardonically turned about face, inside out.

The poems which invoke jazz likewise become the thing they memorialize, though benignly and out of deepest need and affection, as in 'They Forget Too Fast', written in memory of Charlie Parker, 'Jazz Is My Religion' ('it alone do I dig'), or 'Jazz Must Be a Woman', a sound poem made up of the accumulating and run-on names of jazz's greats. One hears, a near perfect blues sense of pitch in the carefully interspaced 'True Blues for Dues Payer', Joans's elegy to Malcolm X written in North Africa:

As I blew   the second chorus   of Old Man River
(on an old gold trumpet loaded with blackass jazz)
a shy   world traveling   white Englishman pushed a French-Moroccan
newspaper   under my Afroamerican eyes
there it said   that you were dead   killed by a group
of black assassins   in black Harlem in the black of night
As I read   the second page   of bluesgiving news
(with wet eyes and trembling cold hands)
I stood   facing east   under quiet & bright African sky
I didn't cry   but inside   said goodbye to you whom I confess
I loved   Malcolm X

Afrodisia reflects more of Joans's African sojourns and his resolve to link
Afro-America back to the mother continent. The opening poem, 'Africa',
so envisions Africa as

> Land of my mothers, where a black god made me.
> My Africa, your Africa, a free continent to be.

'Afrique Accidentale', another Hughes-like montage which parallels the
Mississippi with the Niger, Greenwich Village with the Sudan, re-enacts
his own African *Wanderjahr*, that of a 'jiving AfroAmerican' in search of
the half-mythic and cleverly multispelt Timbuctoo.

> I have traveled a long way on the Beat bread I made
> now I'm deep in the heart of Africa,
> the only Afroamerican spade

he says teasingly, yet pointedly, of his own true black homecoming. The
concluding lines make the point even more emphatic:

> so now lay me down to sleep
> to count black rhinos, not white sheep
> Timbukto, Timbucktoo, Thymbaktou!
> I do dig you!
> Timbuctu, Timbouctou
> I finally made you
> Timbuctoo
> Yeah!!

Throughout, Joans's surrealism shows its paces. In 'No Mo Space for
Toms' he takes an absurdist tilt at colonialism; in 'The Night of the Shark',
he concocts a priapic mock creation parable; and in 'Harlem to Picasso'

he lowers a satiric eye on Euro-American artistic borrowings from Africa with all the accompanying talk of primitivism:

> Hey PICASSO why'd you drop Greco-Roman &
> other academic slop then picked up on my
> black ancestors sculptural bebop?

In 'Jazz Anatomy', the poem itself becomes surreal while invoking surrealism in painting and music. The body, Magritte-like, turns into a combo, a line-up:

> my head is a trumpet
> my heart is a drum
> both arms are pianos
> both legs are bass viols
> my stomach the trombone
> my nose the saxaphone
> both lungs are flutes
> both ears are clarinets
> my penis is a violin
> my chest is a guitar
> vibes are my ribs
> my mouth is the score
> and my soul is where the music lies

Taken with the plentiful erotica, at its best in poems like 'I Am the Lover' and 'Sweet Potato Pie' (and at its quasi-sexist, dated worst in a poem like 'Cuntinent'), Joans has long earned his reputation. 'Whenever I read a poem of my own creation', he has written, 'I intentionally lift it off the page and "blow it" just as I would when I was a jazz trumpeter.' Veteran of both Beat and blues, friend to Kerouac and Ginsberg as to 'Bird', 'Dizzy' and 'Monk', black surrealist and long-time European and Africa sojourner, his continues to be a truly ongoing and live performance.

☆   ☆   ☆

Though born in New Orleans of a Catholic black mother and Jewish white father, raised in the Lower East Side (whose human variety he warms to while condemning the squalor and poverty in pieces like 'East Fifth St. (N.Y.)' and 'TeeVeePeople'), and with 20 years in the Merchant Marine, Bob Kaufman has long been best known as a drugs and poetry doyen of San Francisco. Despite several jail terms, or the self-denying and Buddhist 10 year vow of silence from 1963 to 1973 taken to memorialize John Kennedy's assassination, his adopted city, on his death in January 1986, appointed 18 April 'Bob Kaufman Day' as well as naming a street after him. It was also Kaufman who helped coin the term Beat when editing the magazine *Beatitude* (the journalist Herb Caen claims Beatnik), no doubt appropriately so for the voice which once told America in 'Benediction':

> Everyday your people get more and more
> Cars, television, sickness death dreams.
> You must have been great
> alive.

A degree of fame came in the 1950s and early West Coast 1960s with his work on *Beatitude*, and then Lawrence Ferlinghetti's City Lights Books published his Abomunist poems and broadsides. More, however, resulted from his jazz accompanied and Dadaist poetry readings, not to mention the legendary street and bar 'happenings'. At his death he was usually to be thought of as San Francisco's own one-off bohemian, a Beat irregular.

His different Abomunist papers (*Abomunist Manifesto* (1959), *Second April* (1959) and *Does the Secret Mind Whisper?* (1960)),[28] each an anarcho-surreal parody of all 'isms' and issued under the name Bomkauf, argued for a Beat-derived 'rejectionary philosophy'. A synthesis of terms like bomb, anarchist, communist, Bob, make up the term 'abomunism'. In *Abomunist Manifesto*, telegram style, he lays out its implications as follows:

ABOMUNIST POETS CONFIDENT THAT THE NEW LITERARY
FORM 'FOOTPRINTISM' HAS FREED THE ARTIST OF OUTMODED
RESTRICTIONS SUCH AS: THE ABILITY TO READ AND WRITE, OR
THE DESIRE TO COMMUNICATE, MUST BE PREPARED TO READ THEIR
WORK AT DENTAL COLLEGES, EMBALMING SCHOOLS, HOMES FOR
UNWED MOTHERS, HOMES FOR WED MOTHERS, INSANE ASYLUMS,
USO CANTEENS, KINDERGARTENS, AND COUNTY JAILS.
ABOMUNISTS NEVER COMPROMISE THEIR REJECTIONARY
PHILOSOPHY.

Whatever the noise, the heat, the often dire turns in his life, which went with 'abomunism', Kaufman managed poetry of genuine distinction as borne out in his three principal collections, *Solitudes Crowded with Loneliness, Golden Sardine* (1967) and *The Ancient Rain: Poems 1956–1978* (1981).[29]

In *Solitudes* Kaufman strikes his own Beat affinity in 'Afterwards, They Shall Dance', a poem in which he claims lineage with Dylan Thomas ('Wales-bird'), Billie Holiday ('lost on the subway and stayed there ... forever'), Poe ('died translated, in unpressed pants'), and the *symboliste* master, Baudelaire. Only a dues-paying *black* Beat, however, would end in terms which resemble both Ginsberg's 'Sunflower Sutra' and a dreamy, flighted blues:

>Whether I am a poet or not, I use fifty dollars's worth
>   of air every day, cool.
>In order to exist I hide behind stacks of red and blue poems
>And open little sensuous parasols, singing the nail-in-
>   the-foot-song, drinking cool beatitudes.

Nor can the Beat connection be missed in 'West Coast Sounds – 1956', one of his best-known San Francisco compositions, in which he identifies Ginsberg, Corso, Rexroth, Ferlinghetti, Kerouac, Cassady and himself as co-spirits for a changed America, even to the point of crowding the West Coast. The insider Beat reference, playful throughout, is unmistakable, whether to hipsters or squares, jazz or being high:

>San Fran, hipster land,
>Jazz sounds, wig sounds,
>Earthquake sounds, others,
>Allen on Chesnutt Street,
>Giving poetry to squares
>Corso on knees, pleading,
>God eyes.
>Rexroth, Ferlinghetti,
>Swinging, in cellars,
>Kerouac at Locke's,
>Writing Neil
>On high typewriter,
>Neil, booting a choo-choo,
>On zigzag tracks.
>Now, many cats
>Falling in,
>New York cats,
>Too many cats,
>Monterey scene cooler,
>San Franers, falling down.
>Canneries closing.
>Sardines splitting,
>For Mexico.
>Me too.

This has to be put alongside poems like 'Ginsberg (for Allen)', his surreal, larky homage to the author of 'Howl' ('I have proof that he was Gertrude Stein's medicine chest', 'I love him because his eyes leak'); or 'Jazz *Te Deum* for Inhaling at Mexican Bonfires', a hymn to the human need for exuberance ('Let us walk naked in radiant glacial rains and cool morphic thunderstorms'); or 'A Remembered Beat', with its play of opposites, to the one side Charlie Parker as 'a poet in jazz', Mexico and the 'hidden Pacific', and to the other, coercive 'organization men' and 'television love'; or 'War Memoir', his contemplative, Hiroshima haunted lament at nuclear folly; or 'Jail Poems', his 34 part, movingly self-inquisitorial, sequence:

> I sit here writing, not daring to stop,
> For fear of seeing what's outside my head.

Solitudes Crowded with Loneliness made for an auspicious debut.

Though far less even (a suspicion arises that some of the poems were unfinished), *Golden Sardine* has its own triumphs. The untitled opening poem, a sequence of 'reels' as Kaufman calls them, portrays Caryl Chessman on death row awaiting the electric chair. Norman Mailer's telling of the execution of Gary Gilmore in *The Executioner's Song* (1979) might well have been anticipated.

Kaufman opens his poem in images which deliberately jar, as though writing a kind of deliberately fractured and discontinuous death chant:

> This is a poem about a nobody.
> Charlie Chaplin & Sitting Bull walk hand in hand through
> the World Series.
> The scene opens with Dim Pictures of Animal Sadness, the
> Deathbed of the last Buffalo in Nebraska ... CARYL
> CHESSMAN WAS AN AMERICAN BUFFALO.

Chessman's own voice weaves into the voices about him, a killer but also a sacrificial killing. A mix of verse and prose, its typeface variously in italics or capitalized, the whole exudes a fierce compassion, a gallery of witness and indictment.

Poems like 'Round About Midnight', 'Tequila Jazz', 'His Horn', or 'Blue O'Clock', give testimony to Kaufman's belief in jazz as a healing intimacy, its power to subdue chaos. His poem 'On', a sequence of one line imagist scenes, envisages an America of further disjuncture, beginning 'On yardbird corners of embryonic hopes, drowned in a heroin tear' and moving through to 'On lonely poet corners of low lying leaves & moist prophet eyes'. The view is one from the Beat or hipster margins, appalled at American conformity, 'comic-book seduction' and the 'motion picture corners of lassie & other symbols'.

Kaufman as Beat, however, is perhaps most to be heard in 'Night Sung Sailor's Prayer' in which America's 'born losers, decaying in sorry jails' become some of humanity's holiest (as they do in Ginsberg's 'Footnote to Howl'). The note is indeed beatific, Kaufman as poet of spirit over materiality:

> Sing love and life and life and love
> All that lives is Holy,
> The unholiest, most holy of all.

In his Introduction to *The Ancient Rains: Poems 1956-1978*, Kaufman's editor, Raymond Foye, rightly characterizes the later work as 'some of the finest ... of his career – simple, lofty, resplendent'. Two poems especially do service. In 'War Memoir: Jazz, Don't Listen to at Your Own Risk', he makes jazz a counterweight, a moral balance, to war and rapacity:

> While Jazz blew in the night
> Suddenly we were too busy to hear a sound.

He again focuses on the memory of Hiroshima and Nagasaki:

> busy humans were
> Busy burning Japanese in atomicolorcinescope
> With stereophonic screams,
> What one-hundred-percent red-blooded savage would waste precious time
> Listening to Jazz, with so many important things going on.

For Kaufman, jazz, 'living sound', restores and harmonizes, an act of life over death. Or as he himself puts it:

> Jazz, scratching, digging, bluing, swinging jazz,
> And we listen
> And we feel
> And live.

In 'Like Father, Like Sun', with Lorca as tutelary spirit, he invokes the engendering hope of the Mississippi and the 'Apache, Kiowa, and Sioux ranges' as against a 'rainless', 'fungus' America. The ending looks to a pluralized, uncoercive, universal nation, to America as 'poem' or 'ample geography' as might have been derived from Emerson's visionary essay 'The Poet':[30]

The poem comes
Across centuries of holy lies, and weeping heaven's eyes,
Africa's black handkerchief, washed clean by her children's honor,
As cruelly designed anniversaries spin in my mind,
Airy voice of all those fires of love I burn in memory of.
America is a promised land, a garden torn from naked stone,
A place where the losers in earth's conflicts can enjoy their triumph.
All losers, brown, red, black, and white; the colors from the Master Palette.

Kaufman's 'Like Father, Like Sun' no doubt bespeaks his own pains, his own losses and, throughout, his own will to redemption. But it also brings to bear a quite specific cultural credential: 'Africa's black handkerchief' as progenitor and cornerstone. In shared spirit with Jones/Baraka and Joans, this would signify America made subject to a black beatitude and so reminded of its own best promise as the multicultural apotheosis of all 'colors'.

Acting Out: The Black Drama of the 1960s, the 1960s of Black Drama

> If Bessie Smith had killed some white people she wouldn't have needed that music. She could have talked very straight and plain about the world. No metaphors. No grunts. No wiggles in the dark of her soul. Just straight two and two are four. Money. Power, Luxury. Like that. All of them. Crazy niggers turning their backs on sanity. When all it needs is that simple act. Murder. Just murder! Would make us all sane.
>
> LeRoi Jones/Amiri Baraka, Dutchman (1964)[1]

So, in terms which rarely fail to excite, LeRoi Jones/Imamu Amiri Baraka steers to a climax *Dutchman* – the play which almost single-handedly revolutionized black theatre in postwar America. The speaker is Clay, hitherto a model of black middle-class composure, who finally turns in rage upon Lula, his undulant white temptress, as they travel the subway 'in the flying underbelly of the city'. His belief that 'Murder. Just murder! Would make us all sane' bespeaks an avenging blackness, a once and for all end to white tyranny. No matter that Clay will be stabbed to death by Lula, nor that the cycle of taunt and domination will begin again as this Flying Dutchman train speeds through underground Manhattan only to drop off his corpse and pick up its next black passenger victim.

The play spoke the unspoken, surmised, some said urged, that only unrestrained militancy would truly eradicate America's ancestral colour prejudice. Admirers saw commitment backed up by a radical force of invention. Detractors spoke of black hatred. Yet whichever the ideological assumption, neither viewpoint could deny that here was theatre to match the decade of Black Power.

Dutchman was not to be Jones/Baraka's only Black Power play, nor would it be the only kind of black-authored play on offer by dramatists in the

1960s.[2] But it represents a working touchstone, a marker, for the playwriting which flourished within and beyond this ideological mould. That it aimed to make America *blacker*, as Jones/Baraka himself often insisted, hardly surprises. For black American drama, in context, carries a dialectic of meanings: an inextricable crossover of stagework and politics, art and life.

Besides Jones/Baraka, there emerged a genuinely memorable generation of playwrights: the slightly earlier tier of Langston Hughes, Lorraine Hansberry, James Baldwin and Loften Mitchell, and an array of contemporaries which includes Douglas Turner Ward, Ossie Davis, Lonne Elder and Ed Bullins.[3] Their stage work was set against the 'drama' of the 1960s and the shifting consciousness for virtually all Americans in issues of race and ethnicity, whether the newborn militancy in black communities, North and South, or the response of white America as either liberal support, or angry, threatened backlash. In this respect a mutual refraction was involved: theatre as history, history as theatre. Put another way, the issue involved the unstaging of one kind of entrenched racial history and the staging of its successor.

First, and in keeping with the surge of new confidence in culture and politics, there arose a considerable number of black theatre companies. Including all the community and campus troupes in the 1960s (notably at Howard University and other black campuses) estimates run to more than 500 black theatre groups able to commission and perform new work, crucially, for the most part under the management of their own black playwright-directors. No longer could the minstrelsy and setpiece showtime which had passed as black drama on Broadway be allowed to continue. Broadway had seen the frequent revivals of musicals like DuBose and Dorothy Heyward's *Porgy and Bess* (1927), not to say somewhat inadequate adaptations of Langston Hughes's otherwise richly vernacular story columns from the *Chicago Defender* in the form of *Simple Takes a Wife* (1953) as *Simply Heavenly* (1957).[4]

Nor could white-written plays concerning black life be taken to mean that duty had been done, whether by off-Broadway troupes or, notably, by the historic Provincetown Players from their base in Massachusetts. The latter inevitably calls up the name of Eugene O'Neill, whether his Freudian, operatic drama of black atavism in *The Emperor Jones* (1920), or his portrait of a recriminatory black–white marriage in *All God's Children Got Wings* (1924). Both, at one time, starred Paul Robeson in the title roles. The North Carolina white playwright, Paul Green, also features, notably through *In Abraham's Bosom* (1924), his anatomy of early black community leadership, and through his co-writing, with Richard Wright, of the latter's *Native Son* (1941), an avid, but finally too stilted, dramatization of Bigger Thomas's life, pursuit and fall.

At the outset, one calls into the account the Black Arts Theater of Harlem with Jones/Baraka as its founder and presiding energy. Established independently in 1965 it sought Federal money under the Anti-Poverty Program for a summer community project of theatre and other cultural events in an endeavour to defuse the tensions which had led to riots in Harlem and elsewhere in 1964. The FBI, however, insisted that the enterprise had become a Black Power recruitment drive, with funds being used, among other things, to build a gun arsenal. Before long, Black Arts in Harlem was brought to an end. Jones/Baraka, as a result, returned to his native Newark, New Jersey, relaunching as Spirit House.

But whether in Harlem or Newark, both served as issuing points for black nationalist drama, together with a spate of agitprop, pamphlets, street happenings, poster and mural art. Within the briefest period, other Black Arts centres had sprung up across the country, none more notable than Black Arts West which had strong Black Panther support. Another key upshot was Oakland's Black House Theater under the cultural directorship of Ed Bullins, one of Afro-America's most prolific playwrights. On his discharge from the Navy, Bullins had left his native North Philadelphia for Los Angeles, for a while became the Panthers' Minister of Culture, and made no secret of drawing inspiration from Jones/Baraka.

His move to Harlem, in part out of unease at the ideological rigidity of some of the Black Arts cadre, led to the creation of the Black Theater Workshop and to the staging of a considerable body both of his own work and of various protégés mainly in the New Lafayette Theater.[5] Other leading 1960s Harlem theatres included the Afro-American Studio under Ernie McClintock and the East River Players under Roger Furman and Gertrude Jeanette.

Black Arts Theater also encompassed Black Arts Midwest in Detroit under the direction of Ron Milner and Woodie King (Milner's role came out of his Spirit of Shango Theater); BLKARTSOUTH, in New Orleans, a development of the Free Southern Theater under Tom Dent and Kalamu ya Salaam; Sudan Arts Southwest in Houston; the Theater of Afro Arts in Miami; and Barbara Ann Teer's The National Black Theater on Harlem's 125th Street. Each adhered to a view of theatre as community-serving and driven, a staged politics of consciousness and call to action.

Another related grouping took shape in 1967, the New York based Negro Ensemble Company (NEC), with Douglas Turner Ward and Lonne Elder as its leading writers, and Moses Gunn and Esther Rolle among its actors – theatre frequently given to Brechtian satire and the experimental use of fantasia and cartoon. In this development, as in all the others, there could be no mistaking the shared conviction that black theatre as formula entertainment was at an end.

☆ ☆ ☆

The second implication of 'black American drama' bears on how these plays and companies link into, and transpose, the larger black context of America in the 1960s. In every sense it could not have been more mutual, a whole theatre of national-racial consciousness caught up in the dynamic of change. As coloured or Negro became black or Afro-American so, more or less, all 'the definitions', as James Baldwin had taken to calling them in his essays, came under new scrutiny, a reordering of perspective.

Rosa Park's refusal to accept segregated seating led to the Montgomery Bus Boycott in 1955. Court-ordered desegregation in September 1957 of Central High School in Little Rock, Arkansas, elicited widespread white-liberal approval yet white-Southern resentment. The March on Washington in August 1963, organized by A. Philip Randolph, founder of the BSCP (Brotherhood of Sleeping Car Porters and Maids), and his deputy Bayard Rustin, gave an unprecedented visibility to the Civil Rights movement. Kennedy's meeting with black leadership in 1963, Lyndon Johnson's signing of the Civil Rights Bill in 1964 and the Voting Rights Act in 1965, and his use of 'We Shall Overcome' to a joint session of Congress in March 1965, caught the pulse of the times.

The televised Selma March of January–March 1965 became the cathartic emblem of Black Rights confronting historic Dixie racism and bullying. Headstart, Urban Renewal and CAPs (Community Action Programs) served as the watchwords of new social policy. Despite the eventual shift in focus to Vietnam, Gay and Women's Rights, the gathering Latino, Native American and Asian American movements, or the Nixonism that would eventuate in Watergate, a campaign like the Poor People's March of 1968 with its show of mules and tents and encampment in The Mall in Washington D.C., gave notice that Civil Rights was, even at the end of the decade, and if more diffusedly, still in business.

Theatricalization took an immediate form as black militancy, at once reality and vogue. The groupings became increasingly familiar, whether SNCC (Student Non-Violent Coordinating Committee, founded in 1960, led initially by John Lewis, and then by Stokely Carmichael in 1966, and with James Forman in its ranks), or the Black Panther Party (founded in Oakland in 1966 by Huey Newton and Bobby Seale with Eldridge Cleaver as orator in chief), or the Black Muslims (the revivified Nation of Islam, founded in Detroit in 1930, directed from Chicago by Elijah Muhammad, with Malcolm X as heir apparent until his split to found the Organization of Afro-American Unity in 1964). A 'blackness of the word', impatient, full of warning, was as readily seized upon by the media as by converts and believers. Whether apocalypse, or even, as some believed, hype, it concentrated America's mind.

As spoken by Carmichael, Malcolm X or Panthers like Cleaver and H. Rap Brown, this clenched fist posture also broke with the longstanding gradualism of the NAACP (led by Ralph Wilkins between 1955 and 1977), the National Urban League (under the leadership of Whitney Young), CORE (the Congress of Racial Equality, founded in 1942 and led by James Farmer) or, the rising focus of public attention, the SCLC (Southern Christian Leadership Conference first organized by black clergy in 1957 in the wake of the Montgomery and other boycotts).[6]

The SCLC found its Ghandian leader, and compelling sermonist's voice, in Martin Luther King. His addresses run like an antistrophe to the age, a black folk pulpitry of impassioned heat and eloquence backed by the allusive learning which earned him a University of Boston doctorate in theology. Each homily, full of biblical image and measure, and pitched for call and response, became its own oral-rhetorical drama across a dozen highly public years. The origins lay deep in black church culture, especially those of Atlanta's Ebenezer Baptist Church, where his maternal grandfather and his father had been ministers (and his son would become SCLC president in 1997), and the pastorships King himself held in Montgomery, Alabama.[7]

'I Have a Dream' (1963), inspirational, lyric, full of hope and communal vision, and given from the Lincoln Memorial at the end of the Washington March, took the public imagination by storm. 'Letter from a Birmingham Jail' (1963) spoke biblically of 'love and brotherhood' even as King and other SCLC activists found themselves once more in Southern custody in Alabama. 'Letter from a Selma Jail', carried by the *New York Times* in the form of an advertisement on 5 February 1965, contained the timely reminder that this latest imprisonment for Civil Rights was taking place within two months of King being awarded the 1964 Nobel Peace Prize in Stockholm.

King's 'I See the Promised Land' (1968), again delivered almost messianically within sight of the White House provided the climax to the Poor People's Campaign. 'I've Been to the Mountaintop', the sermon he preached at the Bishop Charles Mason Temple in Memphis, Tennessee, on 3 April 1968, with its 'I may not get there with you. But I want you to know we ... will get to the promised land', held the uncanny prophecy of his own death the very next day by an assassin's gun. Each again bore the imprimatur of Bible, and here specifically Baptist, preachment as indeed a theatre of the word.[8]

Whether King's radical pacificism, or Malcolm's use of Panther and other black radical phrasings like 'by any means necessary' and 'the ballot or the bullet' with all the implication of urban *jihad*, both had called time on America's inherited racial order of supremacist South and ghettoed North. Again, the evolving imprint of change was theatrical, a politics of the media age in which a whole repertoire of visual gesture (Malcolm's Black Power fist, King's prayerful, bowed head) alongside the spoken phrase or address, counted as never before.

CORE pursued its policy, begun in 1961, of sending 'Freedom Riders' across the South to work for desegregation and black voter rights. James Meredith attempted to register at the segregated University of Mississippi in 1962 with 1,200 Federal troops dispatched to keep order. Robert Sheldon as Grand Dragon of the Klan promised a continuing regime of black death in 1963. Governor George Wallace of Alabama blocked the entrance of the University of Alabama at the proposed entry of two black students in June 1963 (wheelchair-bound, in consequence of the attempt on his own life, he would apologize to both in 1996). Fannie Lou Hamer helped create the MFDP (the Mississippi Freedom Democratic Party) to challenge the state's old-time segregationist Democratic Party in 1964. Sheriff Jim Clarke ordered his deputies to club black voter-registration activists in Selma in 1965. Malcolm's Harlem and other Black Muslim demonstrations indicated a new style of black political strength. King took his campaigns North to Mayor Richard M. Daley's Chicago in 1967 in the form of the SCLC's Open Housing Campaign against the city's *ipso facto* segregation and the South Side's substandard living conditions. Edward W. Brooke, a black patrician and Republican of Massachusetts, in 1965 became the first-ever black Senator, and Shirley Chisholm, a Brooklyn Democrat, in 1968 the first-ever black woman elected to Congress.

Television hungrily aided the drama with images of black protesters and their white allies being waterhosed or beaten and for which a 'Public Safety Commissioner' like Bull Connor of Birmingham, Alabama, became notorious. The campaign of lunch counter and other sit-ins started with four black students in a Woolworth's in Greenboro, North Carolina, in February 1960. The sense of *dramatis personae* could not but grow familiar, the protesters, marchers, students and clergy with arms linked, jeering white supremacists, guardsmen with rifles at the ready.

Few events, however, have become more poignant in memory than the deaths of the four African American girls aged 11 to 14 (Denise McNair, Cynthia Wesley, Addie Mae Collins and Carol Robertson), just out of Bible class and in their white dresses and shoes, when Klan segregationists dynamited the Sixteenth Street Baptist Church in Birmingham, Alabama (the city became known as 'Bombingham') on 15 September 1963. Three decades later Spike Lee has returned to the episode in his screen documentary *Four Little Girls* (1997). At the time Nina Simone was among those who best caught the general black sense of Dixie with her angry, but always superbly cadenced, blues rendering of 'Everyone Knows about Mississippi, Goddam'.

In the North, from the Watts riot of August 1965, through to that in Detroit in 1967, and in the outbreaks of Milwaukee, Chicago, Hammond, Washington D.C., Newark and the New York of Bedford-Stuyvesant and Harlem, the cameras showed an America whose cities were burning. Nearly 200 cities bore witness to a new urban script of shoot-out, fires, both black and white looting, cars overturned and aflame.

It hardly took Lyndon Johnson's Kerner Commission, with its brief to examine 'violence' and 'civil disorder', and which reported in 1968, to see a root cause in systematic exclusion, poverty, denial of access to decent housing and schools and a sense of citied imprisonment.[9] A trial like that of 'The Chicago Seven' in 1969–70, with a voluble, declamatory Bobbie Seale, among other Black Panther defendants, bound and gagged in the largely white court, added a further powerfully symbolic spectacle.

No greater ceremonial a drama, however, was to be met with than in the bullet-laden deaths, the funerals and mourning, and then the ensuing spirals of conspiracy theory and accusation, of the age's martyrs. The scenes include the burials of the NAACP's Medgar Evers and President John F. Kennedy at Arlington Cemetery in 1963, the search for the bodies of the student Civil Rights workers Schwerner, Chaney and Goodman in 1964, the Harlem wake for Malcolm X after being gunned down at the Audubon Ballroom in 1965, the encoffined lying-in-state of Robert Kennedy in 1968, and the Memphis killing of Martin Luther King in 1968 and the long campaign to make his birthday, January 15, a national holiday. Each represented a life shared and lost.

Nor did the death end: its shadow continued across the South, the black inner cities, Soledad, San Quentin, Attica and other penitentiaries, Vietnam as black frontline troops disproportionately returned to America in military body bags, and, increasingly, the urban spectacle of gang- and drug-related killing. Yet at the same time, and contradictory as may be, another politics, that of 'Nation Time', equally became a prompt to black affirmation, pride, consciousness, a rising curve of hope.

Not least it was to be heard, and to be seen being acted out, in an emerging new generation of black leaders. Major players in this post-Civil Rights drama include Jesse Jackson, the Carolina-born Chicago minister then spearheading PUSH (People United to Save Humanity), aide to Martin Luther King, and activist in both community and mainstream politics – the latter culminating in his own bids for the American presidency; Julian Bond, son of the distinguished Horace Mann Bond of Lincoln University, already a Civil Rights veteran in his twenties and eventually to become a Georgia State Representative; Andrew Young, SCLC Vice-President from 1967 to 1970, Georgia Congressman, US Ambassador to the UN under President Carter and, in due course, Mayor of Atlanta; and John Lewis, Civil Rights and SNCC veteran, in 1970 Director of the Voter Education Project and, in the 1990s, an eventual Georgia Congressman.[10]

☆   ☆   ☆

The times, thereby, also meant a rebirth of interest in the whole plait of Afro-America's arts – each major literary form, and theatre itself, but also church and related music, painting, dance, journalism, film and, notably, a newly visible 'womanist' art from writing to design. The Black Aesthetic movement had been launched. A black poetry group like the Umbra workshop began in 1961, among its luminaries Ishmael Reed, Tom Dent, David Henderson and Lorenzo Thomas, and out of which *Umbra*, its house magazine, emerged in 1963. The age also saw the increasing popularity of jazz-and-poetry, rarely more dramatically performed than by the Black Arts figure of Gil Scott-Heron in poems like 'The Revolution Will Not Be Televised' and whose ongoing improvisations and balladry supplies a pathway to later generations of rappers, dub and hip-hop artists. Universities, Junior Colleges, even High Schools, developed Black Studies programmes. This new consciousness also showed itself in the bookstores of previously 'raceless' malls, airports and train stations. Each displayed its own black section.

Small publishing houses like Dudley Randall's Broadside Press in Detroit and Don Lee/Haki R. Madhubuti's Third World Press became important forums for black poetry. Anthologies proliferated: John A. Williams's diagnostic essay-collection, *The Angry Black* (1962), and its successor *Beyond the Angry Black* (1967); Abraham Chapman's wide-ranging compendium of verse and other creative work, *Black Voices* (1968) and *New Black Voices* (1972); James A. Emanuel and Theodore Gross's student-oriented *Dark Symphony: Negro Literature in America* (1968); most notably LeRoi Jones/Amiri Baraka and Larry Neal's rallying, ideologically nationalist *Black Fire* (1968), and Toni Cade's timely and restorative *The Black Woman: An Anthology* (1970).[11]

A massive recovery and distribution of black writings also began by houses like Arno/New York Times, AMS Press, Mnemosyne, the Johnson Publishing Company, G.K. Hall, the Chatham Booksellers, and by university presses from Howard (launched in 1972) to those of Illinois, Indiana, Missouri and Michigan. Conglomerates like Random House got into the act through paperback reissues and editions in the form of Vintage, Dell, Signet, Penguin/NAL and Mentor. It did not escape notice that if the black word had become newly visible, newly audible, it had also become newly commercial.

In popular culture 'Black is Beautiful' might have been the presiding anthem: Afros, dashikis, soul music, black food ('soul food'), wall art and graffiti, youth dance, tags like 'right on' and 'cool' (which quickly passed into white youth and campus parlance), rap, and a daring new vein of black comedy in figures like the unreverential Dick Gregory, the laconic Redd Foxx, the early, attractively offbeat Bill Cosby, and the hyper, improvisory Richard Pryor. Black, or at least acting black, was 'in'. Even Frank Yerby, formula romance writer, returned, if briefly, to black themes in *Speak Now* (1969), the story of a black–white love affair set against the 1968 Paris student revolt and the Gaullist backlash, and in *The Dahomean* (1971), a portrait of African dynasty which foreshadows Alex Haley's *Roots* (1976).[12]

Television, however cautiously, used the 1960s to move on. If safety for the networks had lain in the ready popular appeal (and a-politicality) of *Soul Train* (1971–), under the 'cool' hosting of Don Cornelius, as the youth-angled successor to the suitably low key *Nat King Cole Show* (1956–57), further increments of change came with clever but within-bounds studio comedy like *The Flip Wilson Show* (1970–74), a black sitcom series like *Sanford and Son* (1972–77) based on the BBC's *Steptoe and Son*, and, most of all, *The Bill Cosby Show* (1969–71) which, in turn, became *The New Bill Cosby Show* (1972–73), *Cos* (1976) – a children's programme – and then *The Cosby Show* (1984–). The latter has won spectacular ratings, the Huxtable family as an affirming image of middle-class black professional life (Cosby plays a successful gynaecologist) beyond the ghetto or projects. Even so, the show has aroused reservations as too self-absorbed and consumerist.

The 1960s also saw more mixed ethnic casting, notably *I Spy* (1965–68), with, again, Cosby paired alongside Robert Culp in the first TV series to star a black actor, *Mission Impossible* (1966–73), with Greg Morris as the technological brains of the outfit, and *Star Trek* (1966–69), with Michelle Nichols as the communications officer Lieutenant Uhura, and *Star Trek: The Next Generation* (1987–) with LeVar Burton as the 'blind' chief engineer, Geordi LaForge, and Michael Dorn as the Klingon warrior, Lieutenant Worf.

On the political and current-affairs front, Tony Brown, Professor of Communications at Howard, fronted PBS's *Black Journal* (1968–78), directed by the veteran black media figure Bill Greaves, and which, though it shifted from PBS to ABC and back again to PBS, became *Tony Brown's Journal* (1978–), a programme which cultivated an edge of confrontation. CBS, with its seven-part documentary, *Of Black America*, aired in 1968, showed that the commercial networks were beginning to take notice of the new politics of racial change. Local programming played its part, as in the case of *The Black Experience* (1968–73) for WTTV in Indianapolis produced by Mari Evans, author of the poetry collections *Where Is All the Music?* (1968) and *I Am a Black Woman* (1970) and later the editor of the important period anthology *Black Women Writers 1950–1980: A Critical Evaluation* (1984).[13]

The way was further aided through the increasing visibility of black reporters, such as Ed Bradley and Charlayne Hunter-Gault. Bradley began as a reporter with WDAS Radio in Philadelphia in 1963, became a stringer for CBS's Paris Bureau in 1971, reported from Vietnam and Cambodia (1973–75), before becoming anchorman and co-editor of CBS's prizewinning *60 Minutes* (1968–). Hunter-Gault, who was among the first black students to integrate the University of Georgia, headed the Harlem Bureau of the *New York Times* in the 1960s, became an editorial staffer for the *New Yorker*, and eventually took a frontline role in PBS's *MacNeil-Lehrer News Hour* before moving to a new life in South Africa. Both helped pave the way for the current generation of black TV presenters and talkshow hosts, pre-eminently Oprah Winfrey, Arsenio Hall, Montel Williams and Bryant Gumbal.

Politics, churchly or secular, itself became two dramas in one, be it the performative challenge and pitch of a speech by King or Malcolm, each Civil Rights march or confrontation, the increasing frequency of black faces and presence in all the media, the implications of a returning generation of Vietnam 'bloods', or the growing focus on black teenagers. Black Panthers like Cleaver, Newton and Seale also won competing kinds of attention. They headed an estimated 5,000 member organization, a vanguard to admirers, a vigilante force to detractors. If they were perceived to be a threat, they were also genuinely at risk from police racism and from the FBI counter-intelligence unit, COINTEL-PRO, as borne home in the gunning down of 20 year old Fred Hampton, head of the Illinois Panthers, during a raid on their Chicago headquarters in December 1969. Their rhetoric inspired followers even as it enflamed opponents. The scenario involved guns, shoot-outs, pursuits and arrests; but it also involved health clinics, literacy campaigns, food and breakfast programmes. For some they were black soldier-citizens. Others thought they ran close to revolutionary chic with their berets, black leather jackets and dark glasses.

The Panther saga, moreover, continues into the present day. The recent celebrity-supported campaign to stop the execution of Mumia Abu-Jamal, one-time radio reporter and journalist sentenced in 1982 for the alleged shooting of a Pennsylvania cop, partly focuses on how the police used his ex-Panther affiliation (and a suspicion of police informer evidence) in his conviction. Similarly, the release in 1997, after 27 years of incarceration in California, of Elmer Geronimo Pratt, another former Panther (and also a Vietnam Veteran and Amnesty International 'prisoner of conscience'), came about on the grounds that his imprisonment for murder had relied on the word of a witness who, unknown at the time to the jury, both perjured himself and again was an FBI informant.

More political drama attaches to the Black Muslims, one of conversion, discipline, temperance and absolute fealty to a black patriarchal Elijah Muhammad. Throughout the 1960s, and since, often with *Muhammad Speaks* in hand (and at one point edited by the novelist Leon Forrest), they have sought from their network of temples (Malcolm X was Minister of Harlem's Mosque No. 7) would-be converts in street and penitentiary. That Malcolm's killing came about as the likely consequence of an internal Nation of Islam schism, and in which Louis Farrakhan eventually ousted Herbert 'Wallace' Muhammad in the fight for control, adds its own provisional final act or chapter.

Black women, equally, had their respective styles and pathways in the drama. Some drew on deep, ongoing, bible-Christian and churchgoing roots. Rosa Parks, after the Montgomery boycott, helped run the Michigan office of Congressman John Conyers. Daisy Bates, the NAACP's motivating force in Arkansas's Central High School saga, became a continuing stalwart of Civil Rights. Myrlie Evers, who saw her husband, Medgar Evers, gunned down in June 1963, and who had to wait three decades and a third trial before a Jackson, Mississippi court finally convicted his killer, Byron De Le Beckwith, as Evers-Williams was elected Chair of the NAACP in February 1996. Coretta King, throughout each SCLC march, protest and court case, and in her own right and continuingly since the death of Martin Luther King, has always been a major presence. And few would forget the formidable oratory, and passion for Civil Rights, of the late Congresswoman Barbara Jordan of Texas.

Black Muslim women found a stirring incarnation in Betty Shabazz, whose life not only with, but after, Malcolm X would carry its own eventfulness. Heavily pregnant when she witnessed his killing, she raised a family of six girls, and went on to earn a Ph.D. Later came the arrest of her daughter, Qubilah, in a would-be revenge plot against Louis Farrakhan, often thought complicit in Malcolm's assassination. Finally, in June 1997, she met her death from the 80 per cent burns she suffered in a fire started in her Yonkers apartment by a grandson – also called Malcolm. Her Islamic funeral in Harlem, with a gathering of mourners which included Muhammad Ali, New York's ex-mayor David Dinkins and an array of black notables, added to the sense of historical occasion.

Other women expressed their politics through SNCC and other Black Power groupings, despite frequent misgivings about female lack of power, or visibility, not to mention the outright misogyny (Stokely Carmichael's riposte of 'horizontal' when asked about women's position in the movement, jokily intended or not, became a byword for chauvinism). Panther activists and wife-mothers like Kathleen Cleaver, or a Marxist (or at least Marcusean) true believer like Angela Davis, or a leading activist in the sit-in movements like SNCC's Diane Nash, all gave their respective kinds of political edge to the movement.

Black Arts contributed Sonia Sanchez, author of the early call-to-arms play *The Bronx Is Next* (1968) and vernacular 'black talk' poetry like *We a BaddDDD People* (1970), and who also helped start Black Studies at San Francisco State University; Nikki Giovanni, the committed speaking voice of *Black Feeling, Black Talk* (1968) and *Black Judgement* (1969); Sarah Webster Fabio who, although born in Nashville, Tennessee, like the Panthers became an important Oakland presence and whose *Saga of a Black Man* (1968) and *A Mirror: A Soul* (1969) carried the word of black challenge; and Carolyn M. Rodgers, whose early collections like *Paper Soul* (1968), *2 Love Raps* (1969) and *Songs of a Black Bird* (1969) spoke vernacularly of black and feminist revolution.[14]

In Jane Cortez Afro-America looked to one of its leading jazz poets, often accompanied by her husband, the free form composer, saxophonist and trumpeter, Ornette Coleman, and later also by their son, Denardo Cortez, drummer in the band *The Firespitters*. Cortez, in addition, co-founded the Watts Repertory Theater in 1964 for which she wrote the uncompromising tenement and drugs performance piece *Pisstained Stairs and the Monkey Man's Wares* (1969). She also became the owner-founder of Bola Press which was among the first to issue music and text disks. Like her peers Cortez has signified both a black feminism and black femininity, the latter further emphasized in the 1960s habit of wearing Yoruba and other African dress, turbans, sarongs and sashes, along with Afros and braids.[15]

The Mexico Olympics of 1968 supplied another defining tableau. When Tommie Smith and John Carlos, gold medallists for sprint, gave their Black Power salutes with arms outstretched and fists clenched and gloved, was not this a protest too far, the stars and stripes defied? A sports figure like Arthur Ashe – college educated, clean cut – surely better suited the American mainstream, the first black winner that same year of tennis's Men's US Open, however untypical tennis was as a black sport. But again, both the man and his views were more complex, to be borne out in his long held anti-apartheid stance as set out in his autobiography *Days of Grace: A Memoir* (1993), in his insights into the historic role of the African American athlete in *A Hard Road to Glory* (1988), and in the intelligent dignity of his message to his children as he faced death of AIDS after receiving an HIV-infected blood transfusion.[16]

For all the popularity of black action movies like the *Shaft* or *Superfly* series, or the two Godfrey Cambridge/Raymond St. Jacques adaptations of Chester Himes's detective novels, or a martial arts 'amazon' film like *Cleopatra Jones* (1973), starring Tamara Dobson, this kind of film did not reflect the whole story. Gordon Parks, for instance, photographer and writer, directed *The Learning Tree* (1969) based on his own autobiographical novel; Melvin Van Peebles offered *Watermelon Man* (1970), a raucous comic swipe at colour norms in suburbia and the office; and from the dramatist Lonne Elder came the screen adaptation of *Sounder* (1972), a major film of black sharecropper life in Depression-era Louisiana, although originally the work of the white children's book writer William Armstrong. Black music, as always, supplied the acoustic sound wrap, from Motown's *Four Tops* and *The Temptations* to soul's James Brown and Aretha Franklin to rock's Little Richard, with Gospel and spirituals, blues and jazz, always in place as ongoing matrix.

But, inevitably perhaps, it was a media phenomenon which came to summarize the effect of the 1960s: Alex Haley's *Roots: A Family Saga* (1976), the full implications of whose subtitle needed time to be fully recognized, and whose TV spinoff (*Roots*, 1977, and *Roots: The Next Generations*, 1979) continued its phenomenal success. Viewing figures suggest it was watched in whole, or in part, by well over 100 million Americans. Even those who thought *Roots* too assuaging, a studio confection with an 'Africa' which suggested a studio more than a real place, did not deny the appeal it made for revising the view of America's slave and racial legacy.[17]

As confrontation began to ease during the Carter years, and in the need for a lowering of temperature after Vietnam and Watergate, America found itself caught up in more measured contemplation of what lay behind and within the 1960s: to the one side the embedded and unedifying languages of ethnic and other division, to the other the will to change. Prime-time viewing of each life-story in *Roots* – starting with Kunta Kinte in the Gambia, then the scenes of the slave ship and the Middle Passage to Maryland and Virginia, and finally the American years through slavery, Reconstruction and the new century, from Chicken George in North Carolina to the Haley family in Tennessee – gave a new currency to how blackness, indeed race as a whole, could be taken for genealogical dramas in their own right and also of the nation at large. Haley rode, and to an extent helped progress, the interest in black culture released by the age of King and Malcolm.

☆   ☆   ☆

One ongoing saga from the 1960s makes for a special style of cultural theatre: that of Muhammad Ali. For despite the onset of Parkinson's Syndrome, Ali has become Afro-America's best-known and adored athlete king. He has not lacked company, whether earlier boxing names like Joe Louis and Sugar Ray Robinson or, latterly, track's Carl Lewis and Florence ('Flow-Jo') Griffith-Joyner, and basketball's Magic Johnson and Michael Jordan. The flair for publicity began as early as his Olympic days, boxing's bawling man-child, the Louisville Lip, as if his speed in the ring were as much dependent on verbal as physical adrenalin.

To Afro-America, Ali's succession of wins, together with the media hoopla, boasts, verse raps and rhymes, the Howard Cosell and other follow-up interviews, created a triumphalist calendar. First came the 'black' fights, against a supposedly unstoppable Sonny Liston in 1964 and 1965, a serene Floyd Patterson in 1965 and 1970, a fierce, unstinting Smokin' Joe Frazier in 1971, 1974 and 1975, and the 'rumble in the jungle' with George Foreman in the Congo's Kinshasha – with its Conradian heart of darkness echo, its 'blackspectacular' ancillaries like Don King and James Brown, and its stunning, high energy pugilism. When, however, the opposition became a Great White Hope (among them Karl Mildenberger in 1966, Henry Cooper in 1965 and 1966, and Jerry Quarry in 1970 and 1972), the athleticism became more explicitly racialized, a latest or updated 'battle royal'. As in Douglass's fight against Covey, each punch and show of ringcraft bore the not so vicarious relish of hitting back at, not to say downing, white America.

Little wonder that, even in his physical decline, Ali continues to revive the spirits of the most put-upon Harlemite or black Southerner. Connectedly, the early performance rap with Drew Bundini Brown like 'Float like a butterfly, sting like a bee!/Yeah! Rumble, young man, rumble!', or the sass of his insults and predictions of victory, made for a talking-back no less likely to win attention than his grace of hand, or what became the Ali shuffle, or his celebrated tactic of rope-a-dope.

Ali's story like that of Frederick Douglass and Malcolm X, would be one of self-recomposition: the conversion from Christianity to the Nation of Islam in 1964, and acceptance of Elijah Muhammad as both Messenger of Allah and adoptee father; the accompanying name change from Cassius Clay to Muhammad Ali; and, in 1967, at a nearly four year cost of his title, and even though it brought with it the opprobrium of Jackie Robinson and Joe Louis as well as of a number of serving black soldiers, and troubled America at large, his refusal on religious grounds to be drafted for Vietnam. His Muslim conversion, later to be dimly shadowed by that of Mike Tyson, had turned the warrior athlete into the warrior believer.

Nor has Ali as perennially on-stage figure diminished since his best years in the ring. Television, travel, every kind of public role, massive name and face recognition, even his appearance as late as 1997 before a Congressional Committee with his views of child abuse, have all been ways of feting him. Another recent confirmation lies in his lighting of the flame at the 1996 Olympic Games in Atlanta even as, in full media view, he could be seen to suffer the cruel spasms brought on by his disease. It has been a sanctification full of affection, sentimental even, as borne out in the movie *When We Were Kings* (1997) with Norman Mailer and George Plimpton as white literary talking heads and a raft of hitherto unseen documentary footage. The world's one-time fastest heavyweight has continued, in body and voice, to bear the sign, the individual and embodied theatre, of the new black dispensation born of the 1960s of his own youth.[18]

Jones/Baraka's *Dutchman*, to return to theatre drama *per se*, brought black politics and art together as rarely before. Foremost it excoriated the American racist spiral and any black accommodation of its turnings. But it also represented a triumph of stagecraft, whose economy and handling of pace and dénouement were not to be doubted. Thus, behind its resolutely contemporary scenario and its warring colloquy of Clay and Lula, a far more ancient legacy of racial division could be discerned.

First, the piece deploys a pervasive body of allusion to the Underground Railway, Afro-America's earlier Freedom Trail. Slave narrative, inevitably, lies in the mix, be it that of Henson, Douglass or Jacobs, as, echoingly, does the subterraneanism of Wright's 'The Man Who Lived Underground' and Ralph Ellison's *Invisible Man* (whose narrator speaks of 'Dante', 'this underworld', and 'hibernation'). Similarly, much as Clay and Lula embody New York moderns, they also imply biblical typology, an earth-made black Adam, hence Clay, confronting whiteness as an apple-eating bitch Eve. The 'Flying Dutchman' title allusion, with not only Dante's *Inferno* (to which Jones/Baraka returns in his novel *The System of Dante's Hell* with its interplay of medieval hell and Newark ghetto) but Dostoevsky's *Notes from Underground* as supporting terms of reference, gives yet further emphasis to *Dutchman* as theatre parable. Its Pilgrim's Progress along the modern subway ('steaming hot', 'summer on top', as the stage directions say) doubles as a journey along still darker subways within.

At issue is Clay's forced recognition of what he has become as a black bourgeois stalwart, his having settled for less. Lula provokes, tempts, all to bring forth Clay's dissent, her power being to enlighten and then punish for that same enlightenment. Nothing gets spared in her taunting: slavery, the sexual electricities of race, the false coupledom of partying, the deeply emblematic name calling ('Uncle Tom' and 'Uncle Thomas Woolly-Head' from Lula, and 'You dumb bitch' and 'Tullulah Bankhead' from Clay). These exchanges, full of charge and countercharge, point Clay into becoming, as he recognizes, an 'ex-coon', no longer one of the 'half-white trusties' (he even clubs down a white drunk). But his insight is to prove deadly.

'I've heard enough', says Lula before she stabs him, another white murder or castration to pre-empt black reprisal. Clay's mouth, with its newborn words of understanding, is said to go on 'working stupidly'. As his young successor boards the train, in default of any reversal of the *status quo*, the circling, underground journey for black America reassumes its course. It makes for the perfect, if cryptic and accusing, outcome. Much as the vision of *Dutchman* startled, there could be no doubt of the artistry.

☆   ☆   ☆

Jones/Baraka's other main 1960s plays almost tirelessly extend this theatre of catharsis. His only 'raceless' piece, *The Baptism* (1964), launches into Christianity as essentially a massive sexual fetish, hidden, conspiratorially or otherwise, beneath the veil of high spirituality. The Baptist Church in which the action takes place thus converts into a species of violent Gay Court, minister and communicants alike locked in sadomasochist rite and with language to match. With *The Toilet* (1964), set uncompromisingly in a high school latrine, homosexuality again becomes a key image: one boy's love for another hidden by the laws of adolescent gang behaviour, a portrait of victimization implicitly linking sexual with racial oppression.[19]

The Slave, however, actually envisages race war, its principal black figure, Walker Vessels, prepared to assassinate his own children in the very house of his white ex-wife Grace and her present husband Easley. True to his name, Vessels sees himself as the vehicle of a blackness which, lacking any other option, becomes inescapably and brutally murderous; the same impetus as carried in Wright's Bigger Thomas, only this time made aware and articulate. To kill his two girls, then their white professor stepfather Easley, and finally Grace herself, is to achieve a temporary, if bitter, efficacy in the face of all that hitherto has deprived him and his forerunners of self-determining power. To this end, he enters and exits from the play anachronistically as 'an old field slave', as though his incarnation as a killer were the only alternative. Easley at one point speaks reflexively of 'ritual drama', racial blight as historic American dramaturgy.

   Four Black Revolutionary Plays (1969) took Jones/Baraka still further into black nationalism. Two lines from his verse Introduction assume the very persona of militancy:

> i am prophesying the death of white people in this land
> i am prophesying the triumph of black life in this land,
> and over all the world.

Each of the plays, accordingly, becomes a consciously stylized acting-out. *Experimental Death Unit # 1* (1964) envisages a black warrior group which beheads two white addicts, Loco and Duff (their half-comic decadence also linking back to Beckett's Estragon and Vladimir), as they compete for the favours of a black hooker. The play ends with the incantation of 'Black', an anthem or liturgy to reborn African community. *A Black Mass* (1965) looks to an even more pronounced African aegis by re-enacting Black Muslim myth, the creation by Jacoub, one of three Islamic god-like magicians, of a ravening White Beast, against which a *jihad* is demanded by the narrator. *Great Goodness of Life* (1967), 'A Coon Show', according to its subtitle, performs in its own phrase a similar 'cleansing rite', a phantasmagorical trial in which Court Royal, an old-time 'darkie', is made to kill his own son on orders from the judiciary. Equally acerbic is *Madheart* (1967), a kind of masque or harlequin play in which 'Black Man' and 'Black Woman' recognize their mutual plight in the face of the white 'Devil Lady'.[20]

   The play his publishers would not include, to Jones/Baraka's scorn, was *Jello* (performed 1965, published 1970) his scabrous assault on the Jack Benny-'Rochester' comedy series. That American TV's best-known black manservant should turn, savagely, uncomedically, upon his white employer was to challenge one of the culture's most comforting racial equations: all-knowing but still deferential black hireling; put-upon but still custodial white hirer. *Jello*, in other words, sought to reinterpret the relationship as still property equation, slavery in all its offence-defence coonery updated. Perhaps, given the deaths, the fires, it was inevitable that Jones/Baraka would close the decade with *The Death of Malcolm X* (1969), a one-act theatrical caricature which treats the murder of the Black Muslim leader as a species of grotesque media conspiracy.

Other Jones/Baraka plays from the 1960s need to enter the account, notably his farce, *Home on the Range* (1968), first presented at a fundraising benefit for the Black Panthers. The piece again uses a zany black house break-in, and a riotous cross-racial party, to deride any sought-after integration into white America as a fatal wrong turning. Much as the piece actually sidesteps a simple or reductive nationalism, the cry went up that ideology had indeed won the upper hand. Yet here, as in *Dutchman*, the truth remains that Jones/Baraka has always operated more subtly, his theatre a bold metamorphosis of black 1960s America.[21] It cannot surprise that successors as different as the Pittsburgh dramatist, August Wilson, or the film-maker, Spike Lee, continue to insist on Jones/Baraka as an inspiration.[22]

Alternative stylings of black theatre, however, equally mark out the 1960s, even if one first needs a slight step backwards in time. For in Lorraine Hansberry, James Baldwin and Loften Mitchell a more traditional liberalism is to be heard: America as necessarily bound to a shared inter-racial destiny. The accusations, thereby, however real, come over as less severe, a belief in the humanist solubility of racial encounter and division. In this respect Hansberry's *A Raisin in the Sun* (1959), first performed in New York, understandably won plaudits as the best black play to date, a naturalist, upbeat portrait, set in Chicago's South Side, of the Younger family's hopes of betterment.[23]

The plot hinges on an insurance cheque sent to Mama Younger and her resolve to move the family from black Chicago into a hitherto white-only neighbourhood, advance through the would-be bright promise of integration. Each Younger in turn harbours a private aspiration: Mama, herself, of an upward family rise; the son, Walter Lee, working as a chauffeur and long a defeated man, of a business; his wife, Ruth, of an end to a failing marriage and subsistence living; their boy, Travis, of ascent up young ambition's ladder; and Walter Lee's sister, Beneatha Younger, of a medical career and marriage to her African suitor. Each family member, in fact, undermines the other: Mrs. Younger by her need to preside as matriarch; Walter Lee by his self-contempt; Ruth by her despair; Travis by his need to admire a failing father figure; and Beneatha by her whimsy and sentimentalization of Africa.

Yet against the odds, and on the family standard, they find a powerful self-renewal, once a scam robs Walter Lee of his investment in a liquor store and a white neighbourhood group seeks to prevent their purchase of the new house. Mama's 'I be down directly', spoken at the end of the play as they prepare to move, gives the sign of the continued possibility of a new dawn, a black family determined (liberally, optimistically – this was a Civil Rights age) upon a better black tenancy of America.

A 'liberal' ethos also marks out *The Sign in Sidney Brustein's Window* (1964), set in Greenwich Village, and a virtual symposium on the tension of private and public morality.[24] Sidney and Iris Brustein represent the near classic Village couple, he an ineffectual dreamer optimist, Jewish, she a 'resting' actress originally up from poor-white Appalachia and much taken with Freud, and both struggling to save their failing marriage. Around them live Alton Scales, the play's only black figure and an angry political radical who becomes embroiled in a fatal relationship with Iris's sister, Gloria Parodus, a former call girl who commits suicide in the Brustein's apartment once Alton rejects her because of her past; Mavis Parodus, Iris's other, more respectable bourgeois sister; David Ragin, a homosexual and aspiring writer; and Wally O'Hara, Sidney's friend and Greenwich Village politico who sells out to the ward bosses.

In Brustein's turnings as a man of conscience, not to say a failed restaurateur who has bought into the local newspaper, Lansberry argues for moral activism ('We shall make something strong of this sorrow', says Sidney of Gloria's death and her failed affair across the racial divide with Alton) and a stand against old time fixes of political power. Thus a 'raceless' drama, essentially, it subsumes the black need for liberation within a wider humanist process, that which frees every race, gender and minority. Yet however authentic its ethic of cross-racial fraternity, and however well constructed, *Sign* has had an ambiguous fate. Proponents liken it to the theatre of Arthur Miller as a mainstay of the American liberal imagination. But to those in quest of a *black* 'black drama', dutifully – militantly – particular in its attention to black culture and psychology, it remains somewhere at the margin.

As far as subject-matter went, James Baldwin's theatre was to suffer something of a lesser doubt. 'We are walking in terrible darkness here, and this is one man's attempt to bear witness to the reality and the power of the light', runs his 'Notes' for *Blues for Mister Charlie* (1964).[25] Loosely based on the Emmett Till murder in 1955, it was to be dedicated to Baldwin's friend Medgar Evers, who in 1963 also became the victim of a white racist assassination. *Blues* dramatizes the life and killing of Richard Henry, a black, student-age revolutionary lately returned from a drug recovery clinic in the North to his Deep South roots. His murderer is Lyle Britten, white store owner and veteran good ol' boy supremacist. Two worlds thus collide, 'Whitetown' and 'Blacktown', with only occasional intermediaries such as Juanita, Richard's girl, herself an object of white vituperation, and Parnell James, the white liberal newspaper owner, likely to steer a forward path. Against them, Baldwin leaves no doubt, persists the white Dixie of old: violent, sexually fearful and given over to Klan-style phobia.

Few questioned the play's passion, but the cavils, both at the time and since, proliferated. Did not the dialogue dip into banality (Parnell says of his friend Britten 'He suffers – from being in the dark')? Was not Baldwin himself uncertain of the play's moral implications, on the one hand depicting the Reverend Meridian Henry, Richard's father, as eventually abandoning Christian non-violence by taking a gun to church under his Bible ('like the pilgrims of old', he says), and on the other hand holding on, in the Juanita–Parnell connection, to a belief in liberal salvation? What of the charge of formula characterization, whether Lyle Britten as sexually reinvigorated through violence or Parnell's achingly well meant inquiry, 'What is it like to be black?'. Questions, in turn, arose about the play's dramaturgy, about the Whitetown/Blacktown alternation, and possible overlength. But despite misgivings, *Blues for Mister Charlie* was a drama from, and for, the 1960s.

The Amen Corner, written as early as 1952 but not performed until 1965 (or published until 1968), drew directly upon Baldwin's own Harlem upbringing, especially his three years as a boy preacher in his stepfather's storefront church.[26] Centred in Sister Margaret Alexander, evangelical pastor to her black congregation, it explores the call of the world (first to Luke, Margaret's jazzman husband who has returned home sick and dying after ten years on the road, and then to their son David, a music student, who rejects the sanctimony in which he has been raised) as against the call of the spirit which has led Margaret to her vocation. But the congregation's elders, jealous, full of bickering, reject Margaret as mother prophet, accusing her of misuse of authority and even funds, the betrayal of her vaunted churchliness. No single rightness, or righteousness, holds, whether family or church. Even Margaret comes to see her own complicity in her husband's drinking and desertion. In this the best of the play recalls 'The Chant of Saints' in *Go Tell It on the Mountain* (1953), a fervent black Bible Christianity, which for all its certitude is vexed and eluded by the worlds of word and flesh beyond its own churchly terms of reference.

Of an age with Baldwin, Loften Mitchell entered the 1960s with perhaps his strongest work already behind him, *Land Beyond the River* (1957), the reworking of a celebrated South Carolina school busing controversy. But in *Star of the Morning: Scenes in the Life of Bert Williams* (1965) he developed a 'life' of the great vaudeville star, a documentary musical not unlike Langston Hughes's pastiche of Harlem religiosity, *Tambourines to Glory* (1963).[27] Williams's artistry, Mitchell recognises, had to survive both racist managements and audiences bound upon seeing only 'coon' stage acts. Yet whatever the popular persona, songster or black actor self-travestyingly made to wear blackface, Williams is shown to have recognized the game he was playing. 'Every laugh at me and abuse', Mitchell has him say, 'is a nail in white America's coffin'. Honouring Williams, thereby, becomes another kind of recovery of black cultural legacy – tap, acrobatics, song, mimicry, banter, as a kind of black contradance. The play opens up to ironic scrutiny a history in which Williams subverted, even as he seemingly obeyed, the required forms of black self-staging.

☆   ☆   ☆

Black doubling or counter representation has a long ancestry. The cakewalk in slave times offered its own mockery, black slave chattels outwitting their white owner occupiers. A novel such as George Schuyler's *Black No More* (1931) parodies, if from a deeply conservative standpoint, the race industry quite unsparingly. Chester Himes's thrillers, from *For Love of Imabelle* (1957) to *Blind Man with a Pistol* (1969), turn Harlem into a black Vanity Fair. William Melvin Kelley's *dem* (1967), subjects 'dem', or white folks, to the charge of understanding next to nothing about Harlem or about black culture at large. Latterly, the 'black' black comedies of Ishmael Reed, from *The Free-Lance Pallbearers* (1967) to *The Terrible Threes* (1989) to *Japanese by Spring* (1993) have won deserved and widespread success, Afro-America as a voodoo (or voudun) alternative to white, official America.[28] Black drama in the 1960s made its contribution in kind, typically in the plays of Douglas Turner Ward, Ossie Davis and Lonne Elder.

Ward's one-act *Happy Ending* (1964), 'A Satirical Fantasy', adds to the roster.[29] Two domestics, Vi and Ellie, who work for a white couple, the Harrisons, are thrown into near despair by Mrs. Harrison's adultery and the likelihood of a divorce. Their nephew, Junie, professes bafflement. In an age of 'Pride-Race-Dignity' as he calls it, how can his two aunts revert to this *Gone with the Wind* mentality? Slowly, like the veteran troupers they are, they put him to rights about the real calamity at hand. His clothes, food, spare cash, even bedding, in common with that of the family at large, have come from the pair's inspired finagling; just, not to say comic, re-appropriations for all the years of black maid service. Harrison, at their mock solicitude, relents. Equilibrium is restored and the game resumes, America's house of white employer–black employee as an ancestral yet ongoing 'domestic' collusion.

Day of Absence (1968), much in the vein of William Melvin Kelley's novel *A Different Drummer* (1962), envisages a Southern town suddenly emptied of all its blacks.[30] Work comes to a halt. Services, childcare, hospital work, cooking and cleaning, the whole support structure for white daily life, goes awry. The Mayor and Governor give way to rising panic. Radio and television announce deadlines for a black return. Appeals to a supposed Dixie and magnolia past are invoked. Telephone lines jam and conspiracy theories are mooted. Ward works the changes at high speed, a Feydeau or Dario Fo farce which this time mocks traditional Southern shibboleths. The Mayor, for instance, pitches his appeal in formula terms, deploring the absence of 'your cheerful, grinning, happy-go-lucky faces'. The whole works as stylized parody, a kind of adult pantomime which closes with Clem and Luke, two more good ol' boys, left to puzzle upon a vision of missing 'Nigras'. The satire positively exudes theatricality, but only as underwritten by a dark, accusing laughter.

Ossie Davis's *Purlie Victorious* (1961) and Lonne Elder's *Ceremonies in Dark Old Men* (1969) take alternative kinds of aim. In the former, set in Southern Georgia, Davis envisages a latterday plantation with its Ol' Cap'n Cotchipee, Purlie, as the black minister title figure, his son Gitlin, and a caper involving the winsome Lutiebelle Gussie Mae Jankins to win back land on which stands Big Bethel, a black church. Davis's good cheer, and the final appeal to an inter-racial future, marks the play as written in the early years of the Civil Rights movement. The touch is light, witty, companionable.[31]

Elder's irony in *Ceremonies in Dark Old Men* comes over more slow-footedly, a Harlem three-act play about the Parker clan, Russell B. Parker, barbershop regular, and his equally unemployed sons Theo and Bobby. On being evicted by Adele, the hardworking daughter, Parker joins the 'Harlem De-colonization Association', an illegal whisky operation run by a local con-man, Blue Haven. But the liquor scam becomes its own monster, simply another kind of oppression. The point gains force in the death of Bobby, killed while stealing from a neighbourhood store. As embodied in Parker and his sons, and as understandable as may have been their temptation to seek any means available to escape tenement joblessness, this Harlem rounds upon itself like a true predator, head made to devour tail.[32]

☆   ☆   ☆

A further name to be added from the black 1960s inescapably is that of Ed Bullins, especially the collection *Five Plays* (1969) made up of *Goin' a Buffalo, The Wine Time, A Son Come Home, The Electronic Nigger* and *Clara's Ole Man*.[33] This does not overlook the surge of other 1960s black drama: Wellington Mackey's *Requiem for Brother X* (1964), which depicts the ghetto as both outward and inward ruin; Ron Milner's *Who's Got His Own* (1965), the drama of a Detroit family caught generationally between religion and politics; Adrienne Kennedy's *A Rat's Mass* (1967), a piece which echoes Kafka's *The Metamorphosis* (1915) with blacks imaged as a rodent underclass; Ben Caldwell's *The King of Soul, or the Devil and Otis Redding* (1967), a one-act fantasia indicting white commercial degradation of the singer; Marvin X's *The Black Bird* (1969), an elegy to black freedom under Muslim auspices; and Sonia Sanchez's *Sister Sion/Ji* (1969), an early black feminist stagework.[34] But throughout the decade, as thereafter, Bullins's drama ranks alongside that of Jones/Baraka as setting the standard, albeit in a style more resolutely naturalist than experimental.

Bullins deservingly has won the praises of a theatre critic like Irving Wardle for avoiding 'self-affirming racial tracts'. His plays not only acknowledge, but seek to explore in depth, fissures and contradictions within the black community, as he has said 'the dialectical nature' of his people. *Goin' a Buffalo*, set in rundown West Adams, Los Angeles, so delineates a tense, often divided gang family: Curt as the street-hardened leader; Rich his sidekick; Curt's wife Pandora, strip dancer and high-class hooker; Mamma Too Tight, white, Southern born, and a drug addict and whore under the control of the dope dealer Shaky; and Art, a one-time penitentiary inmate with Curt. The play's title points to a dream, Buffalo (like a reverse California) as some mythicized better realm, with Curt and Pandora gentrified into respectable business couple.

That the robbery meant to deliver the necessary cash goes wrong, a probable betrayal by Art, Curt's successor both with Pandora and Mamma Too Tight, points up black criminality as a Pandora's Box, both vain promise and brutal reality. As the play particularizes the ebb and flow of the group, each flare-up, alliance and truce, with 'Buffalo' as the fragile dream, Bullins develops a style to match – the 'tragifantasy' of his subtitle. The play invites close ensemble playing, the more so to convey its 'theatre of cruelty' auspices.

The collection's shorter plays operate in similar mode. *A Son Come Home* amounts to an exercise in the presentation of memory, a sad, lost, mother–son relationship recaptured through a symposium of their own and related past voices. *The Electronic Nigger*, set in a California junior college writing class, becomes the very thing it dramatizes, a sardonic, reflexive exploration of the possible languages of black experience. *Clara's Ole Man: A Play of Lost Innocence*, ostensibly slum Philadelphia in the 1950s, involves an ex-GI, Jack, working his way through college, forced by his interest in Clara to confront a world none of his newly acquired academic vocabulary will account for: the lesbian menagerie which links Clara to Big Girl and Big Girl's retarded sister Baby Girl. It is a world which, as even tougher street-figures make their entrance, leaves him literally beaten into near unconsciousness. Bullins clearly pledged himself from the outset to spare little, or no one, in taking by storm all previous gentility or mere showtime in black theatre.

The same lack of compromise shows in his Cliff Dawson trilogy, *In the Wine Time* (1967), *In New England Winter* (1967) and *The Corner* (1968), overall a ghetto tableau, black 'street' America. The first concerns Cliff's relationship with his pregnant wife Lou, their nephew Ray, and a neighbourhood which includes the one remaining white couple, the fractious Krumps, and acquaintances and relatives from The Avenue, a slightly more respectable thoroughfare. Besotted on jug wine, Cliff fantasizes an escape from the ghetto through his under-aged nephew's enlistment in the navy. Ray himself seeks a way out through the unnamed girl with whom he has fallen in love. But in both cases it amounts to an ironic lyricism, a doomed hopefulness. In the event, the daze brought on by the drinking and the ever present likelihood of violence ends in a knife fight in which Cliff takes the rap for his nephew. A last would-be heroism or not, Cliff's action does nothing to lessen the black inner city as *huis clos*, an imprisoned vitality of sense and body.

Nothing in the other two plays suggests any coming alleviation. *The Corner* depicts an earlier but no less confused Cliff who allows Stella, the girl he philanders with while living with Lou, to be gang raped in accord with male ghetto writ. In *In the New England Winter*, having been abandoned by Lou, he emerges from jail to plan an improbable ideal robbery with his half-brother Steve. Yet bad faith catches him out again: Steve has been Lou's secret lover. Family lines cross, loyalty shades into betrayal. Blackness, in Bullins's theatre, means no single or sentimental oneness.

The trilogy as a whole keeps commendably to this ambiguity of motive and behaviour. Cliff Dawson embodies a man caught out by the odds yet who, at the same time, imposes odds both on himself and others, a self endangered and endangering. Bullins sidesteps a too simple either–or racial militancy. As to the 1960s itself, any hint of a drop in ambition or energy was countermanded in his heady announcement of a multi-part '20th Century Cycle', a kind of black theatrical *roman fleuve* whose opening instalments would include *The Duplex: A Black Love Fable in Four Movements* (1970), *Four Dynamite Plays* (1972) and *The Theme is Blackness* (1972).[35]

Jones/Baraka as a working centre, Hansberry, Baldwin and Mitchell as forerunners, Douglas Turner Ward, Ossie Davis, Lonnie Elder and Ed Bullins as 1960s contemporaries: the era's black theatre bequeaths a composite, yet singular, achievement. If some of the theatre forms are familiar enough, whether masque drama, satire, mixed-media productions, proscenium and street performance, who at the same time would have denied a new pitch or vibrancy to the black cultural signature to hand? And could it be doubted that they have bequeathed a new theatre legacy as borne out in Woodie King Jr.'s *The National Black Drama Anthology: Eleven Plays from America's Leading African-American Theaters* (1995)?[36]

Jones/Baraka in 1965 spoke of 'the aggregate of Black spirit', Ed Bullins in 1972 of 'the collective entity of Black artistic knowledge'.[37] Whatever their individually differing achievements, they, like their contemporaries throughout America's most evident black decade, could not in all its conjoined senses have indeed been more about the staging of that spirit, that knowledge.

Equilibrium Out of Their Chaos: Black Modernism, Black Postmodernism and Leon Forrest's Witherspoon-Bloodworth Trilogy

Descendancy: What's the score?

Leon Forrest: *Re-Creation*,
A Verse Play Set to Music by T.J. Anderson (1978)[1]

And what do I mean by re-creation and reinvention? I mean the powerful use of imagination to take a given form and make something that appears completely new of it – that creates within the reading or listening audience a sense of the magical meaning of life transformed.

Leon Forrest: 'In the Light of the Likeness – Transformed', in
Contemporary Authors Autobiography Series, Vol. 7, (1988)[2]

One of the constants of Afro-American culture is the re-invention of life – or, the cultural attribute of black Americans is to take what is left over ... and make it work for them, as a source of personal or group survival, and then to emboss, upon the basic form revised, a highly individualistic style, always spun of grace, and fabulous rhythms ... a kind of magic realism. The improvisational genius of jazz is what I am getting at here. This is central to the art of Ellington, Armstrong, Lady Day, Sarah Vaughan, Ray Charles, Muddy Waters, Alberta Hunter; I could of course go on.

Leon Forrest: 'Faulkner/Reforestation',
Doreen Fowler and Ann J. Abodie (eds):
Faulkner and Popular Culture: Faulkner and Yoknapatawpha (1990)[3]

'Word-possessed (and word-possessing).' Ralph Ellison's phrasing in his Foreword to *There Is a Tree More Ancient Than Eden* (1973) does every justice.[4] For to enter Forest County, Leon Forrest's black Chicago, at once Northern and yet shaped by a South of Mississippi and New Orleans, is to enter a city also, and in T.S. Eliot's sense, 'unreal'. That is, recognizable as may be Cook County's South Side or black West Side, Forrest's novels at the same time call up a different kind of topography, full of shadow, memory, hallucination and apocalypse.

His mythical kingdom thus aspires to a black city as much of the inner senses as of the apparent hardshell Chicago of Richard Wright's *Native Son* (1940) or, at a different reach, of Saul Bellow's rumbustious Jewish-immigrant in *The Adventures of Augie March* (1953). A Bigger Thomas, or his girl Bessie, might likely still belong, but only as though deliberately magnified, hyperfigures as it were. Forrest's own fictive people appear to be at one with, yet larger than, life: the branded ex-slave patriarch, Jericho Witherspoon; the supremely adaptive jack of all trades, Jamestown Fishbond; the eventually suicidal club owner and abortionist, Abraham Dolphin M.D.; the genealogist, the Rev. Jonathan Bass; the ledger-keeping midwife, Lucia Rivers; a con man as monstrous yet as fertile of invention as W.W.W. Ford; and of greatest relevance in Forest County, hornmen like Ironwood Landlord Rumble and protectresses like Hattie Breedlove Wordlaw and Great-Momma Sweetie Reed.

A similar imaginative regime holds for Forrest's delineation of the black community at large, street life, bars, churches, pool halls, the blues and jazz caught as though a displacement, a non-representational mural of dream and memory. This is a black Chicago made fervid by two Christianities, a Catholicism brought North from Creole Louisiana and a Bible Protestantism from Dixie's Camp Meetings and conversions.

Forrest as a Chicago novelist, without making him in any way too local, also requires its emphasis. From an autobiographical perspective there has been his schooling at Hyde Park School, Roosevelt University and the University of Chicago, his family's joint Catholic and Protestant legacy on the South Side, and his journalism on the *Woodlawn Booster*, the *Englewood Observer* and *Muhammad Speaks* of which (though never himself a Muslim) he became Editor from 1969 to 1972, not to mention a subsequent career as university teacher at Northwestern University, reviewer for *The Chicago Tribune* and other newspapers, and his frequent role as lecturer and broadcaster.

At the same time he can look to a black literary affiliation which includes the heirship of Nella Larsen (a Chicagoan for all her association with the Harlem Renaissance), Richard Wright, Willard Motley, Gwendolyn Brooks and Margaret Walker. Contemporaries include the poet and essayist Carolyn M. Rodgers; Ron L. Fair, whose novel *Hog Butcher* (1966), with its police killing and cover-up in the South Side, and quasi-autobiography, *We Can't Breathe* (1972), the account of another kind of black Chicago upbringing, offer comparisons; and his one-time fellow Professor of African American Studies at Northwestern University, Cyrus Colter, author of *The Rivers of Eros* (1972), a novel of a Chicago black dynasty (descended from the matriarch Clotilda Pilgrim) and of the repetitions of history, and of *The Hippodrome* (1973), with its more fantastical-absurdist ingredients of flight, murder, severed head, sex theatre, and for the protagonist Jackson Yeager, the uncertain border between hard fact and fantasy.[5]

If for Forrest Chicago is a city of the street, of the projects ('perpendicular segregation' was a term once applied to them), of the church or bar, and, always, of the remembrance of slavery and Northward migration, it also doubles as a city of Lex. For like Joyce and Dublin, Forrest and his city as consciously press to be understood in terms of the language of myth and, reciprocally, the myth of language, as of any actual streetmap, be the reference to the El, or to the Robert Taylor and Stateway homes (the largest stretch of public housing in America), or to a white enclave like Bridgeport which has supplied Chicago with five of its mayors, or to the Dan Ryan and Roosevelt Expressways, the South Park Boulevard (now Martin Luther King Jr. Drive), Cook County Hospital, the 408 Club which his parents once owned, Lake Shore Drive and Lake Michigan itself. Forrest's claim lies, finally, in his voicing, his idiom, which led Saul Bellow, in his turn, to speak of 'a fiery writer ... an original'.[6]

This reflexive bodying out of Forest County as both a historic past and present (a third of Chicago's population is black) and, at the same time, fabulatory terrain, amounts to a 'textual' drama in its own right. Little wonder that, alongside the dream sequences, the genealogies, the folklore and the fables of slave legacy and tricksterism, it is the sermon, that acme of black signifying, which recurs as a centrepiece.

Even a first-time reader of *There is a Tree More Ancient Than Eden*, or of the novels which follow, *The Bloodworth Orphans* (1977), *Two Wings to Veil My Face* (1984), the compendious *Divine Days* (1992) and, after his death of cancer in November 1997, the work which will be his posthumous novel, *Meteor in the Madhouse*, together with the essay volume, *Relocations of the Spirit* (1994), would be hard put not to recognize a writer for whom 'the word' lies at the very centre of all his endeavours.[7] Indeed 'the word' might be said to be an energy in itself in all of Forrest's work, iconic, mosaic, his various texts as a holding together, a healing, of all the human breakage passed down from slavery. In this respect he has had good reason to speak of his fiction as 're-creation and reinvention', 'individualistic style', 'grace', 'fabulous rhythms', in all, 'a kind of magic realism'.[8]

Taking up these emphases one might also very properly point to his place within a context of post-Ellison experiment. This implies an African American novel since *Invisible Man* (1952) positioned somewhere between the modernist and postmodern, given to reflexive sleight of hand, time shifts, an often dazzling black dialogic of speech into script. [9] Ishmael Reed offers an immediate companion touchstone, whether *The Free-Lance Pallbearers* (1967), his 'space satire' of Nixonian America and its racism, *Yellow Back Radio Broke-Down* (1969), his spoof Western with black cowboy hero, or *Flight to Canada* (1976), his pastiche slave narrative with its crossovers in time and place, zestful empire of textual play and fabulation, and rich, irreverent syncretisms (helicopters over the quarters, TV in the Big House, Abe Lincoln listening to Country and Western). [10]

The roster of recent self-mirroring black novels has been considerable. Early into the fray was William Melvin Kelley in whose fiction black surrealism takes on a new virtuosity. *A Different Drummer* (1962) envisages a Dixie state whose entire black population ups and leaves in a reprise of past slave escape. *A Drop of Patience* (1965) re-envisages the creative-destructive genius of Charlie Parker in the 'visionary' figure of the blind saxophonist Ludlow Washington. *dem* (1967) plays Harlem against white suburbia, an absurdist vision of America as mutually refractive yet separate 'racial' realms; and *Dunsfords Travels Everywheres* (1969), its vernacular title a parody of a furniture removal company, tackles a wholly imagined sequence of worlds in which apartheid, slave transport, religion and affairs of the heart both white and black are all put under high-fantastical and satiric rules. [11]

LeRoi Jones/Imamu Amiri Baraka's *The System of Dante's Hell* (1965) probes, with a quite intertextual flourish, the modern American city as encircled racial Inferno. William Demby's self-designated 'cubist' *The Catacombs* (1965), its sources in the films of Antonioni and Rosellini and the media theory of Marshall McLuhan as much as in Ellison, explores modern consciousness as a simultaneity of global fragment, sound-bite, image. Clarence Major's *NO* (1973) plays one process of 'detection' into the other, a murder and its unravelling as the metaphor for reality and its unravelling in a literary text. If Charles Wright's novels, *The Messenger* (1963), *The Wig* (1966) and *Absolutely Nothing to Get Alarmed About* (1973) claim a forbear it would be Nathanael West. Each takes its comic-sardonic tilt at 'American Dream' America: *The Messenger* with its phantasmagoric Manhattan of messages without meaning, *The Wig* with its hero, Lester Jefferson, as latterday black Candide, and *Absolutely Nothing to Get Alarmed About* as a contrast of 1960s New York skyscraper opulence with ground-level blight. [12]

Carlene Hatcher Polite's *Sister X and the Victims of Foul Play* (1975) tells the exile Paris life (and death) of Arista Prolo, a black woman dancer whose very life-force has been murdered by mere sex show or striptease, in terms of a free-form 'jazz' narrative. In *Song of Solomon* (1977) Toni Morrison (who was Forrest's editor at Random House) displays the surest inwardness with almost all of modernism's repertoire in how she reanimates

Africanist memory inside the life, searches and literal final flight of her slave-haunted Michigan hero Macon Dead III. Afro-America has one of its radical short-story innovators in James Alan McPherson, as borne out in stories like 'A Matter of Vocabulary', from *Hue and Cry* (1969), with its portrait of the haunted black boyhood in Georgia of two brothers, or 'The Ballad of a Dead Man', from *Elbow Room* (1977), with its circular reworking of the black ballad of feisty, folkloric Billy Renfro.[13]

'I had a real interest in experimenting, in expanding the form of the novel.'[14] John Wideman's ambitions were declared early. *A Glance Away* (1967), his first novel, interiorizes its story of the destructive homecoming of an ex-addict to his presentday inner city roots as a modernist weave of memory and myth. *Hurry Home* (1970) conjures up an Africa-journey from out of black Philadelphia as dream monologue. *The Lynchers* (1973) unfolds the fevered conspiracy of four Philadelphia black men to lynch, retributively and anachronistically, a racist white cop, as polyphonic narrative of a kind Wideman acknowledges among other sources to have derived from T.S. Eliot's 'The Waste Land'.[15]

Interestingly, in his subsequent Pittsburgh-Homewood genealogical trilogy, *Hiding Place* (1981), *Damballah* (1981) and *Sent for You Yesterday* (1983), Wideman has consciously opted for a more vernacular, accessible register, a kind of counter modernist style. Even so he has not forsworn a taste for reflexivity. He casts his story 'Surfiction' as a series of journal annotations under the by-line of 'John Wideman' who, among other autobiographical overlaps, has also taught at the University of Wyoming. In a further doubling, the 'author' then explores his role as the teacher of a pioneer black text like Charles Chesnutt's 'Deep Sleeper' and the novelist-professor who gives creative writing classes and attends conferences on, precisely, surfiction. The underlying question so runs: whose work bespeaks the shrewder textuality, Chesnutt's with its use of slave and other African American codes or that of the postmodern pantheon, nearly all of whom, like conspiratorial sigla and as Wideman/'Wideman' points out, appear to have names beginning with 'B' (whether Beckett, Burroughs, Borges of Berthelme)? 'Surfiction' not only teasingly makes itself over into the very thing it most purports to address, it opens up the more consequential issue of 'black' as against 'white' text.[16]

Responding in a 1978 interview with Maria Mootry to the question 'Do you consider yourself part of a "school of black writing"'?, Forrest replied: 'Well, McPherson, Morrison, Murray, Ellison, Wideman and I are all club-members you might say!'[17]

The answer is lightly phrased, wry, anything but to suggest some insiders-only literary circle. Forrest knew the diversity of all these writers. He speaks, rather, of shared affinities, of a black modernist, and implicitly postmodern, turn of imagination.

☆   ☆   ☆

Doubters have thought Forrest prone to floridity, over entangled or too hurried by his own rhetoric. In his concern to make text of Afro-America's dispossession and survival, with America at large as a crossply of miscegenated orphans, Forrest crowds his novels. The upshot leaves the reader insufficient breathing time or space. But this unflattering view is too limited. For Forrest's play of myth, as of his other imaginative patterns, in fact precisely orders his visions of disorder.

In this Forrest has always freely acknowledged a number of other debts. He has always drawn from the Bible, *The Odyssey* and Dante. His interview with Maria Mootry gives as his modern touchstones 'Joyce, Proust, Twain, Hawthorne, Melville, Faulkner [and] Dylan Thomas'.[18] As to African American literary tradition, besides his admired Ellison, he has often invoked as influences the slave self-articulations of Frederick Douglass and Harriet Jacobs/Linda Brent, the baroque of Jean Toomer in *Cane* (1923), and the urgent, finely caught clarifications of James Baldwin in *Notes of a Native Son* (1955) and the ensuing essay-collections.

Forrest equally insists upon his debt to oral and folk 'Afro-American ranges of eloquence', from street talk and the dozens through to 'the pulpit' and 'the platter'.[19] His resort to different mythic schemae likewise weighs, on the one hand Judaeo-Christian or Hellenic tradition, on the other Egypt's Isis-Osiris-Set triad, the Vodun of Haiti and other New World Africanism and, always, Afro-America's own Brer Rabbit, Stagolee, Shine, High John the Conqueror and John Henry.

In the same register he calls up 'the Black Church, the Negro spiritual, gospel music, the blues and jazz' as, in a beautifully freighted phrase, 'the railroad tracks and wings for my imagination'.[20] Armstrong or Ellington, Billie Holiday or Mahalia Jackson, as his essay 'Faulkner/Reforestation' confirms, the 'improvisational genius of jazz' has been a standard in both his life and writing. In this he offers his own figure of the black musician, none more so than Ironwood 'Landlord' Rumble, the blind jazz master and visionary so vital in the life of Nathaniel Witherspoon as the ongoing persona of all the Forest County novels.

As Nathaniel dwells, intimately, lovingly, upon the remembrance of Ironwood's art (in *The Bloodworth Orphans*), he at the same time refracts Forrest's own improvisational bid to make textual order of history's disorder. 'Magical meaning' takes on a dual signification: Nathaniel's will-to-art shadows Forrest's own, a modernist (even postmodern) collusion of author and character in pursuit of a language, a narrative design, to hold the sheer density and contrariety of black American experience.

Seeking entrance to Refuge Hospital, in which the heroin-addicted jazzman has been incarcerated as a patient, Nathaniel calls to mind 'ole Ironwood's boss-embossing music' and his response of being:

constantly astonished by the furious, heavenly design and the wreckage-resurrecting brilliance of Rumble's beauty blitz, his daredevil leaps, his mocking raps, his dazzling riff escapes, his one-butt shuffle scats, his signifying jagged tremelos, his soul chant crooning inventions. (p. 303)

Forrest's prose palpably re-enacts the finely contrived runs of improvisation played off a fixed rhythm inside any jazz or blues classic, be the model Armstrong, Ellington or Bird, to give three different but symptomatic Forrest favourites. And in the allusions to 'furious ... design', 'raps', 'dazzling riff escapes', 'scats' and 'jagged tremelos', it speaks, analogously, to Forrest's own narrative tactics, his own makings-over, those of a daring, sometimes near pyrotechnic, effort to retrieve order from disorder or, in his own hybrid phrase, the process of 'wreckage-resurrecting'. Little wonder that Forrest has often spoken as an insider of Chicago as the city of Mahalia Jackson, Lady Day, Muddy Waters and Howlin' Wolf and within a jazz and blues tradition stretching from the 1920s to the presentday.

On his way to the apartment of the near-senile Bella-Lenore, Nathaniel has earlier turned his mind to Refuge Hospital:

where old Ironwood 'Landlord' Rumble, the blind virtuoso of nine instruments, poured out a sad musical deluge – a free-flying blitzkrieg, unleashing a grand flood of underground, storehouse figures, long-lost images, homeless visions, signs, and wonders and miracles inside the inferno. (p. 81)

This might serve, reflexively, as a credo for Forrest's own transliteration of improvisory jazz idiom. His language calls up the 'wonders and miracles' of African American life, most of all slavery whether as brute seizure, survival or escape – a past as both 'storehouse' and 'inferno'.

These 'images, visions, signs and wonders and miracles memories', stretching from the earliest African diaspora through Abolition and on to the Great Migration into the cities, declare themselves in abundance in Forrest's fiction; their *locus* is the human workings of Forest County. History, as he seeks to render it, operates as a storm against all the canons of order. His style aspires to work in kind, myth-laden, magic realist as only a black Chicagoan raised on two versions of fervent Christianity could conceive it.

Forrest's will to virtuosity, in other words, runs close to that which has brought on Ironwood's command of his nine instruments so admired by Nathaniel and which will so prevail in the great blues performance given at Refuge Hospital towards the close of *The Bloodworth Orphans*. The ordering of disorder might be thought the necessary remit of any writer worth his calling. But for a black American writer taken up, as Ralph Ellison's brief Foreword to *There Is a Tree* puts it, with 'those dilemmas bred of Christian faith and racial conflict, of social violence ... and dreams of a peaceful kingdom', the task takes on a stirring impetus.

This may well explain why Forrest frequently resorts to hybrids of sacramental and vernacular language, skeins of word play and echo (particularly in the names of characters or churches), and, in *There Is a Tree*, a variety of italicized and other typographical layouts. He gives the impression of wanting to make the very language of his storytelling actually absorb and pattern as much as it can of the chaos and fissure engendered by slavery – whether colour line, sexual phobia, white and black Christianity, or any of the politics of division. At the same time it is pitched to particularize and celebrate the very strategies by which Afro-America *has* survived, the black word in all its multiplicity of form.

Given the initial diaspora out of Africa, the Middle Passage, slavery's ensuing ranks of illegally fathered and mothered offspring, and all the ancestral enigma, curses, and sexual bans and transgressions of colour, which have passed down through all American history, perhaps no literary form can ever pay complete imaginative due. Forrest can hardly be faulted for making the attempt, a fiction in which the footfalls of Joyce and Faulkner, of Douglass and Ellison, cohabit with those of Afro-America community idiom and metaphor.

It is, in fact, precisely this kind of bold eclecticism which, in Robert Frost's phrase, help make Forrest's novels their own kind of stays against confusion.[21] Fashioned of a rhetoric varyingly elevated and vernacular, they both call for, and themselves create, order out of America's reeling, often seemingly unorderable racial inheritance.[22] What, then, *is* the measure of Forrest's unfolding Witherspoon-Bloodworth novels of Forest County, his modernism, his own 'musical deluge'? [23]

☆   ☆   ☆

As 'Richard' serves in relation to Richard Wright, so 'Nathaniel' (or 'Nathan') Turner Witherspoon serves in relation to Forrest, and nowhere more so than in *There Is a Tree More Ancient Than Eden*. Still the most intimate, and lyric, of the novels to date, and in common with novels like Owen Dodson's account of his Brooklyn upbringing in *Boy at the Window* (1951), James Baldwin's uses of his Harlem birth and youth in *Go Tell It on the Mountain* (1953) and Gordon Parks's Kansas farm beginnings in *The Learning Tree* (1963), it draws upon deeply autobiographical sources – most specifically in Nathaniel's rite of passage as a mourner of his recently dead mother.[24]

But when, in imagination, Nathaniel thinks back on black enslavement, its brandings and lynchings and, be it in the South or the Northern cities, its residual workings in the historic colour line, a related but quite other emerging role becomes evident: that of a chronicler of Afro-America itself. Language becomes alchemy for him ('I was always falling in love with the sounds and shapes of people and places' (p. 5) he confides at the outset), a route doubly into history and into his own Portrait of the Artist.

This creation of Nathaniel as mulatto boy in his fifteenth year, born of both Catholic and Protestant roots, and a prism for the Witherspoon dynasty and its enclosing Afro-America, plays through all five of the unfolding acts – 'The Lives', 'The Nightmare', 'The Dream', 'The Visions' and 'Wakefulness' (Forrest has added a sixth, 'Transformation', in the 1987 reissue). As in the schema Joyce had in mind for *Dubliners*, each tells its story as local in space and time and yet linked into the visionary, the millennial. The effect is one of blues-like pilgrimage, at once intensely singular yet always implicitly typological.

As Nathaniel follows the hearse down the DuSable and Black Bottom Streets, on past 'Abe Weinstein's dog', then the Joe Louis Theater and the Salem Cup-Overflowing Tabernacle, comforted throughout by Aunty Breedlove, his new motherlessness reflects both a self-emptying and a spur to self-plenishment. For out of her death comes his own life, a flood of imaginative energy and consciousness about ancestors (his own grandfather and missing father especially), about race, religion, and the mixed-blood and South to North history which has been the making of him.

First, in 'The Lives', Forrest establishes his 'Chant of the Saints' as it were. These span the hideously martyred Master-of-Ceremonies Browne (beaten to death for his sexuality by his own father) to Maxwell 'Black-Ball' Saltport, transformed after drugs and prison into the Black Muslim minister Maxwell 2X. They also include Jamestown and Madge Ann Fishbond, both so black, so feisty and individual, as to bring on the scorn of Nathaniel's own Dupont mulatto relatives (Nathaniel himself, in Jamestown's words, also 'a little yellow boy'). The novel also reaches into history for Louis Armstrong (a 'towering and revolutionary power'), Frederick Douglass ('The North Star'), Harriet Tubman ('Breedlove's antecedent'), and Abraham Lincoln ('assassinated' father and 'Christ-myth'). Each supplies a shaping presence, a voice of memory, for Nathaniel.

It is, however, Nathaniel's own voice which most presides, the agency by which to remember his 'human centerless family'. This includes his defeated father, Arthur Witherspoon, and now his dead mother, but beyond them, and pre-eminently, Jericho Witherspoon ('succumbed' at 117 years of age and at one time a branded and escaped slave 'Wanted Dead or Alive'), and Hattie Breedlove Wordlaw, Dilsey-like, whose life he emblematizes in the single honorific, 'Honor'. Nathaniel makes no secret of his 'fierce desire to mold and sculpt', likening himself, grandly, to Lucifer as the artificer of 'a world of his own within his loneliness', a latest black orphan-narrator.

These imaginings are centrifugal, a gathering focus. In 'The Nightmare' Nathaniel moves out from 'the street' – the Weinstein grocery, the House of the Soul with its ribs and pork advertised through a blood-red pig, the

House of the Brown-Skinned Goddess Salon where nappy hair is styled, the Music Conservatory where Taylor 'Warm-Gravy' James plays blues, the Robert E. Lee High School, the Memphis Raven Snow funeral home, the Dupont residence, and more – into a vision of 'flying', of terror, as brought on by his mother's death with her hands so tightly bound with the rosary.

This 'snaking and hissing', variously likened to a bluesy train and the Mississippi, bespeaks guilt, terror, the boy's self-haunting projection of life's terminus. It plays, too, into 'The Dream', his Bosch-like envisioning of Heaven and Hell in which 'black skeletons appeared like orbit-lost suns' and 'river-deep wounds' haunt his imagination like stigmata. 'Light years from my home', subject to a 'landlocked lostness', he becomes the very sounding-board of black deracination. His own loss, the register suitably one of distortion, plays into a sense of the larger community loss inaugurated by slavery.

'The Vision', its backdrop of a kind with the fanatic, inflamed Georgia of Jean Toomer (and, far from unrelatedly, of Flannery O'Connor), enacts the part for part dismemberment of a black slave Christ with 'a band of blood-bruised angels' as chorus. This interplay of slavery and crucifixion, Dixie and Bethlehem, typifies Forrest at his most 'word-possessing', a rare, truly audacious, effort to locate the monstrous spiritual essence of slavery.

In 'Wakefulness' Nathaniel returns, literally, to the Fleetwood limousine and Breedy, but the journey home again gives way to that taking place in his feelings and brain. As the stream of consciousness last pages of the novel bear out, he has become immersed in the larger significations of all the words in his inheritance, a self now put to transpose them into *imaginative* order.

In adding to the second edition the two-part 'Transition', 'The Epistle of Sweetie Reed' and 'Oh Jeremiah of the Dreamers', Forrest fuses Nathaniel's boyhood visions into two historic later moments, Sweetie Reed's 1967 letter to President Lyndon Johnson on her 100th birthday as a bittersweet, half-comic preachment on the gains and limits of Civil Rights, and a later Nathaniel's witness in the Crossroads Rooster Tavern to the Rev. Pompey c.j. Browne's after hours, impromptu sermon on the twelfth anniversary of Martin Luther King's assassination.

The one highlights Sweetie's memory of slavery and its echo in segregation, the continuing colour line. The other turns upon Browne's elision of a latest black crucifixion into the original. This is indicated by the compounding play of image and allusion in the 'principal homily' he delivers, two martyrdoms and two matching sites, Jesus in Golgotha and King in Memphis, Tennessee. The Browne sermon offers contemporary yet older African American and biblical reference, a preaching of the pathways which have led into, as he says, 'the ruins of the New Jerusalem'.

Unruined, however, is its own art, the black sermon as itself the very image of order replete in cadence, image, design.

> This name of Bloodworth is not unknown to me ... I've heard of this infamous clan, all of my days, including a Hattie Breedlove Wordlaw, a dear woman, whom I always called 'Aunt', even though she was not my blood aunt, but helped raise me and was like a second mother to me ... the story recalls to me something of my own grandfather's saga. (pp. 341–2)

So, as *The Bloodworth Orphans* moves to its close, Nathaniel (or Spoons as he has become) links his own family to that of Noah Ridgerook Grandberry, last of the fated Bloodworths – kin, however, as a result not of blood but through the family's adoption of his father, Pourty Ford Bloodworth, himself doomed to kill, unknowingly, his own father, Arlington Bloodworth II, and a vicious abuser of Noah's mother, Elaine Norwood. Argumentative, accusatory, ready always to seek out each further skein in the story, Nathaniel and Noah (no doubt, intertextually, in some measure derived from Quentin and Shreve in Faulkner's *Absalom, Absalom!*) try to extract some guiding order from the cross-racial, dynastic chaos (Nathaniel's repeated word) which has thrown them together. In the background a city riot threatens, more turbulence in lives already turbulent.

'This name Bloodworth', 'this infamous clan', 'my own grandfather's saga': these and similar terms strike just the right note. For *The Bloodworth Orphans* marks Forrest's move into epic, the genealogy ranging across a century-and-a-half of a line begotten of the slave-owning patriarch, Arlington Bloodworth Sr. (1817–1917), and whose members, white, black and virtually every mix of the two, have become the players in an unabating black-white spiral. Forrest unravels a story begun in antebellum plantation Mississippi, but whose racial legacy of blight, mendacity, human error and coincidence, is lived through to its conclusion in the present of Forest County's postwar Chicago.

Given its intensely imagized styling, word compounds, uses of memory, time shifts and plays on biblical and black folkloric archetypes, the novel demands much of its first-time reader. The effect, even so, is spectacular, Forrest's own *Book of Genesis*. Not the least of the ambitions is to make the Bloodworths a kind of ranking house of America, white, black and a profound ongoing mix and overlap of both.

This is a genealogy drawn from both scriptural and oral sources; but in the gathering litany of slave legacy, miscegenation, death, and the resort to trickster tactics for survival and power, each story becomes subject to Nathaniel's authorial making-over. He becomes as much participant as observer, identifying his own Witherspoon clan with that of the

Bloodworths. Each Bloodworth story becomes the superimposition of the one text upon the other, a process part interfoliation and part palimpsest.

This layering of texts is demonstrated in the extracts from the 'Clearinghouse Book' of the midwife, Lucia Rivers, which Nathaniel finds by accident with its '1000-page document-testament' of births and deaths, a kind of African American Pentateuch or archival naming of names. More comes his way through the research conducted by the Rev. Jonathan Bass which fatally reveals to Amos-Otis Thigpen the incest of his sibling Bloodworths, Regal Pettibone (adopted son and baritone accompanist to 'Mother' Rachel at the River Rock of Eden Baptist Church) and La Donna Scales ('possessed by a terrible premonition: that she would ultimately be abandoned – eternally'), which will lead directly and grotesquely, by gun and then mob attack, to their respective deaths. All three of the triplets and their half-brother, Noah Ridgerook Grandberry, he learns, descend (of two mothers) from Pourty Bloodworth, just one of the many dynastic knots within the Bloodworth lineage. Even so, the Regal–La Donna relationship amounts to 'a beautiful and terrible love-story' in Nathaniel's gloss, its 'beauty' that of the heart's passion even as its 'terror' lies in incest. It is his gloss, too, which links this fatal turn to the original slaveholding, human property as blight.

Nor does his telling of the web, the maverick procreative will, of the Bloodworth lines end there. There is Abraham Dolphin – bastard offspring of the relationship between William Bloodworth ('Body') and his half-sister Carrie Trout Picou – whose contradictory role as successful club owner of the Basement Lounge and abortionist preshadows his despairing eventual suicide ('Burdened with rivers of guilt, Dr. Dolphin thought that perhaps his sonless condition was related to the vast numbers of formless and form-filled babies he had aborted'). There is Rachel Rebecca Carpenter Flowers, mother (by Arlington Bloodworth III) of Industrious Bowman and Carl-Rae Bowman (their surname taken from the 'kindly Negro minister' who adopts them), the former killed in the Santa Fe Railroad Yards and the latter dying as a vagrant in Memphis. Rachel, furthermore, who is won over as a Christian convert by the Rev. Packwood, marries, self-punishingly, the obese, opera-obsessed Bee-More (MoneyCzar) Flowers, and dies brutally of cancer, Nathaniel recognizes for yet another Bloodworth Orphan.

Non-Bloodworths, equally, stir Nathaniel's imagining, foremost among them Maxwell (X) Saltport, the betrayed Muslim minister; Jamestown Fishbond, Korea veteran, linguist and friend, whose body is finally identified only by his dog-tag, having fought against the Portuguese for black African liberation in Angola; Bella-Lenore Boltwood, 89 years of age, close to senility, and who talks to Nathaniel of long-ago imagined loves and courtships; Master-of-Ceremonies Browne, whose singing attracts Nathaniel and whose death at his reverend father's hands has already been told in

There Is a Tree; and, his creative mentor, Ironwood 'Landlord' Rumble, musical prodigy at three and suicide at 47 years of age.

Yet others come to Nathaniel in hearsay and talk. He learns of, and then finds himself utterly held by, the William Body–Carrie Trout Picou liaison with its story of New Orlean prostitution, or the Body–Lavinia Materston affair with its Algerian-French offshoot in Ahmed Picon. Each, for him, becomes part of the web, the enclosing shadow of the Bloodworth patrimony. But above even these, there looms the great *eminence grise* of the novel, W.W.W. Ford, trickster supreme, 'serial hermaphrodite', and a kind of superlative if truly cynical African American warlock in whom Ellison's Rinehart has become a near metaphysical trickster god.[25] In his shifting guises as priest, drug dealer, pimp, adopter of orphans, rhetorician, Tiresian man-woman, Ford is summoned into being by Nathaniel as the very spirit of extravagant survival.

However necessary tricksterism may have been to black survival, Nathaniel comes to recognize that it alone will not suffice. One aspect of his own need to seek the *ur*-story behind the Bloodworth spiral is the quest for some better moral principle, a wiser, saner, American humanity. Even so, the dance continues, chaotically as ever, most evidently in his flight from the riot with Noah and with the black infant they encounter by chance, 'its trembling little hands reaching upwards towards the two sad-faced sobbing men'.

The 'House of Refuge', the decaying, white penitentiary asylum in which the two find themselves held with Ironwood and from which they make their forays for food and drink, acts as Forrest's image of this same 'Bloodworth' America. It serves as the image of a detention centre, in which, historically, blacks have been held, named and renamed, sexually and otherwise abused. Noah, symptomatically, speaks of chaos, 'madness and constant troubled confusions'. Nathaniel agrees, but, counteringly, invokes the music of Ironwood, the jazz and blues of the 'wounded ... blind bard warrior' as offering black spiritual harmonizations amid all the disorder. He also alludes to the 'beautiful but tragic people' who have suffered the blight of the Bloodworths, the epilogue of a narrator hero who even as he glimpses order finds himself obliged once again to take flight against 'more chaos'.

All of their respective commentary, in fact, applies. The Bloodworth genealogy implies not linear history, but rather a chaos writ large and continuingly through all American time and space. Nathaniel understands, even as he is appalled by, the evangelical wiles and tricksterism of W.W.W. Ford, with his false church, staggering rip-offs and sales-pitches, and white girl accomplice, Gay-Rail (a variation of Grail). He also knows that the charade will continue as borne out in Ford's canny, duplicitous adoption ads which Nathaniel and Noah come across towards the end in the personals column of the newspaper.

But the better resistance for Nathaniel lies in the 're-creation and reinvention' of 'what is left over'. He recognizes this in the heroic musicianship of an Ironwood, the church singing of a Rachel Flowers or Regal Pettibone, the politics of a Jamestown Fishbond, or the sermons, well-meant or less so, by the likes of a Rev. Shelton Packwood or Rev. Jonathan Bass (preaching to be compared with that of the Rev. Pompey c.j. Browne in *There Is a Tree* and *Two Wings to Veil My Face*). In their different ways, these each simultaneously resist *and* transform the chaos to hand. They offer truly creative re-creations of the nation's histories within a history.

Above all, Forrest embodies this same process in Nathaniel himself. It falls to him, much as he professes himself unequal to the task, to make a narrative unity of the Bloodworth story. Once again, though on a larger scale than *There Is a Tree*, the complication of an America enravelled in racial confusion actually gets taken into the very form of the novel – in the first instance in Nathaniel's effort against the odds to discover and state the true, underlying plot of the Bloodworths, and behind that, in the orchestration of Forrest's own overall telling.

☆   ☆   ☆

Two Wings to Veil My Face opens with Nathaniel as amanuensis, the memorialist of a bedridden, weakening 91 year old Great-Momma Sweetie Reed. In a room which might itself serve as an echo chamber of past associations and remembrances, it falls to her young grandson, the rejected suitor of Candy Cummings and self-confessed dropout in his early twenties, to record upon a series of aptly named legal yellow pads the life of his own grandmother, or at least the paternal grandmother from whom he believes himself descended and to whom his devotion is total.

That life, of early slavery, the struggle to survive the Reconstruction years, and the move North to Chicago in the wake of her marriage to Nathaniel's grandfather, Jericho Witherspoon, he finds himself writing into being even as he listens, Great-Momma Reed's reader and writer at one and the same time, an inspired overlap which takes Forrest's modernism into still newer reaches.

Sweetie's history in every way profoundly entwines with Nathaniel's own, another black genealogy, that of the Reeds and the Witherspoons, again transposed into order out of the past's disorder by a Nathaniel Witherspoon quite literally called upon to set down the word. In this the novel offers one kind of writer as the secret sharer of another, Nathaniel in the role of Sweetie Reed's personal archivist foreshadowing Nathaniel as the eventual presiding storyteller. Reflexively, again, this dual Nathaniel does the even further duty of standing in for, but kept at a distance from, Forrest himself, Faulknerian *Sole Owner & Proprietor* of yet more Forest County.

Among latterday fictive accounts of the journey up from slavery, Sweetie Reed's readily takes its place alongside that of the tough, enduring Jane Pittman in Ernest Gaines's *The Autobiography of Miss Jane Pittman* or of the ghost haunted Sethe in Toni Morrison's *Beloved*. Despite a specific departure point, the antebellum Rollins plantation of Mississippi, and a specific slave parentage, the Rollins manservant I.V. Reed and his wife Angelina, Sweetie's personal history also signals the enclosing larger black community history: witness at the age of seven, in 1874, to the patrollers' brutal rape and killing of her mother; the long rankling marriage by arrangement at 15, in 1882, to a former escaped slave, the then 55 year old Jericho Witherspoon; her traumatic parting of the ways from him in 1905; and her reluctant, half-delirious attendance in 1944 at the memorial service for the 115 year old patriarch in the Memphis Raven-Snow Funeral Home before an assembly of mourners which includes her diabetic, hysterical 'son', Arthur Witherspoon, Nathaniel's father.

These, and each further contributing tier of her life, she calls to mind before her rapt, impatient grandson in a Chicago of 1958, a cycle of pasts relived as though a simultaneous and ongoing present. Told in slivers of recollection, voices within voices, pauses for inquiry and recapitulation, one-time frame held in abeyance in order to complete the events of another, Great-Momma Sweetie Reed's story profoundly plays into Nathaniel's own, her past deeded to his present as a shared kinship of blood and script.

In the latter respect, her past is a gift of language. The word she bequeaths literally becomes inscribed in his, a process once again involving its own 'magic meaning', its own 'reinvention'. Whether, thereby, as interlocutor to Sweetie or eventual narrator, Nathaniel finds himself compelled to an ordering fusion of her tale inside his telling or, as he calls it, her 'backwater time' and storytelling powers and recollections' inside his 'unfolding'.

'Write it all down' the almost deaf Sweetie enjoins Nathaniel, as though fearful of losing her own other voices in other rooms. So, in obligation, he does, starting with the nineteenth-century plantation owner voices of the 'blackbirding' Rollins Reed, and of his deranged wife, Mistress Sylvia, caught up in her seven-mirrored mansion and her jewels as the war turns against the South. Across, and interplied with them, run the words of Sweetie's parents, I.V. and Angelina, of the conjure-woman Aunt Foisty ('a-huffing and a-chanting some of them broken-down African words'), of the slave-driver Reece Shank Haywood ('a big, muscle-flexing nigger' who near-strangles Rolley), of the mulatto Clea who helps Sweetie bury I.V., of the preacher whose name calls up a familiar other dynasty, the Rev. Stigwood Bloodworth, and of Wayland Woods, author of the near-illiterate but compelling letter long stored by Sweetie and written to Master Rollins demanding the return of his stolen slave daughter.

These, in their turn, echo down into the present century. First, Nathaniel hears Sweetie's invocations of Jericho Witherspoon, both his talk as he rises to prominence as a lawyer and politician in Chicago and his 'lifelong journal' which reads 'as if the very feel of history was ingrained in the texture of the pages'. Nathaniel also discovers adjoining texts like the Reed-Witherspoon freedom papers and family ledgers (crucially that which contains a reference to 1905, and to Arthur Witherspoon, his name written with quotes around it). These, taken with Sweetie's 'world of remembrances' as given in her 'winging call-and-response manner', yield a world once theirs or hers but now also his. Early on in the novel Nathaniel becomes conscious of his role as storyteller:

> But now the young man ... wondered if all the storytelling, the loving, the harsh disciplining, the praying and the direction had been a preparation for the day, *this* day, when he would have to take over her memories. (p. 5)

But the most overwhelming of all these memories for Nathaniel, and which for him most orders all the contributing voices, lies inscribed upon Jericho Witherspoon's back: the branded initials put there by his own white father to prevent escape. Seen through Nathaniel's child eyes at the burial, they become memory itself, or as the boy comes to think them, 'memory wounds on fire'. This 'J.W. script', the 'blister-like italicized brand JW ... vivid as a visitation', seizes him utterly. Sweetie's 'Boswell', as he will at one point call himself, he discerns a composite Afro-America in this 'birthmark', and in each further gathering sign, be it the 'forged chain' or the 'rabbit's-foot bracelet'.

For underlying the 'multilayered collectivity of words' lies the stark, inerasable, 'shadow' of slavery. It is as if Forrest insists that the one encipherment of 'JW' carries all. Can Nathaniel ever wholly understand, and so inscribe, the slave nightmare from which the grandfather's historical branding derives?

Nathaniel Witherspoon will go on to solve the riddle of his own paternity, the mystery of the date 1905 in the Reed-Witherspoon ledger, and Sweetie's own blood kinship with him. At Sweetie's prompting he will begin to understand the mixed bloodlines of the Reeds, the Witherspoons, and the still further outlying family to which he is heir. As the novel's last paragraphs indicate, he will even recognize the complex, larger responsibilities of his own signifying. But there remains the final challenge: how to 'order' into the one resolved narrative all of these paining, contradictory, spirals of legacy for which the 'JW' acts as hieroglyphic.

That, too, is the challenge for the boy who rides to his mother's funeral in *There Is a Tree*, or for the companion of Noah Grandberry who plunges into the riot of the closing chapter in *The Bloodworth Orphans*, or for the Nathaniel literally with the yellow pad transcripts of Great-Momma

Sweetie Reed's remembered history in his hands in *Two Wings to Veil My Face*. As with its predecessors, and in whatever due complication, Nathaniel's rendering of genealogical disorder in *Two Wings* in fact becomes a rare triumph of imaginative ordering; or, more precisely, of Forrest's ordering.

The achievement of the Witherspoon-Bloodworth trilogy, with *Divine Days* there to further extend the reach of Forest County, lies utterly in this overall 're-creation and reinvention'. History is given momentary equilibrium and the seemingly untellable is told. Viewed in more literary terms, Leon Forrest's novels can be said to have put Afro-America under the auspices of his own uniquely modern, modernist, and beckoningly postmodern transformation.

Under Cover, Under Covers: African American Fictions of Passing

> Something more may come of this Masquerade.
> Herman Melville, *The Confidence-Man* (1857)[1]

> The failure of the melting pot, far from closing the great American democratic experiment, means that it has only just begun. Whatever American nationalism turns out to be, we see already that it will have a color richer and more exciting than our ideal has hitherto encompassed ... America is already the world-federation in miniature, the continent where for the first time in history has been achieved that miracle of hope, the peaceful living side by side, with character substantially preserved, of the most heterogeneous peoples under the sun ... Here, notwithstanding our tragic failures of adjustment, the outlines are already too clear not to give us a new vision and a new orientation of the American mind in the world.
> Randolph S. Bourne, 'Trans-National America' (1916)[2]

> Multiple hybrid identities, composed of crossed and recrossed boundaries, have thus become ... the contemporary global as well as American norm.
> Frederick Buell, *National Culture and the New Global System* (1994)[3]

Tiger Woods, 1997 US Masters golf winner, announces on *The Oprah Winfrey Show* that black does not summarize his ethnic make-up and teasingly designates himself 'Cablinasian, a blend of Caucasian, Black, Indian and Asian'. In part to allay talk of Woods's having abandoned his black birthright, Julian Bond, Civil Rights veteran, and himself of mixed ethnicity, speaks of 'sharing' him.

Trey Ellis, positioning himself as New Cultural Mulatto, declares himself unbound from any residual obligation to write only about the colour line. Both of his 'New Black Aesthetic' novels, *Platitudes* (1988) and *Home Repairs* (1993), along with a canny inter-ethnic story like 'Guess Who's Coming to Seder' (1989), provocatively draw upon a syncretic blend of black, white, and magic realist and postmodern sources. Whatever the virtuosity of his fiction Ellis's use of phrasing like Cultural Mulatto arouses consternation. By some fiat of postmodern ethnicity has he ceased to be a 'black' writer?[4]

The poet AI (Florence Anthony), author of *Sin* (1986) and other collections of modern verse Gothic – she casts a typical soliloquy like 'The Good Shepherd' in the cold, manic voice of the anonymous mass-murderer of Atlanta's black children – has a Japanese father ('Ai' is Japanese for love) and a mother of mixed African American, Choctaw and Irish descent. She finds herself listed, often queryingly, in both African American and Asian American reference works.[5]

Alice Walker, notably in her Civil Rights novel, *Meridian* (1976), and her selection of essays, *Living by the Word* (1988), and Clarence Major, a frontline experimentalist in fiction like *Such Was the Season* (1987) and *Painted Turtle: Woman with Guitar* (1988), and the poet of *Some Observations of a Stranger at Zuni in the Latter Part of the Century* (1989), both make imaginative resort not only to African American but also to their mixed African Cherokee legacy[6]. Accordingly, they have challenged assumed niches. Are they to remain listed as African American, cross-listed as Native, or accorded a new kind of recognition as African Native writers?

In *Airing Dirty Laundry* (1993), Ishmael Reed, Afro-America's ranking wit and metafictionist, displays his pleasure in, and wonder at, a lineage which includes both extended black family and stepfamily, a Cherokee great grandmother, a distant Danish woman relative, and the Irish great grandfather engagingly remembered in 'Black Irishman'. He could well have mentioned that Martin Luther King, on his father's side, also had an Irish grandmother. In a riff on the metaphor of American kinship Reed contends: 'there's no such thing as Black America or White America, two nations, with two separate bloodlines. America is a land of distant cousins'.[7]

Toni Morrison puts the argument another way in *Playing in the Dark: Whiteness and the Literary Imagination* (1992), the luminous 1990 Massey lectures she gave at Harvard. There she traces out the 'Africanist presence and personae' behind the classic American authorship of Poe, Melville, Cather and Hemingway. 'American Africanism', she suggests, inhabits all 'white' American discourse, explicitly or otherwise, a metaphor of both presence and absence stretching from the Puritans through to the Declaration of Independence and, in terms of literary fiction, from Poe's *The Narrative of Arthur Gordon Pym* (1838) to Hemingway's posthumous

The Garden of Eden (1987). Her summing-up leaves little to doubt: 'Africanism is inextricable from the definition of Americanness.'[8]

A decade earlier Ralph Ellison, in 'The Little Man at Chehaw Station' (1977), strikes his own anticipatory note. He offers the story of witnessing, one Sunday afternoon on Riverside Drive near 151st Street, 'a light-skinned, blue-eyed, Afro-American-featured individual' dressed in dashiki, breech-tops, Homburg hat, huge Afro, and driving a blue Volkswagen with a Rolls Royce radiator. It leads him to ponder 'the complexity of bloodlines', 'our general confusion over American identity', and of most relevance, 'the appropriation game'.[9]

☆   ☆   ☆

Given these related, if seemingly diverse, bearings upon ethnicity and its styles of expression, a reconsideration of the African American novel of passing, customarily defined as narratives of black impersonation of white, might well suggest some return to a parade gone by. Ethnicity, and within it the history of 'passing', has been transformed under the post-1960s multicultural dispensation, and America is heading towards the twenty-first century in the greater acknowledgement of all its ethnicities and, within them, of each ethnic crossover and interface.[10]

Terms like miscegenation, in consequence, along with the dire sub-lexicon of 'mongrel' or 'halfbreed', look not merely dated but defunct. Slurs, outright hostility even, whether in backwoods Mississippi or suburban New York, obviously continue. But 'mixed' relationships (and 'mixed' offspring) no longer automatically arouse opprobrium, curiosity or spectatorship.

Yet it is a disservice to regard the line of 'passing' inaugurated with William Wells Brown's *Clotel, or The President's Daughter* (1853) as simply or only telling the one story. The transformation whereby black plays white, with its apparent validation of a hierarchically fixed, and so even more reactionary, notion of 'race' in fact serves more as point of departure than arrival. In the case of *Clotel* matters take on the added complication of the two subsequent editions of the text, both with key changes of plot and ending and respectively published as *Clotelle: A Tale of the Southern States* (1864) and *Clotelle: Or, The Colored Heroine. A Tale of the Southern States* (1867).[11]

For *Clotel*, and the subsequent novels, have always reflected a greatly more consequential process, the making, the negotiation, of virtually *all* American identity. This give the true (if not always acknowledged) measure of how they each deploy aspect, colour, voice, family, gender, inner and outer consciousness, tactics of survival and escape, every manner of disguise and, most to the point, *faux* white (and often *faux* black) roles. As the first African American novel of passing, *Clotel* has long invited a wider reading.

Furthermore, *Clotel* links into, and helps construe, the tradition which includes among its best-known landmarks a Reconstruction-set novel like Charles Chesnutt's *The House Behind the Cedars* (1900), James Weldon Johnson's mixed-genre *The Autobiography of an Ex-Coloured Man* (1912, 1927), 'New Negro' fiction like Walter White's *Flight* (1926), Nella Larsen's *Passing* (1929) and Jessie Redmon Fauset's *Plum Bun* (1929), a satire of 1920s 'race fever' like George Schuyler's *Black No More* (1931), and a contemporary-written picaresque like Charles Johnson's *Oxherding Tale* (1982).[12] A latterday route back into these and similar texts has every reason to use the benefit of hindsight, the arising contexts and perspectives of America as a 'first universal nation'.[13]

One departure point, from the 1940s and early 1950s, typically lies in the shock which followed a film like *Lost Boundaries* (1949), with Mel Ferrer and Beatrice Pearson in the principal roles. Its story of the 'black' outing of Albert and Thyra Johnston, initially told in *Reader's Digest* by William L. White in 1947, and then picked up by Hollywood, generally stunned America. The Johnstons had epitomized white New Hampshire respectability, both well known in Republican political circles, both prominent Methodists, he a doctor and she an acclaimed 'family values' homemaker. Passing had long been held to belong to an earlier time. How could black be white?

Similarly the publication of John Howard Griffin's *Black Like Me* (1961) – it had a follow-up in Grace Halsell's *Soul Sister* (1969) – with its Texas author's chameleonism of hiding a white inside a black skin (so reversing Fanon's *Black Skin, White Masks*) gave a unique pathway into the shadowlands of Dixie racism. Griffin attracted widespread praise but also alarm and even violent resentment. His home was attacked a number of times, his name vilified. How, again, could white be black?[14]

'Who's Passing for Who?', Langston Hughes's memorable title from his 1945 Harlem short story, offers the relevant gloss.[15] In an America where identity, interrelatedly individual, collective, racial, cultural, linguistic, gendered, national and regional, has almost by historical rote been subject to continuing (if sometimes arbitrary) processes of change and revision, could the nation ever be imagined without the interplay of these different but always subtly reciprocal and mirroring dramas?

Yet matters rarely have become more charged, or more given to camouflage, than where and when race, and above all the challenge to assumed fixities of black and white, enter the fray. An upshot of the L.A. South Central 1992 riots was the confirmation that black against white, for all its historic (and moral) pedigree from anti-slavery to Civil Rights, cannot continue as the exclusive paradigm for 'race relations'. Black–Asian, and most especially of late in California black–Korean, relations have increasingly come to the fore. Black–brown issues surface over gangs, turf, dress, even language. Within *chicanismo* from Texas to California, Colorado to Arizona, tensions arise between *chicanos* and *sureños*, an old versus a newer Mexican and other Spanish-speaking immigrant America. White–Asian relations turn one way, and then another, lately in a city like Seattle, the first in the United States to have a collective Asian American majority. All of these, not to say the workings of ethnic class mobility, greatly complicate the picture and invite fresh recognition and analysis.

Ethnic Notions, Marlon Riggs's unsparing 1987 film, offers yet another backward glance.[16] Riggs shows how in the form of slave caricature, minstrelsy, foods of the Uncle Ben's rice or Aunt Jemima's syrup variety, or a TV show like *Amos'n'Andy* (dropped in 1953 after a successful NAACP campaign against it), white America managed to image African Americans as Toms, Sambos, Mammies, Coons, Brutes and Pickaninnies. He throws the sharpest light on a history of two-way impersonation which runs from slave-performed cakewalk pastiche of white slave owner gentry to a white-Jewish Al Jolson in blackface in *The Jazz Singer* (1926), and from long-time, if muted, rumours of the white-black genealogy of at least a half dozen American presidents to the black-white physiognomy of Charles Chesnutt, Walter White, A. Philip Randolph, Lena Horne, Adam Clayton Powell Jr., Sterling Brown, or even the 'marinny' Malcolm X (the 'Red' of his Detroit years on account of his complexion and hair). Colour, Riggs is not alone in confirming, has long operated as more permeable, portable and certainly tricksterish than the received wisdom has allowed.

In this regard Melville's *The Confidence-Man* makes its own singular contribution. The novel, throughout, ventriloquizes and impersonates black for white and vice versa. The opening chapter's mute, if deific, white stranger is followed by the earthly and importunate Black Guinea. Thereafter, white from out of black identities proliferate, self-performingly frontier and eastern, secular and transcendental and, in a related vein, Native ('The Metaphysics of Indian Hating') and Asian ('The Story of China Aster').

In its resorts to mask, palindrome, feint, doubling, transformation and *trompe l'oeil*, Melville's Mississippi river-masquerade adds a further touchstone. It can be said to serve, as can Twain's *Pudd'nhead Wilson* (1894) with its figure of Roxie and Faulkner's *Light in August* (1932) with Joe Christmas, alongside Afro-America's own fictions of passing, a complementary text or, perhaps more aptly, a complementary metatext.

An even more contemporary context arises from the shifts and awakenings of the 1960s. Debate in America has increasingly joined about the nation's accelerating ethnic and cultural hybridity. Even *Time* – Henry Luce's one-time journalistic flagship for WASP America, and long given to handing down monocultural stereotypes (African Americans as ghettoites, Asian Americans as model minority gatekeepers, *latinos* as border migrants, Native peoples as vanishing Americans) – recognized that demographically something had changed. Since the 1980s it has run a series of cover stories on the 'browning' of America, on Asian American achievement, and on the 1492–1992 controversy as a way of registering a changing nationhood. A 1991 issue, reflecting more than a hint of the challenge to old custodianship, is entitled 'Whose America?'.[17]

These reflect a signal turn. If the demographers are correct, the process which in all probability will lead by the middle of the twenty-first century to less than one in two Americans being 'white' Euro-American had registered in Middle America's magazine country. A related question ensues. Can there ever be the one, agreed, canonical America, *Mayflower*-birthed, Atlantic, irrevocably shaped by a white (and patrician) Anglocentrism with its footfalls in English culture, English common law, and the English language – itself, somehow, given over to a single standard or usage?

Time is not alone in having to catch up on an accompanying development. This hypothesizes that whiteness, all along, and because of its own massive ethnic diversity (English to Slavic, Scandinavian to Mediterranean, Irish to Jewish) and its different class manifestations (genteel, salaried, urban blue-collar and rural poor white), has been but yet another constructed, albeit composite, American ethnicity. When did darker Italians or Greeks, or Catholic Poles and Orthodox Armenians, or Bavarian Germans and Ashkenazi Jews, all 'pass' into white?[18] In pop culture even Superman, white omnipotent man-god, in the latest TV series ('Lois and Clark: The New Adventures of Superman') is played by Dean Cain, an actor who proclaims himself Japanese American. Little wonder that, challengingly, discussion moves on to speak of regimes of post-whiteness.[19]

The issues pivot around whether race has ever meant the same thing as culture, or whether multiculturalization with or without political correctness is to be welcomed or feared, or whether, in an age not only of ethnic but of sexual and other identity politics and with the millennium pending, America can ever 'again' hope to find a right balance for its nationhood. Diverse polemical hands have been quick into action. The rhetoric blows hot and excited throughout the media, the academy and almost all the political forums.

Vintage references to melting pots and mixing bowls get reinvoked, or rejected, or superseded by terms like those introduced by Werner Sollors of ethnic 'consent' and 'descent'.[20] A careful analytic study like F. James Davis's *Who Is Black? One Nation's Definition* (1991) opens the vistas in yet another direction. Davis enlighteningly calls attention to:

the confusion of biological and cultural categories – 'Negro' came to mean any slave or descendant of a slave no matter how much mixed ... Most parents of black American children have themselves been racially mixed, but often the fractions get complicated because the earlier details of the mixing were obscured generations ago.[21]

A younger black intelligentsia has sought to give the race debate still fresher energy, notably the jurisprudential scholar Patricia J. Williams in *The Alchemy of Race and Rights* (1991), with her 'I am still evolving from being treated as three-fifths of a human, a subpart of the white estate', and the philosopher-theologian Cornel West in *Race Matters* (1994) with his 'As in the ages of Lincoln, Roosevelt and King, we must look to new frameworks and languages to understand our multilayered crisis and overcome our deep malaise.'[22]

Movement, however, has not been all the one way. All kinds of race essentialists speak of threatened loss of identity. Segregationists, first of all, of Louisiana's David Duke variety (with the Klan, the Aryan Brotherhood and its police and other lodges, and many of the survivalists and militia-groups, equally in the frame) allege the beleaguerment of some unitary 'white race'. One nationally known L.A. police chief, symptomatically, hardly bothered throughout the 1980s to rein in his anti-black codes and messages. The O.J. Simpson trial, conducted in summer 1996, whatever its implications about 'the race card', unearths the vintage prejudice of another longserving Los Angeles officer. Both see themselves having been engaged in the delegated hands-on work of preserving whiteness as ordained ascendancy, command-post white 'racial' governance.

Nor has the issue been only white American ascendancy under challenge. The vaunting of whiteness as civilization can be seen to have its exact counterimage in the activities of various latterday Afrocentrists. Few have been more determined, or voluble, than Dr. Leonard Jeffries of the City College of New York with his Manichean opposition of black sun people and white ice people. Likewise, Nation of Islam idealogues, acting on a 'theology' of white (and especially anti-Semitic) master-sorcery, canvas openly for a necessary *jihad* against Jewish Americans in their support of Israel – a conflict which found sharpest partisanship in the widely reported black killing of the young *lubavitcher*, Yankel Rosenbaum, in Crown Heights, Brooklyn, in summer 1991. A perfect counter-spiral, however, lies in the rise of the late Rabbi Meir Kahan's Kach movement, founded also in Brooklyn with the Jewish Defence League in support, which carried the daemonization of all Islam and all Arabs (and Arab Americans) back to Jerusalem and the West Bank.

Asian American traditionalists, like certain Jewish counterparts, for all their experience of orientalist resentment and exclusion (the 1882 Chinese Exclusion Act or Roosevelt's Executive Order 9066 of 1942 interning 120,000 Japanese Americans), invoke the dangers of 'marrying out' with its intermixing of family, language, religious affiliation and children. Frank Chin, Chinese American playwright, along with others, decries the tendency as voluntary self-erasure.

Native America, too, can look to its own divided voices about authenticity. If, historically, a white controlled BIA (Bureau of Indian Affairs) has long been arbitrary about certification of who ranks as 'Indian', so there have been in-house tribal claims and counterclaims about blood quantum, about rights to enrolment, rights to land 'ownership' as in the Navajo–Hopi territorial disputes in Big Mountain, Arizona, and, most of relevance, about the whole issue of mixed-blood (or Métis) status.

In the *latino* spectrum the same process applies. However shared the resentment of 'Anglo' discrimination by Tex-Mex and California *chicanos*, by tenement *puertorriqueños* in New York, or by Cuban exiles in Florida, there have also been internal splits and tensions. Which *hispanidad/latinismo* (acknowledging how contentious has been this European etymology) should, or can, be thought in any way definitive? The landed *chicanismo* of an older New Mexico rubs up against the barrio *chicanismo* of an East Los Angeles (known in local Spanish as 'East Los'), Houston or Albuquerque. How far has the *campesino* leadership of César Chávez and his United Farm Workers retreated into piety, a truly heroic but dated leadership model for an urban (and often middle-class) population? *Puertorriqueñidad*, with Spanish Harlem as its centre and Puerto Rico as island origin, for all the talk of *Borikén* as rallying nationalism, has been faced with various kinds of disquiet. Those of more Native or Jewish identity feel threatened. Tensions arise between returnee *riqueños* and the 'home' population. The fierce anti-Fidel rightism of Florida's exile Cuban American groups, almost all fair-skinned in appearance like the Havana leadership they oppose, looks unforgivingly at a migrant-immigrant leftism brought North from yet other Latin America, that of an often more *indigenista* or 'Indian' Bolivia, Guatemala, Peru or Colombia.

Despite (no doubt equally because of) the evident increase of black-white, amerasian, cross-blood native and *mestizo/a* hybridities, there also persist unquiet ranklings about the colour hierarchy. The scale remains, generally, light over dark, be the latter *latino*, Native, Asian or African American. The ability, because of usually lighter colour and aspect, to move across or between ethnic lines still arouses disquiet. For many of 'settled' ethnicity these Americans of a mix-within-a-mix, however fully possessed of an identity in their own right, cause lingering doubts, the old shadow of mingling as blight.

Multiculturalism, and with it multiracialism, in demography, political and cultural voice, education, gender in the form of the Women's Movement and its gay (and gay ethnic) counterparts, even genetics, may well have become an item on the American agenda of public debate. But much of the work remains to be done. Bill Clinton's greatly trumpeted speech on race at the University of California, San Diego in June 1997 added the presidential voice, yet his working terms could not have been more narrow, even redundant. For he, like others, continues to see the contending forces, actually and figuratively, as broadly of two camps: white and black.

Who better, however, than the ever augmenting number of 'mixed' Americans, born at the ethnic-racial seams, to step through or round that paradigm? For by parentage, or memory, or culture, or by the individual face in the mirror, cannot their perspective be considered broader, more richly eclectic, even more American? 'Passing', old-style, whether rued, relished or tragic, comes to be seen as a mere first step.

☆   ☆   ☆

Another perspective arises from how a number of high-culture mandarins view the supposed loss of 'one nation' canonicity as a step into chaos, a foregoing of *civitas* or good citizenship as well as cultural literacy.[23] Universities, they allege, especially add to the fracture through the creation of multicultural syllabi and Departments of Ethnic Studies, and within those, of African American, Latino, Native and Asian American Studies, accompanied by Bilingual Education, Popular Culture, and Media and Film Studies, as well as Feminist and Gay ideology and writing.[24] Allan Bloom's *The Closing of the American Mind* (1987), the text which began much of the controversy with a sanctioning Preface by Saul Bellow, thus speaks of 'the profoundest crisis', even the breach of a Hobbesian social contract.[25]

Roger Kimball detects a *trahison des clercs*, an ill-given legacy of 1960s specious ethnic-populist relevance, in his *Tenured Radicals: How Politics Has Corrupted Our Higher Education* (1990). Dinesh D'Souza likewise sees in the new multicultural prospect only flight from the rise of 'the best' into petty empire building in his *Illiberal Education: The Politics of Race and Sex on Campus* (1991). One-time Kennedy liberals like Arthur M. Schlesinger Jr. darkly forecast cultural balkanization in his *The Disuniting of America: Reflections on a Multicultural Society* (1992). Harold Bloom, whose Introductions to over 500 Chelsea Press volumes of essays and reprints shows little apparent heed of canonicity, enters the arena with *The Western Canon: The Books and Schools of the Ages* (1995), full of magisterial sweep and disdain for our 'mimic cultural wars' and 'current squalors'.[26]

The counter case has been equally vigorous. America's culture war of 'core values' versus 'cultural diversity' has been long debated as a prophetic essay like Randolph Bourne's 'Trans-National America' (1916) gives powerful evidence.[27] Has not 'canonical' Americanness too readily, and for too long, been defined, and thereby appropriated, by the usual WASP or its successor elites? Is it not, accordingly, merest *canard* to keep hearing that Alice Walker, say, has usurped Shakespeare, or Toni Morrison, say, George Eliot? Above all is there not an unspoken ethnic-racial component to high canonicity, a fear of America as more increasingly than ever a cross- and inter-ethnic multiverse, a nation of cultural pluralities?

In studies like Werner Sollors's *Beyond Ethnicity: Consent and Descent in American Culture* (1986) and Henry Louis Gates Jr.'s *Loose Canons* (1992), furthermore, the argument is put that 'the canonical' (whether as national identity or literary culture), beginning from the battle of Ancients and Moderns, has always been subject to revision and modification.[28] Cultural touchstones, overlappingly Graeco-Roman, Judaeo-Christian and Eurocentric, had to come under question as exclusively best able to serve in an America woven by histories hemispherically Native, African, Pacific Island and Asian as much as Atlantic.[29] Few recent voices, however, have argued more eloquently, or with a firmer sense of the historicity to America's multicultural tradition of seeking to be 'free of the weight of fixed symbols and rigid canons', than Lawrence W. Levine in *The Opening of the American Mind: Canons, Culture, and History* (1996).[30]

Feminist legacy, too, has met with its multiculturization. However overdue the 1960s gender debate – both straight-feminist and gay-lesbian challenges to assumed settled sexual category in the formation of (and the need simply to be accurate about) American national identity – the issues became yet more complicated. Did not modern feminism's first wave, as given in Betty Friedan's *The Feminine Mystique* (1963), turn on analysis not so much generic as of white (and heterosexual) professional women and their discontents?[31] American women of colour, whether black, Native, Asian, *latina*, or of one or another ethnic mix, or straight or gay, would proclaim, and relish, a gender politics of their own.

Symptomatic have been collections like *This Bridge Called My Back: Writings by Radical Women of Color* (1981) under the editorship of Cherrié Moraga and Gloria Anzaldúa.[32] Afro-America found its own working term in 'womanism', most of all in Alice Walker's 1960s and 1970s essays ('Looking for Zora' is pivotal) later gathered as *In Search of Our Mothers' Gardens, Womanist Prose by Alice Walker* (1983). More precise analysis and tactics would be developed in bell hooks's *Ain't I a Woman: Black Women and Feminism* (1981) and June Jordan's *Civil Wars* (1981) and *Technical Difficulties* (1992) – especially her essay 'Wrong or White', and state of the art 'gender discourse' like Patricia Hill Collins's *Black Feminist Thought: Knowledge, Consciousness, and the Politics of Empowerment* (1990).[33]

A further bearing derives from longstanding postcolonial and subaltern intellectuals such as Edward Said, Homi Bhabha and Gayatri Chakravorty Spivak.[34] They have overlapped with the academy's Marxists, such as Frederick Jameson or E. San Juan Jr., who, though opposing the alarmism of Allan Bloom, Roger Kimball or Dinesh D'Souza (with its roots in Arnoldian or the Hutchins/University of Chicago 'Great Books' tradition), also take aim at most notions of multiculturalism itself.[35]

For if this kind of shared critique sees the *status quo* as merely one of cultural power or privilege, multiculturalism itself has also come under reproach. It is seen as having become part of a boutique or consumerist market culture, a 'symbolic ethnicity' in flight from both politics and history. The strictures of E. San Juan Jr. as Filipino materialist critic on Jessica Hagedorn as Filipino American postmodernist, for her novel *Dogeaters* (1990), would be typical.[36]

The most engaging exponents of the multicultural word, however, have been 'ethnic' creative writers. For the best have long undermined, with matching cross-boundary textual verve, any rearguard nostalgia about a prior, and supposedly unethnic, Golden Age or 'core' American demography and a prescribed literature to match. They have been the last to enstatue a Melville or Whitman, recognizing, and indeed often admiring and echoing, the challenging plays of multicultural voice and range in a *Moby-Dick* or *Leaves of Grass*.

One turns, among contemporaries, to Ishmael Reed – essays, editorials, anthologies, and his canniest revamping of received literary genre as in a 'historical' novel like *Flight to Canada* (1976); or to Maxine Hong Kingston in a memory novel like *Tripmaster Monkey: His Fake Book* (1989) with its Chinese American, San Francisco and 'Gold Mountain' talk-story tricksterism and narrative sleights and transformations; or to Guillermo Gómez-Peña, border writer, Mexican, *chicano*, Native, in his own text-as-example urging of 'cross-cultural alliances' in *Warrior for Gringostroika* (1993); or to Gerald Vizenor, Chippewa-Ojibway cross-blood novelist, in an essay-sequence on American 'postindian' idiom and iconography which as readily invokes Jabès, Barthes, Lyotard or Foucault as bear ceremonial, ghost dance or dream-catcher, like *Manifest Manners* (1994).[37]

Recent anthology volumes like the *Heath Anthology of American Literature* (1990) or *The Before Columbus Foundation Fiction Anthology* (1992) and *The Before Columbus Foundation Poetry Anthology* (1992), not only seek to confirm this American multicultural plenty, they enrich and diversify any supposed single American cultural canon.[38] Ishmael Reed, main editorial force and inspiration of the *Before Columbus Foundation* anthologies, suggests the following prospectus:

We hope that the reader will discover that American literature in the last decade is more than a mainstream ... [is] not merely a dominant mother culture with an array of subcultures tagging along.[39]

None of this denies that there have also been 'ethnic' dissenters. Richard Rodriguez, essayist, autobiographer, PBS and *Time* commentator, and raised *chicano* in Sacramento, in his *Hunger of Memory: The Education of Richard Rodriguez* (1982) argues the case for a 'public' rather than 'ethnic' self ('Bilingualists', he insists, 'simplistically scorn the value and the necessity of assimilation').[40] Bharati Mukherjee, Bengali Brahmin, Canadian immigrant, US citizen, novelist, speaks of getting above, or moving on from, multiculturalism to a 'new, sustaining, and unifying national creed'.[41] Believers in 'core' America again applaud. Multiculturalists counter with talk of hegemony, 'uniculturalism' – the refusal to see, or be modified in their views by, America's pluralisms of history, language, gender or ethnicity.

Whichever best holds, Rodriguez and Mukherjee, in common with a 'raceless' conservative like Supreme Court Justice Clarence Thomas (who, under challenge of sexual harassment of Anita Hill, could not resist adding to the racialization of his Senate hearings with loaded talk of 'hi-tech lynching' and the portrayal of his own sister Emma Mae Martin as what one historian calls a 'deadbeat on welfare'), confirm the unabating relevance of 'who's passing for who?'.[42] No longer, runs the shrewder commentary, can 'passing' be thought to remain an issue of skin or colour.[43]

☆   ☆   ☆

In all the cities and towns of the slave states, the real negro, or clear black, does not amount to more than one in every four of the population.[44]

William Wells Brown's observation in *Clotel* gives an essential pointer. Was 'negro', and its ancillary network of 'nigra' or 'nigger' (whatever its vernacular permissions as a term of endearment or reprimand within black on black talk), 'mulatto', 'quadroon', 'octoroon', 'high yellow', 'blue vein', even his 'clear black' (and by implication 'clear white'), ever only a matter of skin pigment or melanin? For his own part, and from the outset, Brown leaves little doubt about his grasp of the constructedness of all racial category and, within it, of sub-category, above all the embedding of 'negro' in a semantics of commodity as much as of colour.

Clotel has its limits, not least where it edges towards formula sentimentality of a kind with *Uncle Tom's Cabin* (1851). The bid to stir heart and tears is patent: the beauteous, fair-skinned Clotel sold in Richmond, allowed a brief if formally unlicensed domestic idyll, and then abandoned by Horatio Green for a white wife; the subsequent slave auction separations from Currer, her mother, Althesa, her sister, and Mary, her own daughter; and the final flight, melodramatic plunge from the bridge and self-drowning in the Potomac.

The novel also has unlikely sudden shifts and dissolves. Yellow Fever carries off first Currer, then Althesa and her abolitionist husband, Henry Morton, in New Orleans. Consumption abruptly ends the life of the benign, slave-freeing Georgiana Charleston. Coincidence gets its measure in the closing encounter, in France, when Clotel's granddaughter, Mary Devenant, by chance meets George Green, the two former slave lovers and escapees. The colloquia about liberty and enslavement, on Mr. Peck's plantation, and in the voices of his neighbour Mr. Jones, Carleton, and the preacher Snyder, can look too staged.

Yet *Clotel* does far more than simply enfigure 'the tragic mulatto' theme. The subtler veins Brown sets himself to tackle envisage slavery, and American slavery in particular, as a world turned both upside down and inside out. In a novel as radically gendered as 'racial' (not one but three generations of women's lives), he shows a keen touch for the 'peculiar institution' as working charade, a collusive play of concealment. Starting from Thomas Jefferson in the role of double patriarch – of American liberty and of white and slave family, drafter of the Declaration of Independence and yet owner of Currer, father of Clotel and Althesa, and grandparent of Mary, Ellen and Jane – Brown's text leaves no doubt of slavery as both life and mime, a helix of 'passings'.

The 'pure Anglo-Saxon' Clotel is first sold at the auction block, lives a mock-marriage and divorce, then sees her daughter, Mary, become the slave servant of her no more white, but 'legitimate', successor, Gertrude. The one family, and within it motherhood and wifehood, mimics the other. A 'white' white woman shadows her 'black' white predecessor who then shadows her. Horatio Green doubles as husband to Clotel yet also Gertrude, father to yet owner of Mary, herself a child severed from her own childhood. Clotel again adds to the about-face, white and yet under the 'one drop' rule black, when she is further racialized in being likened to Italian and Spanish gentry.

A gamut of related other doubles, and doublings, follow. The slave Pompey, who mock-congratulatingly speaks of himself as '"no countefit ... de genewine artekil"', darkens, and so youthens, older slaves for sale. The manservant Jerry is lost and won during a steamboat card game ('I don't know who owns me dis morning'). An escaped slave who is caught by dogs, sentenced by a lynch court, shot and then burnt, passes from live presence to utter absence ('not a vestige remaining to show that such a thing ever existed'). Althesa encounters Salomé Miller, the German-born white woman mistakenly made into a slave who, despite her own restored freedom, then witnesses her daughters sold. On Althesa's death her daughters, in turn, however similarly white of skin, in accord with slaveholding logic (or illogic) are duly sold. In the house where Mary, white-black, is employed, the kitchenwoman, Dinah, delivers a summary all the more brutal for how it turns slavery back on itself. She excoriates 'dees white niggers'.

Escape from this ongoing masquerade, in keeping, requires yet others. Clotel aids William by impersonating a young white man with his slave – William, in a striking anticipation of Melville's Babo in 'Benito Cereno' (1856), has to play, or rather re-play, himself. His disguise, moreover, transgresses not only gender but colour and caste, Clotel as 'white' transvestite master, William as 'black' body-servant. That the episode also anticipates the William and Ellen Craft slave narrative, *Running a Thousand Miles for Freedom* (1860), creates yet another textual overlap: art imitated in life and that again imitated in art.[45] William, in a further variety of transvestism, rather than pay Jim Crow passenger rates on a train, ships himself as human luggage for less. 'This, reader, is no fiction' intervenes a wry, authorial Brown, quick to match the reflexivity of slave history in slave literature.

The portrait of a society caught up in these successive kinds of self-mask continues into the listing of slave ownership by the various churches, the allusion to the letters B.M. and B.W. for 'coloured' church attenders in New York, and, however slavery free, the myriad racism of the Free States. This contrivance of shadow over substance builds into a deft, not to say brisk, whole, every performance in 'white' and 'black', and, in-between, the silhouette of yet others.

The process finds a perfect trope in Brown's allusion to the two arriving ships in the New World of the seventeenth century, the *Mayflower* in Massachusetts and the slave vessel in Jamestown, Virginia. Together, he suggests, they embody America's enravelled, or once again endoubled, 'racial' history: bondage within freedom, enslavement within liberty. The same, he goes on to point out, holds when the slave troops who fought with Andrew Jackson against the British, at New Orleans, found themselves returned to servitude. Which, in either case, 'passes' for rightful history?

These, and the rest of the novel's guises, false fronts and reversals, Brown builds into a narrative continuum whose deftness has not always won due recognition. For *Clotel* offers a drama of masks, a 'slave' America whose every sign of bloodline, race, name and colour calls up its own countersign.

'The unjust spirit of caste': Charles Chesnutt's diary, for 29 May 1880, specifies the essential target of all his fiction.[46] It precisely anticipates *The House Behind the Cedars*, long installed as a 'passing' fable *par excellence*.[47] Rena Walden's life, after all, comes accoutred in mixed-race doomed love, a backdrop of the 'Old South' Carolinas, flight, suitably Gothic ending of storm and forest, and plaintive death scene. Once again, however, any rush to assign the novel merely to formula would be premature.

The story opens with the return of John Warwick, under assumed kingmaker name, to the house of his 'bright mulatto' mother, Molly Walden, and her octoroon daughter, Rena. In bearing he carries all the show of unimpeachable whiteness – skin, the confidence of the lawyer he has become, a 'raceless' marriage (though his wife has died) and child. But, at exactly the same time, Chesnutt adroitly undermines the posture. As Warwick walks towards the 'hidden' family house, he passes a 'colored policeman', Aunt Lyddy as neighbourhood conjure woman in her bandanna, a 'manacled free Negro', a cryptic black undertaker, and Aunt Zilphy, the friend of his mother's. In other words blackness always underwrites his assumed whiteness, a world for all his 'passing' anything but inactive or erased. It serves as the perfect ironic preface.

Similarly, as Rena Walden becomes Rowena Warwick at the mock-Renaissance fair of the Clarence Social Club, and her affair with George Tryon begins, Chesnutt uses the one costume ('South Carolina ... not Ashby-de-la-Zouche') to overlap with, and comment on, the other. Tryon ('A Negro girl had been foisted on him for a white woman'), his supremacist friend, Dr. Green, Warwick himself with his fake plantation background, Judge Straight who out of friendship for Warwick's white father helped him to become a 'white' lawyer, Blanche Leary as George's appropriately named white wife, and Wain, the black fake school owner who pursues Rena into the forest, all engage in a masquerade of their own making ('The influence of Walter Scott was strong upon the old South') and yet, true to Dixie planter-bourbon and black-retainer custom, also actual and historic.

Reading the lawbooks of the two Carolinas concerning when, and when not, blood make-up 'racially' defines a person, Warwick and Judge Straight come to wonderfully opposing conclusions. North Carolina allows entry into whiteness after 'four generations from the Negro'. South Carolina allows 'a person to be white in whom the admixture of blood [does] not exceed one eighth'. '"I am white"', says Warwick. '"You are black"' says the Judge. The absurdity of that exchange of contradictions reveals the novel at its best.

In due course, and in a telling echo, Rena finds herself writing to Tryon 'You are white, and you have given me to understand that I am black.' The black schoolchild, Plato, vernacularly reports to Tryon that his new teacher 'looks lack she's w'ite, but she's black'. In her final delirium the dying Rena mistakes her loyal, artisan black admirer, Frank Fowler, for, respectively, her black suitor Wain and her white lover Tryon, a nicely angled conflation of human colour. Yet in these, and each misconstruing which precedes, *The House Behind the Cedars* underlines a far deeper American history of error. That using Chesnutt's own term, indeed lies in 'caste' as 'unjust', a fatal system of human division.

James Weldon Johnson's *The Autobiography of an Ex-Coloured Man*, understandably, has long been taken for a centrepiece of the 'passing' tradition.[48] The novel could not suggest a more vintage case, the confessional portrait of a turn-of-the-century life lived as 'black' inside 'white', and which seemingly ends in rueful contemplation of a 'true' identity betrayed, a path mischosen. Discussion, in accordance, has long focused on Johnson's treatment of his narrator as one of irony or otherwise, a first-person telling in good or bad faith.

Another interpretation, however, has too rarely been considered: that of the narrator's 'double' life as a way of being in its own existential right and with modes of action and self-understanding to match. Does not his doubling, white and black, yet on occasion also Cuban and Indian, yield a 'passing' beyond the orbit of previous novels? Johnson's narrator, at the very least, is the first to hold up his own harlequinry to self-aware and ironic scrutiny.

Right at the outset, having been called a 'nigger' in school, he ponders his face in his bedroom looking-glass. With almost narcissistic intensity he dwells upon 'the ivory whiteness of [his] skin', the 'beauty' of his mouth, his 'long, black eyelashes', the 'softness and glossiness of [his] dark hair', only to ask his mother, incredulously, '"am I a nigger?"'. Indeed is he? Will either 'whiteness' or 'blackness', not to say the racist derogation implied in the term, anything like wholly suffice? Why simply the one, or, no less plausibly, simply the both? Why not a yet further tier or hybridity?

The Autobiography of an Ex-Coloured Man yields a whole circuit of similar displacements, intimations of an identity beyond the marker of skin. The narrator often acknowledges how he is almost taken aback at the very plurality, and volatility, of his make-up, as though cohabited by not one but several secret sharers. He so gives a Dostoevskian or Poe-like opening gloss to his account: the divulgence of 'the great secret of my life', 'a sort of savage and diabolical desire to gather up all the little tragedies of my life, and turn them into a practical joke on society'. Is this not a call upon identity as Melvilleian confidence-game or mask?

He thinks back on his mixed Georgia birth as 'dreamlike', his sense of being 'the only stranger in the place' at his Connecticut school, his *alter ego* friendships with the white boy 'Red Head' and black boy 'Shiny', his father's dual presence and absence and veiled ownership in the form of the drilled $10 gold and, above all, his youthful musicianship as a way to subject reality to chord and harmony. Atlanta becomes, for him, 'a strange city without money or friends', a city of false friendship (the theft of his money by the Pullman porter), unfulfilled education (Atlanta University) and which, when he finally leaves for Florida, he does so hidden in a basket of soiled linen aboard a departing train.

Jacksonville, similarly, for him blends art into life, his cigar-making as 'artistic skill', 'uproarious conversation'. He enters a new language, Spanish, a new worker-guild community beyond race in his Cuban fellow cigar-makers. He brings his own rare white-black angle on 'The Negro Question' as he passes through the tiers of 'cullud sassiety', its churches, vernaculars, music and cakewalk, and even his own possible marriage to a black schoolteacher. In opting for New York he speaks of 'desire like a fever', a continuing and self-amazing impetus to live at, if not transgress, yet further boundaries.

Manhattan as 'a great witch', 'the most fatally fascinating thing in America', adds to this sense of the world as alien, a realm of displacement. He enters the gambling world, at once a sop to 'some latent dare-devil strain in my blood' yet inhabited by black gamesters who show 'a sort of Chesterfieldian politeness towards each other'. At one point, as his throws of the dice take him into and out of winning ('I felt positively giddy'), he fluctuates between euphoria and diminution, the latter especially when obliged by losses to cover himself in linen dusters (a 'ludicrous predicament'). The ragtime he will make his own, and win him the soubriquet 'The Professor' (p.456), puts him into 'a fitful sort of sleep'.

His odd, equal-unequal relationship with his white mentor, master to valet, party giver to party performer, together with the sight of his own true white father and assumed white sister, and his Grand Tour city to city European travels, give yet further outward form to his circling itineraries within. His millionaire taunts him with 'this idea you have of making a Negro out of yourself'. Yet that, in turn, plays against 'that scene of brutality and savagery' in which he witnesses, and shamingly identifies with, the burning of a black as he travels the South.

Is he, can he be, in his own estimation as much as the world's, only the one colour or the other? That, surely, amounts to the life-dialectic behind the resolve he offers towards the end of his account:

> I finally made up my mind that I would neither disclaim the black race nor claim the white race; but that I would change my name, raise a moustache, and let the world take me for what it would. (p. 499)

Playing white, he summarizes, querulously, and as if in both offence and defence, has been 'a sort of practical joke'. Yet he has a white marriage, white children ('My love for my children makes me glad that I am what I am and makes me from desiring otherwise') and a 'white' real estate fortune. 'Sometimes', he ponders, 'it seems to me that I had never really been a Negro'. At the same time he rues not being overtly black, a Booker T. Washington, a fighter 'for the cause of their race', and dwells on whether he has 'sold [his] birthright for a mess of potage'.

Is this ending, or rather double-ending, although it expresses the narrator's regret, simply another speculative excursus? He can no more wholly *be* black than white, white than black. For as Johnson has his autobiography impersonate a novel, so, just as reflexively, he has his narrator acknowledge his black for white and white for black impersonation as a matching kind of appropriation. Both the text's literary kind, and the 'life' it tells, against category, have engaged in their own species of 'passing'.

☆   ☆   ☆

Walter White's *Flight* rarely attracts plaudits. Even as a tale of four early twentieth-century cities (New Orleans, Atlanta, Philadelphia and Manhattan/Harlem) White is thought to write pedestrianly of the life and 'passing' of his bilingual, Catholic-raised, Creole heroine Mimi Daquin. Yet her moves into, and out of, ethnic self-disguise, refract a larger drama. White delineates not one, but several, American hierarchies of colour, each with its own competing etiquette, language and internal division.

Creole New Orleans, in which Mimi's father, Jean, flourishes, depends upon his *gens de couleur libre* ascendancy rather than the blackness of Mary Robertson, his second wife and Mimi's stepmother ('Mary's darkness of skin prevented her from eating at the old restaurants, Antoine's, Delatoire's, Mme. Begue's'). Jean, too, in his own effeteness, unhesitatingly uses one bias of colour to indict another. He pronounces '"coloured people ... just as full of prejudice against Catholics, Jews, and black Negroes as white people themselves"'. Is this not Creolism as duplicate whiteness, the lower rung in the colour ladder mimicking the higher?

In Atlanta, where they move as a family, the Daquins find no black Catholic church and have no access to a white one; they avail themselves of a Protestant church. They hear the story of Mrs. Adams, black but white-skinned, who is refused access to the Opera House when reported by 'some coloured person'. Although Mimi's own 'cream-coloured skin' allows 'immunities she might not have possessed had she been more distinctly Negro', including being thought white (and actually being apologized to) during the Atlanta race riot, she only slowly begins to learn the music, warmth and ease of a black culture at once part of, and yet hidden within, her own make-up.

Black Philadelphia, and the birth of her son by Carl Hunter, takes the process further. But Harlem ('in the flood-tide of transition to a Negro city within a city') certifies her true awakening. There she learns the fluidity of human colour, even though, as the result of a gossip sheet revealing the illegitimacy of *Petit Jean*, she at first repudiates it. When she herself 'passes' in Manhattan, she also fathoms a matching world of impersonation. Mme. Francine, in whose *haute couture* business she works, turns out to be Irish. Sylvia, her workmate as a finisher, disguises that she is Jewish. Jimmy Forrester, her eventual husband, unveils himself as the clubman racist. She hears the Chinese scholar, Wu Hseh-Chuan, offer a view of 'white' America at odds with its own effortlessly assumed guise as High Civilization.

She sees 'Jews in blackface' in Manhattan, then a 'Negro cabaret in Harlem'. A spiritual heard at a Carnegie Hall concert produces a 'peculiar metempsychosis'. 'Duplicity', run her musings, 'all around her and she had never suspected it'. Her own last return to Harlem ('teeming, exotic'), thereby, becomes a kind of unpassing, a release, of the long-time stranger of colour within herself. It also gives *Flight* its best claim, its mark.

☆   ☆   ☆

Nella Larsen's *Passing*, so often thought a 'simple' race narrative, offers a small gem in deception, delicately seamed in mystery. Its *alter ego* portrait of two high mulatto women, Irene Redfield, New York society wife to a Sugar Hill surgeon who opts not to 'pass', and Clare Kendry, her one-time Chicago friend, who does, but now also wishes to 'pass' back into the black world of Harlem, pursues an almost Jamesian play of equivocation.

Are not Irene and Clare mirror figures, twin yet rival selves, drawn sexually and otherwise to each other even as they spar and divide? Both are white yet black, both moneyed, both have entered the required paths of marriage; both, however, as if compelled, also search for their own hidden or at least undeclared self in the other.

Until roused to jealousy by Clare, Irene more or less acts out her required part as wife to her successful, if conformist, surgeon husband, and mother to their two boys. Hers has been the role of socialite, charity-figure, organizer, typically, of the Negro Welfare League dance. Clare, for her part, plays another kind of wife, another kind of deception, 'white' spouse to Jack Bellew as racist hearty. A one-time child-reject who still seeks family, sisterhood, she is all beguilement, dazzle, risk, nerve, as much a confidence-player in her marriage and extra-marital affairs as in her racial guise. Their pairing lies at the centre of the story.

When the two meet both are playing white in a Chicago hotel restaurant, two faces, as it were, meeting as one. Clare's tireless phone calls to Irene, her letters, the fever of their social meetings, her wish to 'come back' to Harlem as a black woman, all imply a mutual circling, an intense love-hate. As Clare becomes a regular in the Redfield home and social circle, their shared dissatisfaction as 'wives' becomes apparent. Larsen leaves little doubt of a mixed-gender as much as mixed-race identity, for both women have also assumed a kind of sexual 'passing'.

When, at the Christmas party, Clare meets her fatal fall, what, exactly, is to be made of Irene's role? She may be the appalled witness to an accident. She may, indeed, be the killer, the sublimated revenge of a sexually betrayed wife but also herself a lover. She may, however, be as equally involved in a Dorian Gray love-hate, a dual killing, of her own fear of, and yet deep attraction to, Clare's 'white' sexuality ('"I'm not safe"' the 'beautiful and caressing' Clare tells Irene at one point). As Clare 'passes' into death, Irene 'passes' back into life, ironically as the now literally unrivalled and would-be comforter to her husband.

Yet who has won, who lost? Irene returns to the norms of a compromised middle-class black wifehood. Clare becomes victim-martyr of a 'death by misadventure'. White and black have been seen to 'pass' into, and to complicate, realms of public and private female sexuality. Have not, accordingly, both women been caught in, and caught out by, not one but several webs of impersonation? *Passing*, in other words, deals in the masks of gender and desire along with those of race, a double story in like manner doubly told.

For Jessie Fauset in *Plum Bun* a similar disequilibrium comes into play. Angela Murray, under her guise of Angèle Mori, lives two kinds of double identity – black-white and, in parallel, a paragon of turn-of-the-century female respectability yet would-be 1920s 'New Woman'. Fauset shows a deft hand in working each around the other, life as 'more important than colour' in the words of Angela's mother, and, equally, life as self-gendered and thereby free of pre-set gender roles. At its core the novel locates the issue as one of power: '[Angela] knew that men had a better time of it than women, coloured men than coloured women, white men than white women' (p. 88).

Her rite of passage, middle-class, Talented Tenth, and ranging from birthplace Philadelphia to a New York of, varyingly, Greenwich Village and Harlem, and then to Paris, is set within this frame. Angela's 'passing', in all its alternations of plus and minus, involves her in the negotiation both of one arbitrary line of colour for another ('"I am both white and Negro and look white"'), and a girl's dreamworld to a woman's actual world. Fauset's skill lies in offering a suitably zigzag narrative of the pitfalls, snares, false turns and misperceptions involved in both.

This cross-hatch of colour and gender is ingeniously worked throughout. Village-bound 'white' Angela plays against her 'black' sister, the Harlem-bound Virginia. Repulsed as 'coloured' by Mary Hastings at her all-white Philadelphia school Angela recognizes the paradox as 'not because I was coloured but because she didn't know I was coloured'. Her love affair with Roger Fielding turns doubly on his not knowing, as monied racist, that she is 'black' and on her refusal to be further falsely positioned as mistress rather than wife. Her friendship with Rachel Salting throws up a parallel, Jewish daughter of Orthodox parents blighted in her marriage prospects to a Catholic John Adams; yet Rachel suddenly also reveals a savage hatred of blacks.

Of the lecturer Van Meier, race-leader, apostle of blackness, she hears her white friend Martha observe, '"It's the mix that makes him what he is."' She finds herself moved to reveal her own 'colour' when her fellow art student, Miss Powell, is denied a prize because she is black. On the one hand she feels a 'liberation'. On the other the press misrepresentingly reports it as 'Socially Ambitious Negress Confesses to Long Hoax'. The switches in pairings which lead to Jinny's marriage to the black Matthew Henson, and to Angela's prospective marriage to the mixed-race Brazilian artist, Anthony Cross, supplies an appropriate closing irony: a finally affirmative 'passing' in the plies of colour and gender.

'Passing' as farce, comic-grotesque human contrivance, and with race as all-purpose *mot clef*, has few more winning exponents than George Schuyler. His *Black No More*, Menckenite satire to the letter, reduces colour, the ways of American racial caste, to absurdity. The world in which Mark Disher rises to control the skin altering 'Black-no-more, Incorporated' as developed by the rogue geneticist, Dr. Junius Crookman, turns, in a boldly mischievous echo of slavery's freedom cry, on the phrase 'White at last!', the supposed core longing of all (or at the very least all middle-class) Afro-America.

The results produce a wonderful zaniness: mock Klan and NAACP caught up in unholy alliance; 'chromatic democracy' as the ruination of black prosperity from segregated real estate to haircare (as personified in Madame Sisseretta Blandish); DuBois, Garvey, Johnson and the rest of the 'New Negro' leadership all put to satiric account; mulatto children born to formerly black 'white' women; ex-blacks several shades whiter than 'authentic' whites who reverse into the underclass; black confidence-men playing white men lynched in an always lynch-ready Mississippi; and 'stained' skin as eventual chic modishness.

The novel perhaps labours at times. Yet 'passing' as a mirror to American race obsessiveness, and contradiction, rarely has been more exquisitely pilloried.

If a coda, even a *summa*, were sought for the ways of passing in African American fiction few novels would offer more plausible, if challenging, candidature than Charles Johnson's *Oxherding Tale*. As befits an author academically trained in philosophy, and epistemology especially, Johnson in his *Being & Race: Black Writing since 1970* (1987) positively exults in 'the possibility that our art can be dangerously and wickedly diverse, enslaved to no single idea of Being'. [49]

The gloss suits to perfection, *Oxherding Tale* as updated or mock slave-narrative, a baroque, frequently comic, contemplative novel of 'passing' in which colour is seen to act as just one kind of language in the larger workings of human bondage and freedom. It even comes replete with its own 'essayist interlude' or 'intermission', chapters 8 and 11, reflections on slave narrative as form and on the ontology of the slave self. For in the story of the 'black' Andrew Hawkins who becomes the 'white' William Harris, sired as the result of a drunken wife-swap between slaveholder and slave on Jonathan Polkinghorne's Cripplegate plantation, a larger escape narrative emerges. Johnson's cue lies in his title, the ways towards the freed self as given in the image of the oxherd's search for his ox in the ten pictures of the twelfth-century Zen painter Kuo-an Shi-yuan.

Jonathan, educated in Latin and high philosophy from Plato to the Upanishads by his anarcho-transcendental tutor, Ezekiel Sykes-Withers, and witness to a carnivalesque American visit by the young Karl Marx, 'passes' through servitude of several kinds. His learning exposes him to the contradiction of libertarian ideas so often espoused by the slaveholding class (his own image of slavery is the sight of chains 'like a pile of coiled snakes copulating'). His sexual enslavement is experienced with the slave girl Minty, later to physically come apart as she rots of pellagra (the charnel disease of slavery), and the 'noisy eroticism' and drug use of Flo Hatfield, the beautiful yet ageing and grotesque owner-belle of the plantation Leviathan. In Reb, the coffin-maker, he learns the African legacy of the Allmuseri tribe, possessed of a cosmology and logic utterly African and un-western. In the 'soulcatcher', Horace Bannon, he encounters a kind of metaphysical patroller, death in life. In white guise, as Harris, he finds a benign domestic encapturement with Peggy Undercliff and the prospect of his own progeny.

As black into white, boy into man, Andrew/William learns to draw upon, and be larger than, all his 'passings', a self beyond any one servitude yet keyed always to the observation, 'The Negro ... is the finest student of the White World, the one pupil in the class who watches himself watching the others (p. 128). In his slave escape he so 'passes' infinitely beyond black and white, a de-enslavement of any one self in the name of the self's infinite plurality.

The process, moreover, carries its shared implications back into all of Afro-America's novels of passing – *Clotel* to *The Autobiography of an Ex-Coloured Man* to *Black No More*. Others could as readily be enlisted in a tradition from Frances E.W. Harper's *Iola Leroy* to William Melvin Kelley's *dem*. A recent, and quite monumental excavation black-white 'story' like Werner Sollors's *Neither Black Nor White Yet Both: Thematic Explorations of Interracial Literature* (1997) gives further confirmation.[50] It asks if race, and within it colour, as markers of identity have not always been more illusion than reality, less category than category-error.

For as America's black-written fictions of 'passing' have long and dramatically shown, the self beyond race, beyond colour, and in its resort to the varying plies of language, ethnicity, culture, mix, gender or history was, and remains, a wholly other thing, a wholly other impersonation.

Notes

Introduction

1. Toni Morrison, *The Nobel Lecture in Literature* (New York: Alfred A. Knopf, 1994).
2. Toni Morrison, *The Bluest Eye* (New York: Holt, Rinehart and Winston, 1970), *Sula* (New York: Alfred A. Knopf, 1974), *Song of Solomon* (New York: Alfred A. Knopf, 1977), *Beloved* (New York: Alfred A. Knopf, 1987), and *Jazz* (New York: Alfred A. Knopf, 1992).
3. Ralph Ellison, *Invisible Man* (New York: Random House, 1952). Reissued as *Invisible Man*, 30th Anniversary Edition (New York: Random House, 1982).
4. All appropriate references are given in Chapter 1.
5. Henry Louis Gates Jr., General Editor, *The Schomburg Library of Nineteenth-Century Black Women Writers*, 30 Volumes (New York: Oxford University Press, 1988–); William L. Andrews, Frances Smith Foster and Trudier Harris (eds), *The Oxford Companion to African American Literature* (New York: Oxford University Press, 1997); and Henry Louis Gates Jr. and Nellie Y. McKay (eds), *The Norton Anthology of African American Literature* (New York: W.W. Norton & Company, 1997).
6. Phillis Wheatley, *Poems on Various Subjects, Religious and Moral* (London: A. Bell, 1773); Jupiter Hammond, 'An Evening Thought: Salvation by Christ, with Penetential [*sic*] Cries' (1760); *The Interesting Narrative of the Life of Olaudah Equiano, or Gustavus Vassa, the African, Written by Himself* (New York: W. Durrell, 1791); and David Walker, *Walker's Appeal, in Four Articles, together with a Preamble, to the Coloured Citizens of the World, but in particular, and very expressly, to Those of the United States of America* (Boston: David Walker, 1829). For a more complete bibliographical annotation, see Chapter 1, note 6.
7. Frederick Douglass, *Narrative of the Life of Frederick Douglass, an American Slave, Written by Himself* (Boston: The American Anti-Slavery Society, 1845).
8. Claude McKay, *Home to Harlem* (New York: Harper, 1928); and Rosa Guy, *A Measure of Time* (New York: Holt, Rinehart and Winston, 1983).
9. Alice Walker, *In Search of Our Mothers' Gardens, Womanist Prose by Alice Walker* (New York: Harcourt Brace Jovanovich, 1983); Harriet E. Wilson, *Our Nig; or Sketches from the Life of a Free Black, in a Two-Story White House, North* (printed for the author by George C. Rand and Avery Company, 1859); Zora Neale Hurston, *Their Eyes Were Watching God* (Philadelphia: J.B. Lippincott, 1937).

10. Richard Wright, *Native Son* (New York: Harper, 1940).

11. John O. Killens, *And Then We Heard the Thunder* (New York: Alfred A. Knopf, 1963); Gwendolyn Brooks, *A Street in Bronzeville* (New York: Harper, 1945).

12. LeRoi Jones/Imamu Amiri Baraka, *Dutchman*; originally published as *Dutchman* and *The Slave* (New York: Morrow, 1964).

13. Leon Forrest, *There Is a Tree More Ancient Than Eden* (New York: Random House, 1973), *The Bloodworth Orphans* (New York: Random House, 1977), and *Two Wings to Veil My Face* (New York: Random House, 1984); Ishmael Reed, *The Free-Lance Pallbearers* (New York: Doubleday, 1967), *Yellow Back Radio Broke-Down* (New York: Doubleday, 1969).

14. William Wells Brown, *Clotel or, The President's Daughter, a Narrative of Slave Life in the United States* (London: Partridge & Oakey, 1853); Charles Johnson, *Oxherding Tale* (Bloomington, Indiana: Indiana University Press, 1982).

15. Toni Morrison, 'Black and Right and Read All Over', interview-feature with Clive Davis, *The Times*, 28 April 1992, Arts Section, p. 3.

Chapter 1

1. Zora Neale Hurston, *Dust Tracks on a Road* (Philadelphia: J. B. Lippincott, 1942). All references are to Zora Neale Hurston, *Folklore, Memoirs, and other Writings: Mules and Men, Tell My Horse, Dust Tracks on a Road, Selected Articles* (New York: The Library of America, 1993). This is the restored text of *Dust Tracks on a Road*, p. 561.

2. Ralph Ellison, 'Introduction', *Invisible Man*, 30th Anniversary Edition (New York: Random House, [1952] 1982), p. xiii.

3. LeRoi Jones and Larry Neal (eds), *Black Fire: An Anthology of Afro-American Writing* (New York: William Morrow, 1968).

4. LeRoi Jones, 'The Myth of a "Negro Literature"', *Home: Social Essays* (New York: William Morrow, 1966), p. 105.

5. Charles Chesnutt, *The Conjure Woman and Other Tales* (Boston: Houghton Mifflin, 1899), and *The House Behind the Cedars* (Boston: Houghton Mifflin, 1900).

6. Phillis Wheatley, *Poems on Various Subjects, Religious and Moral by Phillis Wheatley, Negro Servant to Mr. John Wheatley, of Boston, in New England* (London: A. Bell, 1773) – all citations are from *The Collected Works of Phillis Wheatley*, ed. John Shields, Schomburg Library of Nineteenth-Century Black Women Writers (New York: Oxford University Press, 1988); Jupiter Hammon, 'An Evening Thought: Salvation by Christ, with Penetential [*sic*] Cries', reprinted in Benjamin Brawley (ed.), *Early Negro American Writers* (Chapel Hill: University of North Carolina Press, 1935, reprinted, New York: Dover Publications, Inc., 1970); *The Interesting Narrative of the Life of Olaudah Equiano, or Gustavus Vassa, the African. Written by Himself. Vol. 1. Five Lines of Scriptural Text from Isaiah XII. 2,4.* (London: printed for and sold by the author, No. 10, Union-Street, Middlesex Hospital; and may be had of all booksellers in town and country. Entered at Stationers' Hall, 1989, 2 Vols). Two versions then followed: *The Interesting Narrative of the Life of Olaudah Equiano or Gustavus Vassa, the African* (London, 1790) and *The Interesting Narrative of the Life of Olaudah Equiano, or Gustavus Vassa, the African, Written by Himself*, 1st American edn (New York: printed and sold by W. Durrell at his books-store and printing office, No. 19, Q Street, 1791, 2 Vols). The text

used here is *The Interesting Narrative of the Life of Olaudah Equiano or Gustavus Vassa, the African, Written by Himself*, reprinted in Henry Louis Gates Jr. (ed.), *The Classic Slave Narratives* (New York: Penguin, 1987); and David Walker, *Walker's Appeal, in Four Articles, together with a Preamble, to the Coloured Citizens of the World, but in particular, and very expressly, to Those of the United States of America* (Boston: David Walker, 1829). Three editions followed. The edition used here is *Walker's Appeal* ed. Charles M. Wiltser (New York: Hill and Wang, 1965).

7. LeRoi Jones, 'The Myth of a "Negro Literature"', p. 113.

8. LeRoi Jones/Amiri Baraka, *Black Magic: Collected Poetry, 1961–1967* (Indianapolis: The Bobbs-Merrill Co., 1969).

9. Addison Gayle Jr., 'Introduction', in Addison Gayle Jr. (ed.), *The Black Aesthetic* (New York: Doubleday, Anchor, 1971), p. xxxii.

10. Hoyt Fuller, 'Towards a Black Aesthetic', *The Critic*, 1968.

11. Maulana Karenga, 'Black Cultural Nationalism', *Negro Digest*, January 1968; republished in Addison Gayle Jr. (ed.), *The Black Aesthetic*.

12. Larry Neal, 'The Black Arts Movement', *The Drama Review*, Vol. 12, No. 4 (Summer 1968).

13. Don Lee/Haki R. Madhubuti, *Black Pride* (Detroit: Broadside, 1968), *Think Black* (Detroit: Broadside, 1968) and *Don't Cry, Scream* (Detroit: Broadside, 1969); Etheridge Knight, *Poems from Prison* (Detroit: Broadside, 1968); George Kent, *Blackness and the Adventure of Western Culture* (Chicago: Third World Press, 1972); and Stephen Henderson, *Understanding the New Black Poetry* (New York: Morrow, 1973). Apart from the texts so far listed the principal Black Aesthetic acccounts include: LeRoi Jones/Amiri Baraka, *Raise, Race, Rays, Raze: Essays Since 1965* (New York: Random House, 1971); Addison Gayle Jr. (ed.), *Black Expression: Essays By and About Black Americans in the Creative Arts* (New York: Weybright and Talley, 1969), (ed.), *The Black Aesthetic* (New York: Doubleday Anchor, 1971), *The Way of the New World: The Black Novel in America* (New York: Doubleday, 1975); Mercer Cook and Stephen E. Henderson (eds), *The Militant Black Writer in the United States* (Madison, Wisconsin: University of Wisconsin Press, 1969); John A. Williams and Charles F. Harris (eds), *Amistad 1: Writings on Black History and Culture* (New York: Vintage, 1970) and *Amistad 2: Writings on Black History and Culture* (New York: Vintage, 1971); *Mid-Continent American Studies Journal*, No. 11 (Fall 1972); Hoyt Fuller's critiques appeared mainly in the following journals: *Negro Digest/Black World*, *Southwest Review*, *Ebony*, *African Forum*, *Nation*, *Journal of American Poetry*, *The New Yorker*, *North American Review*, *Jet* and *The Critic*. Of relevance, too, is his *Journey to Africa* (Chicago: Third World Press, 1971). A further context is to be found in C.W.E. Bigsby (ed.), *The Black American Writer*, Vol. 1, *Fiction*, and Vol. 2, *Poetry and Drama* (Baltimore, Maryland: Penguin, 1971). An overview can be found in Marcus Cunliffe, 'Black Culture and White America', *Encounter*, Vol. 34 (1970), pp. 22–35.

14. William Styron, *The Confessions of Nat Turner* (London: Random House, 1968); John Henrik Clarke (ed.), *William Styron's Nat Turner: Ten Black Writers Respond* (Boston: Beacon Press, 1968). For an overall account of the furore and the competing versions of Turner, see John White, 'The Novelist as Historian: William Styron and American Negro Slavery', *Journal of American Studies*, Vol. 4 (1971), pp. 233–45.

15. For a history of these magazines see Abby Arthur Johnson and Ronald Maberry Johnson, *Propaganda & Aesthetics: The Literary Politics of Afro-*

American Magazines in the Twentieth Century (Amherst, Massachusetts: University of Massachusetts Press, 1979), especially Chapter 6, 'Black Aesthetic: Revolutionary Little Magazines, 1960–1976'.

16.   A helpful diagnosis of these literary wars is to be found in Reginald Martin, *Ishmael Reed & the New Black Aesthetic Critics* (London: Macmillan Press, 1988). See also Madelyn Jablan, *Black Metafiction: Self-Consciousness in African American Literature* (Iowa City: University of Iowa Press, 1987).

17.   My own accounts of the movement are to be found in A. Robert Lee, '"Ask Your Mama": Langston Hughes, the Blues and recent American Studies', *Journal of American Studies*, Vol. 24, Part 2 (August 1990), pp. 251–62, and 'Afro-America, the Before Columbus Foundation and the Literary Multiculturalization of America', *Journal of American Studies*, Vol. 28, Part 3 (December 1994), pp. 433–50.

18.   Clarence Major, *The Dark & Feeling: Reflections on Black American Writers and Their Works* (New York: The Third Press, 1974), p. 28.

19.   Houston Baker, *The Journey Back: Issues in Black Literature and Criticism* (Chicago: University of Chicago Press, 1980).

20.   Robert. B. Stepto, *From Behind the Veil: A Study of Afro-American Narrative* (Urbana, Illinois: University of Illinois Press, 1979).

21.   Barbara Christian, *Black Women Novelists: The Development of a Tradition, 1892–1976* (Westport, Connecticut: Greenwood Press, 1984); Hazel V. Carby, *Reconstructing Womanhood: The Experience of the Afro-American Woman Novelist* (New York: Oxford University Press, 1987). See also Mari Evans (ed.), *Black Women Writers (1950–1980): A Critical Evaluation* (New York: Doubleday, 1984); Marjorie Pryse and Hortense J. Spillers (eds), *Conjuring: Black Women, Fiction, and Literary Tradition* (Bloomington: Indiana University Press, 1985); Cheryl A. Wall (ed.), *Changing Our Own Words: Essays in Criticism, Theory, and Writing by Black Women* (New Jersey: Rutgers University Press, 1989); Elliott Butler-Evans, *Race, Gender, and Desire: Narrative Strategies in the Fiction of Toni Cade Bambara, Toni Morrison, Alice Walker* (Philadelphia: Temple University Press, 1989); and Sandi Russell, *Render Me My Song: African-American Women Writers From Slavery to the Present* (London and New York: St. Martin's Press, 1990).

22.   Henry Louis Gates Jr. (ed.), *Figures in Black: Words, Signs and the 'Racial' Self* (New York: Oxford University Press, 1987), pp. xx–xxvii. See following footnote for a full list of Gates's writings.

23.   The following especially have featured: Houston Baker Jr., *Black Literature in America* (New York: McGraw Hill, 1971), *The Journey Back: Issues in Black Literature and Criticism* (1980), *Workings of the Spirit: The Poetics of Afro-American Women's Writings* (Boston: University of Massachusetts Press, 1982), *Blues, Ideology, and Afro-American Literature: A Vernacular Theory* (Chicago: University of Chicago Press, 1987) and, with Patricia Redmond, *Afro-American Study in the 1990s* (Chicago: University of Chicago Press, 1990); R.B. Stepto, *From Behind the Veil: A Study of Afro-American Narrative* (1979); Henry Louis Gates Jr. (ed.), *Black Literature and Literary Theory* (New York: Methuen, 1984), *Figures in Black* (1987); *Race, Writing and Difference* (Chicago: University of Chicago Press, 1986), *The Signifying Monkey: A Theory of Afro-American Criticism* (New York: Oxford University Press, 1987), (ed.), *The Schomburg Library of Nineteenth-Century Black Women Writers*, 30 Vols (New York: Oxford University Press, 1988–), (ed.), *Reading Black, Reading Feminist: A Critical Anthology* (New York: Meridian, 1990), with Nellie

Y. McKay (eds), *The Norton Anthology of Afro-American Literature* (New York: Norton, 1990), and *Loose Canons: Notes on the Culture Wars* (New York: Oxford University Press, 1992); and, more recently, J. Lee Greene, *Blacks in Eden: The African American Novel's First Century* (Charlottesville, Virgina: University of Virginia Press, 1996).

24. Ishmael Reed, *Flight to Canada* (New York: Random House, 1976). For a useful account, see Richard Walsh, '"A Man's Story is His Gris-Gris": Cultural Slavery, Literary Emancipation and Ishmael Reed's *Flight to Canada*', *Journal of American Studies*, Vol. 27 (April 1993), pp. 57–71.

25. Langston Hughes, *The Selected Poems of Langston Hughes* New York: Knopf, 1965); Countee Cullen, *Color* (New York: Harper, 1925); Jean Toomer, *Cane* (New York: Boni & Liveright, 1923); Claude McKay, *Home to Harlem* (New York: Harper, 1928); Nella Larsen, *Quicksand* (New York: Knopf, 1928) and *Passing* (New York and London: A.A. Knopf. 1929); Jessie Redmon Fauset, *Plum Bun: A Novel without a Moral* (New York: Frederick A. Stokes, 1929); and Walter White, *The Fire in the Flint* (New York: Knopf, 1924). The lynching figures are taken from Samuel Eliot Morrison, *The Oxford History of the American People* (New York: Oxford University Press, 1965).

26. Alain Locke (ed.), *The New Negro: An Interpretation* (New York: Albert and Charles Boni, 1925). 'The Negro Digs Up His Past' is reprinted in Gates and McKay (eds), *The Norton Anthology of African American Literature*, pp. 937–42). For overall assessments see John Henrik Clarke (ed.), *Harlem U.S.A.* (Berlin: Seven Seas, 1964); Gilbert Olefsky, *Harlem: The Making of a Ghetto* (New York: Harper, 1966); Allan Schoener (ed.), *Harlem On My Mind: Cultural Capital of Black America, 1900–1978* (New York: Dell, 1968); Nathan Irving Huggins, *Harlem Renaissance* (New York: Oxford University Press, 1971); Arna Bontemps (ed.), *The Harlem Renaissance Remembered* (New York: Dodd, Mead, 1972); Nathan Irvin Huggins (ed.), *Voices From the Harlem Renaissance* (New York: Oxford University Press, 1976); David Levering Lewis, *When Harlem Was in Vogue* (New York: Knopf, 1981); and Jervis Anderson, *This Was Harlem: A Cultural Portrait, 1900–1950* (New York: Farrar, Straus, Giroux, 1982).

27. Richard Wright, *Native Son* (New York: Harper, 1940), *Black Boy: A Record of Childhood and Youth* (New York and London: Harper, 1945) and *American Hunger* (New York: Harper and Row, 1977). This perspective is more fully explored in Chapter 6, 'Richard Wright's Inside Narratives'.

28. James Baldwin, *Go Tell It on the Mountain* (New York: Knopf, 1953) and *Notes of a Native Son* (Boston: Beacon, 1955).

29. Ralph Ellison, *Invisible Man* (New York: Random House, 1952), *Shadow and Act* (New York: Random House, 1964) and *Going to the Territory* (New York: Random House, 1986).

30. Paule Marshall, *The Chosen Place, the Timeless People* (New York: Harcourt Brace Jovanovich, 1969); Toni Morrison, *Song of Solomon* (New York: Alfred A. Knopf, 1977); Leon Forrest, *Two Wings to Veil My Face* (New York: Random House, 1984); and John Wideman, *Hiding Place* (New York: Avon Books, 1981), *Damballah* (New York: Avon Books, 1981) and *Sent For You Yesterday* (New York: Avon Books, 1983).

31. Ntozake Shange, *Sassafrass, Cypress & Indigo* (New York: St. Martin's Press, 1982); Charles Johnson, *Oxherding Tale: A Novel* (Bloomington: Indiana University Press, 1982) and *The Sorcerer's Apprentice; Tales and Conjurations*

(New York: Atheneum, 1986); and Clay Ellis, *Platitudes* (New York: Vintage, 1988).

32. Harriet E. Wilson, *Our Nig; or, Sketches from the Life of a Free Black, in a Two-Story White House, North. Showing That Slavery's Shadow Falls Even There. By 'Our Nig.'*, originally published in Massachusetts by George C. Rand and Avery 1859. Republished as *Our Nig; or, Sketches from the Life of a Free Black*, ed. Henry Louis Gates Jr. (New York: Vintage Books, 1983). A full analysis is offered in Chapter 4. Zora Neale Hurston, *Their Eyes Were Watching God* (Philadelphia: Lippincott, 1937); Gwendolyn Brooks, *Annie Allen* (New York: Harper, 1949); and Rita Dove, *Thomas and Beulah* (Pittsburgh: Carnegie Mellon Press, 1986).

33. Paul Laurence Dunbar, *The Complete Poems of Paul Laurence Dunbar*, with 'Introduction' to *Lyrics of Lowly Life* by W.D. Howells (New York: Dodd, Mead, 1913); Richard Wright, 'The Ethics of Living Jim Crow' (1937), included as an 'Introduction' to *Uncle Tom's Children* (New York: Harper, 1938); Malcolm X, *The Autobiography of Malcolm X* (New York: Grove, 1965); and George Jackson, *Soledad Brother: The Prison Letters of George Jackson* (New York: Random House, 1970).

34. Briton Hammon, *Narrative of the uncommon suffering and surprizing deliverance of Briton Hammon, a Negro Man-servant to general Winslow, of Marshfield, who returned to Boston, after having been absent almost thirteen years. Containing an account of the many hardships he underwent ... how he was cast away in the Capes of Florida ... inhuman barbarity of the Indians* (Boston: printed by Green & Russell, 1746, 14 pp.); and Maya Angelou, *I Know Why the Caged Bird Sings* (New York: Random House, 1970).

35. Most of these are reprinted in Benjamin Brawley (ed.), *Early Negro American Writers* (Durham: University of North Carolina Press, 1935; reprinted New York: Dover Publications, 1970).

36. For a consideration of Hammon as a founding voice of black theology, see Sondra O'Neale, *Jupiter Hammon and the Biblical Beginnings of African-American Literature* (Metuchen, New Jersey: American Theological Library Association and Scarecrow Press, 1993).

37. Toni Morrison, *Playing in the Dark: Whiteness and the Literary Imagination* (Cambridge, Massachusetts: Harvard University Press, 1992).

Chapter 2

1. Frederick Douglass, *Narrative of the Life of Frederick Douglass, an American Slave, Written by Himself* (Boston: The American Anti-Slavery Society, 1845). Standard edition: Frederick Douglass, *Narrative of the Life of Frederick Douglass, an American Slave* (Cambridge, Massachusetts: Harvard University Press, 1960). For ease of access present page references are to Henry Louis Gates Jr. (ed.), *The Classic Slave Narratives: The Life of Olaudah Equiano, The History of Mary Prince, Narrative of the Life of Frederick Douglass, Incidents in the Life of a Slave Girl* (New York: New American Library/Mentor, 1987), pp. 274–5.

2. Frederick Douglass, *My Bondage and My Freedom. Part 1 – Life as a Slave. Part II – Life as a Freeman. With an Introduction*, by Dr. James M'Cune Smith (New York and Auburn: Miller, Orton & Mulligan, 1855); *Life and Times of Frederick Douglass. Written by himself. His early life as a slave, his escape from bondage, and his complete history to the present time, including his connection with the*

anti-slavery movement. With an introduction by Mr. George L. Ruffin (Hartford, Connecticut: Park Publishing Co., 1881); *Life and Times of Frederick Douglass written by himself. His early life as a slave, his escape from bondage, and his complete history to the present time, including his connection with the anti-slavery movement, with an introduction by Mr. George L. Ruffin*, new revised edition (Boston: DeWolfe, Fiske & Co., 1892).

3. Frances E.W. Harper, *Iola Leroy or Shadows Uplifted* (Boston: James H. Earle, 1892). All citations here and in Chapter 4 are to the following reprint: Hazel V. Carby (ed.), *Iola Leroy or Shadows Uplifted* (Boston: Beacon Press, 1987). This episode appears on p. 45.

4. This consciously 'double' liberation runs through almost all African American autobiography, not only in Douglass but, among others, James Weldon Johnson, Zora Neale Hurston and Ralph Ellison.

5. Ralph Ellison, *Invisible Man*, 30th Anniversary Edition (New York: Random House, [1952] 1982), p. 372.

6. Darryl Pinckney, *High Cotton* (New York and Harmondsworth, Middlesex: Penguin Books, 1992), pp. 212–13.

7. Angela Davis, *An Autobiography* (New York: Random House, 1974).

8. Angela Y. Davis, *If They Come in the Morning: Voices of Resistance* (New York: The Third Press, 1971, reprinted New York: New American Library, Signet, 1971).

9. The following scholarship has been particularly relevant: Rebecca Chambers, *Witnesses for Freedom: Negro Americans in Autobiography* (New York: Harper and Brothers, 1948); Russell C. Brignano, *Black Americans in Autobiography: An Annotated Bibliography of Autobiography and Autobiographical Books Written Since the Civil War* (Durham: Duke University Press, 1974); Sidonie Smith, *Where I'm Bound: Patterns of Slavery and Freedom in Black American Autobiography* (Westport, Connecticut: Greenwood Press, 1974); Stephen Butterfield, *Black Autobiography in America* (Amherst, Massachusetts: University of Massachusetts Press, 1974); Elizabeth Schultz, 'To Be Black and Blue: The Blues Genre in Black American Autobiography', *Kansas Quarterly*, Vol. 7, No. 3 (Summer 1975), reprinted in Albert E. Stone (ed.), *The American Autobiography* (Englewood Cliffs, New Jersey: Prentice Hall, 1981); Robert B. Stepto, *From Behind the Veil: A Study of Afro-American Narrative* (Urbana, Illinois: University of Illinois Press, 1979); C.W.E. Bigsby, *The Second Black Renaissance: Essays in Black Literature* (Westport, Connecticut: Greenwood Press, 1982), especially Chapter 7, 'The Public Self: Black Autobiography'; Albert E. Stone, *From Henry Adams to Nate Shaw* (Philadelphia: University of Pennsylvania Press, 1982); Henry Louis Gates Jr., *Black Literature and Literary Theory* (New York and London: Methuen, 1984); and Carl Plasa and Betty J. Rings (eds), *The Discourse of Slavery* (London and New York: Routledge, 1994).

10. The best recent overviews of slave narrative are William L. Andrews, *To Tell a Free Story: The First Century of Afro-American Autobiography, 1760–1865* (Urbana: University of Illinois Press, 1986) and Charles T. Davis and Henry Louis Gates Jr. (eds), *The Slave's Narrative* (New York: Oxford University Press, 1985).

11. For editions of Olaudah/Vassa's *The Interesting Narrative of the Life of Olaudah Equiano, or Gustavus Vassa ...* , see Chapter 1, Note 6; William Wells Brown, *Narrative of William W. Brown, a Fugitive Slave. Written by Himself* (Boston: The Anti-Slavery Office, 1847) and *Clotel, or The President's Daughter: A*

Narrative of Slave Life in the United States (London: Partridge and Oakey, 1853); the novel was then twice revised as *Clotelle: A Tale of the Southern States* (Boston: J. Redpath, 1864) and *Clotelle: Or, The Colored Heroine. A Tale of The Southern States* (Boston: Lee and Shepard, 1867); and James William Charles Pennington, *The Fugitive Blacksmith; or, Events in the history of James W.C. Pennington, pastor of a Presbyterian church, New York, formerly a slave in the state of Maryland, United States* (London: C. Gilpin, 1849); Among the available anthologies and editions of slave narratives are Julius Lester (ed.), *To Be a Slave* (New York: Dial Press, 1968); Arna Bontemps (ed.), *Great Slave Narratives* (Boston: Beacon Press, 1969); Gilbert Osofsky (ed.), *Puttin' on Ole Massa: The Slave Narratives of Henry Bibbs, William Wells Brown and Solomon Northrup* (New York: Harper, 1969); Norman R. Yetman (ed.), *Life Under the 'Peculiar Institution': Selections from the Slave Narrative Collection* (New York: Holt, Rinehart and Winston, 1970); John F. Bayliss (ed.), *Black Slave Narratives* (New York: Collier Books, 1970); William L. Andrews (ed.), *Sisters of the Spirit: Three Black Women's Autobiographies* (Bloomington: Indiana University Press, 1986); Henry Louis Gates Jr. (ed.), *The Classic Slave Narratives* (New York: Penguin/Mentor, 1987). For overall coverage see George R. Rawick (ed.), *The American Slave: A Composite Autobiography*, 41 Vols (Westport, Connecticut: Greenwood, 1972, 1978, 1979).

12.   Josiah Henson, *The Life of Josiah Henson, formerly a slave, now an inhabitant of Canada, as narrated by himself* (Boston: A.D. Phelps, 1849); also Josiah Henson, *Truth Stranger than Fiction. Father Henson's story of his own life. With an introduction by Mrs. H.B. Stowe* (Boston: J.P. Jewett and Co., 1858); Henry Bibb, *Narrative of the Life and Adventures of Henry Bibb, an American slave, written by himself with an introduction by Lucius C. Matlack* (New York: The Author, 1849); Solomon Northrup, *Twelve Years a Slave. Narrative of Solomon Northrup, a citizen of New-York, kidnapped in Washington in 1841, and rescued in 1853, from a cotton plantation near the Red River, in Louisiana* (Auburn, New York: Derby and Miller; Buffalo, New York: Derby, Orton and Mulligan, 1853); and William and Ellen Craft, *Running a Thousand Miles for Freedom; or the Escape of William and Ellen Craft from Slavery. (With a portrait of Ellen Craft)* (London: William Tweedie, 1860).

13.   See Sarah Bradford, *Scenes in the Life of Harriet Tubman* (Auburn, New York: W.J. Moses, Printer, 1869) and Olive Gilbert, *Narrative of Sojourner Truth, a northern slave, emancipated from bodily servitude by the state of New York, in 1828* (Boston: The Author, 1850). Sojourner Truth's 'Ar'n't I a Woman' (1851) is reprinted in Henry Louis Gates Jr. and Nellie Y. McKay (eds), *The Norton Anthology of African American Literature* (New York: W.W. Norton & Company, 1997).

14.   The definitive edition is now Harriet A. Jacobs, *Incidents in the Life of a Slave Girl, Written by Herself*, ed. by Jean Fagan Yellin (Cambridge, Massachusetts: Harvard University Press, 1987).

15.   All three are collected in John Hope Franklin (ed.), *Three Negro Classics: Up from Slavery; The Souls of Black Folk; The Autobiography of an Ex-Colored Man* (New York: Avon Books, 1965).

16.   W.E.B. DuBois, *Darkwater: Voices from within the Veil* (New York: Harcourt Brace, 1920); *Dusk at Dawn: An Autobiography of a Race Concept* (1940), in Nathan Huggins (ed.) *DuBois: Writings* (New York: Library of America, 1986); and *The Autobiography: A Soliloquy on Viewing My Life from the Last Decade of Its First Century* (n.p.: International Publishers, 1968).

17. James Weldon Johnson, *The Autobiography of an Ex-Coloured Man* (Boston: Sherman French, 1912), reissued, with American spelling, as *The Autobiography of an Ex-Colored Man* (New York: Knopf, 1927).

18. John A. Williams, *The Man Who Cried I Am* (New York; Doubleday, 1967); George Cain, *Blueschild Baby* (New York: Dell, 1970); and Ernest Gaines, *The Autobiography of Miss Jane Pittman* (New York: The Dial Press, 1971).

19. Langston Hughes, *The Big Sea* (New York: Alfred A. Knopf, 1940; reprinted New York: Hill & Wang, 1963); *I Wonder as I Wander* (New York: Rinehart, 1956; reprinted New York: Hill & Wang, 1964). I offer a fuller account in A. Robert Lee, '"Ask Your Mama"; Langston Hughes, the Blues and Recent Afro-American Studies', *Journal of American Studies*, Vol. 24 (1990), pp. 199–209.

20. James Weldon Johnson, *Along this Way: The Autobiography of James Weldon Johnson* (New York: Viking, 1933), *God's Trombones. Seven Negro Sermons in Verse* (New York: Viking, 1927), *The Book of Negro American Poetry* (New York: Harcourt Brace, 1922; Revised Edition, 1931).

21. Claude McKay, *A Long Way from Home* (New York: Lee Furman, 1937), *Home to Harlem* (New York: Harper, 1928), *Banjo* (New York: Harper, 1933), *Banana Bottom* (New York: Harper, 1933), *Gingertown* (New York: Harper, 1932), *Harlem Shadows* (New York: Harcourt, Brace, 1922).

22. George Schuyler, *Black and Conservative* (New Rochelle, New York: Arlington, 1966); 'The Negro-Art Hokum', *The Nation*, Vol. 122 (1926), pp. 662–3; and *Black No More: Being an Account of the Strange and Wonderful Workings of Science in the Land of the Free A.D. 1933–1940* (New York: McCauley Co., 1931).

23. Richard Wright, *Black Boy: A Record of Childhood and Youth* (New York and London: Harper, 1945), p. 284.

24. Richard Wright, *American Hunger* (New York: Harper, 1977).

25. Zora Neale Hurston, *Dust Tracks on a Road, an Autobiography* (Philadelphia and London: Lippincott, 1942). All references are to the restored text published as *Dust Tracks on a Road* in Zora Neale Hurston, *Folklore, Memoirs, and Other Writings: Mules & Men, Tell My Horse, Dust Tracks on a Road, Selected Articles* (New York: Library of America, 1995), p. 561.

26. Robert Hemenway, *Zora Neale Hurston: A Literary Biography* (Urbana: University of Illinois Press, 1984). See also Robert Hemenway, 'Introduction' to Zora Neale Hurston: *Dust Tracks on a Road* (Urbana: University of Illinois Press, 1984). An overview is to be found in Henry Louis Gates Jr., 'A Negro Way of Saying', *The New York Times Book Review*, 21 April 1985, pp. 1, 43, 45.

27. Zora Neale Hurston, *Jonah's Gourd Vine* (Philadelphia: Lippincott, 1934), *Mules & Men* (Philadelphia: Lippincott, 1935).

28. Hemenway, *Zora Neale Hurston*.

29. See Alice Walker, 'Zora Neale Hurston: A Cautionary Tale and Partisan View' and 'Looking for Zora', in *In Search of Our Mothers' Gardens: Womanist Prose* (New York: Harcourt Brace Jovanovich, 1983).

30. Chester Himes, *The Quality of Hurt* (New York: Doubleday, 1972) and *My Life of Absurdity* (New York: Doubleday, 1976).

31. Chester Himes, *The Third Generation* (Cleveland: World Publishing Company, 1954), *Cast the First Stone* (New York: Loward-McCann, 1952), *If He Hollers Let Him Go* (New York: Doubleday, Doran, 1945).

32. Chester Himes, *Une Affaire de viol* (Paris: Editions Les Yeux Ouverts, 1963).

33. Chester Himes, *The Primitive* (New York: New American Library, 1955).

34. Eldridge Cleaver, *Soul on Ice* (New York: McGraw Hill, 1968).

35. Ishmael Reed, *Writin' Is Fightin': Thirty-Seven Years of Boxing on Paper* (New York: Atheneum, 1988).

36. James Baldwin, *Notes of a Native Son* (Boston: Beacon, 1955), p. 150.

37. James Baldwin, *Notes of a Native Son* (1955); *Nobody Knows My Name: More Notes of a Native Son* (New York: Dial, 1961); and *The Fire Next Time* (New York: Dial, 1963).

38. James Baldwin, *Go Tell It on the Mountain* (New York: Alfred A. Knopf, 1953); *A Rap on Race: Margaret Mead and James Baldwin* (Philadelphia: J.B. Lippincott, 1971); and *The Evidence of Things Not Seen* (New York: Holt, Rinehart and Winston, 1985).

39. James Baldwin, *The Price of the Ticket: Collected Non-Fiction 1948–1985* (New York: St. Martin's/Marek, 1985).

40. *The Autobiography of Malcolm X* (New York: Grove Press, 1965).

41. Eldridge Cleaver, *Post-Prison Writings and Speeches* (New York: Random House, 1969); and Lee Lockwood (eds), *Conversation with Eldridge Cleaver, Algiers* (New York: McGraw Hill, 1970).

42. Bobby Seale, *Seize the Time* (New York: Random House, 1970) and *A Lonely Rage* (New York: Times Books, 1978); Huey Newton, *To Die for the People* (New York: Random House, 1972); H. Rap Brown, *Die Nigger Die!* (New York: Dial Press, 1969); Hoyt Fuller, *Journey to Africa* (Chicago: Third World Press, 1971); and George Jackson, *Soledad Brother: The Prison Letters of George Jackson* (New York: Random House, 1970).

43. Nikki Giovanni, *Gemini: An Extended Autobiographical Statement on My First Twenty-Five Years of Being a Black Poet* (New York: Bobbs-Merrill Company, 1971).

44. Charles Mingus, *Beneath the Underdog: His World as Composed by Mingus*, ed. Neil King (New York: Alfred A. Knopf, 1971).

45. Vincent O. Carter, *The Bern Book: A Record of a Voyage of the Mind* (New York: The John Day Company, 1973).

46. Julius Lester, *All Is Well, An Autobiography* (New York: William Morrow and Company, Inc., 1976).

47. June Jordan, *Civil Wars* (Boston: Beacon Press, 1981), p. x.

48. John Wideman, *Brothers & Keepers* (New York: Holt, Rinehart and Winston, 1984) and *Fatheralong: A Meditation on Fathers and Sons, Race and Society* (New York: Holt, Rinehart and Winston, 1995).

49. Audre Lorde, *Zami: A New Spelling of My Name* (Watertown, Massachusetts: Persephone Press Inc., 1982).

50. LeRoi Jones/Amiri Baraka, *The Autobiography of LeRoi Jones/Amiri Baraka* (New York: Alfred A. Knopf, 1984).

51. Lorene Cary, *Black Ice* (New York: Alfred A. Knopf, 1991).

52. Darryl Pinckney, *High Cotton* (New York and Harmondsworth, Middlesex: Penguin, 1992).

53. Ray Shell, *Iced* (New York and London: HarperCollins, Flamingo, 1993).

54. Maya Angelou, *I Know Why the Caged Bird Sings* (New York: Random House, 1969), pp. 24–5.

55. Maya Angelou, *Gather Together in My Name* (New York: Random House, 1974).

56. Maya Angelou, *Singin' and Gettin' Merry Like Christmas* (New York: Random House, 1976); *The Heart of a Woman* (New York: Random House, 1981).

57. Maya Angelou, *All God's Children Need Traveling Shoes* (New York: Random House, 1986).

Chapter 3

1. Alain Locke, *The New Negro: An Interpretation* (New York: Alfred A. Knopf, 1925).
2. LeRoi Jones, 'City of Harlem', *Home: Social Essays* (New York: William Morrow, 1968).
3. Jessie Redmon Fauset, *Plum Bun: A Novel Without a Moral* (New York: Frederick A. Stokes, 1929).
4. For historical reference see John Hope Franklin, *From Slavery to Freedom: A History of Negro Americans* (New York: Knopf, 1947; 3rd edn, 1967); James Egert Allan, *The Negro in New York* (New York: Exposition Press, 1964); and Gilbert Osofsky, *Harlem: The Making of a Ghetto, Negro New York, 1890–1930* (New York: Harper, 1966); also the pictorial compilation, Allan Shoener (ed.), *Harlem on my Mind: Cultural Capital of Black America* (New York: Dell Publishing, 1968, 1979).
5. See, for instance, George Hutchinson, *The Harlem Renaissance in Black and White* (Cambridge, Massachusetts: Harvard University Press, 1996).
6. An early anthology of Harlem writing and photography would be John Henrik Clarke (ed.), *Harlem U.S.A.* (Berlin: Seven Seas Books, 1964).
7. This important artist has long been due a full biography. Fortunately one has recently appeared by a friend and biographer of Baldwin. See David Leeming, *Amazing Grace: A Life of Beauford Delaney* (New York: Oxford University Press, 1997).
8. Two excellent recent cultural histories of Harlem are: David Levering Lewis, *When Harlem Was in Vogue* (New York: Knopf, 1981) and Jervis Anderson, *This Was Harlem: A Cultural Portrait, 1900–1950* (New York: Farrar Straus Giroux, 1982). See also Amritjit Singh, *The Novels of the Harlem Renaissance* (University Park, Pennsylvania: Pennsylvania State University Press, 1976); Lorraine Elena Roses and Ruth Elizabeth Randolph (eds), *Harlem Renaissance and Beyond: Literary Biographies of 100 Black Women Writers, 1900–1945* (Cambridge, Massachusetts: Harvard University Press, 1990); George Hutchinson, *The Harlem Renaissance in Black and White* (Cambridge, Massachusetts: Belknap Press of Harvard University Press, 1995); and Cary D. Wirtz, *Black Culture and the Harlem Renaissance* (College Station, Texas: Texas A & M University Press, 1996).
9. Countee Cullen, *Color* (New York: Harper, 1925); *Copper Sun* (New York: Harper, 1927); *The Ballad of the Brown Girl; an Old Ballad Retold* (New York: Harper, 1927), and *The Black Christ and Other Poems* (New York: Harper, 1929); Claude McKay, *Harlem Shadows* (New York: Harcourt Brace, 1922); Melvin B. Tolson, *Harlem Gallery, Book I* (New York: Twayne, 1965); and LeRoi Jones and Larry Neal (eds), *Black Fire: An Anthology of Afro-American Writing* (New York: William Morrow & Co., 1968).
10. Langston Hughes, *Tambourines to Glory* (New York: John Day, 1958). This was the novel from which Hughes made his adaptation. The play was published as Langston Hughes, *Tambourines to Glory* (New York: Hill and Wang, 1958, 1963); James Baldwin, *The Amen Corner* (New York: Dial, 1968).

11. *Baby Sister* was published for the first time in Chester Himes, *Black on Black: Baby Sister and Selected Writings* (Garden City, New York: Doubleday & Company, 1973).

12. First published in *Commentary*, February 1948, and subsequently in *Notes of a Native Son* (New York: Dial, 1955).

13. Scholarship on the Harlem Renaissance had been increasingly prolific. See, especially, Nathan Irvin Huggins, *Harlem Renaissance* (New York: Oxford University Press, 1971) and Nathan Irvin Huggins (ed.), *Voices from the Harlem Renaissance* (New York: Oxford University Press, 1976); Arna Bontemps (ed.), *The Harlem Renaissance Remembered: Essays Edited with a Memoir* (New York: Dodd, Mead, 1972); Bruce Kelner (ed.), *The Harlem Renaissance: A Historical Dictionary of an Era* (New York: Methuen, London: Routledge & Kegan Paul, 1987).

14. Ishmael Reed, *Mumbo Jumbo* (New York: Doubleday, 1972).

15. James Weldon Johnson, *Black Manhattan* (New York: Knopf, 1930).

16. Claude McKay, *Harlem: Negro Metropolis* (New York: E. P. Dutton, 1940).

17. Carl Van Vechten, *Nigger Heaven* (New York: Knopf, 1926); Claude McKay, *Home to Harlem* (New York: Harper, 1928).

18. Paul Laurence Dunbar, *The Sport of the Gods* (New York: Dodd, Mead, 1902) and James Weldon Johnson, *The Autobiography of an Ex-Coloured Man* (Boston: Sherman French, 1912; New York: Knopf, 1927).

19. Nella Larsen, *Quicksand* (New York and London: Knopf, 1928), reprinted as *Quicksand* (New York: Macmillan/Collier Books, 1971). References here and in Chapter 4 are to this edition. Rudolph Fisher, *The Walls of Jericho* (New York and London: Knopf, 1928) and *The Conjure-Man Dies: A Mystery Tale of Dark Harlem* (New York: Corvici, Friede, 1932).

20. Wallace Thurman, *The Blacker the Berry: A Novel of Negro Life* (New York: Macauley, 1929); George Schuyler, *Black No More: Being an Account of the Strange and Wonderful Workings of Science in the Land of the Free, A.D. 1933–1940* (New York: Macauley Co., 1931); and Countee Cullen, *One Way to Heaven* (New York and London: Harper, 1932).

21. For a full listing of Van Vechten's writing and photography, see Bruce Kellner (ed.), *A Bibliography of the Work of Carl Van Vechten* (Connecticut: Greenwood Press, 1980).

22. Nancy Cunard (ed.), *Negro: Anthology* (1934; reissued, New York: Frederick Ungar, 1970).

23. See, respectively, James Weldon Johnson, *Along This Way* (New York: Viking, 1933); Langston Hughes, *The Big Sea* (New York: Knopf, 1940); Claude McKay, *A Long Way from Home* (New York: Lee Fruman, 1937); and W.E.B. DuBois, 'Review of *Nigger Heaven*', *Crisis*, December 1926.

24. Fauset, *Plum Bun*, p. 97–8.

25. Ann Petry, *The Street* (Boston: Houghton Mifflin, 1946).

26. Louise Meriwether, *Daddy Was a Number Runner* (Englewood-Cliff, New Jersey: Prentice Hall, 1970).

27. Langston Hughes, *Simple Speaks His Mind* (New York: Simon and Schuster, 1950); *Simple Takes a Wife* (New York: Simon and Schuster, 1953); *Simple Stakes a Claim* (New York: Rinehart, 1957); *The Best of Simple* (New York: Hill and Wang, 1961); *Simple's Uncle Sam* (New York: Hill and Wang, 1965). For discussions of Hughes's Simple stories, see James A. Emanuel, *Langston Hughes* (New York: Twayne Publishers, 1967) and Therman O' Daniel, *Langston Hughes, Black Genius: A Critical Evaluation* (New York:

Morrow, 1971). Also, A. Robert Lee, '"Ask Your Mama": Langston Hughes, the Blues and Recent Afro-American Literary Studies', *Journal of American Studies*, Vol. 24, No. 2 (1990), pp. 199–209.

28.   Ralph Ellison, *Invisible Man* (New York: Random House, 1952), p. 140.

29.   A necessary retrospect is to be found in *Invisible Man*, 30th Anniversary Edition (New York: Random House, 1982). Speaking of a novel largely written in, as well as about, Harlem, Ellison observes, 'this has always been a most willful, most self-generating novel, and the proof of that statement is witnessed by the fact that here, thirty astounding years later, it has me writing about it again'.

30.   Ralph Ellison, 'Harlem Is Nowhere', written originally for (but unpublished by) *Magazine of the Year* (1948). The piece is included in *Shadow and Act* (New York: Random House, 1964), pp. 294–317.

31.   Ralph Ellison, 'Harlem's America', *New Leader*, Vol. 48 (26 September 1966), pp. 22–35.

32.   James Baldwin, *Go Tell It on the Mountain* (New York: Knopf, 1953).

33.   James Baldwin, *Another Country* (New York: Dial Press, 1962); *If Beale Street Could Talk* (New York: Dial Press, 1974); and *Just Above My Head* (New York: Dial Press, 1979).

34.   The detective fiction (and *Run Man Run*) have had a complicated history. Titles (and publishers) have changed, and several appeared in French translation before American or British publication. In this listing American editions are given first, then the French and British: 1. *For Love of Imabelle* (Greenwich, Connecticut: Fawcett, 1957). Title changed to *A Rage in Harlem* (New York: Avon Books, 1965). *La Reine des pommes* (Paris: Gallimard, *Série Noire*, 1969) – which won the *Grand Prix de Littérature Policière*. *A Rage in Harlem* (London: Panther Books, 1969). 2. *The Real Cool Killers* (New York: Avon Books, 1959). *Il Pleut des coups durs* (Paris: Gallimard, *Série Noire*, 1958). *The Real Cool Killers* (London: Panther Books, 1969). Himes's original title was *If Trouble Was Money*. 3. *The Crazy Kill* (New York: Avon Books, 1959). *Couché dans le pain* (Paris: Gallimard, *Série Noire*, 1958). *The Crazy Kill* (London: Panther Books, 1969). Himes's original title was *A Jealous Man Can't Win*. 4. *Run Man Run* (New York: Putnam's Sons, 1966). *Dare-Dare* (Paris: Gallimard, *Série Noire*, 1959). *Run Man Run* (London: Frederick Muller, 1967; London: Panther Books, 1969). 5. *The Big Gold Dream* (New York: Avon Books, 1960). *Tout pour plaire* (Paris: Gallimard, *Série Noire*, 1959). *The Big Gold Dream* (London: Panther Books, 1968). 6. *All Shot Up* (New York: Avon Books, 1960). *Imbroglio Negro* (Paris: Gallimard, *Série Noire*, 1960). *All Shot Up* (London: Panther Books, 1969). Himes's original title was *Don't Play with Death*. 7. *The Heat's On* (New York: Putnam's Sons, 1966). Title changed to *Come Back Charleston Blue* (New York: Berkeley Paperback, 1972). *Ne nous enervons pas* (Paris: Gallimard, *Série Noire*, 1961). *The Heat's On* (London: Frederick Muller, 1966; London: Panther Books, 1968). 8. *Cotton Comes to Harlem* (New York: Putnam's Sons, 1965). *Retour en Afrique* (Paris: Editions Plon, 1964). *Cotton Comes to Harlem* (London: Frederick Muller, 1966; London: Panther Books, 1968). 9. *Blind Man with a Pistol* (New York: William Morrow, 1969; New York: Dell Paperback retitled *Hot Day, Hot Night*, 1970). *L'Aveugle au pistolet* (Paris: Gallimard, Série Noire, 1969). *Blind Man with a Pistol* (London: Hodder and Staunton, 1969; London: Panther Books, 1971). The detective stories are admirably studied in Stephen F. Milliken, *Chester Himes: A Critical Appraisal* (Columbia, Missouri:

Missouri University Press, 1976). See also A. Robert Lee, 'Hurts, Absurdities and Violence: The Contrary Dimensions of Chester Himes', *Journal of American Studies*, Vol. 12, No. 1 (April 1978), pp. 99–114.

35. *Sunday Times*, 9 November 1969, p. 69.
36. Chester Himes, *Plan B* (Jackson, Mississippi: University Press of Mississippi, 1993).
37. Warren Miller, *The Cool World* (New York: Little, Brown & Company, 1959); Shane Stevens, *Go Down Dead* (New York: William Morrow & Company, 1967); Edward Lewis Wallant, *The Pawnbroker* (New York: Harcourt, Brace & World, 1961); and Piri Thomas, *Down These Mean Streets* (New York: Alfred A. Knopf, 1967).
38. Charles Wright, *The Messenger* (New York: Farrar, Straus, 1963).
39. William Melvin Kelley, *dem* (New York: Doubleday & Company, 1967).
40. Robert Deane Pharr, *S.R.O.* (New York: Doubleday & Company, 1971). The title refers to a single room occupancy hotel in Harlem.
41. Claude Brown, *The Children of Ham* (New York: Stein and Day, 1976); *Manchild in the Promised Land* (New York: Macmillan Company, 1965).
42. Toni Morrison, *Jazz* (New York: Alfred A. Knopf, 1992).
43. Rosa Guy, *A Measure of Time* (New York: Holt, Rinehart and Winston, 1983).
44. Darryl Pinckney, *High Cotton* (New York and Harmondsworth, Middlesex: Penguin Books, 1992), pp. 132–3.
45. I take the term *rumor* from Lorca's poem 'El Rey de Harlem'. The full line reads 'Harlem ... Me llega tu rumor'. Most translations read something like 'Harlem ... your murmur comes to me'. But *rumor* in this context conveys a great deal more. It incorporates the notion of energy, vitality, the sweep of human feeling and activity. In this sense it denotes perfectly why Harlem has so appealed to the creative imagination. Darryl Pinckney also makes use of this allusion in *High Cotton*, p. 132.

Chapter 4

1. Pauline Hopkins, *Contending Forces: A Romance Illustrative of Negro Life North and South* (Boston: Colored Cooperative Publishing Co., 1900). All references are to *Contending Forces*, ed. Matthew J. Bruccoli, *Lost American Fiction* series (Carbondale and Edwardsville, Illinois: Southern Illinois Press, 1978).
2. 'How It Feels to Be Colored Me', originally published in *The World Tomorrow*, Vol. 11 (May 1928).
3. Alice Walker, *In Search of Our Mothers' Gardens, Womanist Prose by Alice Walker* (New York: Harcourt Brace Jovanovich, 1983), p. xi.
4. Henry Louis Gates Jr., General Editor, *The Schomburg Library of Nineteenth-Century Black Women Writers*, 30 Vols (New York: Oxford University Press, 1988–).
5. Frances E.W. Harper, *Iola Leroy or Shadows Uplifted* (Boston: James H. Earle, 1892). Reissued, with Introduction by Hazel V. Carby, *Iola Leroy or Shadows Uplifted* (Boston, Massachusetts: Beacon Press, 1987). See also Hazel V. Carby (ed.), *The Magazine Novels of Pauline Hopkins*, The Schomburg Library of Nineteenth-Century Black Women Writers (New York: Oxford University Press, 1988).

6. Harriet E. Wilson, *Our Nig; or Sketches from the Life of a Free Black, in a Two-Story White House, North. Showing that Slavery's Shadows Fall Even There. By 'Our Nig.'* Printed for the author by George C. Rand and Avery company, 1859. Recovered and republished as *Our Nig*, edited with Introduction and Notes by Henry Louis Gates Jr. (New York: Random House/Vintage, 1983). 'Literary foremothers' is a term adapted from Claudia Tate, 'Pauline Hopkins: Our Literary Foremother', in Marjorie Pryse and Hortense J. Spillers (eds), *Conjuring: Black Women, Fiction and Literary Tradition* (Bloomington, Indiana: Indiana University Press, 1985), pp. 53–66. Both *Clarence and Corinne; or God's Way* (Philadelphia: American Baptist Publication Society, 1890) and *Megda* (Boston: James H. Earle, 1891) are republished in *The Schomburg Library of Nineteenth-Century Black Women Writers*.

7. Alice Walker with Pratibha Parmas, *Warrior Marks: Female Genital Mutilation and the Sexual Blinding of Women* (New York: Harcourt Brace, 1993) – made into the documentary film *Warrior Marks* (1993); and Alice Walker, *The Same River Twice* (New York: Scribners, 1996).

8. Al Young, *Who Is Angelina?* (New York: Holt, Rinehart & Winston, 1975) and Alice Walker, *Meridian* (New York: Harcourt Brace Jovanovich, 1976). See Elizabeth Schultz, 'Out of the Woods and into the World: A Study of Interracial Friendships between Women in American Novels', in Marjorie Pryse and Hortense J. Spillers (eds), *Black Women, Fiction, and Literary Tradition* (Bloomington, Indiana: Indiana University Press, 1985), pp. 67–85, also Gloria Steinem, 'Do you Know this Woman, She Knows You – A Profile of Alice Walker', *Ms*, Vol. 10, No. 1 (June 1982).

9. Alice Childress, *Rainbow Jordan* (New York: Coward, McGann & Geoghegan, 1981); Rosa Guy, *The Friends* (New York: Holt, Rinehart and Winston, 1973), *Ruby* (New York: Viking, 1976) and *Edith Jackson* (New York: Viking, 1978); Kristin Hunter, *The Soul Brothers and Sister Lou* (New York: Scribner's, 1968), *Boss Cat* (New York: Scribner's, 1971) and *Guests in the Promised Land* (New York: Scribner's, 1973).

10. Jamaica Kinkaid, *The Autobiography of My Mother* (New York: Farrar, Straus & Giroux, 1996) and Toni Morrison, *Sula* (New York: Knopf, 1974).

11. Carlene Hatcher Polite, *The Flagellants* (New York: Farrar, Straus & Giroux, 1967); Alice Walker, *The Color Purple* (New York: Harcourt Brace Jovanovich, 1982); and Gloria Naylor, *Mama Day* (New York: Vintage, 1988).

12. Audre Lorde, *Zami: A New Spelling of My Name* (Watertown, Massachusetts: Persephone Press, 1982). For other commentary on Lorde see Chapter 2. Ann Allen Shockley, *Loving Her* (Indianapolis: Bobbs-Merrill, 1974), *Say Jesus and Come to Me* (New York: Avon, 1982, reprinted Tallahasse, Florida: Naiad Press, 1987). The following offer representative perspectives: bell hooks, *"Aint I a Woman?": Black Women and Feminism* (Boston: South End, 1981); Gloria T. Hull, Patricia Bell Scott and Barbara Smith (eds), *All The Women Are White, All the Blacks Are Men, But Some of Us Are Brave* (Old Westbury, New York: The Feminist Press, 1982); and Joanne M. Braxton and Andree Nicholas McLaughlin (eds), *Wild Women in the Whirlwind: Afra-American Culture and the Contemporary Literary Renaissance* (New Brunswick, New Jersey: Rutgers University Press, 1990).

13. Kristin Hunter, *The Lakestown Rebellion* (New York: Scribner's, 1978) and *The Landlord* (New York: Scribner's, 1966).

14. Zora Neale Hurston, *Their Eyes Were Watching God* (Philadephia and London: Lippincott, 1937). Reprinted Urbana and Chicago: University of Illinois

Press (in arrangement with J.B. Lippincott Company, 1978). All page references are to this later reprint; Paule Marshall, *Brown Girl, Brownstones* (New York: Random House, 1959); Toni Cade Bambara, *The Salt Eaters* (New York: Random House, 1980); and Terry McMillan, *Waiting to Exhale* (New York: Simon and Schuster, 1992).

15. I offer an account of how the 1960s affected women's dress presentation in Chapter 8.

16. Ntozake Shange, *nappy edges* (New York: St. Martin's Press, 1972). I am grateful to Dr. Annette Dula for telling me of these 'scratch' sessions in her own African American childhood in the Carolinas.

17. Nella Larsen, *Quicksand* (New York and London: Knopf, 1928).

18. Jean Toomer, *Cane* (New York: Boni & Liveright, 1923).

19. Dorothy West, *The Living Is Easy* (Boston: Houghton, Mifflin, 1948).

20. Gwendolyn Brooks, *Maud Martha* (New York: Harper, 1953), republished in *The World of Gwendolyn Brooks* (New York: Harper & Row, 1971). For an analysis of Brooks's poetry collection, *A Street in Bronzeville* (New York: Harper, 1945), see Chapter 6.

21. Margaret Walker, *Jubilee* (Boston: Houghton Mifflin, 1966).

22. See, in this respect, Margaret Walker's own Dedication in *Jubilee*, where she speaks of 'my maternal great-grandmother, Margaret Duggans Ware Brown, whose story this is ... ', and her *How I Wrote Jubilee* (Chicago: Third World Press, 1972).

23. Gayl Jones, *Corregidora* (New York: Random House, 1975).

24. Paule Marshall, *Praisesong for the Widow* (New York: G.P. Putnam's, Sons, 1983).

25. Toni Morrison, *Beloved* (New York: Alfred A. Knopf, 1987).

26. Edwidge Danticat, *Breath, Eyes, Memory* (New York: Random House/Vintage, 1995) and *Krik? Krak!* (New York: Random House/ Vintage, 1996); A.J. Verdelle, *The Good Negress* (Chapel Hill, North Carolina: Algonquin Books, 1995).

Chapter 5

1. Richard Wright, *Black Boy* (New York: Harper and Brothers, 1945), p. 274.

2. Richard Wright, *American Hunger* (New York: Harper & Row, 1977), p. 135.

3. The reviews from which these phrases are taken are reprinted in Richard Abcarian (ed.), *Richard Wright's 'Native Son': A Critical Handbook* (Belmont, California: Wadsworth, 1970). Richard Wright, *Native Son* (New York: Harper, 1940).

4. Richard Wright, *12 Million Black Voices: A Folk History of the Negro United States* (New York: Viking, 1941), *The Color Curtain: A Report on the Bandung Conference* (Cleveland and New York: The World Publishing Company, 1956). See, for example, Addison Gayle Jr. (ed.), *Black Expression* (New York: Weybright and Talley, 1969); Addison Gayle Jr. (ed.), *The Black Aesthetic* (New York: Doubleday and Company, 1971); Addison Gayle Jr., *The Way of the World: The Black Novel in America* (New York: Anchor Press/Doubleday and Company, 1971); Mercer Cook and Stephen E. Henderson, *The Militant Black Writer in Africa and the United States* (Madison, Wisconsin: University of Wisconsin Press, 1969); George Kent, *Blackness and the Adventure of Western Culture* (Chicago: Third World Press, 1971); Stephen

Henderson, *Understanding the New Black Poetry* (New York: William Morrow and Company, 1973); Hoyt Fuller's articles in *Black World* (formerly *Negro Digest*); and *MidContinent American Studies Journal*, Vol. 11, No. 2 (Fall, 1972). See also note 13, Chapter 1.

5. Herman Melville, *Moby-Dick* (1851), Chapter 85.

6. Chester Himes, *If He Hollers Let Him Go* (New York: Doubleday, Doran, 1945); Ann Petry, *The Street* (Boston: Houghton, Mifflin, 1946); Alden Bland, *Behold a Cry* (New York: Scribner, 1947); and Willard Motley, *Knock on Any Door* (New York: Appleton-Century, 1947).

7. John A. Williams, *The Angry Ones* (New York: Ace Books, 1960), *Night Song* (New York: Farrar, Straus, 1961), and *Sissie* (New York: Farrar, Straus, 1963); John O. Killens, *Youngblood* (New York: Dial, 1954) and *And Then We Heard the Thunder* (New York: Knopf, 1963).

8. William Gardner Smith, *The Last of the Conquerors* (New York: Farrar, Straus, 1948); Lloyd L. Brown, *Iron City* (New York: Masses and Mainstream, 1951); Julian Mayfield, *The Hit* (New York: Vanguard, 1957); and Herbert Simmons, *Corner Boy* (Boston: Houghton, 1957) and *Man Walking on Eggshells* (Boston: Houghton, 1962).

9. Chester Himes, *The Quality of Hurt* (New York: Doubleday, 1972) and *My Life of Absurdity* (New York: Doubleday, 1976).

10. 'Many Thousands Gone' first appeared in *Partisan Review*, Vol. 18 (November–December 1951), and is reprinted in *Notes of a Native Son* (New York: Dial, 1955). 'Alas, Poor Richard', which incorporates 'Eight Men', originally published as 'The Survival of Richard Wright', *The Reporter*, March 1961, and 'The Exile', *Le Preuve*, February 1961, is reprinted in *Nobody Knows My Name* (New York: Dial, 1961).

11. 'Richard Wright's Blues' first appeared in *Antioch Review*, Vol. 5 (Summer 1945), and is reprinted in *Shadow and Act* (New York: Random House, 1964). 'The World and the Jug', based on an exchange with Irving Howe ('The Writer and the Critic', *The New Leader*, February 1964, and 'A Rejoinder', *The New Leader*, December 1964), also appears in *Shadow and Act*. Ralph Ellison, *Invisible Man*, 30th Anniversary Edition (New York: Random House, [1952] 1982).

12. 'The Man Who Lived Underground' was first published in *Cross-Section* (1945) and republished in *Eight Men* (Cleveland: World, 1961); 'Remembering Richard Wright', *Delta*, Vol. 18 (April 1984). Transcript of a lecture given at the University of Iowa, 18 July 1971. Republished in Ralph Ellison, *Going to the Territory* (New York: Random House, 1986).

13. Eldridge Cleaver, *Soul on Ice* (New York: McGraw Hill, 1968).

14. John A. Williams, *The Man Who Cried I Am* (New York: Doubleday, 1967) and *The Most Native of Sons: A Biography of Richard Wright* (New York: Doubleday, 1970).

15. Addison Gayle, *Richard Wright: Ordeal of a Native Son* (New York: Anchor Press/Doubleday, 1980) and Michel Fabre, *The Unfinished Quest of Richard Wright* (New York: William Morrow & Company, Inc., 1973).

16. Margaret Walker, *Richard Wright: Daemonic Genius* (New York: Warner, 1988).

17. Chester Himes, *The Primitive* (New York: New American Library, 1955); Hal Bennett, *Lord of the High Places* (New York: W.W. Norton & Company, 1971).

18. Herman Melville, *Billy Budd Sailor (An Inside Narrative)*, first published posthumously in 1924. The authoritative edition (and thereby the

authoritative title of the work) is: Harrison Hayford and Merton M. Sealts (eds), *Billy Budd Sailor (An Inside Narrative)* (Chicago and London: University of Chicago Press, 1962).

19. Richard Wright, *Black Power: A Record of Reactions in a Land of Pathos* (New York: Harper, 1954); *Pagan Spain* (New York: Harper & Brothers, 1957).

20. 'How Bigger Was Born' first appeared in *Saturday Review*, 1 June 1940, pp. 3–4, 17–20.

21. 'The Literature of the Negro in the United States' became Chapter 3 in *White Man, Listen!* (New York: Doubleday, 1957).

22. *Uncle Tom's Children: Four Novellas* (New York and London: Harper and Bros., 1938).

23. *Lawd Today* (New York: Walker, 1963); *The Outsider* (New York: Harper, 1953); *Savage Holiday* (New York: Avon, 1954); and *The Long Dream* (New York: Doubleday, 1958).

24. See 'Many Thousands Gone'.

25. For a useful gloss on this, see Graham Clarke, 'Beyond Realism: Recent Black Fiction and the Language of "The Real Thing"', in A. Robert Lee (ed.), *Black Fiction: New Studies in the Afro-American Novel since 1945* (London: Vision Press, 1980), p. 220.

26. George Lamming, *In the Castle of My Skin* (New York: McGraw-Hill Book Company, 1953), p. vi.

Chapter 6

1. James Baldwin, 'Down at the Cross: Letter from a Region in My Mind', *The Fire Next Time* (New York: Dial Press, 1963), pp. 68–9.

2. Relevant histories include Michi Weglyn, *Years of Infamy: The Untold History of America's Concentration Camps* (New York: Quill, 1976); Roger Daniels, *Asian America: Chinese and Japanese in the United States since 1850* (Seattle: University of Washington Press, 1988); and Ronald Takaki, *Strangers from a Distant Shore: A History of Asian Americans* (Boston: Little, Brown, 1989).

3. See, symptomatically, in this connection: Salvatore LaGumina (ed.), *WOP!: A Documentary History of Anti-Italian Discrimination in the United States* (San Francisco: Straight Arrow Books, 1973); and Fred L. Gardaphé, *Dagoes Read: Tradition and the Italian/American Writer* (Toronto: Guernica Editions, 1996).

4. The term 'symbolic' in this context I borrow from Mauricio Mazón, *The Zoot-Suit Riots: The Psychology of Symbolic Annihilation* (Austin, Texas: University of Texas Press, 1984).

5. As good an account as most of the iconography of Native Americans is to be found in Robert F. Berkhover, *The White Man's Indian: Images of the American Indian from Columbus to the Present* (New York: Alfred A. Knopf, 1978). See also Angie Debo, *A History of the Indians in the United States* (Norman, Oklahoma: University of Oklahoma Press, 1970) and Gerald Vizenor, *Manifest Manners: Postindian Warriors of Survivance* (Hanover and London: Wesleyan University Press, 1994). For an excellent account of the Lone Ranger–Tonto story, see Chadwick Allen, 'Hero with Two Faces: The Lone Ranger as Treaty Discourse', *American Literature*, Vol. 68, No. 3 (September 1996), pp. 609–38.

6. A footnote to these refusals occurred at Seymour, Indiana, in August 1997, when a group of former Tuskegee Airmen, meeting in Indianapolis, returned to the Army Air Corps Training Facility where, in April 1945, a number of them had been arrested for entering a segregated club. One of their number, retired Lt. Col. James C. Warwick, spoke of their action as follows: 'We stood up before Rosa Parks sat down.'

7. Quoted in Sterling A. Brown, 'Count Us In', reprinted in Sterling A. Brown, *A Son's Return: Selected Essays of Sterling A. Brown* (Boston: Northeastern University Press, 1996), p. 70.

8. Quoted in Harvey Sitkoff, *A New Deal for Blacks: The Emergence of Civil Rights as a National Issue, the Depression Decade* (Oxford: Oxford University Press, 1978), p. 301.

9. Walter White, *A Rising Wind* (Garden City, New York: Doubleday and Doran, 1945). The best recent history is to be found in Nat Brandt, *Harlem at War: The Black Experience in WWII* (Syracuse, New York: Syracuse University Press, 1996).

10. Betty Friedan, *The Feminine Mystique* (New York: Dell, 1963).

11. This can be compared with the government-sponsored Tuskegee Experiment, begun in the 1930s and continued through the next decade and long after, in which syphilis was left untreated in black male sharecroppers from Macon County, Alabama, and which would wait until 1997 and the Clinton presidency for anything in the way of public apology.

12. Zora Neale Hurston, *Their Eyes Were Watching God* (Philadelphia and London: Lippincott, 1937).

13. Ann Petry, *The Street* (Boston: Houghton, Mifflin, 1946); Dorothy West, *The Living Is Easy* (Boston: Houghton, Mifflin, 1948); Margaret Walker, *Jubilee* (Boston: Houghton Mifflin, 1966); Alex Haley, *Roots* (New York: Doubleday, 1976). Accounts of *The Street* are to be found in Chapter 3 and *The Living Is Easy* and *Jubilee* in Chapter 4.

14. For a full account see Donald Bogle, *Dorothy Dandridge* (New York: Amistad Press, 1994).

15. Frank Yerby, *The Foxes of Harrow* (New York: Dial Press, 1946) – see his 'How and Why I Write the Costume Novel', *Harper's New Monthly Magazine*, Vol. 219 (1959), pp. 145–50; Willard Motley, *Knock on Any Door* (New York: Appleton-Century, 1947); Ann Petry, *Country Place* (Boston: Houghton, Mifflin, 1947); and Zora Neale Hurston, *Seraph on the Suwanee* (New York: Scribner's, 1948).

16. Ralph Ellison, 'Introduction', *Invisible Man*, 30th Anniversary Edition (New York: Random House, [1952] 1982), p. x.

17. Albert Murray, *The Omni-Americans* (New York: Outerbridge & Dienstfey, 1970), p. 23; *South to a Very Old Place* (New York: McGraw-Hill Book Company, 1971).

18. John O. Killens, *And Then We Heard the Thunder* (New York: Alfred A. Knopf, 1963).

19. Norman Mailer, *The Naked and the Dead* (New York: Rinehart, 1948) and James Jones, *From Here to Eternity* (New York: Scribner, 1951).

20. John A. Williams, *Captain Blackman* (New York: Doubleday, 1972).

21. William Gardner Smith, *Last of the Conquerors* (New York: Farrar, Straus & Cudahy, 1948).

22. Richard Wright, *Native Son* (New York: Harper, 1940); Zora Neale Hurston, *Dust Tracks on a Road, an Autobiography* (Philadelphia and London: Lippincott,

1942); Ralph Ellison, 'King of the Bingo Game', *Tomorrow*, Vol. 4 (November 1944), pp. 29–33, and 'Flying Home', in Edwin Seaver (ed.), *Cross-section* (New York: L.B. Fischer, 1944). Both are reprinted in Ralph Ellison, *Flying Home and other Stories* (New York: Random House, 1996).

23. Chester Himes, *If He Hollers Let Him Go* (New York: Doubleday, Doran, 1945) and *Lonely Crusade* (New York: Knopf, 1947).

24. Chester Himes, *Cast the First Stone* (New York: Coward-McCann, 1952); *The Third Generation* (Cleveland: World Publishing Company, 1954); *The Primitive* (New York: New American Library, 1955); *Pinktoes* (Paris: Olympia Press, 1961); *Une Affaire de viol* (Paris: Editions Les Yeux Ouverts, 1963); and *Plan B* (Jackson, Mississippi: University Press of Mississippi, 1993).

25. These three Himes stories are republished in Chester Himes, *Black on Black* (New York: Doubleday, 1973); Ishmael Reed (ed.), *19 Necromancers from Now: An Anthology of Original American Writing for the 1970s* (New York: Doubleday, Anchor Books Edition, 1970).

26. Frantz Fanon, *Peau noire, masques blancs* (Paris: Editions de Seuil, 1952). Trans. *Black Skin, White Masks* (New York: Grove Press, 1970; London: Paladin Books, 1970), pp. 99, 102, 155.

27. Richard Wright, 'Two Novels of the Crushing of Men, One White, the Other Black', *PM* (Spring 1945).

28. Ishmael Reed, 'Chester Himes: Writer', *Black World* (March 1972); republished in *Shrovetide in Old New Orleans* (New York: Doubleday, 1978).

29. For a helpful, spirited synopsis of the historic black–Jewish relationship see Henry Louis Gates Jr., 'Black Demagogues and Pseudo-Scholars', *The New York Times*, 20 July 1992, p. A13.

30. William Attaway, *Blood on the Forge* (New York: Doubleday, Doran, 1941); Owen Dodson, *Boy at the Window* (New York: Farrar, Straus and Giroux, 1951) and *Powerful Long Ladder* (New York: Farrar, Straus and Giroux, 1946).

31. Walter Mosley, *Devil in a Blue Dress* (New York: W.W. Norton & Company, 1990).

32. Sterling A. Brown, Arthur Davis and Ulysses Lee (eds), *The Negro Caravan* (New York: Dryden, 1941).

33. Robert E. Hayden, *A Ballad of Remembrance* (London: Paul Bremen, 1962).

34. Melvin B. Tolson, *Rendezvous with America* (New York: Dodd, Mead & Company, 1944); *Libretto for the Republic of Liberia* (New York: Twayne, 1953); *Harlem Gallery* (New York: Twayne, 1965).

35. Margaret Walker, *For My People* (New Haven: Yale University Press, 1942).

36. George Wylie Henderson, *Jule* (New York: Creative Age Press, Inc., 1946); Langston Hughes, *Not Without Laughter* (New York: Knopf, 1930).

37. Even so the novel has come in for attack. Robert Bone is especially severe in *The Negro Novel in America* (New Haven: Yale University Press, 1958, 1965), p. 123.

38. William Demby, *Beetlecreek* (New York: Rinehart, 1950).

39. Ann Petry, *The Narrows* (Boston: Houghton, Mifflin, 1953).

40. Langston Hughes, *Shakespeare in Harlem* (New York: Alfred A. Knopf, 1942).

41. Langston Hughes, *Jim Crow's Last Stand* (Atlanta: Negro Publication Society of America, 1943).

42. Both these stories are republished in *Laughing to Keep from Crying* (New York: Holt, 1952).

43. Gwendolyn Brooks, *A Street in Bronzeville* (New York: Harper, 1945).

44. Gwendolyn Brooks, *Annie Allen* (New York: Harper, 1949), *Maud Martha* (New York: Harper & Row, 1971), *The Bean Eaters* (New York: Harper, 1960); *In the Mecca* (New York: Harper & Row, 1968), *Report from Part 1: An Autobiography* (Detroit: Broadside Press, 1972), *Primer for Black* (Chicago: Broadside, 1980).

Chapter 7

1. J.J. Phillips, Ishmael Reed, Gundars Strads and Shawn Wong (eds), *The Before Columbus Foundation Poetry* (New York: W.W. Norton, 1992).
2. Imamu Amiri Baraka, *The Autobiography of LeRoi Jones/Amiri Baraka* (New York: Freundlich Books, 1984), p. 159.
3. Ted Joans, *Tape Recording at the Five Spot*, reprinted in Seymour Krim (ed.), *The Beats* (Greenwich, Connecticut: Fawcett World Library, 1960), pp. 211–13.
4. Bob Kaufman, *Solitudes Crowded with Loneliness* (New York: New Directions, 1965).
5. Allen Ginsberg, *Howl and Other Poems* (San Francisco: City Lights Books, 1956); Jack Kerouac, *On the Road* (New York: Viking, 1957) and *The Subterraneans* (New York: Grove, 1958); John Clellon Holmes, 'The Philosophy of the Beat Generation', reprinted together with his two other Beat essays, 'This is the Beat Generation' and 'The Game of the Name' in *Nothing More to Declare* (New York: Dutton, 1967); Gregory Corso, *Gasoline* (San Francisco: City Lights Books, 1958); and Norman Mailer, *The White Negro* (San Francisco: City Lights Books, 1957).
6. Bob Kaufman, 'Bagel Shop Jazz', reprinted in *Solitudes Crowded with Loneliness*, pp. 77–86; A.B. Spellman, *The Beautiful Days* (New York: Poets Press, 1965) and *Four Lives in the Bebop Business* (New York: Schocken, 1966), later retitled *Black Music: Four Lives* (New York: Schocken, 1970).
7. *The Autobiography of LeRoi Jones/Amiri Baraka*, p. 157.
8. A full list of these early magazine publications is to be found in Werner Sollors, *Amiri Baraka/LeRoi Jones: The Quest for a 'Populist Modernism'* (New York: Columbia University Press, 1978), pp. 301–28.
9. LeRoi Jones (ed.), *The Moderns: An Anthology of New Writing in America* (New York: Corinth Books, 1963).
10. *How I Became Hettie Jones* (New York: E.P. Dutton, 1990). The first two chapters, especially, touch on these early years.
11. 'Cuba Libre' first appeared in *Evergreen Review* and was republished in *Home: Social Essays* (New York: William Morrow & Co., 1966).
12. 'BLACK DADA NIHILISMUS', in *The Dead Lecturer* (New York: Grove Press, 1964).
13. *Dutchman* was published in *Dutchman and The Slave* (New York: William Morrow & Co., 1964).
14. *Blues People: Negro Music in White America* (New York: William Morrow & Co., 1963); *Black Music* (New York: William Morrow & Co., 1967).
15. Robert Lowell, 'Memories of West Street and Lepke', in *Life Studies* (New York: Farrar, Straus & Cudahy, 1959).
16. J.D. Salinger, *The Catcher in the Rye* (Boston: Little, Brown, 1951).
17. Full-length contextual anthologies, studies and memoirs include Gene Feldman and Max Gartenberg (eds), *The Beat Generation and the Angry Young*

Men (New York: Citadel, 1958); Lawrence Lipton, *The Holy Barbarians* (New York: Julian Messner, 1959); Krim (ed.), *The Beats*; Donald M. Allen (ed.), *The New American Poetry: 1945–60* (New York: Grove Press, 1960); Elias Wilentz (ed.), *The Beat Scene* (New York: Corinth, 1961); Thomas A. Parkinson (ed.), *A Casebook on the Beat* (New York: Crowell, 1961); LeRoi Jones (ed.), *The Moderns*; Richard Weaver, Terry Southern and Alexander Trocci (eds), *Writers in Revolt* (New York: Frederick Fells, 1963); *Wholly Communion* (London: Lorrimer Films, 1965); *Astronauts of Inner Space: An International Anthology of Avant-Garde Activity* (San Francisco: Stolen Paper Review, 1966); Leslie Garrett, *The Beats* (New York: Scribner's, 1966); Clellon Holmes, *Nothing More to Declare*; Tina Morris and Dave Cunliffe (eds), *Thunderbolts of Peace and Liberation* (Blackburn, England: BB Books, 1967); M.L. Rosenthal, *The New Modern Poetry* (New York: Macmillan, 1967); David Kherdian, *Six Poets of the San Francisco Renaissance* (Fresno, California: Giligia Press, 1967); Diane Di Prima, *Memoirs of a Beatnik* (New York: Olympia Press, 1969); David Metzer (ed.), *The San Francisco Poets* (New York: Ballantine, 1971); Nick Harvey (ed.), *Mark in Time: Portraits & Poetry/San Francisco* (San Francisco: Glide, 1971); Bruce Cook, *The Beat Generation* (New York: Scribner's, 1971); Laurence James (ed.), *Electric Underground: A City Lights Reader* (London: New English Library, 1973); Yves Le Pellec (ed.), *Beat Generation* (New York: McGraw Hill, 1976); Ed Sanders, *Tales of Beatnik Glory* (New York: Stonehill, 1975); David S. Wirshup (ed.), *The Beat Generation & Other Avant-Garde Writers* (Santa Barbara, California: Anacapa Books, 1977); Lee Bartlett (ed.), *The Beats: Essays in Criticism* (Jefferson, North Carolina: McFarland, 1981); Arthur and Kit Knight (eds), *The Beat Vision: A Primary Sourcebook* (New York: Paragon House Publishers, 1987).

18. Amiri Baraka, *The LeRoi Jones/Amiri Baraka Reader*, edited by William J. Harris (New York: Thunder's Mouth Press, 1991).
19. *The Autobiography of LeRoi Jones/Amiri Baraka*, p. 156.
20. Arthur and Kit Knight (eds), *The Beat Vision: A Primary Sourcebook*, p. 131.
21. Allen (ed.), *The New American Poetry*.
22. Allen (ed.), *The New American Poetry*, p. 424.
23. LeRoi Jones, *Preface to a Twenty Volume Suicide Note* (New York: Totem Press/Corinth, 1961).
24. A considerable critical bibliography has now built up around Jones/Baraka. See Donald B. Gibson (ed.), *Five Black Writers* (New York: New York University Press, 1970); Letitia Dace, *LeRoi Jones: A Checklist of Works By and About Him* (London: Nether Press, 1971); Theodore Hudson, *From LeRoi Jones to Amiri Baraka: The Literary Works* (Durham, North Carolina: Duke University Press, 1973); Stephen Henderson, *Understanding the New Black Poetry: Black Speech and Black Music as Poetic References* (New York: Morrow, 1973); Donald B. Gibson (ed.), *Modern Black Poets: A Collection of Critical Essays* (Englewood Cliffs, New Jersey: Prentice Hall, 1973); Esther M. Jackson, 'LeRoi Jones (Imamu Amiri Baraka): Form and Progression of Consciousness', *College Language Association Journal*, Vol. 17, No. 1 (September 1973); Kimberley Benston, *Baraka: The Renegade and the Mask* (New Haven, Connecticut: Yale University Press, 1976); Kimberley Benston (ed.), *Imamu Amiri Baraka (LeRoi Jones): A Collection of Essays* (Englewood Cliffs, New Jersey: Prentice Hall, 1978); Thomas M. Inge *et al.* (eds), *Black American Writers: Bibliographical Essays, Volume 2: Richard Wright, Ralph Ellison, James Baldwin, and Amiri Baraka*

(New York: St. Martin's Press, 1978); Henry C. Lacey, *To Raise, Destroy, and Create: The Poetry, Drama and Fiction of Imamu Amiri Baraka (LeRoi Jones)* (Troy, New York: The Whitson Publishing Company, 1981); William J. Harris, *The Poetry and Poetics of Amiri Baraka: The Jazz Aesthetic* (Columbia, Missouri: University of Missouri Press, 1985).

25. Reprinted in Arthur and Kit Knight (eds), *The Beat Vision*, p. 289. His connection with Kerouac and other Beats is chronicled in the interview which follows with Gerald Nicosia, pp. 270–83.

26. Ted Joans, *Jazz Poems* (New York: Rhino Review, 1959), *All of Ted Joans and No More: Poems and Collages* (New York: Excelsior Press, 1961), *Wow: Selected Poems of Ted Joans* (1991), *Black Pow-Wow: Jazz Poems* (New York: Hill and Wang, 1969) and *Afrodisia* (New York: Hill and Wang, 1970).

27. Ted Joans, 'The Beat Generation and Afro-American Culture', *Beat Scene Magazine*, No. 13 (December 1991), pp. 22–3. The same issue contains a brief profile, 'Ted Joans in Paris', by Jim Burns, p. 13.

28. All three of these manifestos, the originals now collector's items, are republished in Kaufman, *Solitudes Crowded with Loneliness*.

29. *Golden Sardine* (San Francisco: City Lights Books, 1967); and *The Ancient Rain: Poems 1956–1978* (New York: New Directions, 1981). For bearings on Kaufman, see Barbara Christian, 'Whatever Happened to Bob Kaufman?', in Bartlett (ed.), *The Beats*, pp. 107–14; Arthur and Kit Knight (eds), *The Beat Vision*, and Joans, 'The Beat Generation and Afro-American Culture', pp. 22–3.

30. As given in Emerson's 'The Poet', in *Essays: Second Series* (1844): 'America is a poem in our eyes; its ample geography dazzles the imagination'.

Chapter 8

1. Originally published as *Dutchman* and *The Slave* (New York: William Morrow & Co., 1964).

2. Representative anthologies include: William Couch (ed.), *New Black Playwrights: An Anthology* (Baton Rouge, Louisiana: Louisiana State University Press, 1968; republished New York: Bard Books/Avon, 1970); Ed Bullins (ed.), *New Plays from the Black Theater* (New York: Bantam Books, 1969); C.W.E. Bigsby (ed.), *Three Negro Plays* (Harmondsworth, Middlesex: Penguin Books, 1969); Clayton Riley (ed.), *A Black Quartet: Four New Black Plays* (New York: Signet, 1970); Darwin T. Turner (ed.), *Black Drama in America: An Anthology* (Greenwich, Connecticut: Fawcett Books, 1971); Woodie King and Ron Milner (eds), *Black Drama Anthology* (New York and London: Columbia University Press, 1971; New York: Signet Books, 1971).

3. Among the best general accounts are C.W.E. Bigsby, *Confrontation and Commitment: A Study of Contemporary American Drama, 1959–1966* (Columbia, Missouri: University of Missouri Press, 1968); Doris E. Abraham, *Negro Playwrights in the American Theatre, 1929–1959* (New York: Columbia University Press, 1969); C.W.E. Bigsby, *The Black American Writer*, 2 Vols (Baltimore, Maryland: Penguin Books, 1969); Gerald Weales, *The Jumping-Off Place: American Drama in the 1960s* (New York: Macmillan, 1969); George R. Adams, 'Black Militant Drama', *American Imago*, Vol. 28, No. 2 (Summer 1971), pp. 107–28; Travis Bogard, Richard Moody and Walter J. Reserve (eds), *The Revel History of Drama in English, Vol. VIII: American Drama*

(London: Methuen; New York: Barnes and Noble, 1977); and C.W.E. Bigsby, *A Critical Introduction to Twentieth-Century American Drama*, 3 Vols (Cambridge: Cambridge University Press, 1982–85).

4. Although Hughes went on writing drama until his death in 1967, he unquestionably most belongs to an earlier phase. Accordingly he is given only passing mention in this chapter. See, however, the following: Webster Smalley (ed.), *Five Plays by Langston Hughes* (Bloomington, Indiana: Indiana University Press, 1963); Donald C. Dickinson, *A Bio-bibliography of Langston Hughes, 1902–1967* (Hampden, Connecticut: Archon Books, 1967); Therman O'Daniel (ed.), *Langston Hughes, Black Genius: A Critical Evaluation* (New York: Morrow, 1971); Arnold Rampersad, *The Life of Langston Hughes*, Vol. 1: *1902–1941: I, Too, Sing America* (New York: Oxford University Press, 1988), and Vol. 2: *I Dream a World* (New York: Oxford University Press, 1988).

5. The New Lafayette Theater also sponsored the influential journal, *Black Theater*, only six issues in all, but given to the important publication of African American, Caribbean and African drama scripts.

6. A useful summary was offered by Georgia State Representative Tyrone Brooks, a veteran SCLC member: 'The NAACP mostly litigated and negotiated; the Urban League was about employment and job training; but the SCLC was the catalyst, an activist group that engaged in direct action and civil disobedience', *The Washington Post*, 2 November 1997.

7. An excellent analysis of this dimension of King's role can be found in Keith D. Miller, 'Composing Martin Luther King Jr.', *PMLA*, Vol. 105 (January 1990), pp. 70–82.

8. Martin Luther King, *I Have a Dream: Writings and Speeches that Changed the World*, foreword by Coretta Scott King (New York: HarperCollins, 1992).

9. Usually termed the Kerner Commission (Kerner was the then Governor of Illinois), formally this was known as the *Report of the National Advisory Commission on Civil Disorders* (Washington, D.C.: US Government Printing Office, 1968).

10. Relevant accounts of the 1960s include Thomas R. Brooks, *Walls Come Tumbling Down, 1940–1970* (Englewood Cliffs, New Jersey: Prentice Hall, 1974); Sar A. Levitan *et al.* (eds), *Still a Dream: The Changing Status of Blacks since 1960s* (Cambridge, Massachusetts: Harvard University Press, 1975); August Meier and Elliot Rudwick, *Along the Color Line* (Urbana, Illinois: Illinois University Press, 1976); Harvey Sitkoff, *The Struggle for Black Equality, 1945–1980* (New York: Hill & Wang, 1981); and Juan Williams, *Eyes on the Prize: America's Civil Rights Years, 1954–1965* (New York: Viking Penguin, 1987).

11. For bibliographical accounts of this process, see Darwin T. Turner (ed.), *Afro-American Writers* (New York: Appleton-Century Crofts, 1970); Theressa Gunnels Rush, Carol Fairbanks Myers and Esther Spring Arata (eds), *Black American Writers: A Biographical and Bibliographical Dictionary* (Metuchen, New Jersey: Scarecrow Press, Inc., 1975); M. Thomas Inge, Maurice Duke and Jackson R. Bryer (eds), *Black American Writers: Bibliographical Essays*, Vols 1 and 2 (New York: St. Martin's Press, 1978). The anthologies include John A. Williams (ed.), *The Angry Black* (New York: Lancer, 1962) and *Beyond the Angry Black* (New York: Lancer, 1967), revised edition (New York: New American Library, 1971); Herbert Hill (ed.), *Soon, One Morning: New Writing by American Negroes 1940–1962* (New York: Alfred A. Knopf, 1963); Herbert Hill (ed.), *Anger, and Beyond: The Negro Writer in the United*

States (New York: Harper and Row, 1966); Abraham Chapman (ed.), *Black Voices* (New York: New American Library/Mentor, 1968) and *New Black Voices* (New York: New American Library/Mentor, 1972); James A. Emanuel and Theodore Gross (eds), *Dark Symphony: Negro Literature in America* (New York; Free Press, 1968); LeRoi Jones and Larry Neal (eds), *Black Fire: An Anthology of Afro-American Writing* (New York: William Morrow & Co., 1968); and Toni Cade (ed.), *The Black Woman: An Anthology* (New York: Signet, 1970). A typical compilation was John Hope Franklin, *Three Negro Classics: Up from Slavery, The Souls of Black Folks, The Autobiography of an Ex-Colored Man* (New York: Avon Books, 1965).

12. Frank Yerby, *Speak Now: A Modern Novel* (New York: Dial, 1969) and *The Dahomean* (New York: Dial, 1971). Alex Haley, *Roots* (New York: Doubleday, 1976).

13. For a detailed analysis see J. Fred Macdonald, *Blacks and White TV: Afro-Americans in Television since 1948* (Chicago: Nelson-Hall Publishers, 1983). Mari Evans, *Where Is All the Music?* (London: Paul Breman, 1968), *I Am a Black Woman* (New York: Morrow, 1970) and (ed.), *Black Women Writers 1950–1980: A Critical Evaluation* (New York: Anchor Books, 1984).

14. Sonia Sanchez, *The Bronx Is Next*, *The Drama Review*, Vol. 12 (Summer 1968), *We a BaddDD People* (Detroit: Broadside, 1970); Nikki Giovanni, *Black Feeling, Black Talk* (Detroit: Broadside, 1968) and *Black Judgement* (Detroit: Broadside, 1969); Sarah Webster Fabio, *Saga of a Black Man* (San Francisco: Richardson, 1968) and *A Mirror: A Soul, a Two-Part Volume of Poems* (San Francisco: Richardson, 1969); and Carolyn M. Rodgers, *Paper Soul* (Chicago: Third World, 1968), *2 Love Raps* (Chicago: Third World, 1969) and *Songs of a Black Bird* (Chicago: Third World, 1969).

15. Jayne Cortez, *Pisstained Stairs and the Monkey Man's Wares* was originally a chapbook self-published for the Watts Repertory Company in 1969. A number of the poems are included in *Coagulations: New and Selected Poems* (New York: Thunder's Mouth Press, 1994).

16. Arthur Ashe (with Arnold Rampersad), *Days of Grace: A Memoir* (New York: Alfred A. Knopf, 1993) and Arthur Ashe, *A Hard Road to Glory: A History of the African-American Athlete* (New York: Warner, 1988, revised New York: Amistad, 1993, and distributed Penguin, USA).

17. Alex Haley, *Roots* (New York: Doubleday, 1976).

18. The drama continued into Ali's autobiography. See Muhammad Ali (with Richard Durham), *The Greatest: My Own Story* (New York: Random House, 1975). A latest biography is John Stravinsky, *Muhammad Ali* (New York: Park Lane Press, 1997).

19. LeRoi Jones/Amiri Baraka, *The Baptism* and *The Toilet* (New York: Grove, 1964).

20. LeRoi Jones, *Four Black Revolutionary Plays* (Indianapolis: Bobbs-Merrill Co., 1969).

21. For a number of these works, see *Selected Plays and Prose of Amiri Baraka/LeRoi Jones* (New York: William Morrow and Company, 1979), except *Jello* (Chicago: Third World Press, 1970).

22. Among the recent scholarship on Jones/Baraka should be listed: Donald B. Gibson (ed.), *Five Black Writers: Essays on Wright, Ellison, Baldwin, Hughes, LeRoi Jones* (New York: New York University Press, 1970); Theodore Hudson, *From LeRoi Jones to Amiri Baraka: The Literary Works* (Durham, North Carolina: Duke University Press); M. Thomas Inge, Maurice Duke and

Jackson R. Bryer (eds), *Black American Writers: Biographical Essays*, Vol. 2, *Richard Wright, Ralph Ellison, James Baldwin, and Amiri Baraka* (New York: St. Martin's Press, 1978); Werner Sollors, *Amiri Baraka/LeRoi Jones: The Quest for a 'Populist Modernism'* (New York: Columbia University Press, 1978); and Hettie Jones, *How I Became Hettie Jones* (New York: E.P. Dutton, 1990).

23. Lorraine Hansberry, *A Raisin in the Sun* (New York: Random House, 1959).

24. Lorraine Hansberry, *The Sign in Sidney Brustein's Window* (New York: Random House, 1964).

25. James Baldwin, *Blues For Mister Charlie* (New York: Dial, 1964).

26. James Baldwin, *The Amen Corner* (New York: Dial, 1968).

27. Loften Mitchell, *Land Beyond the River* (written 1957, first published Cody, Wyoming: Pioneer Drama Service, 1963), *Star of the Morning* (New York: Free Press, 1965). Mitchell has also written his own account of African American theatre. See Loften Mitchell, *Black Drama: The Story of the American Negro in the Theater* (New York: E.P. Dutton, 1990). Langston Hughes initially wrote *Tambourines to Glory* (New York: Day, 1958) as a novel; he then adapted it for the stage under the same title. See Smalley (ed.) *Five Plays by Langston Hughes*.

28. George Schuyler, *Black No More* (New York: Macauley, 1931); Chester Himes, *For Love of Imabelle* (Greenwich, Connecticut: Fawcett, 1957) and *Blind Man with a Pistol* (New York: William Morrow, 1969); William Melvin Kelley, *dem* (New York: Doubleday, 1967); Ishmael Reed, *The Free-Lance Pallbearers* (Garden City, New York: Doubleday, 1967), *The Terrible Threes* (New York: Atheneum, 1989), and *Japanese by Spring* (New York: Atheneum, 1993).

29. Douglas Turner Ward, *Happy Ending* (New York: Dramatists Play Service, 1964), republished in Couch (ed.), *New Black Playwrights*.

30. Douglas Turner Ward, *Day of Absence* (New York: Dramatists Play Service, 1968), republished in Couch (ed.), *New Black Playwrights*. William Melvin Kelley, *A Different Drummer* (Garden City, New York: Doubleday, 1962).

31. Ossie Davis, *Purlie Victorious: A Comedy in Three Acts* (New York: French, 1961).

32. Lonne Elder, *Ceremonies in Dark Old Men* (New York: Farrar, Straus and Giroux, 1969).

33. Ed Bullins, *Five Plays* (Indianapolis: Bibbs-Merrill, 1969). In England, a year earlier, this became *The Electronic Nigger and Other Plays* (London: Faber and Faber, 1968).

34. Wellington Mackey, *Requiem for Brother X*, republished in King and Milner (eds), *Black Drama Anthology*; Ron Milner, *Who's Got His Own*, republished in King and Milner (eds), *Black Drama Anthology*; Adrienne Kennedy, *A Rat's Mass*, republished in Couch (ed.), *New Black Playwrights*; Ben Caldwell, *The King of Soul, or The Devil and Otis Redding* (New York: Dramatists Play Service, 1967); Marvin X (aka El Mujajir, Marvin Jackman), *The Black Bird* (San Francisco: Julian Richardson, 1969); and Sonia Sanchez, *Sister Sion/Ji*, republished in Bullins (ed.), *New Plays from the Black Theater*.

35. A play long attributed to Bullins from the 1960s, but which he has always alleged was written by a young dramatist who died, is Kingsley B. Bass Jr., *We Righteous Bombers* (1968), a vision of black revolution in America. See also Ed Bullins, *Four Dynamite Plays* (New York: William Morrow & Company, 1972) and *The Theme is Blackness: 'The Corner' and Other Plays* (New York: William Morrow & Company, 1972).

36. Woodie King Jr., *The National Black Drama Anthology: Eleven Plays from America's Leading African-American Theaters* (New York and London: Applause Theater Books, 1995).

37. LeRoi Jones, *Home: Social Essays* (1966) and Ed Bullins, 'Introduction', in *The Theme is Blackness: 'The Corner' and Other Plays* (New York: William Morrow, 1972).

Chapter 9

1. Leon Forrest, *Re-Creation: A Liturgical Music-Drama*, commissioned by Richard Hunt, music by T.J. Anderson, words by Leon Forrest, 1978.

2. Leon Forrest, 'In the Light of the Likeness – Transformed', in Mark Azdronzny (ed.), *Contemporary Authors Autobiography Series* (Detroit, Michigan: Gale Research, 1988), Vol. 7, p. 21–35.

3. Leon Forrest, 'Faulkner/Reforestation', lecture at the annual 'Yoknapatawpha Country' seminar, University of Mississippi, August 1988. Reprinted in Doreen Fowler and Ann J. Abodie (eds), *Faulkner and Popular Culture: Faulkner and Yoknapatawpha* (Jackson, Mississippi and London: University Press of Mississippi, 1990), pp. 207–13.

4. Ralph Ellison, 'Foreword', *There Is a Tree More Ancient Than Eden* (New York: Random House, 1973), p. ii.

5. Ronald L. Fair, *Hog Butcher* (New York: Harcourt, Brace, World, 1966) and *We Can't Breathe* (New York: Harper and Row, 1972); Cyrus Colter, *The Rivers of Eros* (Chicago: Swallow Press, 1972), *The Hippodrome* (Chicago: Swallow Press, 1973).

6. Saul Bellow, dustjacket comment, *There Is a Tree More Ancient Than Eden*.

7. Leon Forrest, *The Bloodworth Orphans* (New York: Random House, 1977); *Two Wings to Veil My Face* (New York: Random House, 1984); *Divine Days* (Oak Park, Illinois: Another Chicago Press, 1992); and *Relocations of the Spirit* (Wakefield, Rhode Island and London: Asphodel Press, 1994). All page references are to these editions. Reissues of the first three novels are to be found as *There Is a Tree More Ancient Than Eden* (Chicago: Another Chicago Press, 1973, 1988); *The Bloodworth Orphans* (Chicago: Another Chicago Press, 1977, 1987); and *Two Wings to Veil My Face* (Chicago: Another Chicago Press, 1983, 1988).

8. These phrases are each to be found in the extracts cited at the head of the chapter.

9. For a recent assessment of Forrest (and in which an earlier version of this chapter appears), see John G. Cawelti (ed.), *Leon Forrest: Introductions and Interpretations* (Bowling Green, Ohio: Bowling Green State University Press, 1997). Ralph Ellison, *Invisible Man*, 30th Anniversary Edition (New York: Random House, [1952] 1982).

10. Ishmael Reed, *The Free-Lance Pallbearers* (New York: Doubleday, 1967), *Yellow Back Radio Broke-Down* (New York: Doubleday, 1969), and *Flight To Canada* (New York: Random House, 1976).

11. William Melvin Kelley, *A Different Drummer* (Garden City, New York: Doubleday, 1962), *A Drop of Patience* (Garden City, New York: Doubleday, 1965), *dem* (Garden City, New York: Doubleday, 1967), and *Dunsfords Travels Everywheres* (Garden City, New York: Doubleday, 1969).

12. LeRoi Jones/Amiri Baraka, *The System of Dante's Hell* (New York: Grove Press, 1965); William Demby, *The Catacombs* (New York: Pantheon, 1965); Clarence Major, *NO* (New York: Emerson Hall, 1973); Charles Wright, *The Messenger* (New York: Farrar, Straus, 1963), *The Wig* (New York: Farrar, Straus & Giroux, 1966) and *Absolutely Nothing to Get Alarmed About* (New York: Farrar, Straus & Giroux, 1973).

13. Carlene Hatcher Polite, *Sister X and the Victims of Foul Play* (New York: Farrar Straus, 1975); Toni Morrison, *Song of Solomon* (New York: Knopf, 1977); James Alan McPherson, *Hue and Cry* (Boston: Little, Brown, 1969) and *Elbow Room* (Boston: Atlantic-Little, Brown, 1977).

14. John O'Brien, *Interviews with Black Writers* (New York: Liveright, 1973), p. 214. A study which tackles Wideman's modernist/postmodern interests and goes some way towards setting him in the general context of black modernism is James W. Coleman, *Blackness and Modernism: The Literary Career of John Edgar Wideman* (Jackson, Mississippi and London: University Press of Mississippi, 1989).

15. John Edgar Wideman, *A Glance Away* (New York: Harcourt, Brace, World, 1967), *Hurry Home* (New York: Harcourt, Brace, World, 1970) and *The Lynchers* (New York: Harcourt, Brace, World, 1973).

16. John Wideman, *Hiding Place* (New York: Avon Books, 1981), *Damballah* (New York: Avon Books, 1981) and *Sent for You Yesterday* (New York: Avon Books, 1983). 'Surfiction' is reprinted in John Wideman, *The Stories of John Edgar Wideman* (New York: Pantheon Books, 1992).

17. Maria Mootry, 'If He Changed My Name: An Interview', *Massachusetts Review*, Vol. 18, (1977), pp. 631–42; republished as 'If He Changed My Name: An Interview with Leon Forrest', in Michael S. Harper and Robert B. Stepto (eds), *Chant of Saints: A Gathering of Afro-American Literature, Art and Scholarship* (Urbana, Illinois: University of Illinois Press, 1979), pp. 146–57.

18. Mootry, *Chant of Saints*, p. 146.

19. Mootry, *Chant of Saints*, p. 150.

20. 'In the Light of the Likeness – Transformed', p. 30.

21. Robert Frost, 'The Figure a Poem Makes', in *The Complete Poems* (London: Jonathan Cape, 1951).

22. This chapter follows on from two of my own brief earlier accounts of Forrest's fiction; see 'Making New: Styles of Innovation in the Contemporary Black American Novel', in A. Robert Lee (ed.), *Black Fiction: New Studies in the Afro-American Novel since 1945* (London: Vision Press, 1980), pp. 222–50 and A. Robert Lee, *Black American Fiction since Richard Wright* (British Association of America Studies pamphlet, No. 11, 1983). I have also profited greatly from Keith E. Byerman, *Fingering the Jagged Grain: Tradition and Form in Recent Black American Fiction* (Athens, Georgia: University of Georgia Press, 1985); Bernard W. Bell, *The Afro-American Novel and Its Tradition* (Amherst, Massachusetts: University of Massachusetts Press, 1987); and John F. Callaghan, *In the Afro-American Grain: The Pursuit of Voice in Twentieth-Century Black Fiction* (Urbana, Illinois: University of Illinois Press, 1988).

23. 'In the Light of the Likeness – Transformed', p. 30.

24. Owen Dodson, *Boy at the Window* (New York: Farrar, Straus & Giroux, 1951); James Baldwin, *Go Tell It on the Mountain* (New York: Alfred A. Knopf, 1953); and Gordon Parks, *The Learning Tree* (New York: Harper & Row, 1963).

25. For an excellent account of the trickster in Forrest see H. Nigel Thomas, *From Folklore to Fiction: A Study of Folk Heroes and Rituals in the Black American Novel* (Westport, Connecticut: Greenwood Press, 1988), pp. 103–8 and pp. 158–73.

Chapter 10

1. Herman Melville, *The Confidence-Man: His Masquerade* (New York: Dix, Edwards, 1857).
2. Randolph S. Bourne, 'Trans-National America', *Atlantic Monthly*, XCVII (July 1916). Reprinted in Randolph S. Bourne, *War and the Intellectuals: Collected Essays, 1915–1919* (New York: Harper & Row, 1964).
3. Frederick Buell, *National Culture and the New Global System* (Baltimore and London: Johns Hopkins University Press, 1994), p. 71.
4. Trey Ellis, *Platitudes* (New York: Vintage Original, 1988), *Home Repairs* (New York: Simon & Schuster, 1993).
5. 'The Good Shepherd' appears in AI, *Sin; Poems* (Boston: Houghton, Mifflin, 1986).
6. Alice Walker, *Meridian* (New York: Harcourt Brace Jovanovich, 1976), *Living by the Word: Selected Writings, 1973–1987* (San Diego: Harcourt Brace Jovanovich, 1988); Clarence Major, *Such Was the Season: A Novel* (San Francisco: Mercury House, 1987), *Painted Turtle: Woman with Guitar: A Novel* (Los Angeles: Sun & Moon Press, 1988) and *Some Observations of a Stranger at Zuni in the Latter Part of the Century* (Los Angeles: Sun & Moon Press, 1989). For a useful summary see the entry 'African-Native American Literature', in William L. Andrews, Frances Smith Foster and Trudier Harris (eds), *The Oxford Companion to African American Literature* (New York: Oxford University Press, 1997), pp. 7–8.
7. Ishmael Reed, 'Distant Cousins', in *Airing Dirty Laundry* (Reading, Massachusetts: Addison-Wesley Publishing Company, 1993), pp. 266–73.
8. Toni Morrison, *Playing in the Dark: Whiteness and the Literary Imagination* (Cambridge, Massachusetts: Harvard University Press, 1992).
9. Ralph Ellison, 'The Little Man at Chehaw Station: The American Artist and His Audience', *American Scholar*, Vol. 47 (Winter 1977–78), pp. 25–48.
10. I have been much helped in this account by the following works of scholarship: Judith R. Berzon, *Neither Black Nor White: The Mulatto Character in American Fiction* (New York: New York University Press, 1978); George M. Frederickson, *The Arrogance of Race: Historical Perspectives on Slavery, Racism, and Social Inequality* (Middletown, Connecticut: Wesleyan University Press, 1988); Dana D. Nelson, *The Word in Black and White: Reading 'Race' in American Literature 1638–1867* (New York and Oxford: Oxford University Press, 1992); Eric Sundquist, *To Wake the Nations: Race in the Making of American Literature* (Baltimore and London: Johns Hopkins University Press, 1993); Naomi Zack, *Race and Mixed Race* (Philadelphia: Temple University Press, 1993); Carl Plasa and Betty J. Ring (eds), *The Discourse of Slavery: Aphra Behn to Toni Morrison* (New York: Routledge, 1994); Elaine K. Ginsberg (ed.), *Passing and the Fictions of Identity* (Durham and London: Duke University Press, 1996); and Juda Bennett, *The Passing Figure: Racial Confusion in Modern American Literature* (New York: Peter Lang, 1996).

11. William Wells Brown, *Clotel or, The President's Daughter, a Narrative of Slave Life in the United States* (London: Partridge & Oakey, 1853); *Clotelle: A Tale of the Southern States* (Boston: James Redpath, 1864); and *Clotelle: Or, The Colored Heroine. A Tale of the Southern States* (Boston: Lee and Shepherd, 1867).

12. Charles Chesnutt, *The House Behind the Cedars* (Boston & New York: Houghton, Mifflin & Company, 1900); James Weldon Johnson, *The Autobiography of an Ex-Coloured Man* (Boston: Sherman French, 1912, and New York: Knopf, 1927) – for an explanation of the spelling of coloured/colored see Chapter 2, Note 17; Walter White, *Flight* (New York: A. A. Knopf, 1926); Nella Larsen, *Passing* (New York and London: A. A. Knopf, 1929; New York: Macmillan-Collier, 1971); Jessie Redmon Fauset, *Plum Bun: A Novel without a Moral* (New York: Frederick A. Stokes, 1929; London: Pandora Press, 1985); George Schuyler, *Black No More: Being an account of the strange and wonderful workings of science in the Land of the Free, A.D. 1933–1940* (New York: Macauley Co., 1931), reprinted as *Black No More* (Boston, Massachusetts: Northeastern University Press, 1989); and Charles R. Johnson, *Oxherding Tale* (Bloomington, Indiana: Indiana University Press, 1982).

13. I take the phrase from Ben Wattenberg's 1992 PBS documentary series on America as multiculture.

14. John Howard Griffin, *Black Like Me* (New York: New American Library, 1961); Grace Halsell, *Soul Sister* (New York: World Publishing Company, 1969); Frantz Fanon, *Black Skin, White Masks* (New York: Grove Press, 1970; London: Paladin Books, 1961); initially published as *Peau noir, masques blancs* (Paris: Editions de Seuil, 1952).

15. Langston Hughes, 'Who's Passing for Who?' (1945), in *Laughing to Keep from Crying* (New York: Holt, 1952).

16. Complementary studies include James Baldwin, *The Devil Finds Work: An Essay* (New York: Dial Press, 1976) and Donald Bogle, *Toms, Coons, Mammies, and Bucks: An Interpretive History of Blacks in American Films* (New York: Viking Press, 1973, revised third edition, New York: Continuum, 1994).

17. *Time*, 8 July 1991.

18. The issue has become increasingly debated. For a timely short essay see Leone Gaiter, 'Stop white-washing American culture', *Los Angeles Times*, 25 October 1997. Gaiter observes: 'The recent media buzz on the subject of "whiteness studies" ... has minimized an issue that's among the most important we face. You can't ask who is "white" without asking, by association, who is "American" ... To principally define yourself as "white" as the majority of Americans have throughout US history, said nothing of your view of God, death, man's place on Earth, magic, your ancestors or your history. It has no cultural significance, and is ethnically meaningless.

Of course, there are infinite bona-fide cultures represented in America, the members of which call themselves "white". Germans, Jews, Irish, Greeks, some Latinos, Russians, Italians, etc., are all "white Americans." Many of the cultures in these groups have little in common. These cultures can share little or nothing, yet all their people are identified as "white." Why? What is the significance of this ridiculously broad, yet empty term?'

19. For an intelligent foray into the terrain see Robert Elliott Fox, 'Becoming Post-White', in Ishmael Reed (ed.), *MultiAmerica: Essays on Cultural Wars and Cultural Peace* (New York: Viking Penguin, 1997), pp. 6–17. A number of like-minded studies supply bearings: David R. Roediger, *Towards the Abolition*

of Whiteness: Essays in Race, Politics and Working Class History (London and New York: Verso, 1990) and *The Ways of Whiteness: Race and the Making of the American Working Class* (London and New York: Verso, 1991); Studs Terkel (ed.), *Race: How Blacks & Whites Think & Feel About the American Obsession* (New York: The New Press, 1992); Phyllis Palmer *et al.*, 'To Deconstruct Race, De-construct Whiteness', *American Quarterly*, Vol. 45, No. 2 (June 1993), pp. 281–94; and Theodore W. Allen, *The Invention of the White Race, Volume One: Racial Oppression and Social Control* (New York and London: Verso, 1994) and *The Invention of the White Race, Volume Two: The Origins of Racial Oppression in Anglo-America* (New York and London: Verso, 1997).

20. Werner Sollors, *Beyond Ethnicity: Consent and Descent in American Culture* (New York: Oxford University Press, 1986).

21. F. James Davis, *Who Is Black? One Nation's Definition* (University Park, Pennsylvania: Pennsylvania State University Press, 1991), p. 6.

22. Patricia J. Williams, *The Alchemy of Race and Rights* (Cambridge, Massachusetts: Harvard University Press, 1991), p. 147, and Cornel West, *Race Matters* (New York: Vintage, 1994), p. 11.

23. See, notably, E.D. Hirsch Jr., *Cultural Literacy* (Boston: Houghton, Mifflin, 1987).

24. For the controversies about bilingualism, see James Crawford, *Hold Your Tongue: Bilingualism and the Politics of 'English Only'* (Reading, Massachusetts: Addison-Wesley, 1992), *Bilingual Education: History, Politics, Theory and Practice*, Third Edition (Los Angeles: Bilingual Educational Services, 1995); Sonia Nieto, *Affirming Diversity: The Sociopolitical Context of Multicultural Education* (New York and London: Longman, 1992); and Colin Baker, *Foundations of Bilingual Education and Bilingualism*, Second Edition (Clevedon, Philadelphia and Adelaide: Multilingual Matters Ltd), 1996.

25. Allan Bloom, *The Closing of the American Mind* (New York: Simon and Schuster, 1987).

26. Roger Kimball, *Tenured Radicals: How Politics Has Corrupted Our Higher Education* (New York: Harper and Row, 1990); Dinesh D'Souza, *Illiberal Education: The Politics of Race and Sex on Campus* (New York: Maxwell, 1991); Arthur M. Schlesinger Jr., *The Disuniting of America: Reflections on a Multicultural Society* (New York: W.W. Norton, 1992); and Harold Bloom, *The Western Canon: The Books and Schools of the Ages* (New York: Macmillan, 1995). My own overview is to be found in A. Robert Lee, 'The Campus as Cockpit', *Times Higher Education Supplement*, No. 1083 (6 August 1993), pp. 16–17.

27. Randolph S. Bourne, 'Trans-National America', *Atlantic Monthly*, CXII (July 1916), pp. 86–97.

28. Henry Louis Gates Jr., *Loose Canons* (New York: Oxford University Press, 1992).

29. In this, studies like the following are especially valuable: Michael Omi and Howard Winant, *Racial Formation in the United States: From the 1960s to the 1980s* (New York: Routledge & Kegan Paul, 1986).

30. Lawrence W. Levine, *The Opening of the American Mind: Canons, Culture, and History* (Boston: Beacon Press, 1996), p. 174.

31. Betty Friedan, *The Feminine Mystique* (New York: Norton, 1963).

32. Cherrié Moraga and Gloria Anzaldúa (eds), *This Bridge Called My Back: Writings by Radical Women of Color* (Watertown, Maine: Persephone Press, 1981).

33. Alice Walker, *In Search of Our Mothers' Gardens, Womanist Prose by Alice Walker* (New York: Harcourt, Brace Jovanovich, 1983), bell hooks, *Ain't I a Woman:*

Black Women and Feminism (Boston: South End Press, 1981); June Jordan, *Civil Wars* (Boston, Beacon Press, 1981) and *Technical Difficulties: African-American Notes on the State of the Union* (New York: Pantheon, 1992); and Patricia Hill Collins, *Black Feminist Thought: Knowledge, Consciousness, and the Politics of Empowerment* (London and New York: Unwin Hyman, 1990).

34. Edward Said, *Orientalism* (New York: Random House/Vintage Books, 1979) and *Culture and Imperialism* (New York: Knopf, 1993); Homi Bhabha (ed.), *Nation and Narrative* (London: Routledge, 1990); and Gayatri Chakravorty Spivak, *In Other Worlds: Essays in Cultural Politics* (New York: Methuen, 1987).

35. Frederick Jameson, *The Political Unconscious: Narrative as a Socially Symbolic Act* (Ithaca, New York: Cornel University Press, 1981) and *Postmodernism, or, The Cultural Logic of Capitalism* (Durham, North Carolina: Duke University Press, 1990); and E. San Juan Jr., *Racial Formations/Critical Transformations: Articulations of Power in Ethnic and Racial Studies in the United States* (Atlantic Highlands, New Jersey: Humanities Press, 1992).

36. Jessica Hagedorn, *Dogeaters* (New York: Viking Penguin, 1990).

37. Ishmael Reed, *Flight to Canada* (New York: Random House, 1976); Maxine Hong Kingston, *Tripmaster Monkey: His Fake Book* (New York: Knopf, 1989); Guillermo Gómez-Peña, *Warrior for Gringostroika* (Saint Paul, Minnesota: Graywolf Press, 1993); Gerald Vizenor, *Manifest Manners: Postindian Warriors of Survivance* (Hanover and London: Wesleyan University Press, 1994).

38. Paul Lauter *et al.* (eds), *Heath Anthology of American Literature* (Lexington, Massachusetts: Heath, 1990); Ishmael Reed, Kathryn Trueblood and Shawn Wong (eds), *The Before Columbus Foundation Fiction Anthology* (New York and London: W.W. Norton & Company, 1992) and J.J. Phillips, Ishmael Reed, Gundar Strads and Shawn Wong (eds), *The Before Columbus Foundation Poetry Anthology* (New York and London: W.W. Norton & Company, 1992).

39. Ishmael Reed, 'The Ocean of American Literature', in *The Before Columbus Foundation Fiction Anthology* (1992) and *The Before Columbus Foundation Poetry Anthology* (1992), pp. xxiv–xxv. I have tried to give due recognition to these anthologies in A. Robert Lee, 'Afro-America, The Before Columbus Foundation and the Literary Multiculturalization of America', *Journal of American Studies*, Vol. 28, No. 3 (December 1994), pp. 433–50.

40. Richard Rodriguez, *Hunger of Memory: The Education of Richard Rodriguez* (New York: David R. Godine, 1982).

41. Bharati Mukherjee, 'Beyond Multiculturalism: Surviving the Nineties', in Ishmael Reed (ed.), *MultiAmerica: Essays on Cultural Wars and Cultural Peace* (New York: Viking Penguin, 1997), pp. 454–61.

42. The phrase 'deadbeat on welfare' is from Nell Irvin Painter, 'Hill, Thomas, and the Use of Racial Stereotype', in Toni Morrison (ed.), *Race-ing, Justice, En-gendering Power: Essays on Anita Hill, Clarence Thomas, and the Construction of Social Reality* (New York: Pantheon Books, 1992), p. 201.

43. A useful compendium on the larger debate is to be found in Ronald Takaki (ed.), *From Different Shores: Perspectives on Race and Ethnicity in America* (New York: Oxford University Press, 1987, Second Edition, 1994).

44. William L. Andrews (ed.), *Three Classic African-American Novels: The Heroic Slave, Clotel* and *Our Nig* (New York: Penguin/Mentor Books, 1990), p. 115.

45. William and Ellen Craft, *Running a Thousand Miles for Freedom; or The Escape of William and Ellen Craft from Slavery* (with a portrait of Ellen Craft), (London: William Tweedie, 1860).

46. I have explored this further across all of Chesnutt's fiction in A. Robert Lee, '"The Desired State of Feeling": Charles Waddell Chesnutt and Afro-American Literary Tradition', *Durham University Journal*, Vol. 35, new series (March 1974), pp. 163–70.

47. Charles W. Chesnutt, *The House Behind the Cedars* (New York: Macmillan/Collier Books, 1969).

48. John Hope Franklin (ed.), *Three Negro Classics: Up from Slavery, The Souls of Black Folks* and *The Autobiography of an Ex-Colored Man* (New York: Avon Books, 1965). All subsequent page references are to this edition.

49. Charles Johnson, *Being & Race: Black Writing since 1970* (Bloomington and Indianapolis: Indiana University Press, 1987), p. 122.

50. Werner Sollors, *Neither Black Nor White Yet Both: Thematic Explorations of Interracial Literature* (New York: Oxford University Press, 1997).

Index

RELATED TITLES FROM PLUTO PRESS

BEAT GENERATION WRITERS
Edited By A. Robert Lee

'Destined to become not only a key pedagogic tool - but also a key player in redirecting the academic construction of the subject itself ... A significant development in Beat literary criticism' **Over Here**

'This intelligently focused collection ... helps to locate the Beat writers in the social and cultural context of their times. It is a very welcome and useful supplement to their work' **Ann Charters**

'At last, an intelligent and peerless compendium of critical essays on the Beat[s], tackling prickly issues of language, gender, race, feminism, anarchy, subjectivity. This is a much needed energetic guide and recondite reading of these controversial writers and cultural icons. I recommend [it] to serious scholars, students and fans of the historic Beat canon' **Anne Waldman, Director, Jack Kerouac School of Disembodied Poetics, Colorado**

1996 • 232pp • 230x150mm • Pb • £13.99 • 0 7453 0661 6 • Hb • £40.00 • 0 7453 0660 8

OTHER BRITAIN, OTHER BRITISH
Contemporary Multicultural Fiction
A. Robert Lee

'[It] opens up potentially new ground ... Interesting and useful' **Wasafiri**

'A useful and significant book, the first that I know of specifically concerned with how British literature is changing and being redefined by its minorities, immigrants, Commonwealth relations, and by such ideas as multiculturalism and postcolonialism' **World Literature Today**

1995 • 192pp • 215x135mm • Pb • £12.99 • 0 7453 0646 2 • Hb • £45.00 • 0 7453 0645 4

Visit the Pluto Press WebSite:
http://www.leevalley.co.uk/plutopress

Pluto Classic
BLACK SKIN WHITE MASKS
Frantz Fanon

'Fanon's analysis of crippled colonial mentalities may be even more salient now than it was then' **New Statesman**

'One feels a brilliant, vivid and hurt mind walking the thin line that separates effective outrage from despair' **New York Times**

'A strange, haunting melange of existential analysis, revolutionary manifesto, metaphysics, prose, poetry and literary criticism' **Newsweek**

1991 • 256pp • 215x135mm • Pb • £13.99 • 0 7453 0035 9 • Hb • £40.00 • 0 7453 1355 8

CALIBAN'S FREEDOM
The Early Political Thought of C.L.R. James
Anthony Bogues

An important analysis of CLR James's early political thought on Marxism and the black radical tradition.

1997 • 216pp • 215x135mm • Pb • £13.99 • 0 7453 0614 4 • Hb • £40.00 • 0 7453 0613 6

Please send this completed order form (prices subject to change) to: (UK only) Pluto Press, FREEPOST, ND 6781, London N6 5BR Outside the UK send to: Pluto Press, 345 Archway Road, London N6 5AA. Or fax on +44 (0) 181 348 9133. Payments must include P&P as follows: UK 10% of order value, min £2; Europe 15% of order value, min £3.50; outside Europe 20% of order value, min £5. I wish to order the following (academics - please tick for inspection copies):   Qty   Insp

Beat Generation ...	£13.99	Pb	0 7453 0661 6	.....	.....
Other Britain ...	£12.99	Pb	0 7453 0646 2	.....	.....
Black Skin ...	£13.99	Pb	0 7453 0035 9	.....	.....
Caliban's Freedom ...	£13.99	Pb	0 7453 0614 4	.....	.....

☐ I enclose a cheque for £_____ (inc P&P, payable to Marston Book Services)
☐ Please debit my credit card (specify type) _____
for £ _____ (inc P&P)   ☐ Please send me the Pluto Press Catalogue
Card Number: _____ Expiry Date: /
Name ....
Signature ....
Card Address ....
....
Delivery (if different) ....
....
E-mail PL.LEE98
Please tick these boxes if you do NOT wish i) to receive any other mailings from Pluto Press ☐ ii) to receive mailings from any organisation using the Pluto Press mailing list ☐